A Practitioner's Guide to
BASEL III AND BEYOND

A Practitioner's Guide to
BASEL III AND BEYOND

Consultant Editor
Richard Barfield
PricewaterhouseCoopers LLP

SWEET & MAXWELL

THOMSON REUTERS

Published in 2011 by Thomson Reuters (Professional) UK Limited
(Registered in England & Wales, Company No 1679046. Registered Office
and address for service: Aldgate House, 33 Aldgate High Street, London, EC3N 1DL)

For further information on our products and services, visit
www.sweetandmaxwell.co.uk

Printed and bound by CPI Group (UK) Ltd, Croydon, CR0 4YY

Reprinted 2011

ISBN 978 0 414 04538 5

No natural forests were destroyed to make this product;
only farmed timber was used and replanted

A CIP catalogue record for this book
is available from the British Library.

Crown copyright material is reproduced with the permission of the Controller of HMSO
and the Queen's Printer for Scotland.

Thomson Reuters and the Thomson Reuters logo are trademarks of Thomson Reuters.
Sweet & Maxwell ® is a registered trademark of Thomson Reuters
(Professional) UK Limited.

Biographies

Richard Barfield
Richard is a director in PwC's risk consulting team at PwC UK in London. He has broad-ranging consulting experience gained over 20 years with PwC. During 2010, he was a key member of the PwC team that worked with the six larger UK banks to assess the implications of Basel III and the wider reform agenda. Richard has also held senior line management positions, for example through secondment as Finance Director to Barclaycard while at Coopers & Lybrand.

Matthew Barling
Matthew is a tax partner in PwC UK's Banking & Capital Markets Tax Practice in London. Matthew specialises in advising on the tax aspects of banking and capital markets transactions, corporate reorganisations and M&A and has over 20 years' experience in the banking and capital markets sector. He advises a range of clients including leading US and European investment and commercial banks and private equity and hedge funds.

Charlie Beach
Charlie is a director in the risk consulting team at PwC UK in London. His main areas of focus are the development of risk frameworks focusing on governance, risk processes and risk MI, and in economic and regulatory capital management. He has been involved in the development of funding and liquidity risk management in response to Basel III and related regulations. Charlie has also served as an officer in the British army.

Christophe Cadiou
Christophe is a Financial Reporting Advisory partner at PwC Japan based in Tokyo, with over 17 years of banking experience in Europe, the US and Asia Pacific. He currently focuses on assisting financial institutions in Japan and Asia Pacific with complex accounting and market reporting issues, such as the

conversion to IFRS and the alignment of Basel II with IFRS. Christophe also led the Global PwC taskforce charged with developing client solutions on the implementation of Pillar 3.

Fernando de la Mora
Fernando is a partner in New York where he leads the US Banking and Capital Markets Risk Practice for PwC US. He has over 15 years of experience conducting risk management, performance management, strategic planning and M&A projects for financial institutions. Most recently, Fernando has advised the boards of several major banks with respect to risk and governance matters related to the credit crisis. He has also advised clients in the areas of Basel, stress testing, ICAAP and economic capital implementation.

Ina de Vry
Ina leads the firm's Advisory Financial Risk Services practice in PwC South Africa. She has 21 years of banking experience of which approximately 10 years were spent with the treasury trading, structuring and market risk management functions. She specialises in bank risk management, particular market and credit risk modelling and derivative valuations. She holds an MsC in Applied Mathematics and a Certificate in Treasury Management.

Sonja du Plessis
Sonja has 24 years' experience in the financial services industry. Previously an external audit partner with Ernst & Young in Johannesburg, Sonja moved to the UK and started her operational risk management career in 1999. Over the last six years she has held senior line roles at Barclays and Lloyds Banking Group, focusing on governance and enterprise-wide risk management. She joined PwC UK in 2010 where she leads operational risk management and focuses on its role in enterprise risk management.

Addison Everett
Addison is a partner in Capital Markets Group in PwC China, based in Beijing, and provides capital markets and accounting advisory services to a range of global clients. Over more than 20 years Addison has advised banking clients on US/IFRS GAAP

conversions, M&A, listings and accounting issues related primarily to financial instruments. These projects included recapitalisations of state-owned banks, involving complex book and regulatory accounting issues. He also established the PwC IFRS technical accounting group in Hong Kong/China.

Patrick Fell

Patrick is a director in Financial Services Regulatory Practice at PwC UK in London, where he leads the capital team and advises banks, investment firms, insurance companies and regulators. He also consults widely on regulatory authorisation, compliance and governance matters and has advised regulators in several countries on policy and supervision matters. He has worked extensively with financial institutions and private equity providers to restructure the balance sheets of troubled institutions.

Nick Forrest

Nick is a director in the UK Economics team at PwC UK and spent two years at the UK Department of Business during the financial crisis. He has been at the heart of the banking reform debate, which has involved working with banks and the UK government on assessing the economic impact of reform proposals, setting bank lending targets and devising a range of bank-led initiatives for improving the business finance environment.

Simon Gealy

Simon is an accounting advisory partner at PwC US, currently based in Atlanta, and has worked exclusively for the last 15 years consulting on large scale change projects at banks principally driven by US listings, adoption of IFRS and by major transactions. Simon is a regular speaker on IFRS Issues as well as the author of several articles and publications around the challenges for Banks of implementing US GAAP and IFRS.

Tom Gosling

Tom is a partner at PwC UK in London, advising companies and their boards on executive compensation issues. His recent work has focused on remuneration design following the financial crisis, including advice to six major European banks. He is also responsible for PwC's extensive research activities in executive compensation, and is a regular conference speaker and media commentator. Prior to joining PwC, Tom was a research fellow in the mathematics department of Cambridge University.

Richard Kibble
Richard is a partner in the financial services strategy team at PwC UK in London, and joined in 2008 to help build the firm's corporate strategy capability and business. He has 20 years' experience advising financial institutions in the UK and Europe on the full range of strategic, operational and organisational issues. His focus covers retail financial services, wholesale and asset management. Prior to joining PwC, Richard was the UK managing partner at Marakon (1990-2007).

Monika Mars
Monika is a director in PwC's financial services practice at PwC Switzerland in Zurich with over 20 years' banking and risk management advisory experience. She is one of PwC's primary experts on the Basel framework and has been advising banks and regulators internationally on the Basel II framework since 2001. Monika is a frequent speaker on Basel-related topics. She is also a member of the IIF Steering Committee on Implementation and the Working Group on Risk Management.

Chris Matten
Chris is a partner at PwC Singapore and is the global leader of PwC's network of risk-based capital management experts. He has over 25 years' experience in the financial services industry, 17 of which were spent working in various risk and finance roles in banks in the UK, Japan, Switzerland, Australia and Singapore. Before joining PwC he was the CFO of OCBC Bank in Singapore.

Duncan McNab
Duncan McNab is a partner at PwC UK in London with over 20 years' experience providing audit and advisory services to wholesale and investment banking clients. He spent over a year on the management team at Lehman Brothers International Europe (in administration) heading up the house positions workstream that traded out of Lehman's bond, equities and derivatives positions. Duncan now focuses on recovery and

resolution planning and assists clients around the world in writing their plans and pilot submissions.

Pramit Mitra

Pramit is a senior associate in the Financial Services Advisory Practice at PwC US in New York. His project experience has covered market and credit risk frameworks and, more in-depth, Basel II implementation, economic capital, FX, liquidity risk management methodologies, measurements, and stress testing. He has also worked as a policy analyst the Center for Strategic and International Studies (CSIS) in Washington, holds a Master's in public policy from Johns Hopkins University and an MBA from Yale.

Agatha Pontiki

Agatha is a consultant in the risk consulting team at PwC UK in London. She joined PwC in Cyprus in 2008 assisting financial services clients on risk management, regulatory compliance and governance. Her prior role was with a rating agency in New York where she managed an international portfolio in the Financial Institutions Group. Agatha has also worked with international regulators. She completed her undergraduate studies in the US as Fulbright scholar and holds an MSc in Finance.

Claire Rieger

Claire is a senior consultant in the risk consulting team at PwC UK in London. She has valuable expertise in developing and implementing liquidity management frameworks, spanning regulatory advice to reporting and stress testing. She has advised clients on liquidity solutions relating to systems and controls, including funds transfer pricing. She has also assessed risk function effectiveness, including review and redesign of governance processes, roles and responsibilities, policies and procedures, supporting infrastructure, management information and reporting requirements.

Anne-Marie Stomeo

Anne-Marie is a senior manager in PwC UK's Banking & Capital Markets Tax Practice. She has extensive experience working with banking groups, brokers and clearing houses in particular in relation to equity finance, international tax planning, M&A and tax accounting issues. Most recently Anne-Marie has been focused on issues related to the UK Bank Levy, as well as helping to lead in establishing and driving PwC's response to bank levies being introduced across Europe.

James Worsnip

James is a director in the valuations team at PwC UK and works with banks and capital markets firms advising on strategic and financial issues. Over the last two years James has been involved with a variety of high profile projects including: the introduction of the Asset Protection Scheme; the assessment of compensation to former shareholders of Bradford and Bingley; and in considering the strategic implications of regulatory change on the UK banking industry and the economy. He was previously seconded to LCH.Clearnet as Group CFO.

Author email and phone details

Richard Barfield: email: richard.barfield@uk.pwc.com;
phone: +44 (0)20 7804 6658

Matthew Barling: email: matthew.barling@uk.pwc.com;
phone: +44 (0) 20 721 25544

Charlie Beach: email: charles.beach@uk.pwc.com;
phone: +44 (0) 20 721 33591

Christophe Cadiou: email: christophe.cadiou@jp.pwc.com;
phone: +81 (90) 4626 6236

Fernando de la Mora: email: fernando.de.la.mora@us.pwc.com;
phone: +1 (646) 471 5257

Ina de Vry: email: ina.de.vry@za.pwc.com;
phone: +27 (11) 797 4036

Sonja du Plessis: email: sonja.duplessis@uk.pwc.com;
phone: +44 (0) 20 721 33051

Addison Everett: email: addison.l.everett@cn.pwc.com;
phone: +86 (10) 6533 2345

Patrick Fell: email: patrick.w.fell@uk.pwc.com;
phone: +44 (0) 20 721 25273

Nick Forrest: email: nick.forrest@uk.pwc.com;
phone: +44 (0) 20 780 45695

Simon Gealy: email: simon.gealy@uk.pwc.com;
phone: +44 (0) 20 721 23513

Tom Gosling: email: tom.gosling@uk.pwc.com;
phone: +44 (0) 20 721 23973

Richard Kibble: email: richard.d.kibble@uk.pwc.com;
phone: +44 (0) 20 721 26644

Monika Mars: email: monika.mars@ch.pwc.com;
phone: +41 (0) 58 792 1622

Chris Matten: email: chris.matten@sg.pwc.com; phone: +65 6236 3878

Duncan McNab: email: duncan.mcnab@uk.pwc.com; phone: +44 (0) 20 780 42516

Pramit Mitra: email: pramit.mitra@us.pwc.com; phone: +1 (646) 471 5679

Agatha Pontiki: email: agatha.pontiki@uk.pwc.com; phone: + 44 (0) 20 7588 5000

Claire Rieger: email: claire.rieger@uk.pwc.com; phone: +44 (0) 20 721 22386

Anne-Marie Stomeo: email: anne-marie.stomeo@uk.pwc.com; phone: +44 (0) 20 721 34976

James Worsnip: email: james.c.worsnip@uk.pwc.com; phone: +44 (0) 20 780 49635

Foreword

Over the past decade, the rulemaking process in the banking area has been far more intense than anyone had expected: Basel II took longer to complete than initially foreseen, while the financial crisis pointed to areas where there was a need for further improvement. It is clear that Basel II cannot be blamed for the crisis, since it was either still in the process of being implemented, or the implementation process had not even been properly started (in fact, this was the case in the country where the crisis first took hold, the USA). However, the crisis made clear the need for a stronger capital rule. And we certainly have that now: Basel III represents a far more stringent regime than Basel I or Basel II. And it has been completed in a short time-frame. The need to deliver a prompt response to the challenges posed by the crisis aligned everybody's incentives and helped those involved to achieve a herculean task in just a little over one year.

Basel III means more capital (far more capital, in fact) and better quality capital, but also introduces stronger rules for the trading book (although, for some commentators, they are not yet stringent enough), new liquidity requirements and new limits on leverage. It is such a stringent rule that the Basel Committee has put in place a long transitional period to make sure that Basel III works as intended, restraining undue risk and leverage, but no more than is necessary to maintain a stable financial system.

The international regulatory community has delivered a strong framework. But looking ahead, none of us (industry, regulators, supervisors) can afford to maintain the speed of rulemaking we have witnessed in the last years. The industry needs to concentrate on managing the impact of the new rules on risk taking, profitability and, why not, on business models as well. I hesitate to use the terminology "regulatory pause", as it brings to mind dark memories of an inadequate policy response to the challenges of a global financial system pre-crisis, but the truth is that we do need to give time for the new rules to bed down.

In fact, the reduction in the speed of new rulemaking does not mean that we remain idle. On the contrary, we all need to focus on the implementation of the new rules. We cannot forget that any rule is only as good as its implementation, and any regulation is only as good as the supervision which ensures that it is being implemented correctly and effectively. We are by no means at the end of the road yet. And I say this not only in my capacity as Chairman of the Standards Implementation Group of the Basel Committee.

Furthermore, we should be aware that stronger capital rules will certainly mean a greater incentive for capital arbitrage, both among the banks, between banks and other solvency regulated institutions (such as insurance companies), and between the regulated sector and the shadow financial system: the higher the capital requirements, the greater the perceived profits to be made from capital arbitrage (and, I might add, the greater the risks of financial instability). Ensuring the integrity of the implementation of Basel III is a necessary, but not sufficient, condition to limit the risks of capital arbitrage.

But the implementation of Basel III is not limited to the new requirements in Pillar I: the case for a stronger Pillar II is even greater under Basel III than under Basel II. Making the case for Pillar II is straightforward: imagine a bank with a Core Equity Tier 1 of 12 per cent, but with a poor internal risk management. Would you feel comfortable, either as a regulator, a client, or a counterparty, when dealing with the bank? Of course not: we need banks with strong capital, but also with strong risk management culture (and, I might add that we need them to be profitable as well!). In fact, this is one of the most important lessons coming from the financial crisis: the need for stronger risk management inside banks.

There is another area, not related to Basel III in particular, of crucial importance going forward: the surveillance of the complex, international and integrated financial system in which banks operate. Before the crisis, the knowledge we had about those complex interactions was too limited, and the spillover effects were as unexpected as they were unsettling. To ensure the stability of the financial system, we need more than just Basel III, more than any rule-based regulation: we need to understand how the complex, integrated and international financial system works. The emergence of global bodies such as the FSB, or regional ones, like the European Systemic Risk Board, will help other pre-existing bodies, such as the IMF and the BIS, to better understand the risks posed by the financial system and, probably more relevant, to deliver the adequate policy responses to mitigate those risks.

To summarise, Basel III is coming, and it is comings fast. But the finalisation of the package of Basel III is just the beginning of a more intense process: the implementation of the new rules. So brace for impact and "bonne chance" (or should we say "bon courage"?).

A Practitioner's Guide to Basel III and Beyond provides a single volume resource that will be very valuable for anyone involved in the banking industry and its supervision. It will help them to prepare for, and implement the major changes flowing from Basel III and related reforms. I therefore welcome its publication.

José María Roldán

Director-General of Banking Regulation, Bank of Spain Chair, Standards Implementation Group, BCBS

Preface

Basel III encompasses a game-changing set of reforms that will have fundamental and long-lasting impacts on the banking industry. Whether Basel III achieves its intended objectives and what its unintended consequences may be are likely to be open questions for years to come.

Basel III cannot be considered in isolation. It is part of a wider set of reforms aimed at addressing the causes of the financial crisis and limiting the impact of future bank failures. So, while this Guide focuses on Basel III, it also considers related changes such as those to remuneration and the accounting frameworks. The Guide also looks at the wider implications of Basel III, such as those for the economy.

This Guide has many authors; each covering one or more chapters, giving the reader access to one extensive range of views and experience from around the world. The authors are principally PwC partners and directors, who are senior and experienced in their respective fields, which range from strategy through risk and regulation to tax and restructuring.

Each chapter is designed to stand alone so that the reader can approach topics of interest easily.

In addition to the authors, an enterprise like this involves the contributions of many PwC colleagues. I would like to thank, in alphabetical order: David Albright, Steve Barnes, Marthina Bathe-Guski, Jo Borzellino, John Bromfield, Diana Chant, Richard Collier, Laura Cox-Kaplan, Jas Ellis, Miles Everson, Rami Feghali, David Franklin, Johannes Goldner, Andrew Gray, Matthew Hardy, Hugh Harley, Andrew Hawkins, John Hitchins, Alastair Howard, Georgina Hutchinson, Anthony Ioannou, David Kenmir, Miles Kennedy, Bill Lewis, Tony Lomas, Thierry Lopez, Matthew McCormick, Charles Morel, Andrew Nevin, Dawn Nicholson, Tim Ogier, Phil Rivett,

Pranjal Shukla, Anne Simpson, Mark Stephen, George Stylianides, Ana Subia, Bob Sullivan, Aamer Rafiq, Henry Risk, Hiltrud Thelen-Pischke, Shyam Venkat, Dan Weiss, Simon Wescott, James Wong, William Zimmern. Special thanks go to Nazli Ozyurek who has assisted me throughout.

Contents

Biographies   v
Author email and phone details   xi
Foreword   xiii
Preface   xvii

1   Introduction   1
    Richard Barfield

    1.1   Overview   1
    1.2   For whom is the Guide intended   1
    1.3   Overview of the reform agenda   2
    1.4   The players   4
    1.5   A brief history of Basel   8
    1.6   Basel III in a nutshell   9
    1.7   Coverage of the Guide   13
    1.8   Looking forward   18
    1.9   Conclusion   19

2   Strategic Context   21
    Richard Kibble and James Worsnip

    2.1   Introduction   21
    2.2   The reforms in context   23
    2.3   Basel III – Impact and response   35
    2.4   Unintended consequences   47
    2.5   Conclusion   52

3   Defining Capital   53
    Chris Matten

    3.1   Introduction   53
    3.2   Overview of the key changes   53
    3.3   Definition of capital under Basel I and Basel II   54
    3.4   Going concern v gone concern   62
    3.5   The definition of capital under Basel III 65

3.6	New minimum capital ratios	78
3.7	Contingent capital	80
3.8	The capital buffers	81
3.9	Practical considerations	82
3.10	Superequivalence	85
3.11	Conclusion	86

4 Trading Book and Securitisation   **89**
Ina de Vry

4.1	Introduction	89
4.2	The Standardised Approach to market risk capital	90
4.3	The internal model approach to market risk capital	92
4.4	The Basel II review of the trading book in 2005	93
4.5	The effect of the crisis	94
4.6	Basel II.5 and Basel III changes	97
4.7	Market risk – looking forward	116

5 Counterparty Credit Risk   **121**
Monika Mars and Agatha Pontiki

5.1	Introduction	121
5.2	Overview of counterparty credit risk	121
5.3	Proposals to enhance counterparty credit risk capture	126
5.4	Implications and practicalities	141

6 Liquidity and Funding   **147**
Charlie Beach and Claire Rieger

6.1	Introduction	147
6.2	Basel III regulations	153
6.3	Implications and practical issues	169

7 Leverage   **181**
Fernando de la Mora

7.1	Introduction	181
7.2	Background	182

| | 7.3 | Basel response | 187 |
| | 7.4 | Conclusion | 192 |

8 **Accounting Considerations** **197**
Simon Gealy and Addison Everett

	8.1	Introduction	197
	8.2	Interaction of Basel III with current and proposed accounting guidance	200
	8.3	Practical implementation considerations	206
	8.4	Conclusion	218

9 **Role of Pillar 2** **219**
Chris Matten

	9.1	Introduction	219
	9.2	The role of Pillar 2 under Basel II	220
	9.3	Impact of Basel III on Pillar 2	223
	9.4	Implications for economic capital	227
	9.5	Importance of risk management – strengthening the SREP	231
	9.6	Conclusion	233

10 **Procyclicality** **237**
Monika Mars

	10.1	Introduction	237
	10.2	Managing procyclicality	238
	10.3	Basel III proposals to address procyclicality	240
	10.4	Conclusion	256

11 **Stress Testing** **259**
Fernando de la Mora, Richard Barfield and Pramit Mitra

	11.1	Introduction	259
	11.2	Basel III guidelines	263
	11.3	Key features off effective stress testing	268
	11.4	Conclusion	283

12   Disclosures and Pillar 3   285
Christophe Cadiou

　12.1   Introduction   285
　12.2   Overview of risk disclosure requirements   288
　12.3   Practical implementation challenges   307
　12.4   Conclusion – the future of risk
　　　　 management disclosures   312

13   Taxation   315
Matthew Barling and Anne-Marie Stomeo

　13.1   Introduction   315
　13.2   The taxation environment for banks   315
　13.3   Tax implications of Basel III proposals   322
　13.4   Conclusion   331

14   Reward   333
Tom Gosling

　14.1   Introduction   333
　14.2   Forces for change   333
　14.3   Incorporating risk into performance
　　　　 measures   337
　14.4   Design of compensation   348
　14.5   Governance of remuneration   356
　14.6   Disclosure of remuneration   362
　14.7   Conclusion   364

15   Recovery and Resolution Planning   367
Duncan McNab

　15.1   Introduction – in peace plan for war   367
　15.2   International overview   369
　15.3   Recovery – financial Business Continuity
　　　　 Planning   374
　15.4   Resolution – planning for your own funeral   379
　15.5   Reality check – lessons learned from the pilots   383
　15.6   Conclusion   384

16   Stakeholder Perspectives   387
Richard Barfield

16.1   Introduction   387
16.2   The funding spectrum   387
16.3   Equity investors   389
16.4   Debt investors and contingent capital   393
16.5   Depositors and borrowers   396
16.6   Government and the taxpayer   399
16.7   Rating agencies   402
16.8   Transparency for stakeholders   404
16.9   Conclusion   407

17   Implications for Risk Management   409
Sonja du Plessis

17.1   Introduction   409
17.2   Establishing an explicit risk culture   412
17.3   Role of the board   415
17.4   Risk appetite   421
17.5   Chief risk officer   424
17.6   Conclusion   434

18   Implications for the Economy   437
Nick Forrest

18.1   Introduction   437
18.2   How banks (and banking regulations)
       impact the economy   441
18.3   Likely response of banks   450
18.4   Impact of previous regulatory changes   452
18.5   Impact on the broader economy   454
18.6   Conclusion   466

19   Implications for Supervision   469
Patrick Fell

19.1   Introduction   469
19.2   The core principles   471
19.3   Rethinking supervision   475
19.4   New style supervision – the glide path   476

19.5	Key principles for macro-prudential supervision	479
19.6	Will the authorities be able to meet the expectations placed on them?	482
19.7	The place of the regulator	492
19.8	International oversight	494
19.9	Conclusion	498

Appendix I – Trends in Pillar 3 reporting and risk disclosures — **501**

Appendix II – List of banks covered in the analysis of Pillar 3 and risk management disclosures — **511**

Appendix III – CEBS observed good practices for disclosures on activities affected by the market turmoil (with mapping to the SSG leading practices) — **513**

Index — **519**

Chapter 1

Introduction

Richard Barfield

1.1   Overview

Basel III represents the biggest regulatory change that the banking industry has seen in decades. It is salutary to remember that it is only one, albeit very important, component of a suite of related reforms that are changing banking, regulation, supervision and the relationship between banks and the state.

In November 2010 the G20 ratified the Basel Committee's proposals for strengthening capital and liquidity standards. In doing so, they committed the global banking industry to significant change and a transition period that extends beyond 2020.

Distant deadlines have the danger of creating complacency and inaction. Leading banks recognise this threat and have no desire to suffer the same fate as the apocryphal simmering frog. The market is also asking how banks will be impacted. The question then, is what practical actions should banks be taking? This Guide aims to provide some answers.

To set the scene, this Chapter introduces Basel III, the reform landscape, the key players, and provides an overview of the Guide.

1.2   For whom is the Guide intended?

This is a Practitioner's Guide to the potential implications of Basel III and beyond: we go beyond the text of the new Basel guidance to consider implications and practical implementation issues. The Guide also goes beyond Basel III to consider closely

1

related reforms such as changes to recovery and resolution (what banks should do when they are at risk of failing or when they have failed). This is therefore a Practitioner's Guide that aims to address the new realities.

The Guide is intended to have broad appeal; the types of reader that we had in mind when putting finger to keyboard included for example:

(a) CEOs and directors wanting to understand the important parts of the G20 reform agenda and its consequences for financial institutions;
(b) CFOs, CROs, Compliance Officers, Treasurers, and COOs grappling with managing one of the most complex change agendas in history; and
(c) supervisors and legal advisers looking for a rounded and coherent overview of Basel III and insights into what it might mean for banks.

1.3   Overview of the reform agenda

It is important to put Basel III in context. The G20's main aim on banking reform is to ensure that governments never again have to bail out the sector. They want to remove the implicit guarantee that governments will back large banks if they get into trouble. The G20 does not want to eradicate bank failure nor does it expect central banks never to have to provide liquidity support to troubled firms, but the G20 is absolutely clear that bank-dependency on taxpayer support on the scale witnessed over the last three years is unacceptable and must not be repeated.

The clarity and unity of purpose of the G20 on the issue is unparalleled. Recent events in Ireland, Greece and Portugal illustrate the importance of achieving this goal. However, for it to happen, that unity of purpose will need to be sustained for a long time.

The causes of the global financial crisis were complex and, because of the interconnectedness of the financial system, its impact was felt far and wide. However, it did not affect all banks or all economies in the same way. Several countries' banks emerged unscathed. Asia generally, Australia, Brazil, Russia,

Canada and South Africa are some notable examples. This is why the G20's unity is remarkable, but unity it has been nonetheless.

Given that the Financial Stability Forum ("FSF") was born at the G7 Finance Ministers' meeting in the wake of the Asian financial crisis of 1999, perhaps we should not be so surprised. Since then, the G7 grouping has grown in both number and scope. In response to the 2007 financial crisis, G20 summits involving heads of state were convened. The summits were preceded by meetings of the G20 Finance Ministers and Central Bank Governors. The G20 was designated the premier forum for international economic cooperation at the Pittsburgh G20 summit in 2009, formally superseding the G7. In the same year, the Financial Stability Board ("FSB") superseded the FSF.

Since the crisis, a plethora of reforms have been proposed from a wide variety of sources, not just the Basel Committee. These included the FSB's proposals on reward; the European Commission's proposals on governance in financial institutions; bank levies proposed globally and locally; and taxes on bankers' bonuses etc. Figure 1.1 gives an idea of the range and complexity of reform that is being pursued. The Basel proposals are one item on this list.

Figure 1.1 The reform agenda

The reform agenda	
Basel II.5 and Basel III	Product market regulation
Pre–funding of deposit insurance	Pro-consumer regulation
Resolution fund	Role of credit rating agencies
Wholesale levy	Securitisation markets
Provisions and other accounting changes	Fund managers to improve fund liquidity
Subsidiarisation	Hedge fund regulation
Central counterparty clearing (OTC contracts)	Bank risk management and governance
Reporting (capital and liquidity) supervision/oversight	Macro-prudential
Remuneration	Supervisory approach
Narrow banking	Cross–border colleges
"Glass–Steagall II"	Recovery and resolution

To give one example of the scale of other reforms: in the US, the Dodd-Frank Act was signed into law on 21 July 2010 and has 2,319 pages (by contrast the 1933 Glass-Steagall Act had a mere 37 pages). The remarkable thing is that the Dodd-Frank Act is just the beginning. Ten US regulatory agencies are now putting the detailed regulatory flesh on the bare legislative bones. As the devils lie in the detail, the final consequences of Dodd-Frank may be unclear for years to come. And, of course, Dodd-Frank does not cover everything in Figure 1.1.

The scope of reforms addressed in other countries may, in some cases, be similar in breadth to the reforms brought about by Dodd-Frank, but these will vary according to local context, history, experience of the crisis, existing central bank and regulatory frameworks etc.

The impact of Basel III in each country will also need to be placed in the context of the local reform agenda. For example, in the European Union, Solvency II (which sets out strengthened risk management and capital adequacy requirements for insurance firms) is being introduced with a proposed "go-live" date of 1 January 2013. This parallel development may have impacts on banks, for example in the availability and pricing of medium-term funding.

There are also much bigger forces at play. There is the rebalancing of the world economic order to the East and the South, large government deficits in several Organisation for Economic Cooperation and Development ("OECD") economies, persistent trade imbalances and mis-valued currencies. This means that reforms are being introduced in "interesting times".

1.4   The players

So, who are the main players in shaping the reform agenda? The G20 sponsors the FSB whose central goals are to improve the functioning of financial markets and to maintain financial stability through coordinating the work of national financial bodies and promoting effective regulatory, supervisory and other financial sector policies.

The Basel Committee on Banking Supervision (the "Committee" or "BCBS") is one of the 42 FSB members and the central forum for regular cooperation on banking supervisory matters. It takes its name from the Swiss border town where its secretariat is based. This is also where Committee members, senior officials responsible for banking supervision or financial stability issues, meet. The members come from central banks and other authorities with formal responsibility for the prudential supervision of banking. Over recent years, it has developed increasingly into a standard-setting body on all aspects of banking supervision. At the time of writing (March 2011), the Chairman of the Committee is Mr Nout Wellink, President of the Netherlands Bank.

The countries represented on the Basel Committee are: Argentina, Australia, Belgium, Brazil, Canada, China, France, Germany, Hong Kong, India, Indonesia, Italy, Japan, Korea, Luxembourg, Mexico, the Netherlands, Russia, Saudi Arabia, Singapore, South Africa, Spain, Sweden, Switzerland, Turkey, the United Kingdom and the United States.

The BCBS reports to a joint committee of central bank governors and heads of supervision (GHOS) from its member countries. The GHOS debates and approves the Committee's recommendations before they are issued.

As the reader can see, there is overlap between GHOS membership and G20 finance ministers and central bank governors. See Figure 1.2

As one would expect, the BCBS is supported by a number of expert committees (see Figure 1.3). From the point of view of Basel III, the most important of these is now the Standards Implementation Group which concentrates on the implementation of Basel standards and guidance, and, as of March 2011, is chaired by José María Roldán.

It is useful to draw a distinction between regulation and supervision. Regulation is the set of rules and standards that govern financial institutions; supervision is the process designed to oversee financial institutions to ensure that the rules and

Figure 1.2 The players

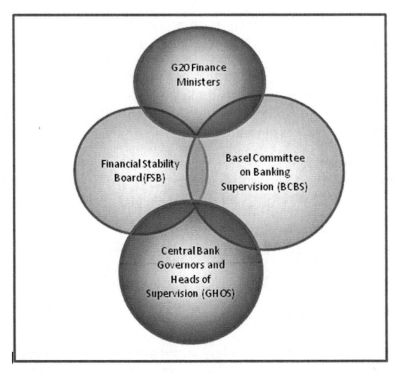

standards are applied. In some countries, these two activities are performed by separate bodies (e.g. China, Germany and Switzerland) and in many by different parts of the same organisation (e.g. Reserve Bank of India, South African Reserve Bank and the Monetary Authority of Singapore). In the UK, the Bank of England and the FSA are represented on the Basel Committee, but the FSA's responsibilities for prudential supervision will soon become part of the Bank of England. It should be clear to the reader that regulation, supervision and financial stability are often closely interlinked.

Another important stakeholder group is the banks themselves. In some countries, criticising banks has long been a national sport and in others the crisis gave criticising banks a much-needed boost. Politicians, previously cheerleaders of the credit-fuelled boom, were, in the natural way of things, not slow in

Figure 1.3 The Basel Committee structure

Basel committee structure

Board of Governors

Basel Committee on
Banking Supervision
(BCBS)

Standards Implementation Group (SIG)	Accounting Task Force (ATF)	Basel Consultative Group (BCG)	Policy Development Group (PDG)
Share information and promote consistency in implementation of BCBS guidance and standards	Ensure intl. accounting and auditing standards promote sound risk mgt. and market discipline	Deepen engagement with supervisors on banking supervisory issues	Identify and review emerging supervisory issues; propose and develop policies

Secretariat

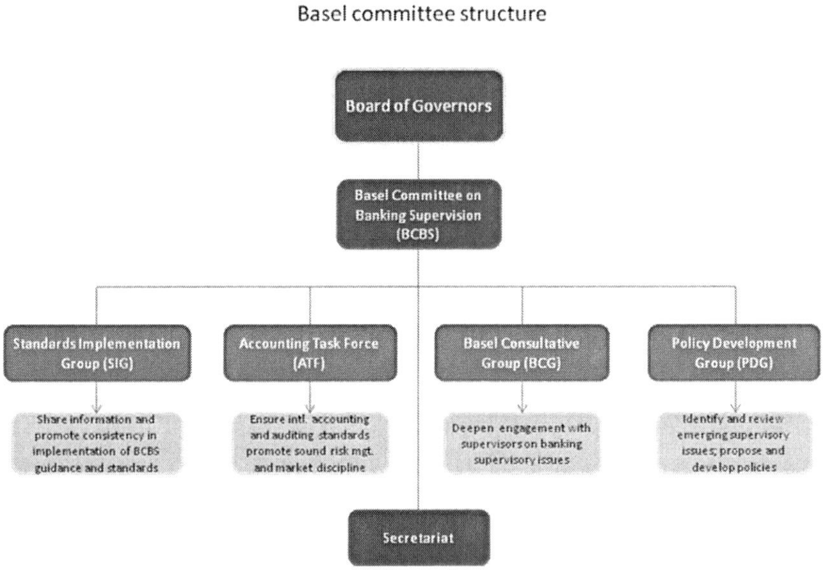

changing their position. As a result of unrelenting bad press in some countries, it is sometimes easy to forget the critical role that banks play in international trade, financial intermediation (linking providers of finance with those that need it) and the economy as a whole. Their participation in the reform debate has also been very important to provide input to finance ministers, central bankers, regulators and their staff to give insights into how the reforms might impact banks and what the wider economic consequences might be.

In most countries there are trade associations of banks (the British Bankers' Association, for example). These play an important role at national level. However, the only global association of financial institutions is the Institute of International Finance ("IIF"). Like the G7 it was born of crisis and was created in 1983 by banks in the wake of the international debt crisis of the early 1980s. The IIF now has over 400 financial institutions as members. Its mission is to support the industry in managing risk, develop best practices and standards for the industry, advocate policies that are in the broad interests of members and foster global financial stability.

1.5   A brief history of Basel

Global standards for capital are a relatively recent innovation. Basel I came into force in 1988, related only to credit risk, and was relatively simple. Before then, there were no standardised rules on capital adequacy for banks. In 1996, market risk rules were added. In December 1998, the BCBS recognised that Basel I needed to be revised to reflect credit risk more effectively and to prevent increasing use of arbitrage by the banks that were using more and more sophisticated internal models to measure and understand risk. The Committee also decided to recommend a capital charge for operational risk.

Basel II was born and took five years to develop and then a further four years to implement. Basel II has only been in place since January 2007 (or 2008 for those on the advanced approaches under Basel II: credit risk regulatory requirements may be calculated using one of three methods which are, in increasing order of sophistication, the Standardised Approach ("SA"); the Foundation Internal Ratings Based approach ("FIRB"); and, Advanced Internal Ratings-Based approach ("AIRB"). Most large international banks use AIRB for the majority of their exposures). In some countries it had not been implemented when the crisis hit (for example the US). Figure 1.4 provides the timeline.

Figure 1.4 Brief history of Basel I and Basel II

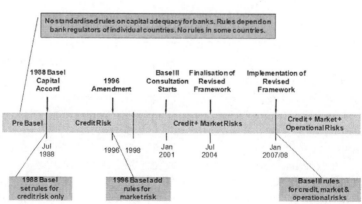

The Committee's remit extends a long way beyond capital adequacy. Its other global standards and consultations include, for example, liquidity risk, deposit insurance, risk management, corporate governance, stress testing and alignment of risk and reward.

The Committee's conclusions and recommendations do not have legal force: its role is to formulate supervisory standards and guidelines. It recommends best practices in the expectation that individual authorities will implement them through detailed national arrangements – statutory or otherwise – which are best suited to their own national systems. The Committee encourages convergence towards common approaches and standards without attempting detailed harmonisation of member countries' supervisory techniques. Even in the EU where Basel III will be enshrined in version four of the Capital Requirements Directive ("CRD"), there are likely to be some differences in national interpretation and implementation.

1.6   Basel III in a nutshell

The main aim of Basel III is to improve financial stability. Views on the causes of the financial crisis are well (and extensively) documented. Commentators still argue over some aspects but there is consensus on the key issues. The Report of the de Larosiere Group on the future of European regulation and supervision, published in February 2009 (Report, the high-level group on financial supervision in the EU, chaired by Jacques de Larosiere, 25 February 2009), was an early and excellent contribution that succinctly identified the principal causes of the financial crisis and made detailed recommendations for reform within the European system and globally.

Before the crisis, there was a period of excess liquidity. As a result liquidity risk had, for many banks and supervisors, become practically invisible. When liquidity became scarce (particularly as wholesale funding dried up) as the crisis developed, banks found that they had insufficient liquidity reserves to meet their obligations.

9

Also, banks had insufficient good quality (i.e. loss absorbing) capital. Low inflation and low returns had led investors to seek ever more risk to generate returns. This led to increased leverage and riskier financial products. High leverage amplified losses as banks tried to sell assets into falling and shrinking markets, which created a vicious circle of reducing capital ratios and a need to de-lever, which increased asset disposals. Mark-to-market accounting meant that there was no hiding place as buyers disappeared, prices dropped and trading asset valuations plummeted.

Due to a lack of transparency, counterparty credit risk was misunderstood and risk concentrations were underestimated. The interconnectedness of the financial system meant that, when trading counterparties defaulted, the shocks were transmitted rapidly through the system; the necessary shock absorbers were not in place, nor was transparency over the linkages.

To make matters worse, the Basel II capital formulae for credit risk are "procyclical". This means that as a downturn develops the probability of borrower default and loss at default both increase, which means that regulatory capital requirements increase. This should be dealt with through Pillar 2 capital planning buffers but the risks had been underestimated by banks and supervisors alike. Under Basel II, Pillar 1 calculates the minimum regulatory capital requirements for credit, market and operational risk; Pillar 2 covers the supervisory review process where supervisors evaluate whether banks should hold more capital than the Pillar 1 minimum; and Pillar 3 aims to encourage market discipline by specifying disclosure requirements to be made by banks to the market.

All the above meant that banks had to turn to their central banks for liquidity support and some to their governments for capital injections or support in dealing with assets of uncertain value for which there were no other buyers. Several major institutions are still dependent on state (i.e. taxpayer) support.

In response to the crisis, the Basel proposals have five main objectives:

(1) raise the quality, quantity, consistency and transparency of the capital base to ensure that banks are in a better position to absorb losses;
(2) strengthen risk coverage of the capital framework by strengthening the capital requirements for counterparty credit risk exposures;
(3) introduce a leverage ratio as a supplementary measure to the Basel II risk-based capital;
(4) introduce a series of measures to promote the build-up of capital buffers in good times that can be drawn upon in periods of stress. Linked to this, the Committee is encouraging the accounting bodies to adopt an expected loss provisioning model to recognise losses sooner; and
(5) set a global minimum liquidity standard for internationally active banks that includes a 30-day liquidity coverage ratio requirement, underpinned by a longer-term structural liquidity ratio.

The Basel changes discussed in this Guide are embodied in Basel II.5 and Basel III. The evolution from Basel I to Basel III is shown in Figure 1.5. Overall there are nine elements to the Basel changes which the Guide covers as follows:

(a) Capital definition (Chapter 3) – item 2 in Figure 1.5
(b) Higher minimum ratios (Chapter 3) – item 3
(c) Trading book and securitisation – Basel II.5 (Chapter 4) – item 1
(d) Counterparty risk (Chapter 5) – item 7
(e) Liquidity Coverage Ratio (Chapter 6) – item 8
(f) Net Stable Funding Ratio (Chapter 6) – item 9
(g) Leverage ratio (Chapter 7) – item 4
(h) Conservation and countercyclical buffers (Chapter 9) – item 5
(i) Systemic risk (Chapter 15) – item 6

Basel II.5 refers to guidance that was issued in July 2009 ("Revisions to Basel II market risk framework"). It included additional capital requirements for the trading book and revisions to the treatment of securitisations that come into effect on 1 January 2012. Basel III also goes further and recommends changes to Pillar 2 (banks' internal assessment of capital

11

Figure 1.5 Basel evolution

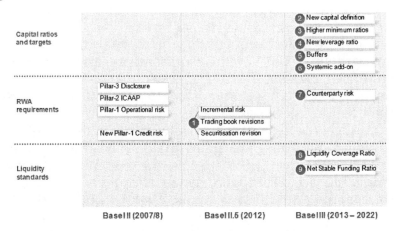

| | Basel II (2007/8) | Basel II.5 (2012) | Basel III (2013 – 2022) |

requirements and supervisory review of risk management and capital assessment) and Pillar 3 (market discipline). The Committee provides additional guidance on key areas to consider as part of Pillar 2 (e.g. risk concentrations): these were expected to be implemented immediately. On Pillar 3, the Committee reiterates banks' responsibility to make sure that their disclosures to market participants evolve to keep up with changes in their risk profile. The Committee also makes detailed recommendations regarding, for example, the disclosure of traded securitisations.

Given the scale of change being proposed in Basel III, the Committee has agreed a lengthy transition period (see Figure 1.6). All but the phasing out of certain capital instruments will be in place by 1 January 2019. The phasing out of capital instruments, such as hybrids and Tier 2 instruments that will no longer qualify will be completed by 1 January 2022. After 1 January 2013, new issues of capital instruments that do not qualify as common Tier 1 equity will be required to include a conversion feature, making them contingent capital.

For the leverage ratio, the Liquidity Coverage Ratio and the Net Stable Funding Ratio, observation periods will be used to monitor carefully how the new measures will work

Figure 1.6 The transition to Basel III

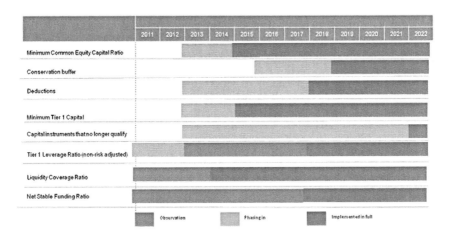

before they are phased in. Given the speed with which agreement was reached on Basel III, it is likely that we will see some changes as the consequences and implementation challenges become better understood through the transition period.

1.7 Coverage of the Guide

In Chapter 2 we consider the big picture: the strategic context into which Basel III and other reforms are being introduced. This Chapter considers questions such as: what are the key trends and challenges facing banking? What will Basel III mean for business models and bank management? Is Basel III likely to achieve its intended consequences and what is the risk of unexpected outcomes? The first step in Basel III is to provide a tighter definition of regulatory capital. This is needed to address the issue that not all Tier 1 regulatory capital proved to be loss-bearing (e.g. preference shares). The Committee also agreed that the rules regarding the definition of available capital resources needed to be sharpened. Chapter 3 examines in detail the definition of capital and discusses the implications for banks.

The requirements to hold capital have also changed. Risk-weighted assets ("RWA") have increased through Basel II.5 for the trading book and securitisations and through Basel III for counterparty credit risk. Chapter 4 covers this aspect of Basel II.5 while Chapter 5 discusses the new treatment for counterparty credit risk. These reforms will have a major impact on investment banks and the funding of financial institutions.

The effect of tougher definitions of capital and increased RWA is to make a 1 per cent Tier 1 ratio under Basel III a lot more expensive than under Basel II (see Figure 1.7). The Basel Quantitative Impact Study ("QIS") published in December 2010 estimated that for Group 1 banks (defined by the Basel Committee as those with Tier 1 capital in excess of €3 billion that are well diversified and internationally active; all other banks are classified as Group 2. The QIS covered 91 Group 1 banks, 74 of which provided the relevant data), double the amount of capital would be required under Basel III due to the tighter definition of capital and the increase in RWA (before any increase in minimum ratios or the impact of the leverage ratio). As one can see, this will depress return on equity and is likely to fundamentally change investors' perceptions of banks.

Figure 1.7 New money, old money

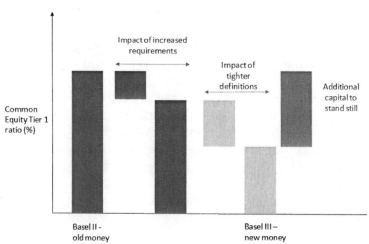

On top of this devaluation, the minimum ratio for common equity more than trebles from 2 per cent to 7 per cent (a minimum of 4.5 per cent plus a conservation buffer of 2.5 per cent). Together these figures imply about a seven-fold increase in Basel minimum capital requirements. Note that this is before the countercyclical buffer and any addition for Systemically Important Financial Institutions ("SIFIs").

A major innovation in Basel III is the introduction of global liquidity standards. Basel III introduces a "Basel I" for liquidity for the first time. This has two aspects: a Liquidity Coverage Ratio ("LCR") and a Net Stable Funding Ratio ("NSFR"). The LCR aims to make sure that banks hold a defined buffer to allow them to be self-sufficient for up to 30 days should a bank-specific stress event and a market downturn occur at the same time. The NSFR takes a longer view and aims to encourage banks to better match the funding characteristics of their assets and liabilities beyond a one year period. The NSFR will reduce the amount of "maturity transformation" provided by the financial sector (the ability of banks to borrow short and lend long). Chapter 6 discusses how the NSFR is likely to work in practice.

The BCBS approach to leverage builds on approaches in use in some countries already (for example the US, Switzerland and Canada). As with liquidity, a global standard is being set for the first time. Chapter 7 assesses this new measure which could have implications for several banks' business models.

Chapter 8 investigates the implications of changes to IFRS and US GAAP. The standard-setters are under pressure to introduce reforms that will eliminate the worst procyclical effects of the current accounting rules. A significant change to the way provisioning is undertaken is expected. This is just one of a series of major changes to financial reporting that will be introduced over the next few years. Together with the developments in Pillar 3 reporting these changes pose a significant operational challenge for banks.

The impact of Basel III on Pillar 2 is discussed in Chapter 9 together with capital planning and the interaction of the new capital buffers: the conservation and countercyclical capital buffers. The qualitative aspects of Pillar 2 – risk management and managing risks that are not captured in Pillar 1 – are areas where greater supervisory attention is likely to be focussed.

Chapter 10 discusses the reforms to the procyclical components of the Basel rules. Procyclicality – the tendency of capital requirements to increase in a downturn and decrease in an upturn – is a fundamental feature of risk-based capital requirements but is probably one of the least understood. This Chapter examines the nature of procyclicality in Pillar 1 capital requirements and modelling (which affects both Standardised and Advanced banks), and the proposed "dampeners" of provisioning and capital buffers.

Stress testing is a key tool to understanding emerging risks and capital requirements over the cycle. Supervisors are increasingly using supervisor-determined stresses to evaluate the relative riskiness of institutions. At the end of 2010, the Federal Reserve required the larger US banks to undertake stresses before it would approve distributions in dividends and bonuses. The European Banking Authority and its predecessor, the Committee for European Banking Supervisors, have conducted European-wide stress tests in 2010 and 2011. These have proved to be very challenging exercises for banks and supervisors. Chapter 11 examines recent developments in leading industry practices for stress testing.

Chapter 12 reviews developments in Pillar 3 for disclosures to market participants. Lack of transparency has been identified as a contributing factor to the crisis and Basel aims to strengthen the market discipline embodied in Pillar 3 by requiring greater disclosures from the banks, many of whom have already begun to do this.

No discussion of capital reforms would be complete without considering the tax implications which are addressed in Chapter 13. In particular, the removal of deferred tax assets as a source of capital for banks that are going concerns has serious consequences for certain banks in certain jurisdictions. This will have consequences, amongst other things, for structure, domicile and funds transfer pricing. Tax is also closely linked to the entity structure of financial institutions which is also under the magnifying glass as part of addressing recovery and resolution plans (see Chapter 15).

Probably one of the most emotive topics in the reform of the banking system is the subject of bankers' pay – or rather the high bonus pay of a relatively small number of bankers. To influence bank management, supervisors are focussing intently on the links between risk and reward and wish to make sure that banks are not offering incentives that would conflict with the goal of increasing financial stability. Chapter 14 delves into leading practice in this critically important and rapidly evolving area.

Planning your own funeral is how resolution plans have been described. Chapter 15 addresses this important and difficult subject. In the wake of the difficulties surrounding the winding up of Lehman, this is the push for banks to develop contingency plans that can be invoked in the event of a future crisis. Recovery refers to contingency plans that need to be deployed when survival is not at stake. These are particularly important for SIFIs, which may be systemically important from either a local or global perspective. SIFIs without sound recovery and resolution plans can expect capital and liquidity surcharges. The detailed recommendations on SIFIs are expected later in 2011.

In Chapter 16 we consider the perspectives of other stake-holders: equity investors, debt investors, government and rating agencies. Regulators seem to have a tendency to ignore the inconvenient question of supply of capital and the interests of capital providers. For example, Mervyn King, the Governor of the Bank of England, in a speech to leading economists, ques-tioned why bankers should be concerned about return on equity ("Banking: from Bagehot to Basel and Back Again", the Second Bagehot Lecture, 25 October 2010). However, for the system to operate effectively, the interests of investors cannot be ignored: this Chapter discusses reform from their perspectives and from those of other stakeholders beyond banks and regulators.

A key response to the crisis has been strengthened risk manage-ment in banks. Chapter 17 examines the implications of reforms for governance, risk management and the role of the CRO. Improved bank risk management is, in our view, likely to be as important a contributor to financial stability as higher capital ratios. It will be central to strengthening the industry and its ability to respond to future challenges.

Too rapid an introduction of reforms such as Basel III in a knee-jerk response to the crisis could cause banks to reduce the amount of credit available and/or increase its price (to achieve the new capital ratios or to pay for the additional capital and liquidity). In turn, this could harm the economy and some sectors would be worse hit than others. Chapter 18 considers likely bank responses to, for example, higher capital requirements and the potential macro-economic implications.

Last but not least, Chapter 19 examines the initiatives that are being taken to improve banking supervision. This is one of the areas of reform where small investments could reap enormous dividends if the investments are made wisely. It is also an area where the challenge of achieving international consensus and maintaining a reasonably level playing field is potentially a major obstacle to the successful implementation of Basel III.

1.8   Looking forward

Much still needs to be done from regulatory and supervisory perspectives to make Basel III a reality. There are the operational details to be agreed on the treatment (and release) of capital buffers. There are definitional details to be refined and sharpened (for example in relation to capital deductions). In Europe, CRD IV needs to be drafted. In the US the timetable for the implementation of Basel III needs to be confirmed. Liquidity buffers, the NSFR, and the leverage ratio need to be monitored and calibrated over the transition period.

An international approach to recovery and resolution and the treatment of SIFIs remains to be agreed; the latest timetable is for this to be done by the end of 2011. And, of course, the market for contingent capital instruments needs to be established.

Banks face the uncertain strategic tasks of deciding what a Basel III world might look like and how they should compete successfully. At a minimum, this requires a long-term view of their capital plans supported by a coherent liquidity and funding strategy. It also requires a view on likely returns on equity, careful management of market expectations and a weather eye to peer performance. Changes to business models are likely for universal and investment banks, but they are unlikely to be alone.

Banks also face extensive operational issues. These range from strengthening risk management and governance to making major changes to capital and liquidity management processes, to enhanced stress testing capabilities, to new funds transfer pricing mechanisms and to multi-year programmes to enhance systems and reporting infrastructures.

1.9   Conclusion

Basel III and other reforms represent an enormous challenge to the whole industry. We trust that this Guide will help you in assessing and addressing your own institution's challenges whether that is as a bank, a supervisor or a regulator.

Chapter 2

Strategic Context

Richard Kibble and James Worsnip

2.1 Introduction

The industry can be confident that Basel III and other reforms will have a significant and permanent impact on the global financial system. However, the precise nature of this impact is currently difficult to determine. As a result, policy-makers and bank management are being forced to make strategic choices under considerable uncertainty. To help the reader in assessing the impact, this Chapter explores the potential strategic implications set against our assessment of the current industry context. These views can only represent our best estimate of what might happen.

One thing is certain: banks will be constrained in their strategic choices by increased capital and liquidity requirements and will face higher costs in the supply of financial products to customer groups. As a result the industry is witnessing a seismic shift from "ubiquity" to "precision".

During the period of credit expansion that preceded the financial crisis, the need for strategic differentiation was eclipsed by a clear belief that capital market innovation would allow banks to supply larger volumes of cheaper credit. As corporate consumers were able to expand activities on this wave of cheap credit, the banks grew more confident in extending credit. Similarly, ever cheaper credit fuelled asset price growth, allowing institutions to support lending decisions through higher collateral backing. Importantly, these conditions also led to funding and liquidity being substantially under-priced. Bank management was assessed in relation to its ability to take advantage of this credit expansion, and little importance was placed on true strategic differentiation. This period of credit expansion and strong profits can be characterised as "ubiquity".

It seems clear that the period of "ubiquity" has ended. As economic recovery is increasingly assured, interest rates will edge upwards, corporate and retail sectors will be more cautious in their dependence on high levels of credit, and banks will be constrained by their capital requirements and funding limitations in the supply of credit. Decisions as to the markets (geographic and product) in which banks deploy their capital will require them to consider relative strengths and make choices on this basis: this period of relatively low growth can be characterised as a period of strategic "precision".

As banks consider their strategic responses, they do so in a dynamic environment where broader regulatory and fiscal reform threatens to cause further fundamental change. The necessary government intervention through the global financial crisis and beyond has ensured that the relationship between government and the industry has continued to be of central importance to banks. As Basel III and other reforms are implemented, bank management teams will not only need to understand the impact across their own institutions but also across the industry. Chief executives will have to maintain cross-functional teams to assess and respond to these changes centrally and throughout their banks.

Basel III is one of many factors that will shape the future of banking. While later Chapters of this Guide address the practical and technical changes that banks will need to make to become Basel III compliant, this Chapter explores the impact of Basel III in a strategic context. The Chapter starts by examining some of the long-term "mega" trends as well as discussing how the economic and interest rate environment in which the reforms are introduced is likely to have an impact.

Having set this context, we then explore the strategic implications of Basel III itself and propose a simple framework by which banks can consider their responses to key questions such as:

(a) With capital and funding constrained, which markets should banks be in?

(b) Which products should they offer and which customer segments should they focus on?

(c) How can banks reconcile the simultaneous and contradictory pressures to increase lending, hold more capital and provide an acceptable return to shareholders?

(d) What will happen to the cost and availability of credit?

The framework first considers the tactical steps that can be taken to ensure efficient compliance with regulations before exploring the strategic questions that banks will need to address. The Chapter concludes by probing the impact of the intended consequences of Basel III such as credit rationing, the future cost of credit and the rise in shadow banking.

2.2 The reforms in context

2.2.1 Section overview

This Section sets out our perspective on the future of banking and then looks more specifically at the likely impact of Basel III. We also propose a simple framework in which banks can assess their response: starting with tactical steps to ensure efficient compliance with the regulation, followed by strategic questions around which markets, which products and which customer segments should be targeted and how to compete.

2.2.2 Drivers affecting the future of banking

Shaping a strategic response to Basel III cannot be done in a vacuum. The environment in which bankers have spent most, if not all, of their careers has changed and senior executives will have to adjust to the new environment. PwC has recently completed extensive research in relation to the evolution of banking – "Project Blue". This research considers the macro-economic and other trends that are likely to drive the global economy and banking in particular. These forces are termed "mega" trends.

23

Where the emerging markets of South America, Africa, Asia and the Middle East (SAAAME) once presented attractive opportunities for Western banks, these banks are now facing stronger, more capable and more confident competition from SAAAME rivals within those markets and, increasingly, in Western markets. Underlying challenges to the Western banks include the tightening grip of government control, mounting pressure on natural resources and declines in working age populations. Figure 2.1 summarises the main drivers that will shape the future of banking. These can be split into two broad categories; current drivers that are reshaping banking now (including Basel III) and mega trends that will reshape banking in the longer term.

2.2.3   Mega trends

2.2.3.1   Rise of the emerging markets

The development of the SAAAME trading bloc threatens all Western banks. Macro-economic analysis (Figure 2.2) highlights seven emerging market economies that might be expected to generate the majority of growth in banking assets

Figure 2.1 Basel III in context: factors shaping the future of banking

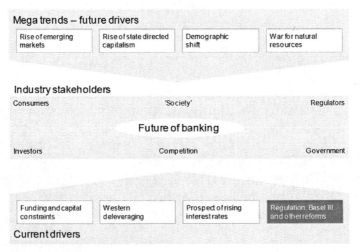

Source: PwC analysis

Figure 2.2 Share of global banking assets by 2050

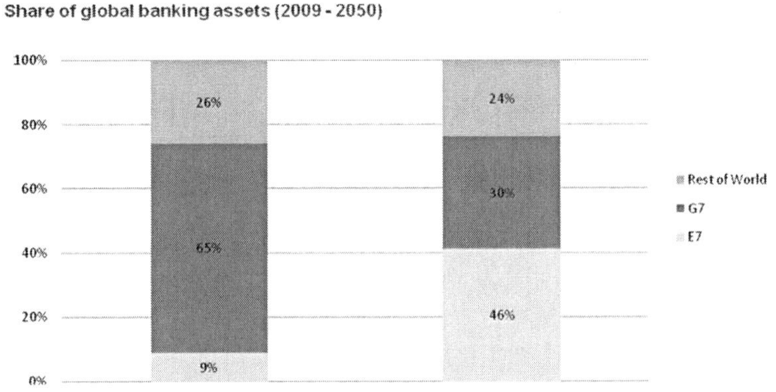

Share of global banking assets (2009 - 2050)

Source: PwC Banking in 2050

through to 2050. This view was shared by Michael Geoghegan, then Group Chief Executive of HSBC Holdings plc, who stated in February 2010:

> "At HSBC, we have long been convinced that the world's centre of gravity is steadily shifting east and south. It's a view we've held since several years BC – BC is after all 'before the crisis.' And, in my view, it is a shift which the crisis has just accelerated".

Most commentators would agree that the main source of growth opportunities derive from the expansion of emerging markets, particularly China. Latest analysis anticipates that the GDP (measured in purchasing power parity terms) of the largest E7 emerging economies will overtake the current G7 economies by 2020. The combination of rapid economic growth and increasingly affluent population within E7 markets creates huge commercial potential. Faced with stagnating growth at home, many G7 banks are looking to strengthen their presence in the SAAAME markets, yet regulation and local competition could make it more difficult for G7 banks to penetrate these markets.

Where institutions already have a strong presence in a market where organic growth can be pursued, the acceleration in the shift of economic power to the South and East may benefit them. Such expansion is not without risk, however, and banks should think carefully before "following the herd". Reform to banking alongside Basel III could further accelerate this development. Western banks will also find themselves on the defensive in their home markets as E7 banks also look to expand overseas. In turn, a growing amount of emerging-to-emerging market business is bypassing the West altogether, which is leaving G7 banks increasingly out of the loop. A sign of the growing financial integration within the SAAAME trading bloc is the Industrial and Commercial Bank of China's ("ICBC") acquisition of a 20 per cent holding in South Africa's Standard Bank, which has given ICBC access to Standard's extensive network across the resource-rich continent.

> "London and New York will have to share their dominant roles with some new financial centres."
> *PwC global banking survey participant*

G7 Countries: **E7 Countries:**

France   China
Germany   India
Italy   Brazil
Japan   Mexico
United Kingdom   Russia
United States   Indonesia
Canada   Turkey

2.2.3.2   Rise of state-directed capitalism

Having supported banks through the crisis, Western governments and voters will expect such banks to demonstrate that they are socially and economically useful. The impact can already be seen in more stringent regulation of capital and liquidity and the threat to break up groups deemed too big to fail or add even more capital requirements. In future, many Western banks may find it more difficult to invest overseas as they are forced to focus on supporting activity in their domestic markets. In the wider economy, an apparent increase has been seen in the number of foreign takeovers being rejected by governments on the grounds of national interest. Prominent examples include the failure of BHP Billiton to get the go-ahead for the purchase of Canada's Potash Corp, the world largest fertiliser maker.

> "Governments will try to move away from the free market economy to a more regulated one as social pressure mounts, people become more risk averse and rely more on the state to take care of them."
> *PwC global banking survey participant*

2.2.3.3 War for natural resources

Supply may not be able to keep pace with rising global demand for natural resources, putting pressure on industrial output, forcing up prices and creating the potential for social unrest and global conflict. It is notable that threats to food and water security and the resulting potential for geopolitical instability feature prominently in the World Economic Forum's Global Risks 2011 Report. Banks will need to think about how to adjust to a world where certain assets become increasingly scarce and valuable. They are also set to face growing pressure to invest in companies that promote sustainable technologies and may need to work out new risk parameters as a result.

> "Global instability will increase and the standard of living in the US and other first world nations is likely to suffer in the coming years."
> *PwC global banking survey participant*

2.2.3.4 Demographic shift

There will be significant opportunities to provide wealth solutions for ageing populations. However, declines in working age populations in both Western and Far Eastern economies could lead to slower growth, depress asset prices and create the potential for severe social tension. Western governments will face fiscal strain as a reduction in the working population suppresses tax revenue, while at the same time the healthcare and pension costs associated with an ageing population continue to increase. The impact of this trend is already evident in rising savings rates and growing uncertainty over the adequacy of retirement income. Banks face a significant impact on their growth prospects, sources of investment and how they manage their assets and interact with their customers.

> "India has 500 million people under the age of 30, creating a huge pool of earners and consumers, which will feed industry and growth and attract more big international companies to set up hubs."
> *PwC global banking survey participant*

2.2.4 Current drivers

2.2.4.1 Funding and capital constraints

Lack of confidence in banking resulted in an interruption in the operation of wholesale markets through the crisis. Institutions had become heavily reliant on the securitisation markets for funding and these markets are yet to recover to anything like the levels of activity that were observed during the credit expansion. Banks will need to look to other sources of long-term funding, including higher levels of capital. The uncertain prospects of Western banking as a sector will limit its attractiveness to investors and banks will need to demonstrate that they can develop cohesive strategies to deploy this capital effectively. With access to wholesale funding constrained there will be a fight for deposits. To some extent, the investment and innovation that helped to develop lending products over the last decade will be redeployed to attract and retain deposits.

2.2.4.2 Western deleveraging

Figure 2.3 illustrates how bank assets have grown almost continually for 30 years outstripping GDP growth before the deleveraging following the great financial crisis. A reversal which is masked by merger activity reflected in the chart. Historically, after recessions and banking crises, bank asset

Figure 2.3 Growth in assets of the top 16 European listed banks aggregated by country

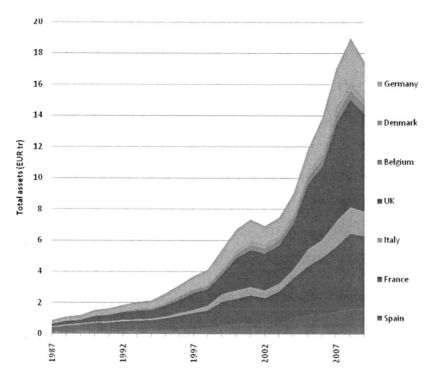

Assets of top 16 European listed banks aggregated by country, 1987 - 2009

	CAGR (1987 - 2007)	CAGR (2008 - 2009)
Germany	14%	-17%
Belgium	16%	-11%
UK	20%	-9%
Italy	19%	-8%
France	13%	-5%
Spain	19%	3%

Source: Capital IQ, PwC analysis

Notes: Graph reflects the balance sheet assets of the largest 16 European banks – no adjustment is made for mergers.

growth returned to its long-term trend above GDP growth. However, looking ahead, the combined effect of capital and funding constraints, rising real interest rates, customer deleveraging (consumers and businesses), and the increasing burden of regulation will mean Western banks may struggle to sustain even modest growth. The low growth environment faced by Western banks will cause further problems as banks attempt to pass through the increased burden of regulation by re-pricing loan books. For banks in faster growing markets the ratio of new lending to back book will allow a more rapid adjustment to the higher cost environment.

2.2.4.3   Rising interest rates

The credit expansion that characterised the decade before the financial crisis allowed banks to expand in a low interest rate environment and to recognise high levels of profit as rates fell. Corporate consumers were able to expand on this wave of cheap credit allowing banks to support further lending decisions on improved collateral backing. Rates will increase as the global economy strengthens and banks will have to adjust to this "new normal" by focusing their scarce resources with ever greater precision.

2.2.4.4   Regulation and other reforms

The package of reforms announced by the Basel Commission on Banking Supervision on 12 September 2010, that form Basel III will only ever be part of the regulatory response to the crisis. Although endorsed by the G20 leaders, this does not mean that implementation will be consistent, nor does it mean that the response of banks will be similar. Implementation of Basel III will be at a local level; variations will inevitably occur and some institutions may be able to take advantage of this lack of international harmony. Further regulatory changes will be made with reference to Basel III (e.g. resolution approaches), so much of its impact will be indirect. Moreover, the structure of the industry may need to respond to address concerns of competition regulators as well as those of financial regulators as seems to be the case in the UK and in Australia.

2.2.5   Framework for response

As banks shape their overall response to Basel III, they do so in an environment where significant uncertainty still remains in terms of government and regulators overall response to the crisis. At the same time, many banks face simultaneous, and seemingly incompatible, pressures to increase lending, hold more capital and to deliver acceptable returns to shareholders. Broadly, we believe banks should consider their response in two stages: first, the degree to which the impact can be mitigated by efficient compliance and secondly what longer-term strategic response might be required. Alongside this decision making process, banks will have to also consider other external pressures which could also have an impact on the structure and working practices within the bank.

2.2.6   Efficient compliance

Institutions will need to consider the extent to which the impact of the reforms can be mitigated by aligning their chosen business model such that they are able to comply with reforms as efficiently as possible. Some forms of tactical response

Figure 2.4 Dimensions of Basel III response

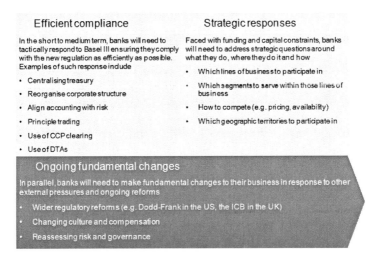

Source: PwC analysis

31

will require changes in the corporate structure and could give rise to operational change. Where banks have considered restructuring programmes in the past, implementation costs – alteration in booking models, technological investment and capital gains taxes – have often stalled or blocked more efficient structures. Basel III will put a higher cost on capital inefficiency and banks may wish to look again at restructuring programmes to ensure that they are able to employ their resources to deliver adequate shareholder return. The liquidity reforms will make the concerns of central treasury influential in determining aspects of the corporate structure to limit trapped pools of liquid assets. Restructuring may also enable banks to accelerate the use of deferred tax assets that will no longer qualify as part of a bank's capital base and to ensure that risk and accounting systems are aligned.

2.2.7   *Strategic response*

Faced with scarcity and increased costs, banks will need to deploy their resources with ever more precision. At the strategic level the choices that face management in an environment of constrained financial resources can be largely boiled down to the traditional strategic choices that face management in all industries:

Which lines of business to participate in? Banks have expanded their reach beyond the traditional role of safekeeping and credit provision into other activities. Given the new constraints, management will need to determine whether these activities strengthen the overall business model and generate acceptable levels of return;

Which geographic territories to participate in? As the crisis developed, banks withdrew from overseas markets favouring the protection of their domestic franchise. Although this was a logical response during the crisis, as the world's economies emerge it will become clear which territories offer a relatively favourable environment for banking. Those banks that already have a strong position in the faster growing economies will look to capitalise on this position; others will have to decide whether to follow;

Which segments to serve within those lines of business? Additional regulatory burden will be borne by all sub sectors of banking. Some elements of banking will only be affected by those reforms that are designed to improve the resilience of the bank as a whole while other activities will be specifically targeted by additional reforms and attract an additional burden. If the reforms were applied consistently across a product market, the burden of the reform might be expected to be borne evenly and the cost passed on to consumers. In some markets this will be true whilst in other markets customer groups may look to adopt nonbank substitutes and restrict the market that banks are able to access profitably;

Where to sit on the risk/reward spectrum? The muted returns on equity achievable in the post-crisis, Basel III world mean that many banks will have to reassess where they wish to sit on the risk/reward spectrum and what target level of return on equity they believe is appropriate; and

How to compete (e.g. pricing, credit availability)? Through the period of credit expansion, banks' focus was on building market share through the issuance of cheap credit and relaxed underwriting criteria. The focus on stable funding may require banks to choose how they compete for customers and in particular their savings and deposits – it will be interesting to see how banks look to adjust their customer proposition to improve the stability of funding.

2.2.8   Ongoing fundamental changes

There is also a political dimension to the ongoing reform programme which cannot be ignored; it seems unlikely that policy makers and regulators will have faith that the market will correct behaviours without state intervention. With the passage of Dodd-Frank in July 2010, the US established a framework for reform that would confine and regulate banking activities and reverse the liberalism that had been adopted in the pre-crisis years of ubiquity. Although Western democracies will not reject capitalism, it does seem likely that they will seek to exert increasing control over banks and the real economy. Some commentators argue that the implicit government guarantee to creditors of institutions that are too interconnected to fail represents a distortion to the free market that ought to be corrected.

Banks will need to win back the trust of the state and demonstrate their social utility; supporting lending through periods of stress and committing to real change in remuneration structures. Alongside these reforms, banks will need to choose how they engage with policy makers and regulators such that they continue to be able to point to unintended consequences of reform and seek refinement to avoid asymmetries that might otherwise arise. Commentators argue that to achieve sea change in the management of risk, fundamental reform is required through the culture of institutions. Fundamental reform can only be achieved if incentives are aligned and banks are looking at innovative ways to link reward to longer-term shareholder value. Although some banks may look to defer bonuses or introduce longer-term incentive plans, others could follow Barclays in linking the risk of failure to deferred reward; in the Barclays example through the issuance of contingent convertible capital to senior bankers.

Where activities are prohibited, e.g., the Dodd-Frank prohibition of principal trading, banks have a choice between carving out activities through other business lines, disposal (to related entities or otherwise) or winding up such operations. Where investment banks were once able to generate returns from illiquid or specialised OTC markets, reforms push for increased homogeneity; standardisation that will allow banks to reduce counterparty risk through the use of centralised clearing.

2.2.9 *Impact on regulators*

Regulatory authorities (local, regional and global) will need to change to address the failings that became manifest during the financial crisis. They also carry a heavy burden in that it will be their responsibility to ensure that Basel III is implemented in a manner that affords flexibility and discretion without giving rise to international inconsistency. Regulators are likely to need different and perhaps greater resources to meet greater and different responsibilities:

(a) broader remit – macro prudential regulation;
(b) deeper resource with new capabilities – more intrusive regulation;

(c) new domains need to be more effectively covered (e.g. liquidity risk); and

(d) greater need for international collaboration.

The challenges for regulators are discussed in detail in Chapter 19.

2.2.10 Unintended consequences

Lastly, and critically, there are likely to be several unintended consequences of Basel III including effects on the supply of financing to certain segments (e.g. SME, unsecured lending to consumers) and the viability of certain products and related business models. Where demand is unmet by the traditional banking sector, consumers may look outside the regulated sector undermining the reforms at the margin and spreading risk. Section 2.4 below discusses some of the concerns that commentators have raised in this respect.

2.3 Basel III – Impact and response

2.3.1 Section overview

Considering the impact of regulation against the strategic context outlined above allows banks to assess the strategic responses and tactical considerations that might be appropriate. This section identifies the impact that Basel III is likely to have on banks and considers how banks might react. The key reforms can be grouped in terms of their impact: higher levels of capital; strengthened liquidity requirements and funding restraint; and higher quality capital.

2.3.2 Summary of impact

The reforms could have a very different impact on some institutions, depending in part on their current balance sheet strength but also on their mix of activities. Also the impacts of Basel III will vary considerably depending on the region and country question. Figure 2.5 provides a generic perspective.

Figure 2.5 The impact of reforms on generic types of banking institutions

Regulatory reform	Retail banking	Corporate banking	Investment banking
Higher levels of capital			
Higher minimum levels of capital	Medium	Medium	Medium
Capital conservation buffer	Medium	Medium	Medium
Countercyclical buffers	Small	Small	Medium
Strengthened liquidity requirements			
Higher levels of liquid assets	Small	Institution specific	Large
Introduced stable funding ratio	Small	Institution specific	Large
Securitisation reforms	Institution specific	Institution specific	Large
Quality of capital			
Higher quality capital	Small	Institution specific	Large
Altering risk weighting of assets	Institution specific	Medium	Large
Structure			
Subsidiarisation	Institution specific	Institution specific	Medium
Structural reform	Small	Medium	Large

Large impact   Medium impact   Small impact   Institution specific

Source: PwC analysis

2.3.3 *Higher levels of capital*

Basel III will require banks to hold higher levels of capital. Within this mandate there are three distinct factors driving the requirement to hold higher capital levels: higher minimum levels of capital; the capital conservation buffer; and counter-cyclical buffers.

The minimum levels of capital that banks will be required to hold will be far higher than those held pre-crisis and perhaps higher than some regulators would have thought desirable. Banks will need to hold enough capital to comply and absorb unforeseen shocks while at the same time maximising returns for shareholders. Shareholders might be prepared to accept the need for higher levels of capital than regulatory minima would suggest, but management will need to express the strategic benefits associated with this, for example improved rating and more assured access to funds. Where excess capital is trapped rather than being deployed strategically, shareholders will be entitled to take management to task.

In making the transition to this higher capital ratio environment, banks will look to generate higher levels of earnings and retain a greater proportion of those earnings to meet reforms. The capital retained to support growth over and beyond the minimum required to meet the reforms is likely to be limited, but stronger institutions may see opportunities in this environment to cement their market position. Demonstrating this, Standard Chartered raised £3.25bn at the end of 2010 in a rights issue targeted at accommodating regulatory changes. The Standard Chartered statement read:

> "The Board believes that under the current regulatory regime the Group could sustain good growth whilst maintaining capital ratios broadly constant at their current strong levels through internal capital generation. However, the regulatory environment remains in flux and the Board believes that the Group's principal regulators will raise requirements relating to minimum capital ratio levels, through revised definitions of capital and incorporating further regulatory buffers, and in addition may accelerate the transition timetable announced by the Basel Committee on Banking Supervision (the "BCBS") on 12 September 2010. To accommodate such increases in effective capital ratios, the Group may have to constrain risk-weighted asset growth, sacrificing attractive growth opportunities, unless new capital is raised."
>
> *Source:* FT "Standard Chartered is off to the capital races" 13 October 2010

Several banks looked to protect and build their capital strength as the financial crisis deepened. For some, this strengthening was pre-emptive, whilst for others it was a response to a crisis of confidence that could have induced panic. The more pessimistic economic scenarios appear to have been avoided in the majority of large economies, and the losses that threatened to erode capital have not been as great as some had feared. Most banks are now in a position where they hold far higher levels of capital than they would have thought appropriate before the financial crisis, as illustrated in Figure 2.6. From these current levels of capital, banks can develop plans to achieve the still higher levels that Basel III prescribes. For many institutions, the strategic plan will include a focus on the core franchise with divestments and exits in other areas. The real challenge for many will be achieving an appropriate funding structure and higher levels of liquid assets.

The aspects of the reforms that have drawn the greatest comment are those aspects that oblige banks to hold higher levels of capital to support their activities. Banks are only able to generate higher capital ratios immediately in two ways: either to raise fresh capital from the markets, or reduce the size of their lending activities. With access to capital markets restricted to some banks, immediate compliance with a higher level of capital would only be achievable by forced deleveraging, the implications of which for those banks and the wider economy could be severe (see Chapter 18 – Implications for the economy).

The extended transition period introduced by the Committee means that a third option becomes available to institutions: retention of earnings to build their capital bases more quickly than they expand their asset bases. The Committee believes that, in aggregate, the Basel III timeframe should allow the banking sector to comply with Basel III without major delever-

Figure 2.6 Capital ratios for selected banking systems, 2005–2010

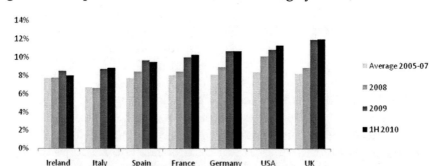

Source: Bank of England, Financial Stability Report, December 2010

Notes: a) Includes banks with total assets of more than US$100bn at end 2009, b) Aggregated from individual banks (risk-weighted) capital ratios, weighted by total assets, c) UK data excludes Northern Rock, aging, even as the definition of capital hardens. It is important to note that compliance with the reforms will be a bigger challenge for some institutions than others and that further economic disruption could make the situation worse. In some cases, shareholders will be asked to accept a period of low dividends or low growth (possibly both) as institutions seek to build their capital bases. For other institutions, the stressed position of their competitors will open up opportunities.

Compliance with Basel III will require further bolstering over the transition timeframe. The extent of this requirement will be driven by three elements:

3.2.3.1 *The starting point of the bank and strategy for capital strength*

In response to more stringent stress tests and the need to demonstrate stability to counterparts, banks have undertaken major exercises to bolster their capital positions, running down risk positions and injecting fresh equity. Some banks have undertaken more radical exercises than others to improve capital ratios. In some instances, this has been driven by the concerns in the market that more complex balance sheets may include unrecognised losses, which could quickly erode capital strength. In others, the bank management has taken a strategic view that capital strength may allow them to attract new business or allow them to be opportunistic. Banks with higher levels of capital should attract a better credit rating and lower their cost of funding. Security over longer-term sources of funding will become increasingly important.

2.3.3.2 *The attitude of local regulators in forcing compliance/super equivalence*

The fact that the G20 endorsed the proposals should set in train the necessary legislative and regulatory reform that ensures consistent application of the standards on a global basis. There remains a very real risk that global consistency will not be achieved and we may see significant differences in application. Through the rounds of consultation and debate in relation to Basel III it became clear that some continental European authorities (notably those in France and Germany) would have preferred a less radical reform agenda whilst others (notably the UK and Switzerland) would have welcomed more stringent reform. The need for compromise could lead to a situation whereby national authorities seek to apply higher standards or use other discretionary powers to force higher levels of capital. It is important to recognise that Basel II was not adopted consistently across the globe and a drive to achieve consistency for some banks in these countries could present an additional challenge.

2.3.3.3   *The activities of the bank*

Banks with a stronger focus on retail banking and commercial banking will be less impacted by the reforms than those with a strong focus on investment banking. Cash and derivative trading will be hit by specific reforms that require banks to recognise higher levels of market risk. These reforms are compounded by the introduction of Credit Valuation Adjustments, requiring banks to recognise the market risk element associated within counterparty credit risk. Other reforms apply across the bank affecting their activities, either through enhancing the quality of capital by forcing the deduction of assets from the capital base, or through lifting the overall ratios that the bank must reach to ensure compliance. These reforms amplify the impact of those specific reforms that are attributable to particular activities.

Although the impact on different institutions will vary, the choices that restricted capital will be similar. Banks will have to decide how to deploy scarce capital to generate the optimal risk adjusted return. These choices will depend on the extent to which a higher capital charge can be passed on to an end consumer. In making this assessment, managers will have to consider the strategic environment of the business sectors in the following ways:

- **How will competitors respond to the regulatory change?**
  Marginal players in a market may choose to exit a geography or product market in order to focus resources elsewhere. As institutions exit and capacity is withdrawn the intensity of competition may fall, allowing incumbents operating at appropriate scale to benefit from higher margins. Higher margins may help to offset the increased capital charges that

they are forced to bear, and to some may continue to offer attractive returns. In some markets, for example specialist mortgage banking in the UK, the financial crisis resulted in the withdrawal of firms, and so now spreads for those with access to funding has increased significantly.

- **What alternatives are available to clients?**
  In other markets, alternatives may be available to customers. For example, larger corporate clients may choose to make greater use of bond markets, such that the extent to which banks are able to pass on the additional cost of providing credit is limited. Lending to large corporates may become less attractive from a strict return on capital employed metric, and institutions will have to assess the value of the relationship to the bank as a whole, perhaps as a client of their broader banking and capital markets business.
- **Will the market shrink as price levels rise?**
  Other markets in which banks participate could become less viable, shrink markedly or be abandoned by banks and customers alike. The reforms that look to push derivative activity through centrally cleared models impose significant capital cost on activities that cannot be moved away from an OTC (i.e. bespoke) environment. Corporate treasurers use banks to hedge risk, but the higher cost of doing so may encourage some businesses to carry more of this risk themselves or seek bilateral arrangements to reduce exposures.

2.3.4 Strengthened liquidity requirements and funding restraint

Although the recapitalisation of the banks has allowed a restoration in confidence between banks it has not unlocked the wholesale funding channels to supply the volumes of credit at anything like pre-crisis levels. Some commentators fear that banks will face a refinancing cliff as central banks' schemes come to an end. Although attempts by institutions to diversify their funding profiles have been welcomed (see *www.bankofengland.co.uk/ publications/fsr/2010/fsr28sec4.pdf*), there remains reticence and a concern that the innovation that had been observed has the effect of redistributing rather than eliminating risk within the system. More permanent solutions to the need for "sustainable" funding may require fundamental change in the banking models adopted. In the meantime, it will be important for banks to work with policy makers to improve transparency, and work towards restoring investor confidence in a badly damaged ABS market.

By tapping these markets directly and through structured products, banks were able to expand their activities and allowed their capital to work harder. One of the most alarming features of the financial crisis was the pace at which the loss of confidence in certain elements of securitised mortgage lending spread to cause effective seizure across this funding channel, and then spread through into the interbank market. With this seizure, central banks were called upon to support the system with the launch of temporary measures to ensure that sufficient liquidity would be available to meet the requirements of otherwise solvent banks, and thereby restore confidence in the system. Closing the liquidity shortfall – estimated as being €1.7 trillion across the world's largest banks (169 banks formed the sample reviewed through the Quantitative Impact Study (Dec 2010)) – will require institutions to hold far greater quantities of highly liquid, low-yielding assets. Along with those measures which increase the level of capital held by banks, the liquidity reforms will depress returns in areas where cost cannot be passed on to end consumers.

Perhaps of even greater significance are the reforms that force banks to address their funding profile. One of the central functions of banking is to allow individuals and firms to take out loans that they are only obliged to repay over a term. The maturity mismatch that banks manage is a critical element to the operation of the economy and banks are rewarded for managing this risk. Banks took confidence that funding sources would remain secure and this confidence allowed them to increase lending without a corresponding increase in deposits. The focus of bank analysts and management was drawn to growth and market share and away from the monitoring of stability ratios. The introduction of the NSFR establishes a framework to regulate how assets are funded, and in doing so will drive banks to hold a greater proportion of assets in more liquid form (perhaps beyond that required by the LCR) and create a funding profile that includes more long-term funding, part of which will come from the expansion in the capital base. In effect the NSFR will act as a further constraint on balance sheet growth and in the asset types that they choose to hold.

While treasury functions will have the challenge of generating the funding required to close the gap, management will also have to consider whether the additional constraints can be eased by refinements to the business model or more funda-mental strategic change. The importance of a stable deposit base has been highlighted through the crisis, and it became clear that deposits gathered through branches were far more stable than reliance on interbank facilities and internet account balances. Banks may choose to focus more closely on building stability within their deposit base, providing additional services to create stickiness. Should the race for deposits develop into a price war then this will place further pressure on bank returns and may do little to improve the stability of funding.

2.3.5 Higher quality capital

Reporting the results of their Quantitative Impact Study in December 2010, the BCBS announced that, whilst on a Basel II basis the sampled banks aggregate Core Tier 1 (referred to as Core Equity Tier 1) ratio would have been 11.1 per cent, the impact of the Basel III rules on risk-weighted assets and on deductions from equity would be to reduce this ratio to 5.7 per cent for its sample of larger, internationally active banks. The elements associated with these deductions are discussed in more detail in the Chapters that follow. Two particularly impor-tant challenges will arise around securitisation and trading activities (see also Chapters 4 – Trading book and securitisation and 5 – Counterparty credit risk, which discuss these issues in more detail).

- **Securitisation activities**
  The dependence on access to wholesale funding became apparent with the seizure of the securitisation markets. Considerable efforts are being made to restore the confi-dence in these markets, requiring originators to retain a minimum interest of 5 per cent in the securitisation. This, combined with the higher levels of capital required to

support assets retained, will increase the cost of securitisation to institutions. The funding challenges associated with mortgage banking remain, and banks will need to consider the extent to which the limitations to their access to cheap funding will drive mortgage rates higher and restrict access to those with established and stable sources of deposits

- **Trading activities**

  Where a bank acts as a market maker holding inventory to facilitate client trading, the costs of such positions will increase and depress profitability. By challenging the holding of such box positions, the regulations will challenge market makers to consider the breadth of securities covered and the spreads that they seek to maintain. Within derivative trading, the implementation of CRD III from January 2012 will require banks to hold far higher levels of capital against market risk. Through Basel III regulators will also seek additional capital in relation to the market risk component of credit risk through Credit Value Adjustments on counterparty risk. In view of these reforms, the risk weighting associated with trading activities will increase significantly, particularly where market participants are unable to make use of central counterparty clearing, suppressing the profitability of such businesses. Banks will need to consider the extent to which they are able to pass on the additional costs associated with the higher levels of capital, or adjust their business model as such that they are no longer acting as principal in transactions. By improving the efficiency of netting through central counterparties, banks may hope to mitigate some of the increased costs and achieve the transparency that regulators seek. This is likely to be most effective where there is greater standardisation within the product portfolio traded, but may offer little support where bespoke positions are taken to assist a client to manage a particular risk.

Alongside those reforms that require banks to recognise that their activities give rise to greater risks are reforms that challenge the quality of the balance sheet that supports those activities. Banks are unable to rely on certain assets to form part of the capital base and, as a result, they will need to replace this capital (see Chapter 3 – Defining capital). As noted above, the two most biting deductions are likely to be:

(a) Material holdings and insurance subsidiaries – Where banks hold an investment of more than 10 per cent of another financial institution but do not consolidate that entity within their group accounts the excess above the 10 per cent threshold will become a deduction. Deductions will also be required in relation to insurance subsidiaries (again above a 10 per cent threshold) such that the "double leverage" that banks have been able to benefit from will no longer be available to them. In some instances, some realignment through corporate restructuring may help mitigate the impact of the reforms, whilst in others divestment may be the more rational approach. This could be particularly challenging for those banks who have sought to make the bancassurance model work.

(b) Deferred Tax Assets ("DTAs") – although DTAs form part of the equity of a bank from an accounting perspective, they offer no protection to creditors once a bank has ceased to be a going concern. In view of this, banks are likely to seek to organise themselves so that they can accelerate the use of these assets.

2.3.6 *An ongoing reform agenda*

Banks will need to ask themselves what they anticipate the end-game will be, both for themselves as institutions and for the wider industry. The key questions to be addressed in the ongoing reform agenda can be grouped across the following issues:

(a) an effective resolution regime, including the need for subsidiarisation;

(b) new forms of loss absorbent capital; and

(c) structural reform of the industry.

These open questions are relevant to banks in two respects: first, they create uncertainty and limit the ability of bank management to develop strategies with confidence; and, secondly, further reform is likely to require additional financial (and other) resources to meet regulatory requirements for business models that are inherently less efficient than the existing ones.

Chapter 15 – Recovery and resolution planning, considers the developments that are underway to address the need for more extensive preparation for recovery and resolution. These developments are being considered in parallel to Basel III. Regulators can seek to mitigate risk – the probability that failure might happen – and the impact of such an event. The failure of a bank is regrettable and disruptive, but it is not economically desirable to require banks to hold so much capital that failure is virtually impossible. Banks should be able to fail in such a way that the disruption that failure creates is not systemic; that a bank's positions can be unwound in an orderly way. National authorities have been given the discretion to determine the levels of countercyclical buffers that might be employed during a period of credit expansion and the timing of buffer release during a crisis. Regulatory intervention is likely to be influenced by the measures that are in place to allow the institution to draw on further risk absorbent capital.

Bank management will need to consider how these wider concerns can be addressed through organisational restructuring (including subsidiarisation) and through the issuance of new loss absorbent securities. Chapter 16 – Stakeholder perspectives, discusses contingent capital.

In several countries, restructuring of the industry is being proposed or debated. The structure of the US banking industry has been challenged through Dodd-Frank and US banks are already responding to the reforms in their business models. In the UK, the Independent Commission on Banking ("ICB") is considering recommendations for structural reform that are aimed not only at enhanced financial stability but also greater competition. The ICB recommendations will have fundamental implications for those banks that fall under its direct remit and could have wider policy implications internationally. In Australia, the Treasury has launched proposals to reform the structure of its banking industry, which are also designed to promote competition.

2.4 Unintended consequences

2.4.1 *Section overview*

There are a number of unintended consequences that are a direct result of Basel III. Basel III imposes capital and liquidity restrictions which are at odds with the pressure national governments are placing on banks to increase lending. By placing further burden on the "traditional" banking services, Basel III could have significant detrimental effect on specific areas of an economy heavily reliant on the availability of credit, for example small and medium-sized businesses. In addition, Basel III is likely to impact services which would usually complement capital and liquidity restraints in a tight lending environment, such as trade finance.

This Section groups these unintended consequences into three key areas of concern: credit rationing; the future cost of credit; and shadow banking. Banks should consider these issues in the context of wider evolution of the market as they develop their strategic responses to Basel III.

2.4.2 *Credit rationing*

One of the main concerns policy-makers were keen to address was the risk of encouraging or even forcing deleveraging – the withdrawal of credit from critical segments of the economy. As discussed in Chapter 18 – Implications for the economy, if banks are forced to meet the reforms in a short period of time, this could have a considerable negative impact on the economy. But by electing to implement such a radical package of reforms over an extended timeframe to 2019, regulators hope to mitigate this risk by allowing banks to comply with the reforms over a longer period through gradual accumulation of retained earnings. In this case the main impact on the economy is likely to be a gradual rise in credit prices, which is expected to have far more moderate economic impact than forced deleveraging across the banking sector.

The ability of banks to generate profits is dependent on the level and future path of interest rates. The ability of banks to re-price business in a rising interest rate environment and broaden spreads to accommodate the greater cost burden associated with regulation depends on their mix of business and how the shape of the yield curve changes. Some institutions will be presented with a number of strategic options: increase the proportion of earnings retained; ignore opportunities for otherwise profitable growth by negative net lending; where possible, cutting trading activities that give rise to high RWA (and profits); or reduce RWA by divestment of portfolios.

The base from which banks will begin addressing these issues is fundamental to how they are able to respond. Where institutions are well funded and face less of a challenge re-pricing business to comply with the reforms, it seems that they will be in a strong position to take advantage of other institutions who do not have the capital available to maintain market share or are forced to dispose of portfolios. In the event that interest rates and spreads rise quickly, bank profits will be challenged and disposal of portfolios will become more difficult without crystallising losses. In such circumstances, the sector may still be forced to ration the credit that it supplies to the economy.

2.4.3   Future cost of credit

The burden of reform will increase costs for banks and threaten profitability. The ability of banks to pass on these costs to consumers will depend on the substitutes that are available to them, the capacity of borrowers to absorb this increased burden and the lender's ability to re-price their assets. In some instances the substitutes available may be attractive to policy-makers (creating a deeper corporate bond market), whereas for others forcing activity outside the regulated sector is far from desirable (see Section on shadow banking below). The impact will be varied between sectors, with SME lending and unsecured credit expected to be disproportionally affected. Where SMEs find themselves badly affected by the economic slowdown and operate at a level of gearing where servicing of debt has become difficult, a rising interest rate environment could push them into insolvency.

Unsecured lending is another area where an increased burden is likely to rest on consumers; both in terms of the availability and the cost of credit. Lenders will target their scarce capital with precision, and will be increasingly selective in terms of who they lend to. This will effectively re-draw the boundaries of what constitutes prime and sub-prime (see Figure 2.7). Simultaneously, as consumers have struggled to cope with challenging economic conditions, credit scores may have deteriorated. The combined effect will mean that a growing number of consumers will be unable to access credit from mainstream banks, leading to a potential rise in financial exclusion. If the recovery continues to gain ground and demand for credit begins to return, this mismatch between supply and demand will come to the fore. For customers who do fall into bank's target segments, credit offers are likely to be highly attractive as lenders compete for their custom.

Credit card borrowers (especially sub-prime) have seen increasing interest costs as lenders have looked to meet increased charge-offs through wider interest spreads. Such price rises have not yet stopped and it is estimated that further increases in the cost of unsecured credit may be as much as 200–300 basis points over the next few years (Source: Precious Plastic 2011, PwC). Higher spreads over increasing interest rates will be required in order to pass on the burden of reform, and banks may choose to leave some customer groups un-served.

Figure 2.7 Illustrative shifts in lenders cut off and credit scores

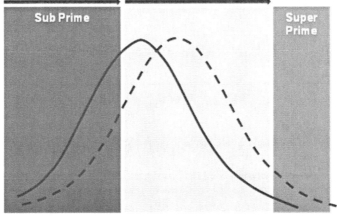

Source: PwC analysis

49

Non-bank lenders who are not subject to the same reform and who may not be regulated as stringently as banks are well placed to extend credit to these individuals. A dearth of credit may yet result in a slow down on the high street. Other areas that could be affected include auto-finance where manufacturers may choose to subsidise captive business models to support dealer networks in selling cars.

Trade finance is another area of activity that is likely to be adversely affected by the reforms. By issuing letters of credit to other financial institutions, banks are able to support the trading activities of their clients, which is an important aspect of international trade. Under Basel II, letters of credit held between well-rated financial institutions would attract relatively low risk weighting. The new reforms not only increase the risk weighting and associated capital charge, but also force recognition of this off balance sheet commitment within liquidity calculations.

Capital market activities will also be affected by the reforms. Banks will be disincentivised (and could be prohibited) from carrying principal exposures. Where banks operate as market makers they maintain principal (box) positions that allow them to facilitate client trading as efficiently as possible. The additional regulatory burden (direct and indirect) associated with this activity could be passed on to clients through higher trading costs and perhaps wider spreads. By increasing the cost of trading a security, the reforms could make certain markets less liquid and less efficient.

2.4.4   Shadow banking

Basel III and the majority of other banking reforms focus on reducing risk and increasing stability among traditional banks. One very real concern is that increasing regulation will do little to reduce overall risk in the system as activity is pushed into the less regulated and more opaque shadow banking sector. The shadow banking sector is large and not well understood. In July 2010 the Federal Reserve Bank of New York undertook a study of shadow banking, and the resulting wall chart that mapped the connectivity of shadow banks with the rest of the financial sector was 4ft by 3ft in size. According to estimates from US Federal Reserve

(Figure 2.8), shadow banking liabilities exceed those of traditional banks, rising to \$20 trillion before the global financial crisis. Risk taking in the shadow banking market expanded even more quickly than traditional banking through SIVs, ABS conduits and hedge funds. Tax-efficient structures, high leverage and low operating costs allowed innovative bankers to step outside the more tightly regulated deposit taking banking environment.

While global regulators are currently examining the shadow banking sector to assess how they might work together to manage the risk posed, there is increasing evidence that the sector is competing more directly with traditional banks e.g., by lending money directly to companies and through heavy trading in commodities and bonds.

Regulators care about the lack of transparency and volatile nature of these vehicles, but they also recognise that the connectivity with banking is difficult to break and that governments may be forced to salvage failing vehicles to prevent contagion. It may not be possible for regulators to successfully regulate shadow banking because it is difficult to define and it attracts innovation to avoid the constraints that they might otherwise face. As a reaction to the reforms to strengthen formal banking, the credit expansion and maturity transformation of the next

Figure 2.8 Liabilities in US shadow and traditional banks

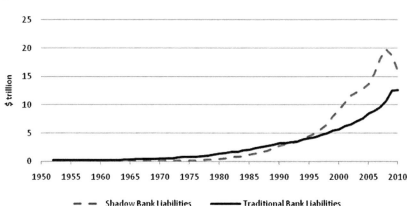

Source: Shadow Banking; Federal Reserve Bank of New York Staff Reports, no. 458; July 2010

boom might come through vehicles that are beyond the regulators, but still represent a systemic risk.

2.5 Conclusion

During the credit expansion, innovation in the capital markets and globalisation supplied ever cheaper credit in increasing volume. Corporate borrowers were able to ride this wave of cheap credit to expand their activities and deliver profit growth, and increases in asset values provided collateral to support lending decisions. Through this low interest rate environment, banks were able to expand and recognised higher levels of profit on existing business as rates fell. This period of falling interest rates is at an end, and, as the global economy strengthens, interest rates will edge upwards and banks will have to adjust to the new norm. It is against this challenging environment that the reforms are introduced.

To meet the requirements of Basel III, many banks will be forced to adopt conservative growth strategies and retain a greater proportion of earnings to meet the hardening definition of capital and higher capital ratios. Demands on restricted financial resources will force institutions to consider carefully the geographic and product markets that they serve, to ensure that they can deliver appropriate returns on the capital that they deploy. It will only be possible to pass on the full burden of higher levels of capital and liquidity where customers lack access to alternatives and the costs do not become prohibitive. Banks may exit other markets, choosing to focus on areas where differentiation gives them a strategic advantage. This strategic realignment is likely to be accompanied with structural changes to ensure that the reforms are implemented as efficiently as possible, minimising the impact of stranded capital and avoiding pools of trapped liquidity.

Those banks which have aligned their strategy with regional economic growth, or those which have developed advantaged operating models to serve particular product markets, including new contracts, may be able to take advantage of an industry shakeout whereas marginal performers may be forced to exit.

Chapter 3

Defining Capital

Chris Matten

3.1   Introduction

It is worthwhile bearing in mind that, despite its far-reaching ramifications, Basel III does not change the framework under which capital adequacy is assessed, namely:

$$\frac{\text{Qualifying capital}}{\text{Risk-weighted assets}} \geq x\%$$

While Basel II was all about the changes to the definition and calculation of risk-weighted assets (the denominator), from a capital adequacy perspective Basel III is mostly about the other two components of the capital adequacy computation, namely the definition of capital (the numerator) and the minimum percentages required to be held (although there are some changes to the definition and calculation for risk-weighted assets ("RWA"), which primarily affect investment banking activities – see Chapters 4 and 5).

This Chapter will look at the changes to the definition of capital, with an emphasis on the distinction between "going concern" and "gone concern capital", and then at the minimum ratios and transitional arrangements. It will conclude by looking at the key implications and practical considerations.

3.2   Overview of the key changes

The key changes under Basel III are set out in Part 1 of the final Basel III package issued on 16 December 2010.

In short, the changes are:

(a) introduction of a new "core" Tier 1 measure called "Common Equity Tier 1" (CET1), with a minimum ratio of 4.5 per cent;
(b) stricter requirements on the instruments eligible for Tier 1, with a minimum ratio of 6 per cent;
(c) simplification of Tier 2 into a single band (i.e. no longer Upper and Lower Tier 2) and stricter criteria for eligibility;
(d) abolition of Tier 3;
(e) harmonisation of what classifies as a deduction from capital;
(f) virtually all deductions from capital to be made from Common Equity;
(g) prevention of inclusion of minority interest as CET1 issued by subsidiaries in the consolidated capital adequacy computation unless those subsidiaries are themselves banks and only in respect of that subsidiary's capital; and
(h) restriction on inclusion of capital instruments issued by subsidiaries to third parties, in the parent bank's consolidated capital adequacy computation. The parent bank can include only its share of any surplus capital above the minimum capital requirement of those subsidiaries and exclude the share attributable to third parties.

As will be seen, the impact of these changes is significant, especially in the area of Common Equity Tier 1. By the Basel Committee's own estimates, the effect of the changes will be to reduce the Common Equity Tier 1 ratio of larger banks by a factor of close to one half (Per the Basel Committee's quantitative impact study published in December 2010).

However, before the impact of the changes brought about by Basel III can be understood, it is worthwhile briefly re-capping the situation that had hitherto existed.

3.3   Definition of capital under Basel I and II

The definition of qualifying capital had, until Basel III, barely changed in over two decades. Basel II did not introduce any significant changes to the definition of capital, other than some of the deductions from capital, and the framework was largely the same as under the original Basel Accord of 1998 (Basel I).

Under Basel I and II, qualifying capital consisted of Tier 1 (equity and equity-like elements), Tier 2 (divided into upper and lower Tier 2) and Tier 3, with some deductions made from either Tier 1 or total capital.

There were two key capital ratios:

(1) the total capital adequacy ratio, being all of the components of capital (after deductions) divided by RWA; and
(2) the Tier 1 ratio, being Tier 1 capital (after deductions) divided by RWA.

The minimum ratio for (1) was 8 per cent and, as the total of non-Tier 1 could not exceed Tier 1, the effective minimum Tier 1 ratio was 4 per cent. However, this was never actually specifically set out – it was a consequence of the limitation on other capital components not exceeding Tier 1. A further restriction was that lower Tier 2 could not exceed 50 per cent of Tier 2.

3.3.1 Tier 1

Tier 1 capital was defined under Basel I and II as:

(a) paid-up capital/common stock and perpetual non-cumulative preference shares; and
(b) disclosed reserves.

Recognising that different jurisdictions have different rules around "general reserves" (e.g. some jurisdictions required banks to put a fixed percentage of profits into a "statutory reserve" which could not be used to pay dividends), the rules allowed these to be included as long as they met the following criteria:

(a) allocations to the funds must be made out of post-tax retained earnings;
(b) the movements in and out of the funds must be disclosed separately;

(c) the funds must be available to meet losses for unrestricted and immediate use as soon as they occur; and

(d) losses cannot be directly charged to the funds but must be taken through the P&L account.

For consolidated accounts, Tier 1 included minority interests. While it might seem vague as to whether, for example, real estate revaluation reserves should be included, the rules specifically also stated that, "this basic definition of capital excludes revaluation reserves and cumulative preference shares". The exclusion of the first of these is a logical extension of criterion (c) above (funds must be available to meet losses); how, for example, could a bank use its real estate revaluation reserves to absorb a large credit loss? The only way to do this in practice would be to sell the buildings and realise the gain, which might not be feasible given that (a) if the bank has incurred large losses, the chances are the economy as a whole is in trouble and (b) it takes time.

However, it should be clear to the astute reader that there are a number of loopholes in the above definitions. The inclusion of minority interests allowed a bank to create Tier 1 capital by issuing notes out of a partially-owned subsidiary, and non-cumulative preference shares were not excluded.

Banks seized on these loopholes, starting in the mid-1990's, to issue equity-like structures generically referred to as "hybrid equity" – instruments that in the hands of investors looked and behaved like deeply subordinated debt, but which could be accounted for as equity, and thus met the criteria for inclusion in Tier 1 capital. It is difficult to find aggregate figures, but according to a consultation paper issued by the Committee of European Banking Supervisors in 2008 ("Proposal for a common EU definition of Tier 1 hybrids", March 2008), some €213 billion of this type of capital was outstanding from European banks alone as of December 2006, accounting for 11.3 per cent of total capital. Estimated new issue volume across the globe peaked at around $90 billion in 2006, according to another study ("Hybrid Capital Securities: a guide for investors", by Steve Sahara, Calyon, found at *www.scribd.com/doc/38259838/IFR-Definitive-Guide*). These figures suggest that the global volume of such instruments outstanding must be in the order of $600 – 800 billion.

3.3.2 Hybrid Tier 1

The range of instruments that was issued was impressively diverse, reflecting differences in both accounting and tax rules in different jurisdictions. Generally, these instruments were designed to be tax-deductible, and were arguably closer to deeply subordinated debt than equity. It is not the subject of this Guide to go into these structures in too much detail, but for the interested reader we look at a fairly typical example known as "Trust Preferred Securities" in the box.

Hybrid equity structures – Trust Preferred Securities.

In such structures, the bank creates a special-purpose vehicle ("SPV"), which it owns 100 per cent. The SPV (often a trust established in Delaware for American investors or the Cayman Islands for international investors) then issues a security to investors, known as preferred stock. This stock carries a fixed dividend or coupon (like a preference share) which is not cumulative. In some structures, the stock can be converted into ordinary equity if the bank files for bankruptcy. The proceeds of the issue are lent to the bank, in exchange for subordinated debt securities. As taxation is based on legal entities, the bank can claim a tax deduction for the interest payments on the debt securities. The SPV, however, is structured in such a way that it is not itself subject to tax, so the interest received on the subordinated debt held by the SPV is passed on to the trust preferred securities holders as the coupon on those securities. From an accounting point of view, however, the preferred securities appear as equity on the consolidated balance sheet (but not the standalone balance sheet of the bank). Figure 3.1 depicts a typical trust-preferred hybrid equity structure.

Figure 3.1 Hybrid equity structure

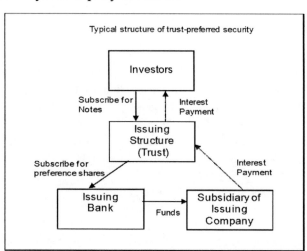

These structures provide a boost to capital ratios at the consolidated level, which is useful for non-operating bank holding companies or where national regulations require only compliance with capital adequacy ratios on a consolidated basis. However, they are less useful when the bank holding company is itself an operating bank (parent bank) subject to standalone capital adequacy ratios, as typically the capital ratios are tighter at the parent bank level than the consolidated level (because the consolidated accounts incorporate all of the group's retained earnings, while the parent bank can include these only if they have been paid up as dividends, and because goodwill is deducted from Tier 1 in both cases, more of which later).

There were also some structures created which achieved many of the same features but also allowed for treatment as Tier 1 at the parent bank level. For example, in June 1999 the National Australia Bank issued AUD 2 billion of hybrid equity that consisted of a debt-like note issued by one of its overseas branches stapled to an unpaid preference share. Should the bank file for bankruptcy, the note would become immediately repayable but the preference share would become immediately payable, simply swapping debt for equity on such an event.

The Basel Committee tried to put some restrictions around this, setting out the following requirements:

(a) they must be unsecured, subordinated and fully paid-up;
(b) they are not redeemable at the initiative of the holder without the prior consent of the supervisory authority;
(c) they are able to participate in losses without the bank being forced to cease trading; and
(d) they should be non-cumulative.

However, it can be seen from this list that these instruments are much closer in nature to deeply subordinated debt than equity, and this is also borne out by the yields on these instruments. While a bank's cost of equity, at least before the global financial crisis, might have been 10 per cent after tax, its hybrid equity would be costing 150–200 bps over its senior debt. This suggests that the market agreed that these instruments are much closer to debt than equity.

For banks' capital management departments, this was as close as one could get to a free lunch, and they naturally took advantage of it.

3.3.3   Restrictions on hybrid Tier 1

In October 1998, the Basel Committee tried to put some further restrictions around hybrid instruments. However, this was only in the form of a press release, not a formal amendment to the framework. The press release was interpreted at the time as being somewhat ambiguous, as although it tightened (a bit) the requirements for inclusion as hybrid equity, and reinforced the desire to have Tier 1 made up predominantly of paid-up common stock, the only explicit limitation was that instruments with "step up" features should not exceed 15 per cent of Tier 1 (step-ups are typically an increase in coupons after a fixed period, e.g., 10 years, which strongly indicate that the bank intends to redeem the notes at that time, notwithstanding the fact that they might have a 30 or even 50 year maturity). Even the 15 per cent limit was not clear, as it was not specified as to whether the limitation applied to Tier 1 before or after deductions. To illustrate how important this is, imagine a bank which has $1000 in RWA and wishes to keep a

Tier 1 ratio of at least 5 per cent (i.e. $50). Being an acquisitive organisation, it also has $50 of goodwill, which must be deducted from Tier 1, so it needs $100 of Tier 1 capital before deductions. If the 15 per cent applies to the Tier 1 before deductions, it can issue up to $15 of hybrid Tier 1 with step-ups, which means that its Tier 1 capital after deductions will be $35 of ordinary equity and $15 of hybrids, or 30 per cent of its net Tier 1. And remember, this limitation did not apply to hybrid equity without any step-up features.

Basel II incorporated the Basel I definitions and the October 1998 press release by reference, rather than using the opportunity to clean up the definitions and tighten the rules. However, it did make it clear that the 15 per cent limit was to be based on Tier 1 *after* deductions (§39) (All paragraph references to Basel II are to the consolidated package issued in June 2006).

3.3.4   Deductions from Tier 1

Initially, the only deduction from Tier 1 was goodwill. This makes sense, as goodwill represents a permanent outflow of shareholders' funds which will only be replenished if the acquired entity generates profits over time, which will accrue to retained earnings and thus offset the goodwill deduction. (However, it does tend to discourage acquisitions of asset-light, brand-heavy businesses, such as asset management, as such acquisitions tend to involve a very high percentage of goodwill which has to be funded out of equity).

Under Basel II, the following changes were made:

(a) deductions for material investments in non-banking subsidiaries or affiliates (or banking subsidiaries, where the measurement is on a standalone basis), which were previously deducted 100 per cent from total capital, would now be deducted 50 per cent from Tier 1 and 50 per cent from total capital;

(b) the excess of expected loss over actual provisions for IRB banks (§43), as well the expected loss amount for equity exposures under the PD/LGD approach (§386), are deducted 50 per cent from Tier 1 and 50 per cent from total capital; and

(c) there were some additional deductions for securitisation exposures (§49(xv)(ii)).

3.3.5   Tier 2

Under Basel II, Tier 2 consisted of:

(a) qualifying long-term hybrid debt (i.e. those instruments similar to hybrid equity but which do not meet the criteria for Tier 1 – §49(xi));
(b) revaluation reserves, as long as they are "prudently valued, fully reflecting the possibility of price fluctuations and forced sale" (§49)v);
(c) unrealised gains on equity investments held at cost, but limited to 45 per cent of the gain (§49(vi));
(d) general loan loss reserves (for non-IRB banks), capped at 1.25 per cent of RWA (§49(x)); and
(e) excess of actual provisions over expected loss (for IRB banks), capped at 0.6 per cent of IRB RWA (§43).

Undisclosed reserves were specifically excluded.

In addition, banks could have up to 50 per cent of their Tier 2 debt (after deductions) in the form of dated subordinated debt, which counted as lower Tier 2. The basic requirements for such instruments were that they must:

(a) be subordinated to all debt which does not count as capital;
(b) be unsecured; and
(c) have an initial maturity of at least five years.

Furthermore, for the last five years before maturity they would be discounted for capital adequacy purposes by 20 per cent p.a. (i.e. subordinated debt with only three years to go before maturity will be discounted by 40 per cent etc).

Due to the haircut in the last five years, the standard subordinated debt instruments are either 10 year, callable after the first five, or 15 years callable after the first five years. These are typically abbreviated to "10NC5" and "15NC5", respectively.

3.3.6   Tier 3

This element of capital was introduced to meet the capital requirement for market risk after its introduction in 1998 and, subject to approval by national supervisors, consisted of short term subordinated debt. The cap was that Tier 3 cannot exceed 250 per cent of the Tier 1 capital required to support market risk. It has not been widely used.

3.3.7   Deductions from capital

Under Basel II, the deductions from Total Capital were:

(a)   the remaining 50 per cent of material investments in non-banking subsidiaries or affiliates (or banking subsidiaries, where the measurement is on a standalone basis); and

(b)   the remaining 50 per cent of the excess of expected loss over actual provisions for IRB banks (§43), as well the expected loss amount for equity exposures under the PD/LGD approach (§386).

Therefore this is the balance of the deductions made 50 per cent from Tier 1. In addition, although not clearly spelt out under Basel II, there are other items which have over time been treated as deductions from capital in some countries, such as:

(a)   mortgage servicing rights; and

(b)   deferred tax assets arising from timing differences.

However, the reader should take care to familiarise themselves with the specific national regulations, as there has been a wide range of interpretation and discrepancies between different national regulators.

3.4   Going concern v gone concern

A key weakness of the Basel I/II regime was that it considered capital only from a solvency perspective, i.e., it was focussed on setting capital to be sufficient to support the bank in meeting its liabilities, thus ensuring depositor protection at the point of insolvency. As the global financial crisis made clear, however, the order in which losses are deducted from capital components is critical. As any accountant knows, the order is as follows, with the first category absorbing losses until it is fully depleted, and then moving to the next one until it too is fully depleted, and so on:

(a)   from current year profits;
(b)   from retained earnings;
(c)   from paid-in ordinary shareholders' funds;
(d)   from preference shares and hybrid equity instruments;
(e)   from Upper Tier 2 debt;
(f)   from Lower Tier 2 debt; and
(g)   from other (senior) debt.

However, a critical point is reached long before (g), typically at some point during (b) or (c). This is because it is these components that make up core Tier 1 and so before long a bank can reach a point where, while it is technically still solvent and has adequate capital to protect depositors, its core Tier 1 ratio is so low that investor confidence evaporates and the authorities have to make a decision either to rescue the bank or allow it to fail. We call this tipping point "regulatory insolvency". The key point here is that "regulatory insolvency" is not necessarily triggered when Tier 1 reaches the legal minimum, but it can be at a much higher level than that. It may differ from bank to bank, and will also depend on the external economic environment. In other words, there is a point where the Tier 1 ratio falls below "x per cent" and the authorities have to step in.

This is illustrated in Figure 3.2 below, which depicts a typical overall loss distribution, with the frequency of losses on the y-axis and the size of losses (increasing from left to right) on the x-axis. Expected losses are absorbed out of expected earnings and at certain points losses can exceed expectations by an amount equal to expected profits, wiping out the profit. As losses increase further, they are absorbed out of retained earnings, until the point is reached where the bank's capital ratios are dangerously depleted and the point of regulatory insolvency is reached.

Figure 3.2 Going concern and gone concern capital – Basel II

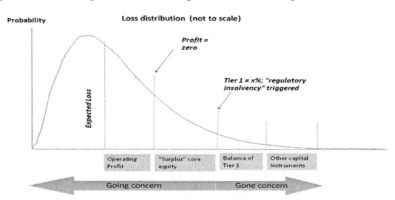

While the Basel Committee does not have a term for the tipping point, it has recognised that capital can effectively be split into two components: "going concern" capital, which can absorb losses while the bank continues to operate; and "gone concern" capital which is there to protect depositors once the decision to let the bank fail has been reached.

This is a correct way to look at the issues, but the Committee has not taken such a purist approach in the Basel III Framework, as they classify all of Tier 1 as "going concern". Some practitioners could argue that, in theory at least, a portion of Tier 1 would need to be in the "gone concern" component, as it is inconceivable that a bank could run its Tier 1 ratio down to 0 per cent before the tipping point is reached. However, as the "x per cent" cannot be defined in advance and will be different from bank to bank, for any one bank over time, and as markets change and develop, it makes sense that for practical purposes the Committee has defined all of Tier 1 as "going concern" capital.

The Committee has determined that, as a baseline at least (more on this later), 8 per cent is still the right number for the overall capital level, but the "going concern" portion needs to be significantly increased, as illustrated below.

Essentially, what the Committee is trying to do is move the tipping point further to the right, thereby decreasing the probability that it will be reached, by increasing the buffer provided by "going concern" capital.

Figure 3.3 Going concern and gone concern capital – Basel III

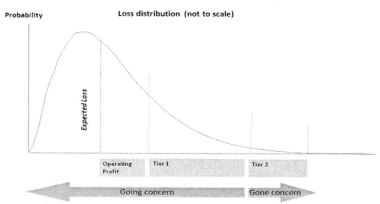

3.5 The definition of capital under Basel III

As set out by the Committee, the elements of capital under the new rules are:

(a) Tier 1 Capital:
    (i) Common Equity Tier 1 (CET1); and
    (ii) Additional Tier 1 (AT1).
(b) Tier 2 Capital (T2).

3.5.1 Common Equity Tier 1

In essence, for a joint stock company, Common Equity Tier 1 consists of ordinary shareholders' funds (paid up ordinary shares plus retained earnings). The rules are worded a little bit more flexibly to incorporate other types of legal entity such as co-operatives, but the essence is the same (see box for details). This is very similar to the concept of "tangible common equity" which the ratings agencies have for many years used as the key ratio to measure the health of a bank's capital ratios. Disclosed reserves are also included, but the Committee has signalled that it will give further consideration to the inclusion of unrealised gains on securities that are not marked-to-market through the profit and loss account, taking into account the evolution of accounting standards.

Criteria for inclusion in CET1 ("Basel III: A global regulatory framework for more resilient banks and banking systems" published by Basel Committee on Banking Supervision):

(1) Represents the most subordinated claim in liquidation of the bank.

(2) Entitled to a claim on the residual assets that is proportional with its share of issued capital, after all senior claims have been repaid in liquidation (i.e. has an unlimited and variable claim, not a fixed or capped claim).

(3) Principal is perpetual and never repaid outside of liquidation (setting aside discretionary repurchases or other means of effectively reducing capital in a discretionary manner that is allowable under relevant law).

(4) The bank does nothing to create an expectation at issuance that the instrument will be bought back, redeemed or cancelled, nor do the statutory or contractual terms provide any feature which might give rise to such an expectation.

(5) Distributions are paid out of distributable items (retained earnings included). The level of distributions is not in any way tied or linked to the amount paid in at issuance and is not subject to a contractual cap (except to the extent that a bank is unable to pay distributions that exceed the level of distributable items).

(6) There are no circumstances under which the distributions are obligatory. Non-payment is therefore not an event of default.

(7) Distributions are paid only after all legal and contractual obligations have been met and payments on more senior capital instruments have been made. This means that there are no preferential distributions,

---

including in respect of other elements classified as the highest quality issued capital.

(8) It is the issued capital that takes the first and proportionately greatest share of any losses as they occur. Within the highest quality capital, each instrument absorbs losses on a going concern basis proportionately and pari passu with all the others.

(9) The paid in amount is recognised as equity capital (i.e. not recognised as a liability) for determining balance sheet insolvency.

(10) The paid in amount is classified as equity under the relevant accounting standards.

(11) It is directly issued and paid-in and the bank can not directly or indirectly have funded the purchase of the instrument.

(12) The paid in amount is neither secured nor covered by a guarantee of the issuer or related entity or subject to any other arrangement that legally or economically enhances the seniority of the claim.

(13) It is only issued with the approval of the owners of the issuing bank, either given directly by the owners or, if permitted by applicable law, given by the board of directors or by other persons duly authorised by the owners.

(14) It is clearly and separately disclosed on the bank's balance sheet.

3.5.2 Minority interests and CET1 of subsidiaries

Minority interest and CET1 capital held by subsidiaries are now only included in CET1 if (1) the instrument meets all of the above criteria for CET1 and (2) the issuer is itself a bank (or an entity subject to the same prudential standards and level of supervision as a bank). This closes the existing loophole of issuing debt-like instruments out of an SPV and then including the bank's interest in the equity of the SPV as Tier 1.

There is a further restriction in that the proportion of any surplus CET1/minority interest over and above the minimum CET1 of the subsidiary attributable to third parties is excluded in the parent bank's consolidated CET1. The minimum is defined here as the overall minimum (4.5 per cent) plus the capital conservation buffer (2.5 per cent – see below), i.e., 7 per cent. In other words, the portion of any surplus capital issued to third parties by the subsidiary cannot be included in the consolidated capital adequacy ratio.

The effect of these new restrictions will be to reduce significantly the inclusion of minority interest in CET1, reflecting the fact that minority interest has very little loss-absorbing capacity at the level of the parent bank.

3.5.3 Additional Tier 1

Additional Tier 1 consists of:

(a) instruments issued by the bank that meet the criteria for inclusion in Additional Tier 1 capital (and are not included in Common Equity Tier 1) (see box);
(b) stock surplus (share premium) resulting from the issue of instruments included in Additional Tier 1 capital;
(c) instruments issued by consolidated subsidiaries of the bank and held by third parties that meet the criteria for inclusion in Additional Tier 1 capital and are not included in Common Equity Tier 1; and
(d) regulatory adjustments applied in the calculation of Additional Tier 1 Capital.

Very few, if any, of the existing hybrid equity instruments in issue today would meet the criteria, for example because they include step-ups and/or have a stated maturity, both of which fall foul of criterion 4. The new criterion 15 – that all Additional Tier 1 instruments must be so-called "contingent convertibles" – will also mean that existing capital instruments are unlikely to comply (see Section 3.7 below for a discussion on this new feature).

Criteria for Additional Tier 1 capital instruments ("Basel III: A global regulatory framework for more resilient banks and banking systems" published by Basel Committee on Banking Supervision):

(1) Issued and paid-in.
(2) Subordinated to depositors, general creditors and subordinated debt of the bank.
(3) Neither secured nor covered by a guarantee of the issuer or related entity or other arrangement that legally or economically enhances the seniority of the claim vis-à-vis bank creditors.
(4) Perpetual, i.e., there is no maturity date and there are no step-ups or other incentives to redeem.
(5) May be callable at the initiative of the issuer only after a minimum of five years:

   (i) to exercise a call option a bank must receive prior supervisory approval; and
  (ii) a bank must not do anything which creates an expectation that the call will be exercised; and
 (iii) banks must not exercise a call unless:

   • they replace the called instrument with capital of the same or better quality and the replacement of this capital is done at conditions which are sustainable for the income capacity of the bank (replacement issues can be concurrent with but not after the instrument is called); or
   • the bank demonstrates that its capital position is well above the minimum capital requirements (as defined by the national supervisor) after the call option is exercised.

(6) Any repayment of principal (e.g. through repurchase or redemption) must be with prior supervisory approval and banks should not assume or create market expectations that supervisory approval will be given.
(7) Dividend/coupon discretion:

   (i)   the bank must have full discretion at all times to cancel distributions/payments: (A consequence of full discretion at all times to cancel distributions/payments is that "dividend pushers" are prohibited. An instrument with a dividend pusher obliges the issuing bank to make a dividend/coupon payment on the instrument if it has made a payment on another (typically more junior) capital instrument or share. This obligation is inconsistent with the requirement for full discretion at all times. Furthermore, the term "cancel distributions/payments" means extinguish these payments. It does not permit features that require the bank to make distributions/payments in kind);

  (ii) cancellation of discretionary payments must not be an event of default;

 (iii) banks must have full access to cancelled payments to meet obligations as they fall due; and

 (iv) cancellation of distributions/payments must not impose restrictions on the bank except in relation to distributions to common stockholders.

(8) Dividends/coupons must be paid out of distributable items.

(9) The instrument cannot have a credit sensitive dividend feature, that is a dividend/coupon that is reset periodically based in whole or in part on the banking organisation's credit standing.

(10) The instrument cannot contribute to liabilities exceeding assets if such a balance sheet test forms part of national insolvency law.

(11) Instruments classified as liabilities for accounting purposes must have principal loss absorption through either (1) conversion to common shares at an objective pre-specified trigger point or (2) a write-down mechanism which allocates losses to the instrument at a pre-specified trigger point. The write-down will have the following effects:

> (i) reduce the claim of the instrument in liquidation;
> (ii) reduce the amount re-paid when a call is exercised; and
> (iii) partially or fully reduce coupon/dividend payments on the instrument.
>
> (12) Neither the bank nor a related party over which the bank exercises control or significant influence can have purchased the instrument, nor can the bank directly or indirectly have funded the purchase of the instrument.
>
> (13) The instrument cannot have any features that hinder recapitalisation, such as provisions that require the issuer to compensate investors if a new instrument is issued at a lower price during a specified time frame.
>
> (14) If the instrument is not issued out of an operating entity or the holding company in the consolidated group (e.g. an SPV), proceeds must be immediately available without limitation to an operating entity or the holding company in the consolidated group in a form which meets or exceeds all of the other criteria for inclusion in Additional Tier 1 capital.
>
> (15) The instrument must be convertible into CET1 or written down on the occurrence of a 'trigger event', unless this is already provided for in national laws and confirmed as such by a peer review of those laws. A trigger event is the earlier of (1) a decision that a write-off is necessary, as determined by the relevant authority (i.e. in most cases the national supervisor), to prevent the bank becoming non-viable; or (2) the decision to make a public sector injection of capital, again as determined by the relevant authority.

Criterion 15 was announced separately by the Committee in a press release on 13 January 2011. Astute readers will have noticed that it conflicts with criterion 11 and this conflict remains unresolved at the time of writing (i.e. must the instrument comply with both criteria, or does 15 replace 11?).

3.5.4   Additional Tier 1 issued by subsidiaries

As with minority interest and CET1 of subsidiaries, there are new restrictions on the inclusion of AT1 issued by subsidiaries.

As with CET1, the amount of any capital issued to third parties that can be included in the consolidated capital ratios is restricted to the minimum required Tier 1 ratio, defined as 8.5 per cent (the minimum 6 per cent plus the 2.5 per cent capital conservation buffer – see Section 3.8 below), i.e., the portion of surplus capital attributable to third parties is excluded in the consolidated capital adequacy calculation. To avoid double-counting, a bank must first work out how much Tier 1 can be included and then how much of this is CET1; with the balance qualifying as AT1.

3.5.5   Tier 2 capital

Tier 2, which is now a single category instead of the old Upper Tier 2 and Lower Tier 2, consists of instruments which meet the qualifying criteria (see box below) as well as certain loan loss provisions. Instruments can be issued by the bank (for stand-alone capital adequacy measurement) as well as by its subsidiaries (for consolidated measurement), but the previous rules preventing double-counting remain (i.e. a company in a banking group cannot issue subordinate debt to other members of the same group and still count this as capital). Although not clearly spelt out, it would appear that a subsidiary of a bank can still issue Tier 2 debt to its parent and include this in its own capital ratios, when capital adequacy is measured at the level of the subsidiary bank.

Most of the new criteria for Tier 2 are not too dissimilar to the old rules, but the inclusion of a convertible feature (see point (10) below) means that it is unlikely that much existing Tier 2 debt will continue to qualify.

Criteria for Tier 2 capital instruments ("Basel III: A global regulatory framework for more resilient banks and banking systems" published by Basel Committee on Banking Supervision):

(1) Issued and paid-in.

(2) Subordinated to depositors and general creditors of the bank.

(3) Neither secured nor covered by a guarantee of the issuer or related entity or other arrangement that legally or economically enhances the seniority of the claim vis-à-vis depositors and general bank creditors.

(4) Maturity:

　(i) minimum original maturity of at least five years;

　(ii) recognition in regulatory capital in the remaining five years before maturity will be amortised on a straight line basis; and

　(iii) there are no step-ups or other incentives to redeem.

(5) May be callable at the initiative of the issuer only after a minimum of five years:

　(i) to exercise a call option a bank must receive prior supervisory approval;

　(ii) a bank must not do anything that creates an expectation that the call will be exercised; and

　(iii) banks must not exercise a call unless:

　　• they replace the called instrument with capital of the same or better quality and the replacement of this capital is done at conditions which are sustainable for the income capacity of the bank; or

　　• the bank demonstrates that its capital position is well above the minimum capital requirements (as defined by the national supervisor) after the call option is exercised.

(6) The investor must have no rights to accelerate the repayment of future scheduled payments (coupon or principal), except in bankruptcy and liquidation.

(7) The instrument cannot have a credit sensitive dividend feature, that is a dividend/coupon that is reset periodically based in whole or in part on the banking organisation's credit standing.

(8) Neither the bank nor a related party over which the bank exercises control or significant influence can have purchased the instrument, nor can the bank directly or indirectly have funded the purchase of the instrument.

(9) If the instrument is not issued out of an operating entity or the holding company in the consolidated group (eg a special purpose vehicle – SPV), proceeds must be immediately available without limitation to an operating entity or the holding company in the consolidated group in a form which meets or exceeds all of the other criteria for inclusion in Tier 2 Capital.

(10) The instrument must be convertible into CET1 or written down on the occurrence of a "trigger event", unless this is already provided for in national laws and confirmed as such by a peer review of those laws. A trigger event is the earlier of (1) a decision that a write-off is necessary, as determined by the relevant authority (i.e. in most cases the national supervisor), to prevent the bank becoming non-viable; or (2) the decision to make a public sector injection of capital, again as determined by the relevant authority. This additional criterion was announced by the BCBS in a press release on 13 January 2011.

3.5.6 Tier 2 issued by subsidiaries

In parallel with the rules for CET1 and AT1, any excess T2 capital held in subsidiaries issued to third parties is excluded from the consolidated capital adequacy calculation. For these purposes, the minimum total capital requirement for the subsidiary is 10.5 per cent (the minimum 8 per cent plus the 2.5 per cent capital conservation buffer – see Section 3.8 below).

3.5.7 Deductions from capital

As noted earlier, virtually all deductions from capital will henceforth be made entirely from CET1. These include:

(a)   goodwill and other intangibles (net of any deferred tax liability), except mortgage servicing rights;
(b)   deferred tax assets, other than those resulting from temporary timing differences;
(c)   cash flow hedge reserves not relating to assets held at fair value (but any negative amounts can be added to capital);
(d)   shortfall of actual provisions in relation to expected loss (for IRB banks only);
(e)   increases in equity resulting from a securitisation transaction (such as future margin income);
(f)   increases/decreases in equity resulting from fair value of own financial liabilities;
(g)   defined pension fund surpluses; and
(h)   investments in own shares (treasury stock).

Certain other deductions are made on a pro-rata basis:

(a)   Non-consolidated investments in other financial entities, where the bank does not own more than 10 per cent of the common shares of those entities; these are only deducted from capital where the aggregate of such investments exceeds ten per cent of the bank's own CET1 (after above deductions), and then only the amount exceeding ten per cent is deducted. The "corresponding approach" is used, whereby the components of capital of the invested entities (CET1, AT1 etc) are deducted from the same components of the investing bank.
(b)   Non-consolidated investments in other financial entities where the bank owns more than ten per cent of the common shares are fully deducted, using the corresponding approach except for investments in common equity of these entities, where the threshold deduction (see below) applies.

Interestingly, the deduction for the excess of expected loss over actual provisions (for IRB banks) is now gross of any tax benefits, whereas previously it was net, which increases the size of the deduction. This was introduced into the final rules in December 2010 but was not in the earlier consultation paper.

3.5.8 Threshold deductions

Some deductions which would normally be made from common equity may instead be relaxed under certain conditions. These are:

(a) significant investments in the common shares of unconsolidated financial institutions;
(b) mortgage servicing rights; and
(c) deferred tax assets that arise from temporary timing differences.

The cap is two-fold. First, each of these items is subject to a cap of 10 per cent of a bank's CET1 (net of deductions). Secondly, the aggregate amount is capped at 15 per cent of the bank's CET1 (net of deductions). As a transitional arrangement, from 1 January 2013 the aggregate cap is 15 per cent of CET1 net of all deductions but before these three items, whereas from 1 January 2018 it is 15 per cent of CET1 net of all deductions. In other words, banks should first deduct everything, and then calculate the cap as 17.65 per cent of the net amount of CET1, being 15/85. As an example, if a bank's overall CET1 after all deductions is 85, the cap is 17.65 per cent of 85 i.e. 15. This amount can then be removed from the deductions and treated as an RWA instead, by multiplying by 250 per cent.

3.5.9 50/50 deduction under Basel II

Certain items which were treated as 50 per cent deductions from Tier 1 and 50 per cent from total capital under Basel II are now treated as risk-weighted assets instead, with a 1250 per cent risk-weighting. These are:

(a) certain securitisation exposures;
(b) certain equity exposures under the PD/LGD approach;

(c) non-payment/delivery on non-DvP or PvP transactions; and
(d) significant investments in commercial entities.

The retention of 1250 per cent is interesting, as this is the inverse of the old eight per cent minimum capital ratio. In other words, banks would in theory have been indifferent between treating an item as a deduction from total capital and treating it as RWA, as the impact on the capital ratio would have been the same. However, for banks that were capitalised above the minimum amount (as would invariably be the case in anything but a crisis scenario), it was actually disadvantageous to treat the item as RWA rather than a deduction. Under the new capital ratios (see below) the effective minimum capital ratio is 10.5 per cent, and therefore this disadvantage holds even for banks which are capitalised at the minimum level, as well as those which are more strongly capitalised.

This can be illustrated with a simple example. Consider a bank which has 70 in CET1 and 130 in total capital before deductions, a 10 item which could either be deducted or treated as an RWA, and 1,000 in other RWA. The Figure below shows the different impact under Basel II and Basel III, comparing the deduction approach with the RWA approach.

Figure 3.4 Deductions under Basel II and III

	Under Basel II		Under Basel III	
	Deduction approach	RWA approach	Deduction approach	RWA approach
Available CET1 before deductions	70	70	70	70
Deduction	(5)		(10)	
Net CET1	65	70	60	70
RWA	1,000	1,062.5	1,000	1,125
CET1 ratio	6.5%	6.6%	6.0%	6.2%
Available Tier 2	60	60	60	60
capitalDeduction	(5)	–	–	–
Total capital	120	130	120	130
RWA	1,000	1,125	1,000	1,125
Total capital ratio	12%	11.5%	12.0%	11.5%

With the new rules, the deduction approach is no longer available, with a consequential negative impact on capital ratios.

3.6 New minimum capital ratios

The new capital ratios are as follows:

Figure 3.5 New minimum capital ratios under Basel III

Target Capital Ratios			
	Common Equity (after deductions)	Tier 1 capital	Total capital
Minimum	4.5%	6%	8%
Capital conservation buffer	2.5%		
Minimum plus conservation buffer	7%	8.5%	10.5%
Countercyclical capital buffer	0% - 2.5%		
Upper end of minimum capital	9.5%	11%	13%

However, recognising that not all banks can meet these ratios, and that premature implementation could lead to a credit squeeze and undermine the still-fragile economic recovery in Western Europe and the United States, the Committee opted for quite a long implementation period, as shown below, with the transitional ratios shaded:

Figure 3.6 Transitional arrangements for capital

	2011	2012	2013	2014	2015	2016	2017	2018	2019
Min Common Equity Ratio			3.5%	4.0%	4.5%	4.5%	4.5%	4.5%	4.5%
Capital conservation buffer						0.625%	1.25%	1.875%	2.5%
Min common equity + cap conservation buffer			3.5%	4.0%	4.5%	5.125%	5.75%	6.375%	7.0%
Phase in of deductions from Common Equity				20%	40%	60%	80%	100%	100%
Minimum Tier 1	4.0%	4.0%	4.5%	5.5%	6.0%	6.0%	6.0%	6.0%	6.0%
Minimum Total Capital	8.0%	8.0%	8.0%	8.0%	8.0%	8.0%	8.0%	8.0%	8.0%
Min Total Capital + cap conservation buffer	8.0%	8.0%	8.0%	8.0%	8.0%	8.625%	9.25%	9.875%	10.5%
Capital instruments that no longer qualify as Tier 1 or Tier 2			Phased out over 10 year period starting 2013						

The new framework can be compared with the Basel II framework as follows:

Figure 3.7 Capital structure under Basel II

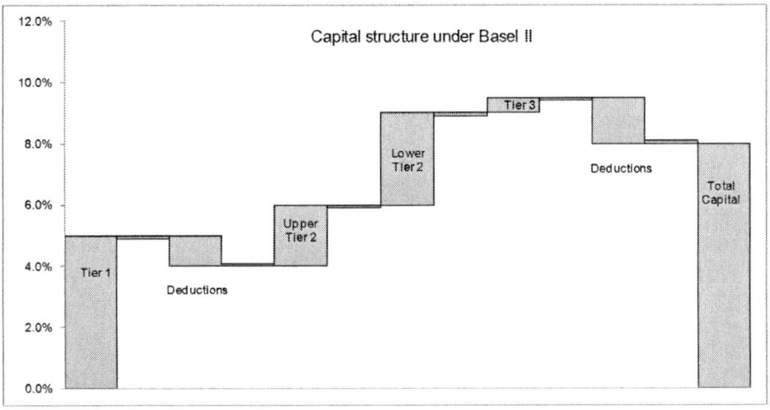

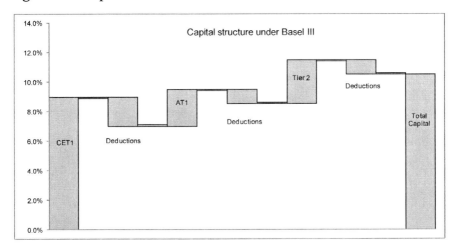

Figure 3.8 Capital structure under Basel III

It should be clear from this diagrammatic representation that:

(a) even before buffers, the key constraint is going to be Common Equity;

(b) the definitional changes (of what constitutes Tier 1) and the change in the deductions (from Tier 1/total capital to

Common Equity) are going to have a very significant impact on existing ratios;

(c) because all of the ratios are subject to the two buffers (see below), this means that in effect the buffers have to be met entirely out of Common Equity; and

(d) Tier 2 becomes relatively unimportant – only two per cent of the minimum eight per cent before buffers, and only two per cent of the minimum thirteen per cent if both buffers are fully deployed.

3.7   Contingent capital

A consultation paper was issued by the BCBS in August 2010, to "ensure the loss absorbency of regulatory capital at the point of non-viability" – a long-winded way of saying that when the taxpayer has to step in to rescue a bank, the bondholders should suffer too. In this paper, "bondholders" refers only to holders of Hybrid Tier 1 and/or Tier 2 debt. Such bonds are generally referred to as "Contingent Capital" or more simply "CoCo Bonds" (an idea which *The Economist* magazine referred to as "CoCoNuts").

In a press release on 13 January 2011 the BCBS confirmed that, in order to qualify for non-core Tier 1 or Tier 2, capital instruments must have a clause that requires them to be converted into common equity or written down on occurrence of a "trigger event". Trigger event means the earlier of (1) the decision to make a public-sector injection of capital or (2) the point where the regulatory authority deems that a write-down is necessary to prevent the firm failing.

The comments that have been posted on the BCBS website are not very supportive of this proposal, and objections range across a number of areas such as:

(a) the potential for the trigger to become a self-fulfilling event when a bank is under stress and the market gets nervous;

(b) the injustice of bondholders taking a 100 per cent write off when equity holders might still recover something (an argument which speaks in favour of the conversion approach rather than the write-off approach);

(c) the problems of aligning the new instruments with existing disclosure and securities laws;

(d) the problems of finding a market that is sufficiently large (many institutional funds cannot buy paper with a conversion clause in it, as they are not allowed to hold equities, although in recent months there has been a handful of successful issues);

(e) the lack of a clear distinction between Tier 1 and Tier 2, as both would have conversion features; and

(f) the fact that the proposal distracts attention from the far more important (and far more difficult) search for a functioning cross-border mechanism for dealing with resolution of bank failures.

Notwithstanding these concerns, the requirement is now part of Basel III. All new capital instruments issued after 1 January 2013 must meet this criterion in order to qualify (as well as all the other criteria described above). Existing capital instruments will start to be haircut by ten per cent starting from 1 January 2013, with the haircut increasing by ten per cent p.a. thereafter. This means that virtually all existing hybrid Tier 1 and Tier 2 debt – which is estimated to be over $2 trillion in total – will need to be refinanced over the next twelve years, with as much as possible being refinanced by the end of 2012 to avoid the haircuts, and thus expensive capital sitting on the balance sheet which will no longer fully qualify.

3.8 The capital buffers

There are two capital buffers in the new framework, each adding up to two and a half percentage points to the minimum ratios.

The capital conservation buffer is intended to be built up in good times to enable a more resilient banking sector to weather the storms of a downturn or even another crisis. Although the transition rules indicate that the buffer must be fully in place by the end of 2018, it is not clear how – or even whether – this buffer can be eroded in adverse conditions without attracting sanctions. If banks do allow their capital ratios to fall below the buffer, they will face restrictions on the extent to which they can make distributions (defined as dividends, share buy-backs and discretionary bonuses).

The counter-cyclical capital buffer is a macro-level buffer that will be built up when there are signs of "excessive" credit growth. A buffer of up to 2.5 per cent of RWA would be added to a bank's capital requirements, based on a country-specific assessment of credit expansion by the national authorities in that country. Thus if, for example, the UK were to decide that there was a danger of excessive credit building up in the UK, they could declare a buffer and, for the sake of example, they set the full 2.5 per cent. A UK bank that has all of its exposures in the UK would have to add a 2.5 per cent buffer to its capital ratios. A German bank that has 50 per cent of its exposures in the UK would have to add 1.25 per cent; an Australian bank with ten per cent of its exposures in the UK would have to add 0.25 per cent, and so on.

Further details are given in Chapter 10 on Procyclicality, but for the purposes of this Section let us just recall that these buffers will have to be funded entirely by Common Equity.

3.9 Practical considerations

There are clearly a number of key practical issues to be considered, and while it is difficult to go into these in any detail given the lack of detail to date from the BCBS, it is clear that banks should be thinking about the following:

(a) capital planning;
(b) managing the "buffer-on-a-buffer-on-a-buffer" approach;
(c) views of ratings agencies; and
(d) meeting the demands of the market.

3.9.1 *Capital planning*

Banking is a capital intensive business and is about to become much more so. This means that capital planning and stress–testing, both of which should be an integral part of managing a bank (see Chapter 9 on Pillar 2), have become even more important.

Although the level of detail is not yet complete, the outlines are visible and banks can, and should, start planning now. A capital plan should be developed covering the entire transition period through to at least 2019 (and one would not be surprised if supervisors do not start asking for it soon, if they have not already done so).

Such plans need to address the *supply* as well as the *demand* for capital. Supply can be both internal (profits, less dividends) and external (capital raisings). Given the definitional changes, this needs to be done at quite a granular level, as for example "hybrid equity" or "upper tier 2 debt" may not qualify as such in the future. The supply side of the model should factor in each individual instrument in the current capital structure, separated by type of instrument, maturity, any call options or non-call periods, etc. Thus for example, instead of the lump-sum "lower Tier 2 debt" that might normally be used in such planning (on the assumption that, historically, it has been easy to replace lower Tier 2 debt once it reaches the five years to maturity mark), one would need to look at each issue separately.

As noted earlier, the size of the Hybrid Tier 1 market is estimated to be around $600–800 billion outstanding, most of which will not qualify as Tier 1 due to the prohibition of step-up features or fixed maturity (most hybrid equity instruments feature one or both of these) as well as the imposition of a conversion feature. This is a significant amount to refinance over ten years.

Reliable estimates of the total size of the Lower Tier 2 market are not available, but it most probably exceeds that of the hybrid equity market by two or three times. This adds another $1.5 trillion or so of Tier 2 that will need to be refinanced, and with the imposition of a haircut from 1 January 2013 the pressure will be on to do this as quickly as possible.

Demand is, of course, notoriously difficult to forecast, and the further out the time horizon of the planning, the harder this is.

To accommodate this uncertainty, flex-planning should be adopted, where instead of a fixed scenario for each year there are a range of outcomes. Capital management activities would then be split into those which the bank is committed to do in any circumstances, and options which can be utilised should, for example, RWA growth be greater than anticipated.

3.9.2 Managing the buffer-on-a-buffer approach

This seems quite straightforward at first sight, as one can simply plug the buffers into the minimum required capital ratios and then use these to develop the plan. The problem, however, is the degree of uncertainty over these buffers. As previously noted, the capital conservation buffer is supposed to be fully in place by the end of 2018, but under what circumstances can it be eroded?

The same is doubly true of the countercyclical capital buffer; here we cannot foresee either when it is going to be imposed, or when it will be released, as even if final details of the exact mechanism were known (which they are not) we cannot foresee when a credit bubble will arise in the future.

In the meantime, we would suggest the following pragmatic assumptions:

(a) For the capital conservation buffer, assume it has to be built up and held, but do not assume a crisis scenario as part of the planning horizon. One can certainly perform the "normal" capital stress tests (see Chapter 10 – Procyclicality and Chapter 11 – Stress testing) to show that capital ratios will not go below the minima in a mild downturn, but if the capital conservation buffer is intended to absorb a severe crisis then it would be double-counting to model such a crisis but keep the buffer intact. In this sense, a pragmatic solution is to treat the capital conservation buffer as a hedge against a severe downturn or crisis.

(b) Similarly with the countercyclical capital buffer, but this time reversing the logic as this buffer only applies when there is "excessive" credit growth. So by not including expectations of excessive credit growth in the capital plan (and the extra profits that go with it), banks can also decide not to include the countercyclical capital buffer in the plan.

In both of these assumptions, all we are really doing is making sure that our assumptions as to the supply of capital are consistent with the assumptions as to the demand for capital.

3.10 Superequivalence

A major concern for many practitioners is the danger of "superequivalence", or the extent to which national regulators set even higher standards than the Basel framework. Of course, Basel III is meant to be a minimum standard and national regulators may want to go higher, but given the large increase in capital ratios, and the risk of double- (or even triple-) counting, there is a danger of serious distortion to the "level playing field" set out as one of the twin goals of Basel I and II (the other being the safety and soundness of the international financial systems).

At the time of writing, some examples of superequivalence in respect of Basel III have already been seen. On 4 October 2010, an expert commission reporting to the Swiss Government recommended that UBS and Credit Suisse be subject to a minimum Common Equity ratio of 10 per cent (including the 2.5 capital conservation buffer, which compares with seven per cent under Basel III) and a total capital adequacy ratio of 19 per cent (again including the 2.5 per cent buffer).

Even more surprisingly, the CBRC, China's national banking regulator, issued new minimum capital ratios for the large Chinese banks which are broadly the same as Basel III, but the announcement was surprising because (1) it was made on 31 August 2010, two weeks before the new Basel III ratios were announced, and (2) the large Chinese banks have to meet these ratios by the end of 2012, not 2018.

It would seem that the G20 welcomes – and even encourages – such developments. In the G20 Seoul Summit Document (November 2010), appended to the communiqué, it says at para.9 that, "we are committed . . . . to raise standards . . . . . in a way that ensures a level playing field, *a race to the top* and avoids fragmentation of markets . . . ." (author's emphasis). So there we have it – a race to the top is seen as a good thing to have, whatever the consequences.

3.11   Conclusion

It should be clear that the new definition of capital is much more restrictive than the pre-existing regime. Not only are minimum capital ratios much higher, but the definition of what qualifies as capital is much narrower, and the deductions are taken almost entirely from Common Equity.

The impact of this is illustrated by the Basel Committee's own quantitative impact study ("QIS") which was issued at the same time as the full Basel III package in December 2010. This covered a total of 263 banks from 23 countries, being 94 Group 1 banks (those with Tier 1 capital exceeding €3 billion, and being both internationally active and considered well-diversified), and the balance Group 2.

Based on the actual numbers as of 31 December 2009 and ignoring any transitional arrangements (i.e. assuming that the full rules were implemented immediately as of that date), the Group 1 banks would have to raise an additional €165 billion to meet a CET1 target of 4.5 per cent, or €577 billion to meet a CET1 target of 7 per cent. This is equivalent to nearly three times these banks' combined net profits in 2009. The change in the deductions from capital, moving these to CET1, have the effect of nearly halving these banks' available CET1 (down by 41.3 per cent, according to the QIS). This would reduce their CET1 ratios from an aggregate 11.1 per cent to 5.7 per cent.

The changes to Tier 1 and total capital are less dramatic, but still not insignificant, with Tier 1 ratios falling from 10.5 per cent to 6.3 per cent, and total capital from 14 per cent to 8.4 per cent.

To put this in perspective, the Group 1 banks need €165 billion for each one per cent improvement in their CET1 ratios. If, in aggregate, their current gross CET1 ratios (before deductions) are 11.1 per cent, this implies that their aggregate available CET1 is €1,485 billion. In order to raise €577 billion, these banks will have to increase their available CET1 by nearly 40 per cent – a significant amount (which also makes no allowance for buffers to be held above the seven per cent level).

The comparison with 2009 profits given in the QIS is somewhat misleading, as it could lead one to conclude that over the nine year transition period banks would be able to fund the additional capital requirements by retaining roughly three years' worth of profits, which seems eminently feasible. However, this does not take into account the need for the banks to (1) retain profits to fund growth in their balance sheets and (2) pay dividends to keep their shareholders onside. One conclusion is inescapable: banks need to start preparing a full capital plan for the duration of the transition period, and if that shows that they will need to raise fresh equity (as in many cases it will undoubtedly do), it may be better to go the market sooner rather than later, to avoid the crush.

Chapter 4

Trading book and securitisation

Ina de Vry

4.1   Introduction

Market risk (the risk that the value of a portfolio, in this case the trading portfolio, will decrease due to the change in value of the market risk factors) was first included for regulatory capital purposes when the market risk amendment for Basel I was published in 1996[1] and became effective in 1997 for many jurisdictions. Market risk capital can be calculated in two ways: one using the Standardised Approach (sometimes referred to as the standardised method) and the other using an internal Value-at-Risk ("VaR") approach, where capital requirements are based on the firm's own assessment of market risk.

Market risk regulation remained unchanged until 2005 when the Basel Committee in conjunction with the International Organisation of Securities Commissions ("IOSCO") published the Basel II trading book review. These changes were implemented in the European Union in 2007.

After analysing sources of losses caused by the financial crisis, the Basel Committee released the final revision of the market risk framework in July 2009[2]. This is often referred to as Basel II.5. An annex was also published in June 2010[3] with additional changes. The Committee's impact studies

---

[1] "Amendment to the Capital Accord to Incorporate Market Risks", Basel Committee on Banking Supervision (1996)

[2] "Revisions to the Basel II market risk framework – final version", Basel Committee on Banking Supervision (2009)

[3] "Changes to the Revisions to the Basel II market risk framework", Basel Committee on Banking Supervision (2010)

conducted on these changes estimated that market risk capital will increase on average by 223 per cent, resulting in an overall increase of 11.5 per cent in overall capital[4].

The Committee agreed to a start-date of not later than 31 December 2011 for all elements of the July 2009 trading book package. This consists of the "Revisions to the Basel II market risk framework" and the "Guidelines for computing capital for incremental risk in the trading book".

This Chapter covers the following:

(a) brief background of the capital framework up to the introduction of the revision of the Basel II market risk framework in July 2009;

(b) discussion of the effect of the crisis on traded market risk; and

(c) detailed discussions of the proposed changes published in July 2009 and subsequent updates on securitisation in Basel III.

4.2 The Standardised Approach to market risk capital

The Standardised Approach for market risk[5] applies strict criteria, which generally only allow positions to be offset with each other when risks are:

(a) linear[6];

(b) equal (e.g. the same instrument with some allowances for interest rate instruments[7]); and

---

[4] "Analysis of the trading book quantitative impact study", Basel Committee on Banking Supervision (2009)

[5] Market risk includes general and specific risk. General market risk refers to changes in market values due to large market movements (e.g. interest rates or equity market indices). Specific market risk refers to change in the value of a financial instrument due to factors related to the issuer of the security (e.g. a change to the issuer's credit rating).

[6] Linear in this context means that the unit of risk for a defined relative change stays the same regardless of the level of the risk factor. Examples are equities or interest rate futures. Financial instruments such as options tend to exhibit non-linear risk characteristics.

[7] Interest rate risk arising from a portfolio of different instruments could be reduced applying some form of bucketing with vertical and horizontal offsets.

(c)   opposite (e.g. one is directionally "long" and one is directionally "short").

In the case of options, non-linear risks are either approximated by linear risks and therefore allowed to offset, or are only permitted to partially off-set using the delta of the position[8]. There are also charges for vega and gamma[9] risks.

Each net position (i.e. after offsetting) is subject to a capital charge based on a simple look-up table that is the same for all firms.

There is also a charge for specific risk, namely the risk of a change in the deterioration of the creditworthiness of an issuer (of a corporate bond or equity), which is based on standard formulae provided by the regulator. This applies to equity and interest rate positions where specific risk applies.

The specific risk charges for securitisations were the same as for other issuer paper, which therefore created an incentive for banks to include securitisation paper in their trading book portfolios.

Capital is arrived at by adding up the charges for each market risk type.

The Standardised Approach relies on fixed risk weights and aggregation techniques which either ignore correlations or take a simplistic approach. As a result the Standardised Approach resulted in prohibitively large amounts of capital for the trading book and provided an incentive for banks to develop their own internal VaR model for calculating regulatory capital. The standardised method is really only suitable for banks with trading portfolios containing no complex products or that are of a relatively small size.

---

[8] The delta represents the net position in the underlying reference instrument that would describe the change in value of the option at that market level.

[9] The vega represents the change in the value of the option due to volatility changes. The gamma represents the change in value of the option due to the changes in the delta of the option.

4.3 The internal model approach to market risk capital

When a bank uses its own VaR model in the assessment of regulatory capital, the capital shall be estimated using the following formula:

$$C = \max(VaR_{t-1}, m_c * VaR_{avg})^{10}$$

The VaR methodology is subject to both qualitative and quantitative standards that ensure the risk sensitivity and appropriateness of the model. In addition to producing VaR on a daily basis the bank is required to perform back-testing (comparing the VaR estimate to the actual profit and loss outcomes) and submit it to the regulator. In addition, the model can only be used once the bank has completed a formal approval process and has been granted permission by the regulator to use the model.

VaR is estimated at a 99 per cent confidence level over a 10-day holding period. The risk factors that were recognised under the amendment were equities, commodities, foreign exchange and interest rates.

There are three possible approaches used for the estimation of VaR amongst the banks for regulatory purposes, namely variance-covariance, historical simulation and Monte-Carlo simulation. Historical simulation has been by far the most popular model for regulatory VaR models.[11]

Although VaR models are very sophisticated, they still have some shortcomings, which have to be considered. In particular:

- VaR models do not take into account the underlying liquidity of positions. The 10-day holding period assumes that all positions can either be liquidated or hedged within

---

[10] The multiplication factor m_c is set at 3 plus an add-on stipulated by the regulator based on its assessment of model soundness. The average VaR is calculated over 60day rolling average.

[11] "DP 10/4 The prudential regime for trading activities – A fundamental review", Financial Services Authority (2010)

10 days. Should this not be the case the risk will be under-stated.

- Due to the development in trading credit, VaR models did not usually incorporate all aspects of credit risk as risk factors. In particular default and migration risk were often excluded and, in trading books where very exotic credit products are traded, the effects of correlation were not included. This led to understatement of the credit-related aspects of market risk.
- The models are not able to take into account concentrations where a bank has a material portion of the market.

This led the regulators to perform a review of the market risk amendment.[12]

4.4   The Basel II review of the trading book in 2005

In 2005 the BCBS published revised market risk requirements, which addressed some of the pre-crisis concerns of regulators.

The document included guidelines on prudent valuation of positions. These guidelines addressed several aspects such as:

(a) control environment and the existence of policies and procedures controlling the valuation process;
(b) assessing the availability and liquidity of mark-to-market rates;
(c) controls around the model development process for positions that are marked to model and the assessment of model uncertainty;
(d) independent price verification; and
(e) valuation adjustments assessing the impact of position size on liquidation prices, market liquidity and valuation uncertainty.

Several changes to the modelling of specific risk under the internal models approach were also introduced. For example, allowance was made for the use of credit VaR to estimate

---

[12] These amendments were first published in November of 2005.

specific risk and the incremental default charge was introduced. The purpose of the incremental default charge was to ensure that the effect of issuer default was included as a separate charge. The charge calculates the incremental default risk of obligors in the trading book that was not covered by specific risk.

4.5   The effect of the crisis

Even though there had been a review of the regulatory capital for the trading book conducted in 2005, as the crisis unfolded it was realised that even these amendments may not be sufficient.

A high level analysis by the FSA during the crisis revealed that the level of losses was 160 per cent of the average credit and market risk capital. The study did not include any of the defaulted institutions and the losses were offset by the yearly profit, so that the institutions in the study remained solvent. See Figure 4.1 below. Of the losses, 77 per cent originated in the trading book.

It was evident from the crisis that there were particular products where the capital was insufficient. The Bank of England reported in 2008 that the range of mark-to-market losses on super-senior tranches of securitisations, which were rated AAA

Figure 4.1 Average capital versus total losses

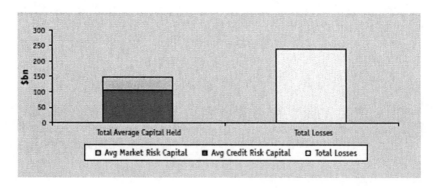

Figure 4.2 Implied losses at March 2008 for AAA tranches of sub-prime RMBS (per cent of notional)

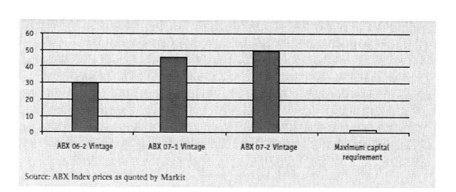

Source: ABX Index prices as quoted by Markit

in 2007, amounted to 20–80 per cent of notional. The capital held against these particular instruments was about 1.6 per cent of notional in the trading book.

The crisis showed that the shortcomings of the VaR methodology could lead to significant losses. As stated previously, one of the principal shortcomings of VaR models is that they assume a constant liquidity factor of ten days. During the crisis it was clear that many products experienced a lack of liquidity and banks were unable to hedge these products within a ten day time-frame.

Even though the incremental default charge was introduced before the crisis, losses in trading portfolios not only stemmed from defaults, but also from value losses in credit migration of these instruments. The losses were exacerbated by the lack of liquidity in the market for these instruments.

Because a VaR model's estimates are typically based on histor-ical volatilities of risk factors and the past five years had expe-rienced benign conditions, VaR underestimated the size of the losses when the market came under stress. Market liquidity also evaporated and banks could not hedge or sell their positions within this time-frame.

Due to the complexity of some instruments, the models used to estimate the risk of complex products were simplified for computational purposes. This meant that some of the really large value changes were not picked up, leading to underestimation. For example, during the financial crisis equity derivative traders suffered large losses on risks such as dividends where this was not included in the VaR model as a risk factor. In addition interest rate traders suffered large losses on products, such as constant maturity swaps ("CMS"), where the convexity effects of interest rates were not fully captured, or spread options where the correlation between interest rates were not included. Many credit products that ended up in the trading books were modelled by proxies such as rated corporate bonds. Risk managers reported losses exceeding VaR by up to ten times during the crisis resulting from this assumption. These and other examples led to the underestimation of risk and contributed to insufficient capitalisation of the trading book.

Valuation also emerged as an issue. Even though prudent valuation guidance was incorporated in the 2005 changes, it was found that valuations still did not adequately incorporate adjustments for issues such as model uncertainty and market liquidity. Trading positions were valued in accordance with accounting standards such as International Financial Reporting Standards ("IFRS") and then incorporated into regulatory reporting. These valuations did not, therefore, meet regulatory requirements for prudent valuations.

All these factors have led to the document issued by BCBS in July 2009 on revisions to the Basel II market risk framework, commonly referred to as Basel II.5. The revisions introduced are aimed at addressing many of the shortcomings discussed above. In the release of the Basel III document in December 2010 changes such as CVA have also been introduced to deal with the effect of market value changes on counterparties of the bank. This is discussed more fully in Chapter 5 – Counterparty credit risk.

These regulations were originally intended to come into effect in January 2011, but this was postponed by a year to allow for simultaneous implementation in the US and Europe. The regulations will now have a start date no later than 31 December

2011, with one exception, relating to the transition period for non-correlation securitisation products, which will end on 31 December 2013.

4.6 Basel II.5 and Basel III changes

4.6.1 *Changes to the definition of the trading book*

No changes have been made to the definition of the trading book[13], but in the explanatory footnote, positions in securitisation warehouses are noted as not meeting the requirements of trading positions.

Many banks use the accounting classification under IFRS accounting standards as a basis for allocating trades to the trading book. However, IFRS need to be used carefully. Consideration should be given to prudent valuation guidelines to consider the value placed on any position in the trading book where the market may be thin or positions cannot be marked to market reliably. One should consider carefully whether such positions should be allocated to the trading book. For example, a banking book treatment may not be aligned with the business model of a bank that is engaged in developing a traded market for new instruments. This may be one of the areas affected by further reviews of the market risk regime by regulators.

4.6.2 *Changes to the standardised measurement for market risk*

In terms of the capital calculation under the Standardised Approach the current calculation is maintained where there is a charge for general market risk and a charge for specific risk.

The major changes have been introduced in relation to the calculation of specific risk. This is the area where banks did not hold sufficient capital and where large losses arose from trading

---

[13] A trading book consists of financial instruments and commodities held either with trading intent or in order to hedge other elements in the trading book. The Committee specifies a number of conditions that must be met for an instrument to be classified as a trading book item.

credit derivatives and securitisation positions. There are changes to the specific risk rules for securitisation exposures, the preferential charge of 4 per cent for a well-diversified equity portfolio is discontinued, and the specific risk charges for securitisations are harmonised with the banking book charges for securitisation. The correlation trading portfolio is defined for specific risk purposes and is treated separately.

4.6.2.1 The correlation trading portfolio

The correlation trading portfolio is defined by the Committee to include securitisations and nth-to-default[14] credit derivatives with the following criteria:

- The positions should not be re-securitisation positions, nor derivatives of securitisation exposures that do not provide a pro-rata share in the proceeds of a securitisation tranche.
- All reference entities are single name products, including credit derivatives, for which a liquid two-way market exists. It also includes traded indices based on these reference entities.
- Hedges for these instruments are also included, provided they also meet the criteria set out above.

The definition of trades to be included in the correlation trading portfolio means that options on securitisation tranches and synthetic leveraged tranches are excluded.

Specific risk for the correlation trading portfolio under the Standardised Approach is determined as the larger absolute number of the specific risk charge for long and short positions. These risk weights are the same as for non-correlation securitisations set out in Section 4.6.2.2

Under the internal model approach, the correlation trading portfolio is a limited exception that applies to securitised products where banks may be allowed to calculate a comprehensive risk charge (see Section 4.6.3.6).

---

[14] An nth-to-default credit derivative contract is one where the derivative is triggered in the event of a specified number (n) of defaults out of a pool of underlying assets.

4.6.2.2   Amendment to the specific risk charges for securitisations

The last twenty years have witnessed explosive growth and innovation in the credit and securitisation markets. This was, in part, driven by the demand for yield by investors and the desire of banks to move assets off their balance sheets to free up capital. This resulted in rapid growth in the overall market for credit securities and a significant increase in complexity and growth in credit derivatives enabling firms to hedge many of their credit-related exposures.

Recently this market has contracted sharply, but it is here to stay – albeit with a slower growth rate. One of the prime reasons for ensuring robust capital treatment for these positions is because the banks' share of the market for credit securities exceeds their share of any other market. Contrary to popular belief, most of the credit risk was retained in the banking system (albeit in super senior form) prior to the crisis and did not leave the system to be taken up by other types of institutions. As a result many of these positions found their way into the trading books of banks. That was one of the primary reasons for the large mark-to-market losses experienced within the banking sector.

The specific risk of the securitisation positions in the trading book is to be calculated according to the method used for such positions in the banking book, except for specific requirements for the trading book as set out below.

In order to eliminate trading book/banking book arbitrage the Basel Committee introduced changes to the specific risk charges for securitisations in the trading book, which are aligned with the banking book risk weights. Figure 4.3 describes the risk weights to be used. These weights are to be applied if a bank uses the Standardised Approach for credit risk.

Where banks have approval to use an Internal Ratings Based Approach ("IRB") in the banking book a more granular table of risk weights can be used for positions rated by external ratings as set out below.

Figure 4.3 Securitisation risk weights – Standardised Approach

External credit assessment	AAA to AA A-1/P-1	A+ to A– A-2/P-2	BBB+ to BBB– A-3/P-3	BB+ to BB–	Below BB– Below A-3/P-3 or unrated
Securitisation exposures	1.6%	4%		8%	8% (B+ to B– and unrated) 12% (Below B–)
Resecuritisation exposures	3.2%			8%	18%

Figure 4.4 Securitisation risk weights – IRB

Specific risk capital charges based on external credit ratings					
External rating (illustrative)	Securitisation exposures			Resecuritasation exposures	
	Senior granular	Non-senior, Granular	Non-granular	Senior	Non-senior
AAA/A-1/P-1	0.56%	0.96%	1.60%	1.60%	2.40%
AA	0.64%	1.20%	2.00%	2.00%	3.20%
A+	0.80%	1.44%	2.80%	2.80%	4.00%
A/A-2/P-2	0.96%	1.60%		3.20%	5.20%
A–	1.60%	2.80%		4.80%	8.00%
BBB+	2.80%	4.00%		8.00%	12.00%
BBB/A-3/P-3	4.80%	6.00%		12.00%	18.00%
BBB–	8.00%			16.00%	28.00%
BB+	20.00%			24.00%	40.00%
BB	34.00%			40.00%	52.00%
BB–	52.00%			60.00%	68.00%
Below BB-/ A-3/P-3	Deduction				

For unrated positions the specific risk charges are covered as follows:

- For banks using an IRB approach for those asset classes, the bank may use the supervisory formula approach, provided that the bank meets the minimum criteria of the IRB approach.
- Should the bank's VaR model include specific risk modelling and it meets the criteria for such models the bank may use these estimates in the supervisory formula.
- In all other cases the risk weights can be calculated as 8 per cent of the weighted average risk weight under the Standardised Approach, multiplied by a concentration ratio.[15] This charge must not be lower than any charge applicable to a rated, more senior tranche. If this calculation is not possible the position must be deducted from capital.

The capital for securitisations that are not contained in the correlation portfolio will be calculated as the sum of the charge for the long positions and the short positions respectively. For a transitional period until 31 December 2013, banks will be allowed to calculate the capital charge as the larger of the charge for the long positions and the charge of the short positions. This should be shown separately from the charge for the correlation trading portfolio.

This rating derived method would lead to punitive treatment of unrated charges, whilst offering limited capital relief for hedges. For businesses that rely on offsetting long and short positions this approach could be a showstopper. If you own one tranche with 100 names and are short another with 99 of the same names the risk is limited, but the approach will ignore the benefit of the netting effect.

4.6.2.3   Amendment to the specific risk charges for credit derivatives

For first-to-default credit derivatives, the specific risk charge is set as the lesser of the sum of the specific risk charges for all of

---

[15] The concentration ration is the sum of the nominals of all the tranches divided by the sum of all the junior tranches to or pari passu with the tranche in which the position is held, including the tranche itself.

individual reference credit instruments in the basket and the maximum possible credit event payment under the contract. There is some offset allowed if the reference entities hedge parts of the bank's exposure. With respect to the hedged amount, the bank is allowed to reduce both the capital charge for specific risk of the reference instrument and the part of the specific risk charge of the credit derivative that relates to this reference instrument. Should there be more reference entities acting as hedges, the offset is applied only to the instrument with the lowest specific risk charge.

A similar scheme is implemented for nth-to-default derivatives, where the charge for the specific risk is the lesser of the sum of the specific risk capital charge for the individual credit reference instrument but disregarding (n-1) obligations with the lowest specific risk charges and the maximum possible credit event payment under the contract. No offsets are allowed for these derivatives if it hedges a reference entity in the trading book.

If these derivatives are rated, the protection seller must calculate the charge based on the rating and apply securitisation risk weights.

4.6.2.4   Impact and challenges of the changes

The impact study, conducted by the BIS prior to issuing the final version of Basel II.5 and released in October 2009, indicated that the revised treatment of equity specific risk contribution to market risk requirements would rise on average from 2.85 per cent to about 7.76 per cent and that re-securitisations would on average increase market risk capital by about 118 per cent, with 72.75 per cent of that allocated to rated re-securitisations.

In the Basel III Quantitative Impact Study released in December 2010 the change in equity specific risk resulted in a 0.2 per cent change in risk weighted assets for Group 1 banks and 0.1 per cent for Group 2 banks. The impact of securitisations in the trading book was not measured separately but was included together with the increase for the incremental risk charge.

The biggest impact on trading activities still remains the effect of using the standardised measurement for correlation trading portfolios. Whilst some relief is afforded by removing it from the more general standardised treatment, the fact that no offset is allowed makes it hugely punitive.

Banks are able to include the correlation trading portfolio under the internal measurement approach using the comprehensive risk management charge but this is also not without its challenges (as discussed in Section 4.6.3.6).

4.6.3 Changes to the internal models approach for market risk

There were several changes proposed to the requirements for internal VaR models, both in terms of the specification of market risk factors and the quantitative standards. The more important changes are discussed in this Section.

One of the key impacts of these changes is the increased emphasis this places on the bank's validation of its internal model. Back-testing is no longer deemed the only evidence required to ensure that the model performs adequately. Banks will have to test their model assumptions more fully and will have to prove that all the assumptions still result in reasonable risk estimates that can be reconciled back to actual profits and losses.

4.6.3.1 Specification of market risk factors

The wording of the amendment has been modified to require that factors deemed relevant for the pricing of instruments should be incorporated as risk factors in the VaR model. Where this is not the case, the bank should justify the exclusion to the satisfaction of the regulator. To do this, the bank should prove that the exclusion still leads to reasonable risk estimation and should base it on the actual profit and loss of the instruments. In addition, the amendment re-emphasises that the model must capture the non-linear risks of options and other relevant products. It should also capture the correlation risk and basis risk of products. Where proxies are used, a good track record for estimating the risk of the actual position should exist. This statement is now more general and can be interpreted to include securitisation products and other products where non-linear risks may exist.

Proxies and approximations have always been a feature of VaR models. A common example would be using a similarly-rated bond pricing model to approximate securitisation issues. In some instances the difficulty in estimating the volatilities of risk factors where market liquidity is low lead to the use of cruder add-ons. In many markets implied volatilities move infrequently and exhibit jumps due to a lack of market disclosure.

Difficulty in estimation is no longer seen as a reason for simplifying models or assumptions. A more rigorous approach in terms of estimating volatilities for risk factors and modelling instruments more accurately should be receiving particular attention. The validation and testing of models and assumptions will have to be done at a far more granular level. Whereas validation has often focussed narrowly on the modelling of the instruments in terms of valuation, it will have to be expanded to include test on risk estimation at an instrument level. Stress tests will have to be expanded to include areas of significant model uncertainty.

4.6.3.2 *Amendments of the quantitative standards*

The regulatory capital requirement is based on estimating a 10-day 99 per cent VaR figure. In most implementations of VaR models this is achieved by calculating the one-day VaR and scaling it up by the square root of 10. Using the square root of time makes a number of implicit assumptions. In the new regulations the bank has to prove that there is no underestimation of the risk when using this method.

Market data update periods have been shortened to one month from three months. The aim of this is to ensure that the models adjust more quickly to increased market volatility. The bank must also make provision to be able to update it more frequently if required. Banks that have been operating in emerging markets that are inherently more volatile and risky than developed markets have implemented these kinds of practices (even under Basel I). If a sudden surge in volatility occurs, infrequent market updates result in far more back-testing exceptions, as the model only incorporates the increase in risk once the dataset is updated.

4.6.3.3 *Stressed VaR*

One of the key changes introduced aimed at reducing the procyclicality of the risk measure and to increase the overall level of capital is Stressed VaR ("sVaR"). The sVaR must be calculated using a historic period of significant stress for the positions in the bank's portfolio. This estimate must be calculated at least weekly. Regulators therefore now require the bank to hold capital for stressed times.

In terms of capital requirements, the capital estimate for sVaR is added to the capital requirements for VaR:

$$c = \max\{VaR_{t-1}; m_c.VaR_{avg}\} + max\ \{sVaR_{t-1}; m_s.sVaR_{avg}\}$$

Both averages are estimated over the past 60 trading days and the multipliers both have an absolute minimum of three with a maximum of four at supervisory discretion. The supervisory discretionary add-on is determined based on the back-testing of only normal VaR.

One of the key requirements of this measurement is to ensure it truly reflects a period of stress for the portfolio. The exact details of this calculation are left to each bank itself. The approach used to calculate sVaR must be agreed with the regulator.

Regulators will want assurance that it does not overly favour a particular directional position of the bank, so consideration to include antithetic movements could be important to provide this assurance. By antithetic, the Committee means that price movements are considered irrespective of their direction.

The implementation of sVaR is not without its challenges. The stressed period has to resemble a period of stress relevant to the portfolio of the bank. Banks favour this as it would make sense but they would have to identify the most stressful period and justify why it is appropriate. This could become a huge computational task. Another consideration could be to choose stressed periods appropriate for different business lines, but aggregation of the results would then be problematic.

One of the challenges of implementing sVaR is how to account for structural changes in markets such as including products that have been introduced subsequent to the stressed period and for which no historical stressed data exists. This will mean that proxies will have to be chosen for new instruments and proposed. Thus housekeeping measures such as controls and documentation around the stressed dataset are going to be important and a focus for validation. If complete structural shifts in markets have occurred, the relevance of the results will also have to be questioned.

All of the above will probably result in real guidance only when regulators consider the approval of the model implementations. That could, of course, again lead to inconsistent implementation across jurisdictions, which has been raised by regulators and the industry as a major concern. There is, of course, a great deal of overlap between the VaR measure and the sVaR measure. As a result, in periods of stress these numbers could be quite similar and the Basel II.5 formulae could be seen as double counting.

In the quantitative impact study conducted in 2009, sVaR would result in a 110 per cent increase in market risk capital and would on average be 2.6 times higher than the normal VaR number. However, there was more variation in results with the maximum being seven times higher. In the comprehensive quantitative impact study released in December 2010 sVaR would, in aggregate, result in an overall increase of 2.3 per cent in overall capital requirements. Comments from the regulator on the results included that one of the expectations of the sVaR number is that there should be significantly less diversification benefit in the numbers compared to VaR. However, the results indicated that this was not the case.

4.6.3.4   Treatment of specific risk

Banks are allowed to include specific risk for equity and interest rate risk positions in their VaR model. For interest rate risk to be included the regulator has to be satisfied that both the general risk model and the IRC model meet regulatory requirements. Securitisations and nth-to-default credit derivatives are allowed to be included in the VaR model, but a bank will still be required to hold capital under the standardised methodology.

The specific risk VaR model must include all material components of price risk[16] and be sensitive to changes in market conditions and portfolio composition. The model should:

(a)   explain historical price variation in the portfolio;
(b)   capture concentrations;
(c)   be robust under adverse conditions;
(d)   capture name related basis risk;
(e)   capture event risk; and
(f)   be validated through back-testing.

To meet these requirements is a tough task. Not only does one have to model portfolio changes, but the underlying data used should reflect the effect of seniority and contract terms. One also has to prove that the model would reflect adverse conditions and that the underlying data used to model the default risk cover at least a full credit cycle. In addition, the regulations require that the bank assesses the effect of liquidity and limited price transparency into its process. The standards require meeting minimum data standards and limiting the use of proxies to cases where the bank can justify that the available data is insufficient.

In terms of validation of specific risk the regulator requires two types of validation. The first is focussed on the modelling of specific risk and the second on back-testing[17]. In the first regulators require specific tests such as goodness of fit to measure how

---

[16] This excludes default and migration risk for positions subject to the incremental risk charge.
[17] This refers to specific risk only, as Back-testing is not a requirement for the IRC.

well the chosen risk factors explain changes in profit and loss for specific risk estimates. In the second they would like to see the back-testing results for portfolios where specific risk is modelled and an evaluation of whether the specific risk model explains the portfolio value changes. These sub-portfolio results should be split at least between debt and equity portfolios, but should the bank have more granular portfolios such as different currencies or markets, then it should also produce back-testing for these. Minimal changes should be made to the portfolio structure. This is quite an interesting requirement since it is not required for the general market risk component. This may be due to the fact that it is necessary to report VaR at a risk type level.

Back-testing should be reported on an aggregated basis (including general market risk) and on specific risk alone. Should the specific risk back-testing have exceptions that would classify the model as unacceptable (falling into the red zone with 10 or more exceptions), the bank should take immediate action to correct the problem and ensure there is a sufficient capital buffer to absorb the risk that the back-test identified.

Should a bank model specific risk under the internal models approach, there is also a requirement to model default and migration risk under the incremental risk charge, which is discussed in the following section.

4.6.3.5   Incremental Risk Charge

4.6.3.5.1   What is the Incremental Risk Charge and why was it introduced?

During the financial crisis a number of major banking organisations experienced large losses, most of which were sustained in banks' trading books. Most of those losses were not captured in the 99 per cent 10-day VaR since the losses had not arisen from actual defaults but rather from credit migrations combined with widening of credit spreads and the loss of liquidity.[18]

---

[18] Default risk is the potential for direct loss due to an obligor's default, as well as the potential for indirect losses that may arise from a default event; and credit migration risk is the potential for direct loss due to an internal/external rating downgrade or upgrade as well as the potential for indirect losses that may arise from a credit migration event.

Even the implementation of the incremental default charge ("IDC"), as introduced in 2005, was not sufficient to ensure that these risks were captured. In addition, reaction of banks on the introduction of the IDC indicated that quantifying default risk separately was inconsistent with their internal practices.

The introduction of the Incremental Risk Charge ("IRC") will ensure that some of the shortcomings of the regulatory capital model are addressed as it will produce an estimate of the default and migration risks of unsecuritised credit products over a one-year capital horizon at a 99.9 per cent confidence level. It will also take into account the liquidity horizons of individual positions or portfolios.

The IRC will be estimated as:

$$C = \max(IRC_{t-1,}\, m_c * IRC_{avg})^{19}$$

4.6.3.5.2   What positions does the IRC cover?

The IRC will be calculated on all positions that are subject to a capital charge for specific interest rate risk according to the internal models approach to specific market risk, but that are not subject to the treatment outlined for unrated securities in paras 712(iii)–712(vii) of the Basel II Framework, regardless of their perceived liquidity.

With supervisory approval, the bank may choose to include all listed equity and derivative positions, based on the listed equity of a company, in its incremental risk model when the inclusion is consistent with how the bank internally measures and manages risk at the trading desk level. If equity securities are included in the computation of incremental risk, default is deemed to occur if the related debt defaults (as defined in paragraphs 452 and 453 of the Basel II Framework).

Securitisation positions are excluded from the IRC, even when they are viewed as hedging underlying credit instruments held in the trading account. These will be subject to the securitisation

---

[19]   The multiplication factor m_c is set at 1. The average IRC is calculated as the 12 week rolling average.

framework introduced under the Standardised Approach. A possible separate treatment, called the comprehensive risk measure ("CRM"), can be applied to the correlation trading portfolio, as discussed in Section 4.6.3.6.

4.6.3.5.3   Key supervisory requirements for calculating the IRC

Soundness standard

One of the major regulatory objectives is to ensure that there is consistency between capital charges for similar positions in the banking and trading books. For this reason the first requirement is that IRC must adhere to a soundness standard comparable to IRB approaches in the banking book.

The confidence level and holding period are therefore consistent with the IRB approach namely 99.9 per cent confidence and a one year holding period.

Constant level of risk over a one-year capital horizon

This measurement must take into account the liquidity horizons applicable to individual trading positions. Trading positions are rebalanced at the end of their liquidity horizons to achieve a constant level of risk. This is also consistent with the IRB approach where the definition of Exposure at Default ("EAD") assumes that positions are rolled over if they mature within the one year capital period.

This approach is also deemed to incorporate the behaviour of banks at a time when it experiences large losses. It is not reasonable to assume that the bank will reduce its VaR substantially after large losses, as it will need to sustain its existing trading book and continue its trading operations to generate income as a going concern. This does not imply that banks do not cut specific positions to limit specific losses. In addition it may not be possible for a bank to raise capital in stressed market conditions.

Liquidity horizons

Appropriate liquidity horizons have to be assumed for the various positions subject to the IRC. The liquidity horizon represents the time required to sell the position or to hedge all material risks covered by the IRC model in a stressed market. A regulatory floor of three months is imposed on the liquidity horizon.

In particular, banks should consider the following when setting these liquidity horizons:

(a) the credit quality of the position;
(b) evidence of market liquidity during stressed periods;
(c) applying conservatism to new products that have not experienced a downturn;
(d) concentration risk of positions in the portfolio for both issuers and market concentration; and
(e) assumptions made in terms of liquidity under the prudent valuation guidelines.

Liquidity horizons can be assigned on an aggregated basis provided that the aggregation is sensible. There is an expectation that non-investment grade products would have a longer liquidity period than investment grade products.

Correlation

The IRC should include correlations between defaults and migrations, which are caused by economic and financial dependence among obligors. The capital charge should reflect the effect of concentrations by attracting higher capital for concentrated positions.

The correlations between default or migration risks and other market factors in the VaR model are excluded and no diversification is allowed when capital is calculated. Hence the IRC is added to the other market risk capital charges.

Diversification and risk mitigation

Netting of exposures is only allowed if the instruments are exactly the same. The diversification for long and short positions in different instruments for the same obligor must be handled within the modelling framework and not through netting.

111

The model should take significant basis risks into account within the IRC model, for example those caused by seniority, product, rating, maturity or payoff triggers.

Rebalancing of the portfolio within the liquidity period may be taken into account if the rebalancing is modelled consistently over the portfolio and the market for the hedge instruments is liquid enough to accommodate the hedging process (even under periods of stress).

If an instrument matures prior to the end of the liquidity horizon or has a maturity longer than the liquidity period that is not contractually assured, the model should take the associated risks into account.

Optionality

The IRC has to reflect the impact of optionality. This should include the non-linear impact of options and other non-linear behaviour. The banks should have an understanding of the model risk associated with the estimation of price risks.

4.6.3.5.4 *Modelling the IRC*

Modelling the IRC is a complex task and two models have been implemented by banks to do this. The first is a jump diffusion model and the second is a Merton model.

The jump diffusion model has not been very popular due to several issues, such as problems with the calibration of the jumps to actual migration or default probabilities, modelling correlation between jumps and the fact that spread changes do not only relate to migration and default.

The majority of banks that model the IRC use a simulation technique that uses concepts developed by Robert Merton. In deriving data to use in the IRC model one should use market estimates for estimating probabilities of default and hence implied migration probabilities. Some banks have used their banking book models for this purpose, but these do not provide market estimates.

This approach results in estimating point-in-time default probabilities that are higher than real world data, but these are what would be used to trade and hedge products in the trading book. This will also cause the measurement to be more volatile than using a through-the-cycle measure based on real world probabilities. The market data from products such as CDS strips can be used to determine forward default probabilities. Choice of data sources will of course depend on availability of market data. In some markets only bond data may be available. And even this may not be sufficient in some emerging markets, leaving no alternative than to use real world credit data.

Achieving the constant level of risk assumption can be accomplished in two ways:

(1) Replacing migrated or defaulted bonds with instruments that will ensure that the initial risk level is maintained. When doing this a bank should consider the portfolio exposure by credit rating and concentration.
(2) Deriving for example the three-month loss distribution and then sampling it four times using a simulation to derive a one year loss distribution if the liquidity horizon is set at three months.

The effect of seniority or other instrument specific characteristics must be incorporated within the estimates for loss given default.

4.6.3.6 *Correlation trading and the Comprehensive Risk Measure*

Under the internal model approach, banks are allowed to apply the Comprehensive Risk Measure ("CRM") to their correlation trading portfolios. In broad terms this allows banks to combine the measurement of specific risk and the incremental risk charge for these portfolios.

The requirements set out for the calculation of the CRM are challenging. Modelling CRM must ensure that the following is captured in the model:

(a) cumulative risk arising from multiple defaults, including defaults in tranched products;
(b) credit spread risk, including gamma and cross-gamma effects;
(c) volatility of correlations, including the cross effect between spreads and correlations;
(d) basis risk between indices and constituents or other bespoke portfolios;
(e) recovery rate volatility; and
(f) hedging slippage and costs of rebalancing.

On an overall basis CRM must comply with all requirements for the IRC: ensure that there is sufficient data availability to model all factors; conduct back-testing to ensure the measure explains price variations; and, ensure that these portfolios are properly separated from portfolios where the IRC and specific risk will apply.

In addition banks will be required to design stress scenarios for these portfolios and examine the effect of these scenarios on default rates, recovery rates, credit spreads and correlations. These tests must be applied weekly and the results submitted to the regulator, who has supervisory discretion to apply a supplemental capital charge if he deems it necessary. No adjustments for double counting will be allowed.

A floor on this measure was introduced, being 8 per cent of the measurement under the standardised measurement method. This was published in the press release of 18 June 2010.[20]

4.6.3.6.1   Validation of the IRC

One of the key requirements of model acceptance is the use test. Banks must ensure that they are using this approach in managing their positions. Direct validation through back-testing is not required as it is not feasible for a measurement with such a long holding period and high confidence level.

---

[20] Adjustments to the document, "Revisions to Basel II market risk framework", announced by the Basel committee

Therefore banks have been advised to use the type of validation approaches applicable to the IRB approaches in the banking book. Firms should develop internal modelling benchmarks to assess the soundness and accuracy of the IRC model. Extensive use should also be made of sensitivity tests and stress testing to establish the reasonability of model outputs. These should not be based on historical experience only.

In terms of validation the bank should ensure that assumptions made about liquidity should reflect actual prices and experience during period of both systematic and idiosyncratic stresses. This will entail banks analysing historical data to confirm modelling assumptions.

If the bank uses rebalancing of positions associated with a liquidity horizon shorter than one year, the validation should compare the outcome of their model, with the results of a fixed portfolio with no rebalancing.

A particular area of concern to the regulator is the correlation approach used in the model and banks should address the appropriateness of the model inputs and methodology here with appropriate rigour. Where the liquidity period is shorter than one year, tests to be performed include estimating the annual implied correlations resulting from the model and comparing those with observed annual correlations. Particular care should be exercised in documenting the modelling approach in a transparent way.

4.6.3.7   Impact of the IRC and CRM

One of the key assumptions that could have a substantial effect on the capital charge is the choice of liquidity horizon and therefore the choices exercised should be carefully considered

For the quantitative impact study conducted by the BIS during 2009, banks were asked to use several different liquidity horizons to calculate the IRC. The IRC were seen to increase by about 20 per cent if the liquidity horizons are increased – even though there is large variability in the results due to granularity and modelling assumptions.

115

Figure 4.5 Incremental risk capital

Table 3

Incremental risk capital charge for different liquidity horizons compared to the overall market risk capital requirements, in per cent

	Capital charge SMM (fallback option)	Specific risk surcharge	Incremental risk capital charge including default and migration risk for a liquidity horizon of...			Default-only charge, 3m liquidity horizon
			1m	3m	6m	
Mean	422	23	136	126	156	97
Median	181	17	92	84	98	66
StDev	714	20	131	132	159	92
Min	26	1	9	5	5	7
Max	2973	78	522	565	613	375

In the quantitative impact study released in December 2010, the increase in market risk capital relating to the IRC and CRM methodologies is estimated at 28.8 per cent and 25.5 per cent respectively, which represents a significant increase in capital.

There have been many concerns raised around the implementation of the IRC, but even more vocal have been the criticisms levelled at the CRM. The standard that has been set for the CRM is very high and banks expect that significant computational and IT requirements will need to be met. The 8 per cent floor is estimated to be far above the CRM measurement, rendering the results of the model useless. Ironically the floor will still result in the most favourable treatment of the correlation portfolio. The unwelcome consequence of all of this is that banks will be required to spend millions to implement a CRM approach only to apply an 8 per cent floor and discard the model result.

Making the situation worse is the inclusion of the correlation portfolio in the VaR and stressed VaR models. Many banks feel a better approach would be to develop a truly comprehensive measure by including general market risk in the CRM.

4.7   Market risk – looking forward

Banks have been inundated with new rules during the last three years, but for trading risk it is not the end of road for regulatory change. Many of the changes introduced have been criticised by both regulators and banks who argue that market risk regulation has now been broken up into several pieces, whereas banks manage their trading books on an integrated basis.

A particular area of concern is the introduction of many systems within the market risk process. Previously market risk departments have been reliant on one regulatory risk system, but they can now have up to five systems to manage. This in itself is likely to increase the operational risk associated with market risk. Even though these measures are being introduced to ensure more comprehensive measurement, their complexity may cause banks to miss positions and, as always, there will be loopholes in the systems, harder to find but also harder to catch. The CVA measurement requirements for internal models also rely heavily on the specific risk VaR models for trading risk. However, it is going to be a complicated task to keep track of the requirements for CVA measurement in terms of counterparties not expressly covered under the specific risk VaR model, and to ensure accurate separation of CVA hedges. In addition, applying all these models separately will not enable banks to consider properly the impact of correlations between VaR, specific risk VaR and CVA.

A big concern is still the effects of double-counting between VaR and sVaR, and the possible double-counting between CRM and VaR. In determining regulatory capital, these effects will eliminate much of the diversification benefits in trading books.

Trading activity in all risk classes has grown significantly over the last two decades. In equity markets we have seen the introduction of high frequency trading ("HFT") driven by technological advances. This activity is increasingly attracting scrutiny from regulators. Not only are the HFT operations of different banks co-located with the exchanges that they trade on, leading to an increase in operational risk, but it is argued that the market liquidity HFT provides dries up in crisis times and could lead to idiosyncratic price movements (as illustrated in the flash crash in May 2010 in US equities).

Simple foreign exchange and interest rate products are now being built into structured products sold to bank clients.

Structured products often lead to illiquid one-way positions that are difficult to hedge in stressed markets.

Banks do not usually retain most of the risk of products they write, except in the case of credit products. It was always believed that eventually most of the risk of products was taken by counterparties outside the banking system, but figures published by the FSA in their recent discussion paper, DP04/10, show that this is not the case. This has strengthened the case for a banking book approach to credit.

One of the other concerns is that the current trading book/banking book split does not address areas within the banking book where fair value drives balance sheet values (e.g. fair value of assets in the banking book such as corporate bonds or interest rate swaps serving as hedges). So the fundamental question is whether it would not be more appropriate to subject all fair-valued positions to trading book capital charges.

Figure 4.6 Counterparty breakdown of OTC derivative revenues by asset class

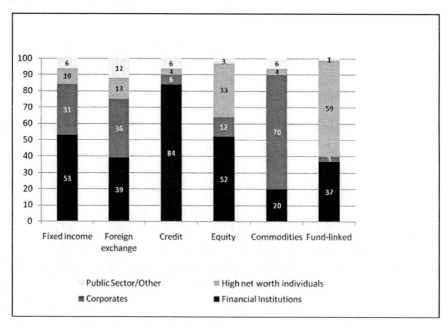

Source: FSA DP04/10

118

Based on all these developments, the Committee has embarked on a fundamental review of the trading book regulatory environment to be conducted in 2011. The review is focussed on issues such as:

(a) Valuation uncertainty. This is a risk to which all trading books are exposed and the question remains whether there should be a capital charge against this risk. Regulators are concerned about the rate of progress in the convergence of accounting standards and inconsistent application of valuation adjustments across jurisdictions.

(b) Consistent treatment of market liquidity. There may still be inconsistencies between implementing market liquidity measures for prudent valuation and the modelling of market risk. Greater emphasis may be placed on ensuring that liquidity horizons are incorporated into general market risk modelling.

(c) Decoupling of market risk oversight by regulators from market risk model approval. In other words, this means widening the net of oversight to banks under the Standardised Approach.

(d) Handling of contingent market risk if a significant counterparty fails.

The industry awaits feedback from the Committee on these issues in 2011 as banks continue their efforts to implement appropriate risk management practices in their own organisations.

Chapter 5

Counterparty Credit Risk

Monika Mars and Agatha Pontiki

5.1 Introduction

This Chapter considers one of the fundamental weaknesses in risk management witnessed during the crisis: the industry's practices relating to the recognition and measurement of counterparty credit risk ("CCR"), principally for derivatives. The Chapter begins with a discussion of the issues that arose during the crisis and provides an overview of the new requirements under Basel III that aim to strengthen and standardise CCR management across banks. The rules are explored in some detail, with a separate discussion provided on the quantitative and qualitative requirements. The Chapter concludes with a discussion of practical challenges and implications including the potential effects on the evolution of the derivatives market given regulatory support for central counterparty clearing houses[1].

5.2 Overview of counterparty credit risk

Counterparty credit risk is the risk that a counterparty to a transaction will default prior to the final settlement and therefore will not make any current or future payments required by the contract.

---

[1] A clearing house stands between parties to a trade, taking on the financial risk if one party defaults. It uses funds, known as margin or collateral, posted by members of the clearing house to ensure deals are completed in the event of default.

The large losses experienced by many global financial institutions during the financial crisis of 2007–2009 highlighted the weaknesses behind understanding, measuring and managing CCR. A significant portion of financial losses registered by the banks during the crisis was in fact generated by credit value adjustments ("CVA") relating to mark-to-market losses on counterparties that did not default. The CCR incurred from trading over-the-counter ("OTC") derivative products and banks' repo style transactions was therefore more detrimental to banks' bottom line results than losses on defaulted counterparties. Unlike most banking products, which are sold to counterparties outside the banking system, with credit derivatives the counterparties are largely the banks themselves. This means that both sides of CVA losses effectively stay in the banking system.

The use of derivative products has become increasingly widespread over the last two decades. The majority of non-financial users continue to apply these products only for the hedging of specific risks (risk insurance) but it is the speculative trading (proprietary trading) undertaken by a number of financial institutions that has brought them under scrutiny. Figure 5.1 below shows the growth trend of global derivative markets. The growth

Figure 5.1 Amounts outstanding of OTC derivatives (notional amounts in billions of US dollars)

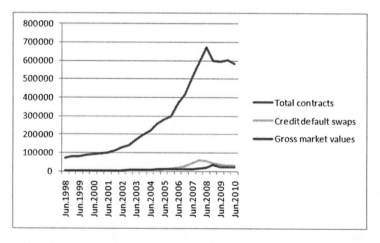

Source: BIS Quarterly Review (December 2010)

rate between 2006 and the market's peak in mid-2008, is notable. The growth in credit default swaps ("CDS") exhibits a similar trend; the notional value of outstanding CDS grew by a factor of 100 between 2001 and 2007 with the growth accelerating from 2006. Since the peak, volumes have fallen but the majority of these contracts (approximately 90 per cent of notional value) continues to be traded OTC on a bilateral contract basis.

The derivatives market is characterised by five main classes of products: interest-rate; foreign-exchange; credit; equity and commodities. What is clear from the graph though is that CDS are not significant in terms of overall volume, as they constitute less than 10 per cent of the OTC derivatives market. Other products, such as interest rate and currency swaps, which remained robust under market crisis conditions, are much more significant and should be the main focus of impact considerations in the context of regulatory reform, including Basel III. Interest rate products account for the majority of exposures both in OTC and exchange-traded terms. They represented 73 per cent and 87 per cent of the two respectively in terms of notional values as of end 2009.

The majority of risk associated with derivatives trading is known to be concentrated among the larger international banks acting as dealers[2] though insurance firms such as AIG and the monolines[3] also played a significant role leading up to the crisis. Among dealers, Lehman Brothers for example, was reported to have a notional amount of $800 billion of OTC derivatives when it filed for bankruptcy in September 2008.

It should be noted that the reference to gross notional amounts is not a measure of market risk as notional amount refers to the underlying quantity upon which interest payments are calculated. Notional amounts are not exchanged; as such, initial amounts are not required to be borrowed either. Notional amounts can therefore be misleading as they overstate the

---

[2] JPMorgan, Goldman Sachs, Morgan Stanley, Citigroup and Bank of America are the five larger US dealers for derivatives business and dwarf the rest of the market. (Source: Filings with Federal Reserve Bank of New York)

[3] A monoline is a financial services firm which specialises in one particular area of the industry.

size of the trading activity and in theory reflect a much larger exposure than what can be funded in the cash market. Notional amounts are useful in terms of reporting however, as they are easily quantifiable, consistently calculated across all institutions and do not change over the life of the agreement. As contracts tend to be on a long-term basis, the notional figures capture non-expired contracts and therefore also reflect a good historical view of cumulative business.

A meaningful market risk indicator would be the "gross market value" which represents the total value that could be received or paid if the transaction was to be unwound on the reporting date. From Figure 5.1, it can be seen that gross market value in 2010 was about 5 per cent of notional amount. Gross market value also overstates market risk as it does not account for offsetting positions (netting). On a similar note of caution for comparisons, open interest figures typically reported in exchange-traded futures and options markets are also different to the meaning of notional amounts. Open interest represents the total number of contracts that have not been settled or liquidated, but since this type of contract typically expires over very short time-frames, open interest figures reflect only an instant view of market activity at any defined point of time.

In the aftermath of Lehman, the OTC derivatives market came under much scrutiny not just for the sheer growth in the volume of transactions leading up to the credit crisis but more significantly for the opaqueness that characterised the market and the complexity of bespoke products. The role of special purpose vehicles ("SPVs")[4] which were used to hold the assets relating to Asset Backed Securities ("ABS") and Collateralised Debt Obligations ("CDOs")[5], amongst other traded structured

---

[4] Qualified Special Purpose Entity ("QSPE"), Variable Interest Entity ("VIE") are among the similar commonly referred structures in financial disclosures of US broker-dealers and which were vehicles designated to hold off-balance sheet assets.

[5] The bubble created by the demand for CDS and which peaked in 2007 is explained by the role of SPVs. Instead of the actual mortgage bonds associated with securitisation transactions, SPVs largely held CDS on the underlying mortgage bonds, thus creating a synthetic CDO. The CDS in this case, provided them with a similar albeit leveraged exposure to the underlying mortgage pool. As demand for these structured products evaporated and SPVs had to be unwound, the level of CDS holdings dropped from 2007 onwards.

products, the inter-relatedness of market participants in these trades, and the subsequent need for the unwinding of collateral positions were all contributors to the systemic shock and market dislocation that followed. Bilateral collateralisation practices, which assume that parties on both sides of a trade mark-to-market ("MTM") their contracts to monitor changes in residual value, were an area where banks exhibited poor performance either due to differing valuation practices or infrequent margining. The actual level of collateral posted for OTC trades which is generally viewed as too low[6], remains another issue of concern. Overall, regulatory oversight had failed to monitor any of these developments.

To address the shortcomings in risk management practices prevailing as of the time of the crisis and to strengthen the risk coverage of the Basel II framework, the Basel Committee issued in July 2009 a set of proposals to raise banks' capital requirements for trading book exposures, re-securitisations and liquidity lines to the asset-backed commercial paper ("ABCP") market. A much more comprehensive set of rules to address counterparty credit risk arising from derivative, repo and securities financing transactions followed in the consultative document BCBS issued in December 2009. The primary objective of these rules was to formalise the link between market and credit risk in trading activities and to ensure banks effectively capture and price counterparty risk, as such, to enhance risk coverage, and to introduce detailed standards on collateralisation.

Although the Committee made revisions to its original proposals especially in view of the results of the Comprehensive Quantitative Impact Study and concerns raised by the industry, the final Basel III text issued in December 2010 introduces a formidable framework with significant implementation challenges. At the same time, calculations under certain aspects of the framework will have to be monitored and further calibrated.

---

[6] On the basis of ISDA data, more than two-thirds of OTC trade exposures were collateralised as of end 2009; however, levels vary by product, asset class and end-user. In contrast, for centrally cleared trades both counterparties post collateral, initial and variation margin. It should be noted that for information purposes, ISDA's margin surveys reflect a double-counting i.e. collateral delivered and received.

The new counterparty risk framework comes into effect on 1 January 2013.

5.3 Proposals to enhance counterparty credit risk capture

5.3.1 *Quantitative requirements*

The Basel II framework addressed counterparty credit risk by assessing the risk of counterparty default and to a lesser degree, credit migration. It did not, however, foresee the risk of market-value losses in the trading book as credit spreads of counterparties widened to reflect deteriorating credit quality, yet stopping short of default. One of the new rules in the Basel III framework – the charge for Credit Value Adjustments ("CVA") – addresses this shortfall. It is widely regarded as the one rule with potentially the largest impact on the industry, it could also impact the future evolution of the derivative markets. In parallel, the Committee made significant modifications to existing Basel II rules to enhance risk capture particularly with having the "back-mirror" view of CCR levels becoming elevated as volatility increased within a stressed market environment. In this sense, the Committee acknowledged that the Basel II framework did not adequately incorporate generalised "wrong-way" risk either.

Below is a list of the quantitative requirements in the Basel III framework, which are described in more detail in the sections that follow in this chapter. Most of the new rules apply to banks which have permission to use the internal models method (hereafter referred to as "IMM banks") to calculate counterparty credit risk regulatory capital.

(a) a new Pillar 1 capital add-on charge to capture the potential increase in CVA due to the changes in counterparty credit spreads;

(b) the concept of stressed 'Expected Positive Exposure' (EPE) to calculate counterparty risk exposures;

(c) increased Asset Value Correlations (AVC) for exposures to systemically important financial institutions (SIFI) and non-regulated financial entities;

126

(d) a Pillar 1 charge for specific wrong-way risk;
(e) standard haircuts for securitisation collateral;
(f) increased margin period of risk for collateralised trades; and
(g) capital charges for exposures to central counterparty clearing houses ("CCPs").

It should be noted that external ratings continue to be important in the Basel III framework. As a result of lessons from the crisis, the BCBS has also introduced changes to tighten standards for the use of ratings. The most important changes featured in the Risk Coverage section of the new rules include:

(a) Recognition of External Credit Assessment Institutions ("ECAI"): the IOSCO Code of Conduct for Credit Rating Agencies ("CRA") has been explicitly introduced to strengthen eligibility criteria for the use of ECAI.
(b) CRA "merry-go-round": banks must choose ECAI and use their ratings consistently in order to eliminate "cherry picking" of assessments. In parallel, the use of unsolicited ratings is allowed subject to certain conditions and supervisory control.
(c) Non-rated exposures: incentives have been put in place to ensure that there is no deliberate avoidance of getting exposures rated. This specifically eliminates conflicts where unrated exposures could have received lower risk-weights than those of non-investment grade ratings.
(d) "Cliff effects": the requirement for eligible guarantors to be rated A- or better has been removed except in the case of securitisation exposures.

5.3.1.1 EPE calculated based on stressed inputs

> **General wrong way risk** is the risk that arises when the probability of default of counterparties is positively correlated with general market risk factors (such as interest rates or equity indices). In Basel II terms, there is a positive expected correlation between Exposure at Default ("EAD") and Probability of Default ("PD").

Significant general wrong-way risk was evidenced during the financial crisis as exposure to counterparties increased as their creditworthiness deteriorated. It appeared that in calculating their counterparty risk exposures, IMM banks did not take fully into account market volatility and potential illiquidity during a time of stress. Under the revised guidelines, the Basel Committee, which has retained Effective "Expected Positive Exposure"[7] ("EEPE") as the metric for EAD, addresses this shortcoming by introducing a requirement for estimating EEPE under stressed parameters. The approach is meant to be similar to the revision the Committee made to the market risk framework for stressed Value-at-Risk ("VaR").

Under the new rule, EEPE needs to be calculated using a three-year period that includes a one-year stress period. Given that the stressed period of risk could have occurred several years in the past, IMM banks must also calculate EAD using current market data and compare this with the EAD using the stressed parameters. Wherever stressed EEPE exceeds the EEPE calculated using current period market data, the former must be used for the portfolio-level capital charge.

It should be noted that under the Basel II framework, wrong way risk was accounted through the alpha factor[8] in the counterparty risk formula, which is a multiplier applied to the exposure amount. In revising the framework, the Committee concluded that it is extremely difficult to address general wrong-way risk through explicit capital charges and as such, the alpha factor remains the best available option. As an added impetus to the use of the alpha factor, the Committee highlights the need for "supervisors to be alert to the significant variation in estimates of alpha that arises from the opportunity for

---

[7] Effective Expected Positive Exposure is the weighted average over time of effective expected exposure over the first year, or, if all the contracts in the netting set mature before one year, over the time period of the longest maturity contract in the netting set where the weights are the proportion than an individual expected exposure represents of the entire time interval.

[8] This is a ratio (bank's internal estimate of economic capital based on stochastic exposures / economic capital based on EPE). It is currently set at 1.4 for banks that do not have own internal estimates and at a floor of 1.2 for banks that make their own internal estimates.

mis-specification in the models used for the numerator, especially where convexity is present"[9].

5.3.1.2 Specific charge for CVA

During the financial crisis, roughly two-thirds of CCR losses were due to CVA losses and only about one third were due to defaults of counterparties. The Basel II framework did not fully provide for market value losses in the banks' trading book as counterparties' credit spreads widened. Given this lapse as well as banks' diverse practices for calculating CVA, the Basel Committee introduced in its original proposal in December 2009 a "bond equivalent of the counterparty exposure" approach to standardise the methodology for measuring CVA risk and for banks to calculate a Pillar 1 capital add-on charge. Banks may exclude from this capital charge transactions with a central counterparty ("CCP") and securities financing transactions ("SFT") unless the supervisor determines that CVA loss exposures arising from the latter are material.

CVA is the difference between the risk-free portfolio and the true portfolio value that takes into account the possibility of the counterparty's default. CVA is therefore the monetised value of the counterparty credit risk. It is commonly expressed as: Probability of Default ("PD") x Loss Given Default ("LGD") x discounted Expected Exposure ("EE").

In the final "Basel III" text, the approach to measuring CVA risk was revised. The CVA capital charge is to be calculated depending on a bank's approved method of calculating capital charges for counterparty credit risk and specific interest-rate risk of bonds. Indicatively, banks with IMM approval will employ the "Advanced CVA risk capital charge" method[10]

---

[9] Enhanced counterparty credit risk management requirements, Paragraph 114 from 'Basel III – A global regulatory framework for more resilient banks and banking systems', Basel Committee on Banking Supervision, December 2010

[10] For the mathematical formula, see Paragraph 98 in the original text of 'Basel III – A global regulatory framework for more resilient banks and banking systems', Basel Committee on Banking Supervision, December 2010

together with eligible CVA hedges using the bank's VaR model for bonds. The VaR model is restricted to changes in the counterparties' credit spreads and does not model the sensitivity of CVA to changes in other market factors (e.g. the value of reference asset, commodity, currency or interest rate of a derivative). The standards for qualifying hedges are specific; only hedges used for mitigating CVA risk, and managed as such, are eligible for inclusion in the VaR model. The hedges may consist of single name CDS, single name contingent CDS, other equivalent hedging instruments referencing the counterparty directly, and index CDS' (with restrictions). Tranched or nth-to-default CDS are not eligible. Hedges that are eligible for inclusion in the CVA capital charge must be removed from the bank's market risk capital charge. The CVA risk capital charge consists of both general and specific credit spread risks, including stressed VaR but excluding IRC. An appropriate scaling factor (at least three) must be used in the calculations of a bond VaR and a stressed VaR.

All other banks will employ the "Standardised CVA risk capital charge" method. This method is also to be used in those cases where a bank's approved market risk VaR model does not appropriately reflect the specific risk of debt instruments issued by the counterparty. In other words, only exposures to counterparties for which the bank has supervisory approval for modelling the specific risk of debt instruments can be included in the advanced CVA risk charge. Under the "Standardised CVA risk capital charge"[11], a one-year time horizon is used. For calculation purposes, counterparties are mapped to one of seven weights based on external ratings ranging from 0.7 per cent for example for "AAA" and "AA" rated counterparties, to 2.0 per cent for below investment grade ratings ('BB' rated) and to 18 per cent for counterparties in default ("CCC" rated).

---

[11] For the mathematical formula, see Paragraph 104 in the original text of 'Basel III – A global regulatory framework for more resilient banks and banking systems', Basel Committee on Banking Supervision, December 2010

5.3.1.3 *Pillar 1 charge for specific wrong-way risk*

> **Specific wrong-way risk** arises when the exposure to a particular counterparty is positively correlated with the probability of default of the counterparty due to the nature of the transactions with that counterparty.

During the financial crisis, significant credit losses were incurred from transactions with counterparties such as financial guarantors ("FGs") whose credit quality was positively correlated with the exposure amount. As the Committee's view is that specific wrong-way risk can and should be explicitly recognised and measured by banks, the Committee raised the standards to address this. Banks are required to perform stress testing and scenario analysis to identify specific wrong-way risk, to manage the risk by product, region, industry or any other relevant category as well as report to senior management as part of ongoing credit risk assessment. For transactions where specific wrong-way risk has been identified, the Committee introduced higher exposure measurements that translate into higher capital charges and effectively penalise those executed outside of a central clearing platform.

Specifically, for single-name credit default swaps ("CDS"), EAD equals the full expected loss in the remaining fair value of the underlying instruments assuming the underlying issuer is in liquidation. Accordingly, LGD must be set at 100 per cent for such swap transactions (For banks using Standardised Approach, the risk weight is that for an unsecured transaction). For equity derivatives, bond options, SFT referencing a single company, EAD equals the value of the transaction under the assumption of a jump-to-default of the underlying security.

> **The monolines**
>
> Financial Guarantors ("FGs") guarantee the timely payment of principal and interest on a bond in the event that the underlying issuer defaults. A bond with such a

guarantee is referred to as being "wrapped". Monolines are guarantors focusing on capital markets. In contrast, multi-line insurers offer insurance in a range of sectors but are not permitted to offer financial guarantees. More importantly, monolines provide an irrevocable and unconditional guarantee to pay the claims on default of the underlying issuer in a timely manner, whereas multilines pay claims after a period of loss adjustment. As such, monolines have played an important role in reducing funding costs for issuers and giving them access to capital markets that otherwise would have been too costly to achieve.

Historically, FGs serviced the US municipal bond market but with the growth in credit derivative markets and participants looking for well-established and highly-rated counterparties to provide credit protection, the monoline business underwent a rapid transformation. With abundant liquidity in the market and their credit spreads narrowing, monolines started expanding their underwriting business to include newer asset classes such as CDOs backed by US subprime mortgage collateral and subprime residential mortgage backed securities ("RMBS"). By end-2005, FGs maintained over $300 billion in gross credit protection that was largely rated "AAA". With the sharp rise in loan delinquency rates, the fall in demand and eventually the demise of the market for the related structured products, monolines came under severe stress. They had to recognise significant mark-to-market ("MTM") losses from the embedded CDS in CDOs (which had served to enhance the credit structure of the product), as well as create reserves directly against RMBS exposures. With their solvency in question, monolines lost their top-notch ratings. It should be noted that unlike most CDS contracts, those entered into with monolines did not require the guarantor to post collateral. Should this have been the case, the monolines might have not benefited from their "AAA" external ratings for as long as they did.

The downgrade in their ratings triggered a spiral effect in the market with the "wrapped" deals losing their investment-grade ratings and in their turn, the buyers of credit protection having to recognise losses, i.e., just as they were due to collect insurance when the asset quality of the underlying security was impaired. Market players were therefore exposed to specific wrong-way risk given the nature of the transactions they entered into with monolines. Wrong-way risk causes CVA to increase substantially (a technical discussion can be found in "Counterparty credit risk, The New Challenge for Global Financial Markets" authored by Jon Gregor and published by John Wiley and Sons (2010)).

It should also be noted that direct financial guarantees from an insurance company are not eligible for MTM accounting. The monolines however, had created separate legal entities to write the CDS contracts and then guaranteed their separate legal subsidiaries. This provided banks with CDS eligible for MTM accounting and the reason behind originally active trades with such CDS.

Banks do not report exposures to monolines (or related "wrapped" portfolios) in a consistent manner. In some cases, meaningful disclosure from "vintage" years is absent altogether. This makes it difficult to compare what were core businesses at some of the larger international investment banks (including defunct US broker-dealers). However, the size and significance of the industry exposure to FGs has become evident as some of the leading market players have come forward with more detailed disclosures. For example, in its 2009 annual financial statements, Deutsche Bank reported that it recorded €1.2bn in CVA against aggregate monoline exposures for 2009 after another €2.2bn CVA charge for 2008. Similarly, UBS reported cumulative CVA of $2.8bn for 2009 and $7bn for 2008.

5.3.1.4   Increase in asset value correlation for exposures to large financial firms

Studies conducted by the Committee indicated that during the financial crisis, financial institutions were more correlated than reflected in the Basel II internal ratings-based ("IRB") framework. The studies concluded that the asset value correlation ("AVC") for financial firms was 25 per cent or more higher than for non-financial firms. For this reason, the Committee introduced a 1.25 multiplier to the formula computing the correlation for exposures that is to be applied to all regulated financial intermediaries with assets over $100bn. Exposures to unregulated financial intermediaries would always be subject to a higher AVC regardless of asset size. Unregulated financial entities are defined as legal entities whose main business includes the management of financial assets, lending, factoring, leasing, provision of credit enhancements, securitisation, investments, financial custody, central counterparty services, proprietary trading and other financial services activities identified by supervisors.

Given the non-linear relationship between AVC and capital, it is understood that this rule can increase capital requirements significantly as AVC would range from 15–30 per cent compared to the 12–24 per cent range under the Basel II framework. Under the IRB formula, AVC captures the default risk part of capital whereas the "maturity adjustment" captures migration risk. By increasing the correlation values, it therefore suggests an increase of the default losses and not of the migration losses (i.e. BCBS' targeted "interconnectedness" lever) that materialised during the crisis.

5.3.1.5   Increased margin period of risk for collateralised trades

The financial crisis showed that the close-outs amounted to longer risk horizons than the mandated margin periods used for regulatory capital calculations. For transactions subject to daily re-margining and MTM valuation, the supervisory floor was ten days for OTC derivatives and five days for securities financing transactions ("SFTs"). The Committee observed that the liquidity of trades, the costs of hedging open positions, the size of netting sets and the length of disputes were causes for the longer close-out horizons. Where close-outs were completed rapidly in periods of volatility, this was at the cost of price discounts.

The Committee therefore considered that there was a need to establish additional "bright line" indicators of when to compel the banks to extend the margin period of risk. Specifically, in the new rules the margin period of risk has been extended to 20 business days for netting sets where; (a) the number of trades exceeds 5,000 or (b) the set contains illiquid collateral or OTC derivatives that cannot be easily replaced in the marketplace (bespoke or exotic derivatives or those concentrated with a counterparty which exited the market precipitously). Banks which have a history of margin call disputes on a netting set that exceed the margin period of risk would be required to double the applicable margin period of risk for the affected netting set.

The minimum holding period for various products is summarised in Figure 5.2:

Figure 5.2 Product minimum holding periods

Transaction type	Minimum holding period	Condition
Repo-style transaction	5 business days	Daily re-margining
Other capital market transactions	5 business days	Daily re-margining
Secured Lending	20 business days	Daily revaluation

5.3.1.6 Standard haircuts for securitisation collateral

Under the Basel II supervisory haircuts method, the same haircuts are applied to repo-style transactions of securitisations and to corporate debt of the same rating. With the onset of the financial crisis, the valuation of securitisation exposures became substantially more volatile than similarly rated corporate debt. Given problems with the banks' collateral management frameworks, banks used different standards to transform non-cash collateral into cash-equivalent amounts. To better reflect the realities of the market, the Committee has introduced a new set of recalibrated supervisory haircuts (assuming daily mark-to-market, daily re-margining and a 10-business day holding period) expressed as a percentage (see Figure 5.3).

Figure 5.3 Supervisory haircuts for collateral

Issue rating for debt securities	Residual maturity	Sovereigns issuers	Other exposures	Securitisation
AAA to AA-/A-1	<1 year	0.5	1	2
	>1 year<5 years	2	4	8
	>5 years	4	8	16
A+to BBB-/	<1 year	1	2	4
A-2/A-3/P-3 and	>1 year<5 years	3	6	12
unrated bank	>5 years	6	12	24
securities				
BB+ to BB-	All	15	Not eligible	Not eligible
Main index equities		15		
Other equities		25		
UCITS/ mutual funds	Highest haircut applicable to any security in fund			
Cash in the same currency		0		

(The footnotes associated with the table are not included; however, securitisation exposures would be defined as those exposures that meet the definition set out in the securitisation framework.)

The revised haircuts will be implemented together with a ban on the use of re-securitisations as eligible financial collateral, irrespective of their credit ratings. The prohibition applies whether the bank is using the supervisory haircuts method, their own estimates of haircuts method, the repo VaR method or the internal model method. The use of downgrade triggers in the estimation of EAD is also prohibited. Banks on the IMM approach will be expected to model collateral in order to recognise the effect of collateral on EAD calculations with all other banks applying the mandatory haircuts for non-cash collateral.

5.3.1.7 *Capital charges for exposures to CCP*

In an effort to reduce systemic risks and bring more transparency to derivative trading activities, the new rules provide banks with strong incentives to move trades to a central counterparty clearing house ("CCP") with exposures to CCPs assigned fairly low risk-weights. To complement this, the Committee supports enhanced capital standards and rigorous risk management for CCPs. It has therefore specified that the favourable treatment of exposures to CCPs applies only where the CCP complies with the standards set by the Committee on Payment and Settlement Systems ("CPSS") and the International Organisation of Securities Commissions ("IOSCO"). Such entities will be denoted as "qualifying" CCPs.

In early March 2011, the Basel Committee published the consultative report on "Principles for Financial Market Infrastructures" that was prepared by CPSS and IOSCO. The consultation period ends in mid-2011 and the objective is for CPSS and IOSCO to review all comments and publish a final report in early 2012. Once final, the principles will replace existing standards[12] for systemically important payment systems, central securities depositories, securities settlement systems, central counterparties and trade repositories.

Separately, in December 2010 the Basel Committee also issued for public consultation a detailed set of rules relating to the capitalisation of bank exposures. The main features of these proposals are:

(a) trade exposures to a qualifying CCP will receive a 2 per cent risk weight (under Basel II they were risk-free);

---

[12] These standards are the 'Core principles for systemically important payment systems' (2001); the 'Recommendations for securities settlement systems' (2001); and the 'Recommendations for central counterparties' (2004).

(b) default fund exposures to a CCP will, in accordance with a risk-sensitive waterfall approach (based on a CCP's actual financial resources and hypothetical capital requirements), be capitalised according to a method that consistently and simply estimates risk arising from such default fund; and

(c) exposures to any non-qualifying CCP should, regardless of whether it has some attributes of a CCP or is for some other purposes considered to be a CCP, be capitalised as is the case with any other bilateral exposure.

Once the consultation process and a relevant impact study based on year-end 2010 data are complete, the Committee expects to release the final standards by September 2011. The Committee aims to monitor how the proposed framework will affect bank capital levels by completing observations at 30 June 2011, 31 December 2011 and 30 June 2012. The final rules will be implemented in line with the rest of the counterparty credit risk framework.

5.3.2 Qualitative requirements

Aside from the quantitative rules that better capitalise for the risks banks incurred during the crisis, the Basel Committee also evaluated and adopted a series of qualitative measures to address shortcomings in banks' margining practices, back-testing and stress testing programs. These qualitative require-ments, which are fairly prescriptive in some respects, direct the banks in upgrading risk management practices and provide them with incentives to reduce operational risk. Again, all of the measures are applicable to banks using the internal model method ("IMM").

5.3.2.1 Enhanced collateral management requirements

Banks must have a collateral management unit that is respon-sible for calculating and making margin calls, managing call disputes and on a daily basis, reporting levels of independent amounts, initial margins and variation margins. The unit must also track the extent of reuse of collateral and the concentration to individual asset classes accepted by the firm. The enhanced collateral management process is meant to provide banks with more reliable data which they can use in their PFE and EPE calculations.

The banks are therefore called upon to make important investments in terms of human capital and technology in this area. As outlined in the Committee's recommendations, the units must be adequately staffed to ensure that they can process calls and disputes in a timely manner even under severe market crisis and to maintain appropriate collateral management information that is reported on a regular basis to senior management. All of the new requirements are incorporated in the independent review of the CCR management system that a bank's Internal Audit department must conduct regularly (not less than once a year).

5.3.2.2 Enhanced requirements regarding re-use (re-hypothecation) of collateral

Banks should not only have well-functioning collateral management units in place but the units should also operate within the guidelines of a liquidity management strategy developed by senior management. To this end, controls regarding the reuse of collateral should be in place and ensure that the nature and horizon of collateral reuse is consistent with a bank's liquidity needs and does not jeopardise the institution's ability to post or return collateral in a timely manner.

5.3.2.3 Treatment of highly-leveraged counterparties

For highly-leveraged counterparties such as hedge funds, the Committee's view is that the use of an increased margin period of risk will result in a more appropriate capital requirement. The Committee also added a qualitative requirement in that the PD for highly-leveraged counterparties (or counterparties whose assets are predominantly traded assets) should be estimated using a stressed period of performance of assets.

5.3.2.4 Requirements for stress testing of CCR models

The Basel Committee has elaborated a detailed set of rules in order to upgrade stress testing of the models banks use for the identification, measurement and control of CCR and to make stress testing an integral part of a bank's risk management process. These requirements are fairly explicit in terms of describing the parameters (e.g. exposure aggregation for all forms of CCR, not just OTC derivatives) and the exposure factors that stress testing employs (e.g. single factor; multi-factor; non-directional risks) as well as the frequency with which the test should be conducted. Guidelines on the governance of the stress testing program are also described with the active involvement of senior management emphasised.

5.3.2.5   Back-testing and model validation guidance for CCR

The Basel Accord specified that IMM banks back-test their EPE models, where back-testing is defined to be the comparison[13] of the IMM model's output against realised values. With back-testing being one of the elements of the validation process, the Basel Committee identified significant shortcomings in the banks' ability to conduct these tests following review of banks' programmes. Specifically, the Committee highlighted the inappropriateness of the approach to VaR back-testing as a method for back-testing the CCR models. In the context of assurances that supervisory authorities must have for allowing banks to use a models-based approach, the Committee elaborated qualitative criteria that banks must first meet in order to receive supervisory approval. For this reason, back-testing and model validation criteria in the new accord are rigorous and detailed.

As with stress testing, the requirements encompass all aspects of the back-testing programme: model architecture; frequency of the back-testing; procedures that need to be followed; the governance of the programme; the required independence for units running the tests; reporting; and the use of results by senior management as well as its active involvement throughout.

---

[13] This comparison is either the comparison of a distribution with a single realised value at a point in time, as for market risk factor or exposure distribution back-testing, or the comparison of a single predicted value against some realised value at a point in time, as for back-testing EPE or pricing models.

To illustrate the degree of detail and the breadth that some of these requirements have, a rule describes that, "back-testing of a model must be performed not only against realised risk measures but also hypothetical changes based on static positions. Risk measures refer not only to EEPE (the risk measure used to derive regulatory capital) but also to the other risk measures used in the calculation of EEPE such as exposure distribution, the positive exposure distribution, the market risk factors used to derive those exposures and the values of the constituent trades". Similarly, "banks should document the process for initial and on-going validation of their IMM model (and all the models that input into the calculation of EPE) to a level of detail that would enable a third party to recreate the analysis."

5.4   Implications and practicalities

The new CCR rules will impact the most those banks with a large business in derivative sales and trading. The results of the Comprehensive Quantitative Impact Study ("QIS") that the BCBS released in December 2010 confirmed this. Based on the QIS, the sample of banks included in the CCR analysis resulted in an 11.0 per cent average increase in credit risk-weighted assets ("RWA") for Group 1 banks[14] and a much smaller (1.1 per cent) increase in credit RWA for Group 2 banks. It should be noted that the number of banks included in the counterparty credit risk analysis is smaller than the number that took part in the QIS as CCR is relevant only to banks engaged in OTC derivatives activities or securities financing transactions.

The table below summarises the QIS results for the change in overall RWA attributable to key elements of the Basel III framework (including those outlined in this chapter).The increase relative to overall RWA for Group 1 is 7.6% and 0.3% for Group 2 banks.

---

[14] For the purposes of the comprehensive QIS, Group 1 banks are those that have Tier 1 capital in excess of €3bn, are well diversified, and are internationally active. All other banks are considered Group 2 banks.

Figure 5.4 Change in overall RWA, in percent

Type of banks	Number of banks	Overall %	Definition of capital %	CCR[15]	Securitisation in banking book %	Stressed VaR %	Equity standard measurement method %	IRC & securitisation in trading book %
Group 1	74	23.0	6.0	7.6	1.7	2.3	0.2	5.1
Group 2	133	4.0	3.2	0.3	0.1	0.3	0.1	0.1

Note: The average impact of the trading book and counterparty credit risk rules could not be estimated by all banks in the sample. Therefore, the sample of banks is smaller than the overall sample and the average definition of capital impact is different.

Source: Results of the Comprehensive Quantitative Impact Study, BCBS December 2010

Aside from the increase in RWA and capital requirements, banks will need to invest (some heavily) in technology and resources to upgrade and meet qualitative requirements, as well as enhance clearing services to clients. Other firms will need to decide on what third-party clearing services are to be used. The changes are anticipated to have huge implications for the banking industry and for the size and behaviour of derivative markets in the longer term.

To alleviate some of the capital burden that the enhanced CCR rules place on banks, the Basel III framework supports incentives to promote the use of qualified CCPs. While the promotion of standardisation and improvement of transparency have been driving the global regulatory initiative in this respect, such change raises new issues in view of the large amounts of risk that will be transferred to CCPs and

---

[15] This column measures the increased capital charge for CCR and the higher capital charge that results from applying a higher AVC parameter against exposures to financial institutions under the IRB approaches to credit risk. The calculation uses a modified version of the December 2009 proposed bond equivalent capital charge for MTM losses associated with deterioration in the credit worthiness of a counterparty (i.e. CVA risk) and a threshold of USD 100billion for applying the increased AVC to regulated financial institution exposures. As this does not reflect all refinements since the initial proposal, the impact of the final rules will likely be overestimated to some extent.

the dangers that may consequently arise as CCPs evolve into systemically important market entities. In the prospect of CCPs evolving into "too-big-to-fail" institutions themselves, resolution agreements and implied government support, or the mechanism through which CCPs can have access to "a lender of last resort" needs to be addressed. Some of the regulation that has been developed to address these issues is not yet satisfactory. For example, ISDA, in its October 2010 response to the "European Commission proposal for regulation on OTC derivatives, CCPs and trade repositories", points out that CCPs should be required to hold more than €5 million in initial capital and be required to participate in the default waterfall with an own funds/equity contribution, to be used immediately after a defaulting member's contribution and prior to non-defaulting members' contributions. Such equity should be in reasonable proportion to the size of the default funds and no less than 10 per cent of the fund size.

In its September 2009 statement, the G20 called for all standardised OTC derivative contracts to be traded on exchanges or electronic trading platforms where appropriate, and cleared through CCPs by the end of 2012. A large shift of the derivatives business away from the OTC market and onto CCP platforms is unlikely to occur in this short timeframe. A number of regulatory issues have to be further discussed and resolved regarding the eligibility of contracts for central clearing and the interoperability of CCPs. The fungibility issue is also critical in terms of market participants endorsing exchange-trading; this means setting for the whole industry minimum standards of the legal parameters contained in the contracts. Fungibility is a prerequisite to novation, netting and for the substitution of contracts traded in different locations with different parties.

Clearly, full standardisation is not attainable (nor desirable) as the need for bespoke derivatives that cater to the specific needs of end-users will remain. This is particularly relevant where non-financial firms use the products to hedge economic risks for their business (e.g. oil derivatives). Standardisation of contracts and therefore hedges on CCPs would still leave banks with basis risk for any transactions they enter into with such end-users.

Whether derivative trading and clearing through a CCP delivers the expected benefits, such as risk mitigation and transparency will need to be assessed by product segment. In the case of FX swaps and forwards (where the FX market has many transactions which are simple and short-term and where the trade involves the exchange of cash flows) CCPs do not add benefit. For this product, settlement risk is the key concern and CLS Bank was specifically set-up to manage and mitigate it. In other cases, for example interest rate swaps as well as futures and options, CCPs are already operational[16]. Trade repositories have also been developing along the different asset classes. Although mandatory reporting of OTC transactions is aimed at providing more transparency on the various product exposures, this in itself does not address the issues of cross-asset or cross-market linkages, an appreciation of which is necessary to fully understand counterparty and systemic risk.

In all instances, non-financial firms are unlikely to become members of CCPs. Given that clearing houses impose initial and variation margins on members, the increased collateral cost could potentially outweigh the benefit of other efficiencies in the long term. Member banks are also expected to re-price their products to pass at least some of the new costs (e.g. exchange fees, clearing fees) to non-member end-users meaning that the cost of hedging for non-financial firms will increase until volumes and cause transaction costs to decline. In addition, members face upfront costs (e.g. legal fees) to achieve and maintain compliance given more stringent registration requirements.

Other important implications for banks arise from a simplification of the rules where the Committee aims to standardise

---

[16] In view of the lion's share interest rate products have in terms of overall derivative exposures, three exchanges namely, CME, Eurex and NYSE Liffe, account for up to 90% of all exchanged-traded volume.

compared with a more sophisticated industry practice (e.g. the bond equivalent method for CVAs) or from detailed guidance on a "one size fits all" basis (e.g. stress and back-testing; size of margin sets).

There is also a risk of unintended consequences. Two such examples are the treatment of highly-leveraged counterparties and the increased asset value correlations for exposures to financial institutions. The choice of treatment for higher leveraged (hence "riskier") counterparties under the new framework creates an uneven playing field. Leverage on its own does not necessarily mean lack of active risk management of trading positions and the experience of the crisis does not support the unfavourable bias towards hedge funds. The biggest CCR problems and credit losses during the crisis did not originate from the hedge fund industry but from banks. In contrast, some hedge fund managers[17] were among the first to identify the risk management deficiencies of banks and regulatory oversight shortcomings and to work them to their advantage. The assessment of whether a company is highly leveraged or not should be made on an individual basis and reflected in a counterparty's rating which results in PD. The rule on increased AVC for unregulated financial intermediaries such as hedge funds and financial guarantors regardless of their asset size (vs. the US$100bn set for banks) creates a similar bias.

More importantly, to implement the Basel III rules for CCR successfully, banks will have to transform themselves operationally by upgrading their data, systems and know-how. The integrity of data and the building of uniform calculation engines will be key drivers of successful compliance. Banks will need, for example, to have systems with common risk factors for consistent stress tests and back-testing and which allow them to develop common models, e.g., using the same parameters for market risk valuations and for counterparty credit risk.

---

[17] "The greatest trade ever: The Behind-the-Scenes Story of How John Paulson Defied Wall Street and Made Financial History" (Author: Gregory Zuckerman) and "I saw the crisis coming. Why didn't the Fed?" Dr. Michael J. Burry, The New York Times, Opinion, 3 April 2010

The systems must become particularly adept at supporting "what-if" analyses, allowing the banks to run scenarios to quantify the impact of incremental trades or changes in hedging. The additional human and IT resources in areas such as collateral management units will translate into significantly increased operational costs. The organisational and operational implications may well be as significant financially as the capital add-on charge for higher CCR.

Chapter 6

Liquidity and Funding

Charlie Beach and Claire Rieger

6.1   Introduction

Perhaps the most significant addition to the Basel framework under Basel III is the inclusion of liquidity rules. Basel II was focused on capital adequacy and the associated risk management and measurement frameworks. Whilst many countries had in place some form of liquidity regulation prior to Basel III, there was little consistency across territories and the financial crisis led to a broad recognition that the existing liquidity rules were largely inadequate.

This Chapter explores the Basel III liquidity standards and the associated implications and practical issues for firms in the implementation of a strengthened liquidity framework. As regulators in the UK, USA, Germany, the Netherlands and Australia have already introduced strengthened standards following the recent crisis, we will use the experiences of implementing these regulations as a benchmark to highlight the implications for Basel III implementation more widely.

6.1.1   Background

Liquidity risk is the "risk that a firm, although solvent, either does not have available sufficient financial resources to enable it to meet its obligations as they fall due, or can secure such resources only at excessive cost" (FSA Glossary (*www.fsahandbook.info/FSA/html/handbook/Glossary*)).

Liquidity and funding issues came close to causing a meltdown of the financial system down in 2007–2008, with infamous examples, such as the collapse of Northern Rock and Lehman Brothers. In the case of Northern Rock, the funding model played a key role in the collapse of the bank, in particular an over-reliance on wholesale short-term funding to fund long-term assets. The issue worsened when the financial position of the bank came into question, leading to a loss of customer confidence and the first run on deposits experienced by the UK banking industry for more than a century.

Liquidity risk also ultimately led to the collapse of Lehman Brothers, again where a loss of confidence led the bank's counterparties to demand additional collateral and guarantees (against funding and trading positions with the firm that it could not meet in the short-term). The episode also saw $8bn of cash repatriated as part of Lehman's normal treasury operations from the UK to the USA over the weekend prior to the collapse. This was one of the factors leading to the urgent redefinition of the liquidity regulatory regime in the UK in advance of the Basel III consultation, with a particular focus on legal entities and local self-sufficiency. Prior to the crisis, it had become increasingly common for banks to create global funding frameworks relying on a small number of funding and liquidity "hubs" to supply the liquidity needs of legal entities and business operations across multiple territories.

During the crisis, funding became more expensive as some significant sources of financing such as securitisation became unavailable and credit extension became more straitened. Firms significantly increased the stock of liquid assets on their balance sheets to improve their resilience to liquidity shocks and there has been a systemic increase in the cost of funding to which banks will need to adjust permanently.

The importance of liquidity to the safety and soundness of banks has led to significant regulatory scrutiny and the new liquidity rules form a key aspect of the Basel III reform agenda. The Basel III accord puts in place qualitative and quantitative standards that will require significant improvements to liquidity risk management and also to the levels of liquidity held by banks. This will undoubtedly go some way to address the current gap in the Basel regulatory framework, but the new rules have also raised concerns across the banking industry, for example in relation to the strict definition of liquid assets for the numerator of the Liquidity Coverage Ratio ("LCR") or the less favourable treatment of financial institutions.

In particular, the implications of the quantitative standards will not be fully understood until some way through the implementation phase: whilst the implementation has been deliberately planned over an extended timeframe, with built-in observation periods and resulting calibrations, there are concerns that some of the quantitative standards described in this Chapter will render certain existing banking activities unviable due to prohibitively high costs. Also, since the standards will, in practice, be interpreted and adopted by individual territory regulators, the usual level playing field concerns exist. In addition, in a global banking group, legal entity considerations are likely to lead to trapped liquidity in several territories as supervisors apply rules to legal entities in their respective jurisdictions and require them to have stand-alone financing capabilities with large buffers of liquid assets.

6.1.2 Overview of the regulation and quantitative implications

In the "International Framework for Liquidity Risk Measurement, Standards and Monitoring" published on 16 December 2010, the Basel Committee sets out a strengthened liquidity framework which introduces quantitative standards to supplement the qualitative "Principles for Sound Liquidity Risk Management and Supervision" issued in 2008. The standards consist of two measures:

(a) The Liquidity Coverage Ratio ("LCR"): this is a measure of the ratio of available liquid assets to the estimated net cash outflow over a 30-day period, based on a number of prescribed cash-flow assumptions – it is designed to ensure short-term resilience against liquidity disruptions.
(b) The Net Stable Funding Ratio ("NSFR"): this is a longer-term structural liquidity ratio which aims to ensure the use of sufficient stable, longer-term funding sources to cover less liquid assets.

Furthermore, the Committee introduces a set of monitoring metrics to assist supervisors in the analysis of bank-specific and system-wide liquidity risk trends. These are described in detail in the following Section.

The potential shortfall of liquidity and funding arising from the implementation of these two ratios is difficult to assess accurately and analyses vary significantly. However, the Quantitative Impact Study ("QIS") results published on 16 December 2010 indicate at the end of 2009 a shortfall of liquid assets of 1.73 trillion and stable funding of 2.89 trillion for the banks that do not meet the 100 per cent LCR and NSFR requirement respectively. In addition, analyses show disparities among European, North American and Asian institutions: in a Staff Position Note ("Impact of Regulatory Reforms on Large and Complex Financial Institutions", IMF, 3 November 2010), the IMF states that European banks would be most affected by the NSFR requirement, with an average estimated NSFR of 89 per cent against a requirement of 100 per cent, which reflects a greater reliance on wholesale funding and higher loan-to-deposit ratios than exist in other regions. By contrast, most North American banks and some Asian banks would already meet the 100 per cent NSFR requirement (average ratios of 112 per cent and 113 per cent respectively). This can be explained by a favourable balance sheet structure, with a relatively higher share of securities on the asset side that requires less stable funding and deposits on the liabilities side, which provide a more stable source of funding. The new rules will also have particular impacts on economies such as South Arica, which display unusual structural characteristics: small bond markets, no deposit insurance and stickier wholesale deposits than in other countries due to exchange control. Where deemed relevant, the Committee will define alternative treatments for such jurisdictions during the transition period.

In general, banks that do not yet meet the NSFR requirement will need to make structural changes to their balance sheet, by increasing stable funding and reducing the average maturity of lending. This will restrict banks' ability to undertake all but short-term lending and will particularly affect those asset classes that significantly contribute to increasing average maturity. The IMF survey also notes that the disparities within regions can be significant: whilst the European banks included in the sample would, on average, not meet the 100 per cent requirement, some banks have much lower ratios than others: for example those with greater amounts of long-term lending and high reliance on wholesale funding. A similar structure is observed in some Asian banks which finance long-term assets mainly through wholesale funding. Overall, the implementation of the ratios is likely to force a reduction in wholesale funding (in particular short-term), an increase in deposits, a reduction in longer-term loans and an increase in liquid assets.

For many financial institutions, the liquidity challenge may be greater than for capital as supply constraints (such as the availability of deposits, medium-term funding and high-quality liquid assets) are likely to be key issues. To meet the new quantitative standards, banks will need to compete more for deposits, work harder to re-finance medium-term funding at favourable rates and potentially enhance their capability to trade in liquid assets.

Despite the extended implementation timeframe, many financial institutions are tackling the balance sheet consequences of the new regime sooner rather than later. This is necessary to identify potential conflicts between current funding structures and what will be required under the new regulatory regimes thereby minimising the need to hold liquidity in locations that are sub-optimal for the firm. The need to make these changes early to avoid prohibitive financing costs and unfavourable peer comparisons by the market is likely to be the overarching concern, rather than the formal regulatory timetable.

Whilst addressing the new quantitative requirements firms will also need to focus on implementing a robust liquidity management framework: regulators have made it clear that they expect banks to comply with the Basel Committee's *Principles for Sound Liquidity Risk Management and Supervision* (the "Sound Principles") in conjunction with the implementation of the new Basel III quantitative standards and monitoring tools.

The main tool for managing liquidity is the mismatch report (which can be based on contractual or behavioural attributes) and can be used to analyse assets and liabilities, derive mismatch gaps, carry out stress testing and define the liquid assets buffer requirement. Figure 6.1 below illustrates how a mismatch report may be used.

Figure 6.1 Simplified contractual mismatch and potential application

Contractual mismatch report – simplified example	1 Day	2 Days	3 Days	4 Days	5 Days	1-2 Wks	> 2 wks -1 Mth	>1 Mth -3 Mth	>3Mth -6Mth
Marketable assets (split by category)									
Contractual inflows (split by category)									
Contractual outflows (split by category)									
Net contractual outflows / inflows									
Contingent liabilities									

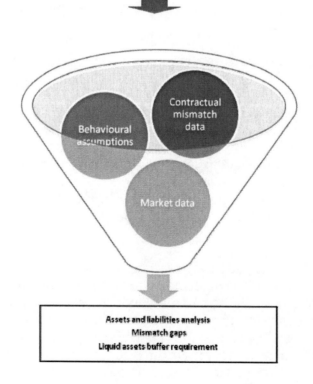

The new quantitative standards will place much greater liquidity and funding constraints on the financial position of the firm. It will therefore be important for firms to manage liquidity and funding proactively, both at the structural and tactical levels. This means:

(a) embedding funding and liquidity planning into business planning;
(b) putting in place limits (e.g. weighted average maturity limits) and incentives (e.g. through funds transfer pricing frameworks) to manage balance sheet structure proactively; and
(c) improving processes and controls around the day-to-day management of liquidity across businesses, legal entities and currencies.

The implications of failing to get liquidity management right can lead to a build-up of hidden risks in the balance sheet: for example, arising from sudden shifts in market breadth and depth as well as product valuation concerns for certain types of derivatives and structured products. From a regulatory perspective, poor systems and controls could result in increased quantitative requirements, such as higher liquidity buffers or restrictive funding profiles.

The next Section focuses on the Basel III quantitative standards, while Section 6.3 explores the implications of these on the balance sheet and the risk management framework.

6.2   Basel III regulations

This Section provides a detailed description and discussion of the key characteristics of the two Basel III quantitative measures ("LCR" and "NSFR") and the monitoring tools proposed by the Committee.

The LCR and NSFR have been calibrated and tested as part of the 2010 Quantitative Impact Study ("QIS"), which was completed on a "best-efforts" basis by firms based on consolidated data as at 31 December 2009; the Basel Committee now intends to further validate the metrics over an "observation period" which will be used to make refinements and amendments before the formal introduction of the metrics.

Figure 6.2 Timeline for implementation of liquidity quantitative standards

	2010	2011	2012	2013	2014	2015	2016	2017	2018	2019
LCR		Observation period				Minimum standard in place				
NSFR			Observation period						Minimum standard in place	

Source: BCBS, International Framework for Liquidity Risk Measurement, Standards and Monitoring, 16 December 2010, p.2

Figure 6.2 describes the timeline for implementation. The observation periods for the LCR and NSFR will begin on 1 January 2011 and 1 January 2012 respectively; the information reported to supervisors will include the overall percentages of the LCR and NSFR, as well as information on all their components (similar to the information gathered for the QIS). The firms will be required to comply with the minimum standards beginning 1 January 2015 and 1 January 2018 respectively. The Basel principles will be adopted by supervisors in their respective jurisdictions and although Basel III provides prescriptive minima, some items are subject to national discretion. Examples include assumptions in relation to deposit run-off rates, contingent funding obligations and market valuation changes on derivative transactions.

6.2.1 Liquidity Coverage Ratio

6.2.1.1 Definition

The 30-day LCR requirement is designed to ensure that a financial institution has sufficient unencumbered, high-quality liquid resources to survive significantly severe liquidity stress scenario lasting for one month.

The LCR identifies the amount of unencumbered, high-quality liquid assets (see below for a full definition) an institution holds that can be used to offset the net cash outflows it would encounter under a short-term (30 days) stress scenario specified by supervisors, including both institution-specific and systemic (or market-wide) shocks.

The LCR is calculated as follows:

$$\frac{Stock\ of\ high\ quality\ liquid\ assets}{Total\ net\ cash\ outflows\ over\ the\ next\ 30\ calendar\ days} \gg 100\%$$

6.2.1.2   Applying the ratio

The ratio is applied by undertaking a scenario-based liquidity stress test using prescribed assumptions in relation to run-off rates and liquidation haircuts to assess the net cash outflow over 30 days. Figure 6.3 provides a simplified overview of the LCR and key underlying assumptions.

Figure 6.3 Simplified overview of LCR

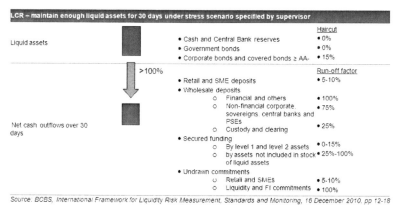

Source: BCBS, International Framework for Liquidity Risk Measurement, Standards and Monitoring, 16 December 2010, pp 12-18

In the above table, the haircut is the percentage that is subtracted from the value of the liquid assets: cash and high quality government bonds are given liquidity credit for their full value while qualifying corporate bonds and covered bonds receive a 15 per cent haircut (i.e. 85 per cent of their value is recognised as available liquid assets).

The run-off factor refers to the percentage of liabilities that are assumed to be withdrawn from the balance sheet in a stressed situation (see 6.2.1.4 below). For example, for maturing retail and SME deposits only 90-95 per cent of the value at the maturity point during the stress period is assumed to roll over.

The following worked example in Figure 6.4 illustrates how the ratio is applied in practice. In this example, we use a simple balance sheet, where only the first line of assets ("liquid assets") is eligible for the numerator.

Figure 6.4 Example LCR calculation

Liquid assets   150 (a)

Cash outflows over 30 days:

	Liabilities	Run-off factor	Outflows
Stable retail deposits	300	5%	15
Less stable retail deposits	500	10%	50
Unsecured wholesale funding	100	75%	75
Total	900		140 (b)

LCR (a)/(b)   107%

Using the simple example above, it is possible to derive some broad-brush conclusions about how the LCR may affect two different types of banking activity.

On the asset side, the numerator depends only on the amount and quality of highly liquid unencumbered assets, rather than the type of assets on balance sheet. A compliant ratio (i.e. a ratio over 100 per cent) will therefore be dependent on the liquid asset buffer and the funding mix.

Retail and commercial banks: These banks are likely to have a large amount of stable retail deposits, which are sticky with a relatively low outflow percentage. It is likely that these institutions will seek to strengthen their deposit base and reduce their wholesale funding, especially to other financial institutions, as this type of funding attracts a 100 per cent outflow under the LCR.

Investment banks: These firms, that are often funded through secured funding and debt issuance and provide commitments to various sorts of clients or vehicles, usually have a smaller deposit base than retail and commercial banks. They will therefore have to work hard to optimise their funding mix. It is likely that they will need to hold a relatively large buffer of liquid assets to maintain their activities.

6.2.1.3   Liquid assets

Liquid assets are assets that can be liquidated at any time – including times of stress – easily and immediately with little or no loss of value. Figure 6.5 describes the fundamental and market-related characteristics of liquid assets.

Figure 6.5 Liquid asset characteristics

Fundamental characteristics	Market-related characteristics
Low credit and market risk:	**Active and sizeable market:**
Less risky assets tend to have higher liquidity.	Asset should have active outright sale and repo markets
Credit risk: high credit standing of the issuer and a low	at all times (which means having a large number of
degree of subordination increases an asset's liquidity.	market participants and a high trading volume).
Market risk: low duration, low volatility, low inflation	Market breadth (price impact per unit of liquidity) and
risk and denominated in currency with low foreign	market depth (units of the asset can be traded for a
exchange rate risk all enhance liquidity.	given price impact) should be good.
Ease and certainty of valuation:	**Presence of committed market makers:**
Asset's liquidity increases if market participants are	Quotes are always available for buying and/or selling
more likely to agree on its valuation.	the asset.
A liquid asset's pricing formula must be easy to calculate	
with no strong assumptions and inputs must be publicly	
available. (i.e. no exotic products)	
Low correlation with risky assets:	**Low market concentration:**
High quality liquid assets should not be subject to	Diverse group of buyers and sellers in an asset's market
wrong-way risk. Assets issued by financial firms are	increases the reliability of its liquidity.
more likely to be illiquid in times of liquidity stress.	
Listed on a developed and recognised exchange	**Flight to quality:**
market:	Historically, the market has shown tendencies to move
Being listed increases an asset's transparency due to	into these types of assets in a systemic crisis.
standards in place.	

Source: BCBS, *International Framework for Liquidity Risk Measurement, Standards and Monitoring*, 16 December 2010, pp

8-10

The Basel Committee requires that the liquid assets stock should be made of at least 60 per cent of Level 1 assets and no more than 40 per cent of Level 2 assets as defined below. Figure 6.6 below provides an overview of the characteristics of Level 1 and Level 2 assets.

Figure 6.6 Level 1 and Level 2 assets

Level 1 assets	Level 2 assets
• Cash	• Government assets qualifying for 20 per cent risk weighting under Basel II's standardised approach for credit risk, with 15 per cent haircut
• Central bank reserves to be drawn down in times of stress	• Non-financial corporate and covered bonds not issued by the bank itself, rated AA- and above, also 15 per cent haircut.

• Marketable securities: claims issued or guaranteed by sovereigns, central banks, non-central government public sector entities (PSEs), the Bank for International Settlements, the IMF, the European Commission, or multilateral development banks with all the following criteria:
  o 0 per cent risk-weighted under the Basel II standardised approach;
  o Deep repo-markets exist for these securities; and
  o The securities are not issued by banks or other financial service entities.
	Conditions for level 2 assets:
	
	• Not issued by a bank, investment or insurance firm.
	• Proven as reliable source of liquidity in the markets (repo and sale) even during stressed market conditions, i.e. maximum decline of price or increase in haircut over a 30-day period not exceeding 10 per cent (or during a relevant period of significant liquidity stress).

• Domestic sovereign debt for non 0 per cent risk-weighted countries, issued in foreign currency that matches the currency for the bank's operations	

Liquidity buffer assets are also subject to operational requirements. In particular, liquidity buffer assets should be: managed as contingency funds and only for the purpose of creating a buffer; made available to the relevant function (e.g. Treasury) as and when required; and, should not be amalgamated with hedges on trading positions. This could imply that assets are managed in a separate book or desk, but this needs to be clarified. Liquid assets should be turned over on a periodic basis to test their liquidity and ensure that they can be realised during a crisis. The Committee has not yet stated clearly the timeframe required to reinstate the ratio if the buffer is used but gives banks 30 days to replace an asset that becomes ineligible, for example, due to a downgrade.

The Basel III definition of liquid assets is wider than some of the current regulatory regimes' definition; for example UK FSA's definition of liquid assets is limited to eligible government bonds and cash held at central banks. This raises level playing field concerns. It could allow banks subject to regimes that adopt the Basel definition (or an even wider definition) to incorporate a wider set of asset classes into its liquid assets pool. It is difficult to assess at this stage how significant the differences in implementation will be, or what degree of alignment between different territories will be achieved in the roll-out of the Basel III framework (despite front-running the Basel rules, the UK FSA has indicated that it will seek to align with Basel).

6.2.1.4 Scenario proposed and liquidity driver analysis

Over a 30-day period, firms are required to model a scenario that combines idiosyncratic and market-wide shocks with the following characteristics:

(a) significant downgrade (three-notch) of the institution's credit rating leading to additional contractual outflows;
(b) partial loss of retail deposits;
(c) partial loss of unsecured wholesale funding;
(d) partial loss of secured short-term financing with a significant increase in secured funding haircuts;
(e) increases in derivative collateral calls and substantial calls on contractual and non-contractual off-balance sheet exposures, including committed credit and liquidity facilities; and
(f) the need for the institution to buy back debt or fund balance sheet growth arising from non-contractual obligations honoured in the interest of mitigating reputational risk.

159

Under the above scenario, the Basel III framework provides minimum or actual run-off assumptions for liabilities and haircut assumptions for liquid assets as shown in Figure 6.3. These drive net cash outflows (which consist of cumulative expected cash outflows minus expected cash inflows; the expected cash inflows are capped at 75 per cent of the expected cash outflows). Whilst most factors are prescribed by the Basel framework, some of them, such as deposit run-off rates, contingent funding obligations or market valuation changes on derivative transactions, are subject to national discretion. Each asset type is assigned a percentage of contractual inflows and each liability type a run-off factor. Figure 6.3 provides an overview of key run-off rates for liabilities.

In comparison, as an example of a national regime, the FSA liquidity regime requires firms to estimate net cash outflows for ten identified liquidity risk drivers over both a two-week and three-month period across three stress scenarios: idiosyncratic, market-wide and combined. The estimated outflows resulting from this stress test are then used as a key component to derive the amount of liquid assets (or liquidity buffer) to be held by the firm.

Through the application of run-off rates to the liabilities and the definition of contractual inflows, Basel III addresses some but not all of the risk drivers identified by the FSA Individual Liquidity Adequacy Standard ("ILAS"). The following FSA risk drivers are not addressed directly via the LCR: intra-group liquidity risk, funding concentration risk, intra-day liquidity risk (although the Committee is currently considering whether this risk should be captured as part of the LCR), and cross-currency risk (but the liquid assets should be held in various currencies to allow a firm to meet its outflows if currencies cannot be converted and the LCR should also be calculated per significant currency as part of the monitoring tools). These risk drivers are, in effect, captured by the Principles for Sound Liquidity Risk Management and Supervision. Other differences between the LCR and the ILAS include a different time period (one month for Basel III and two weeks and three months for the FSA) and a different number of scenarios (one for Basel III and three for the FSA).

160

For two of the main risk drivers, wholesale funding risk and retail funding risk, and for the inflows, Figure 6.7 compares the run-off rates between the LCR and the FSA benchmark to show how different regulators may approach the issue in different ways.

Figure 6.7 Comparison of Basel III and FSA outflow and inflow parameters

Examples of outflows and inflows	LCR	FSA benchmark
Outflows		
Retail deposit	% Run-off factor (assumed by scenario)	Outflow characteristic and run-off rate
Stable deposits	5% and higher	Deposits type B Sizeable outflow Benchmark – 10%
Less stable deposits	10% and higher	Deposits type A Sizeable outflow Benchmark – 20%
Unsecured wholesale funding	% Run-off factor (assumed by scenario)	Outflow characteristic and run-off rate
Small business customers	5%, 10%	22.5 %
Non-financial corporate customers: Sovereigns, Central banks and public sector entities with operational relationships:	25% or 5%	100% (2 weeks) 60% (2 weeks to 3 months)
Non-financial corporate customers	75%	Large corporates: Type B - 22.5% Type A (less stable) - 100%- 50%
Other legal entity customers (including financial inst)	100%	100 % (2weeks) c.60% (3months)
Inflows	% Contractual inflows	% Contractual inflows
Retail inflows	100%	0%
Wholesale inflows	100%	100%
Reverse repos and secured lending	0%-100% (100% if against illiquid assets)	100%
Other assets	0%	No explicit requirement
Own account securities	NA	100%
Commercial lending	0% [as part of other assets]	0%
Intra-group inflows	0% [as part of other assets]	0%

Overall, the FSA run-off factors appear to be more stringent than those of Basel III. If national regulators take different views, international banks will need to understand and manage around

161

these. It is worth noting that Basel III and the FSA have adopted the same approach to inter-bank contingent liquidity or credit facilities. The assumption is 100 per cent outflow for undrawn committed facilities, but 0 per cent inflow is recognised from committed facilities provided by other banks and financial institutions. Such level playing field issues are a significant concern for banks.

The following table considers some of the potential implications of the LCR for banks, the markets and wider economy.

Figure 6.8 Implications of LCR

Implications for banks

- A potential shift in the balance sheet structure is to be expected, with the following characteristics:
    - More use of liquid securities, which are lower yielding assets and may also create a concentration of exposure to sovereign risk across the industry;
    - Less use of bank paper exacerbating the funding challenges for banks.
- A transformation of the interbank market because wholesale funding impacts the LCR negatively.

Implications for the markets and the wider economy

- Potential correlations across financial markets (e.g. concentrations in holding of eligible assets, concentration in certain funding markets, etc.) resulting in increased exposure to sovereign risk;

- Reduce liquidity in certain market segments;

- Decrease in bank profitability leading to increased interest rates and effectively decreasing credit supply to the economy;

- Shift of banking activities with negative impact on the LCR to the shadow banking sector; and

- The increased competition for retail deposits may push up the cost for banks and lead to a reduction of the traditional stickiness of these deposits as depositors become more accustomed to changing bank.

6.2.2   Net Stable Funding Ratio

6.2.2.1   Definition

The NSFR aims at measuring the amount of longer-term, stable sources of funding employed relative to the funding required by a given asset profile, including the potential for contingent calls on funding liquidity arising from off-balance-sheet commitments and obligations. The standard complements the LCR and aims at promoting structural changes in banks' liquidity risk profiles toward more stable, longer-term funding.

The NSFR is a new concept for most regulators and, more than the LCR, goes to the heart of what banking is and how banks make profits, by placing a formal limit on the extent of maturity transformation they are allowed to undertake. As a result this is an area where the regulators' (public) and the bankers' (private) interests are likely to be in conflict.

The NSFR is calculated by applying prescribed weightings (set out below) to a bank's liabilities to calculate the amount of available stable funding and to its assets to obtain a figure for the required amount of stable funding. The NSFR, which is expected to be greater than 100 per cent, is then obtained by dividing available funding by required funding as follows:

$$\frac{Available\ amount\ of\ stable\ funding}{Required\ amount\ of\ stable\ funding} > 100\%$$

6.2.2.2   Applying the ratio

Figure 6.9 provides a simplified overview of the NSFR. The required stable funding ("RSF") factors relate to the amount of stable funding considered to be required for a certain type of assets. For example, cash and highly liquid securities are assigned a 0 per cent factor as they are not considered to require stable funding for more than one year. The available stable funding ("ASF") factors refer to the degree of stability of the funding source. For example, capital is assigned a 100 per cent factor as it

Figure 6.9 NSFR overview (simplified)

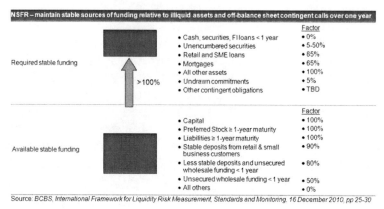

NSFR – maintain stable sources of funding relative to illiquid assets and off-balance sheet contingent calls over one year		

		Factor
Required stable funding	• Cash, securities, FI loans < 1 year	• 0%
	• Unencumbered securities	• 5-50%
	• Retail and SME loans	• 85%
	• Mortgages	• 65%
	• All other assets	• 100%
	• Undrawn commitments	• 5%
	• Other contingent obligations	• TBD

		Factor
Available stable funding	• Capital	• 100%
	• Preferred Stock ≥ 1-year maturity	• 100%
	• Liabilities ≥ 1-year maturity	• 100%
	• Stable deposits from retail & small business customers	• 90%
	• Less stable deposits and unsecured wholesale funding < 1 year	• 80%
	• Unsecured wholesale funding < 1 year	• 50%
	• All others	• 0%

>100%

Source: BCBS, *International Framework for Liquidity Risk Measurement, Standards and Monitoring, 16 December 2010, pp 25-30*

is the most stable funding source. Unsecured wholesale funding of less than one year is assigned a factor of 50 per cent and is considered to be a less stable source of funding than deposits of less than one year.

The implementation of the NSFR is still under review by the Committee during the observation period and several aspects remain uncertain. For example, securitisation is another area of discussion, where although assets and liability-related cash flows may be perfectly matched, for NSFR purposes the assets have to be funded 85 per cent. More generally the Committee is still assessing whether some amount of recognition should be applied to matched funding. Banks that rely heavily on securitisation or on wholesale funding may have difficulties in meeting the NSFR.

6.2.2.3 The NSFR scenario

The NSFR is designed to encourage firms to maintain stable sources of funding relative to illiquid assets and off-balance sheet contingent calls under a one year scenario displaying the following characteristics:

(a) material event which calls into question the reputation or credit quality of the institution;

(b) potential downgrade in a debt, counterparty credit or deposit rating by any nationally recognised credit rating organization; and

(c) significant decline in profitability or solvency arising from heighted credit risk, market risk, operational risk and/or other risk exposures.

Furthermore, the scenario assumes no reliance on the central bank as a source of funding: extended borrowing from central bank lending facilities outside regular open market operations are not considered in this ratio.

RSF reflects the illiquidity of assets and is calculated as the value of assets multiplied by liquidity risk factors assigned to asset types. The RSF factors assigned to various types of assets are parameters intended to assess the amount of a particular asset that could not be monetised in the NSFR scenario through sale or used as collateral in secured borrowing on an extended basis. Assets that are more liquid and more readily available to act as a source of extended liquidity in the stress scenario receive lower RSF factors (and require less stable funding); those that are less liquid receive higher factors.

Required stable funding = (Sum of the value of the assets held and funded by the institution × Specific RSF factor) + (Amount of off balance sheet activity × associated RSF factor)

ASF includes the types of equity and liability that are expected to be reliable sources of funding over the next year under conditions of extended stress (primarily Tier 1 and Tier 2 capital and stable deposits). ASF is defined as follows:

Available stable funding = Capital + Preferred stock (maturity ≥ 1 year) + Liabilities (effective maturities ≥ 1 year) + Stable open maturity deposits (maturity < 1 year) + Term deposits (maturity < 1 year) + Wholesale funding (maturity < 1 year)

NB. Items with a maturity < 1 year are expected to stay with the institution for an extended period in an idiosyncratic stress event

ASF is calculated by weighting an institution's equity and liabilities according to one of five factors as presented in figure 6.9 above.

6.2.2.4   Impact of NSFR

From a systemic perspective, the NSFR (and the LCR) will increase competition for and the pricing of retail deposits. In addition, repo financing of securities positions will become more costly. However, at this stage, the impact on the structure of wholesale funding markets is unclear given preferential treatment for more stable sources of funding. The rationalisation of wholesale loan products, including committed credit and back-up liquidity lines, is likely to push activities towards the shadow banking sector.

From a firm perspective, it is likely that the cost of funding will increase for all institutions with the extent of increase depending on balance sheet structure and funding strategy. It is also likely that the implementation of legal entity NSFR requirements will lead to trapped liquidity at banking subsidiary level.

Based on the structure of the ratio, it appears that banks will have two main options to manage the NSFR. First, banks can adjust business strategy, by reducing businesses with unfavourable liquidity treatment (these include committed credit and liquidity facilities such as a letter of credit or a standby bond purchase agreement), and adjusting pricing to compensate for higher cost of funding. The NSFR is also likely to encourage firms to move towards more stable sources of funding by raising additional funding, such as retail deposits, long-term debt and capital, and reducing their reliance on less stable funding, such as wholesale credit. Many large financial institutions have already been developing stable funding sources since the 2008 crisis and the NSFR should consolidate this trend.

6.2.3   Link between LCR and NSFR

A firm can have a low LCR and a high NSFR: this would be the case if it had a small pool of liquid assets but a large amount of stable funding. However, working towards achieving a better

NSFR will have an impact on the LCR: as discussed above, the LCR is driven by the liquidity buffer on the asset side and the outflow on the liability side. More stable long-term funding will lead to less outflow during the LCR stress period, hence a higher LCR but also a smaller mismatch, which is one of the key monitoring tools described in Section 6.2.4.

In addition, the implementation of the liquidity ratios will force firms to adapt their internal management frameworks and manage the divergence between the regulatory requirements and their own internal measures. This is especially relevant for funds transfer pricing, which will need to be calibrated to take into account the impact of the ratios. This issue is covered in detail in the Section on practical implications.

6.2.4 Qualitative requirements/monitoring tools

The Committee has proposed a suite of monitoring tools to capture information related to cash flows (contractual maturity mismatch), balance sheet structure (concentration of funding), available unencumbered assets and certain market indicators. These are in more detail as follows:

- Contractual maturity mismatch: the contractual maturity mismatch profile identifies the gaps between the contractual inflows and outflows of liquidity for defined time bands. No behavioural assumptions are applied, which will allow supervisors to apply their own assumptions to perform analysis across the market.
- Concentration of funding: this metric aims at identifying funding concentrations by counterparty or type of instrument/product in relation to wholesale funding across material currencies (accounting for 5 per cent or more of bank's total liabilities). The proposal to implement this metric has some identified shortcomings (for example, it does not provide an indication of how the funding from a counterparty could be replaced) and will be used as a basis for discussion between banks and the regulators.
- Available unencumbered assets: this metric relates to the amount and key characteristics of unencumbered assets, including currency denomination and location. Banks

should also provide expected haircuts required on the secondary market or by the central bank and the expected monetised value of the collateral.

- Market-related monitoring tools: these will be broken down into market-wide, financial sector and bank-specific information and will used by supervisors to monitor potential liquidity difficulties at banks.
- LCR by material currencies.

Some existing regimes, such as the UK's, are super-equivalent and this raises questions of alignment during the Basel III implementation. Firms subject to multiple regulatory regimes could be faced with highly complex reporting requirements if there is no alignment or agreement to waive reporting requirements between their different regulators. Figure 6.10 provides a high-level comparison between the monitoring tools set out under Basel III and those already required under the FSA liquidity regime:

Figure 6.10 Comparison of Basel III and FSA monitoring

Basel III common metrics to monitor the liquidity risk profiles	Corresponding FSA reporting regime
Contractual Maturity Mismatch • Distinction between inflows and outflows by time bucket	FSA048 • Enhanced mismatch report
Concentration of funding • Concentration by significant counterparty, product, currency and/or terms	FSA 051 • Wholesale and repo – by counterparty FSA053 • Retail and corporate including SME FSA054 • Assets and liabilities by currency
Available Unencumbered Assets • Amount, type, location and currency of liquid assets. Include estimated haircut under BAU	FSA050 • Market value of liquid asset buffer securities by issuer (country)
Market-related monitoring tools • Equity prices, debt markets, CDS spreads, FX markets	Under FSA's supervision

As demonstrated in Figure 6.10, the range of information required for Basel III will be similar to the range for the FSA reporting requirements. Based on the authors' experience, these are extensive requirements that provide a good overview of liquidity and funding information for a firm and allow it to produce stress testing and draw comparisons with other firms. However, implementing these reporting requirements has proved a huge challenge in the UK, due to the amount of data needed but also to the frequency of reporting (weekly and often daily) and firms should start identifying any gaps in data requirements and infrastructure sooner rather than later. This issue is explored further in the next Section.

6.3 Implications and practical issues

This Section focuses on the implications and practical issues that firms may face in implementing the new liquidity standards and a robust liquidity management framework in line with the Sound Principles, and how the Basel ratios and monitoring tools might influence the shape of this framework and associated systems and controls. As the Sound Principles do not apply directly to firms and will be implemented differently across jurisdictions the example of the FSA is used, where relevant, to illustrate how these could be implemented. Where the European Banking Authority ("EBA") (formerly Committee of European Banking Supervisors ("CEBS")) has provided additional guidelines, such as in relation to Funds Transfer pricing ("FTP") (CEBS's "Guidelines on Liquidity Cost Benefit Allocation", October 2010), we also refer to them.

6.3.1 Impact on the balance sheet

Basel III establishes new liquidity standards that will drive new balance sheet strategies to limit the extent of illiquid assets, restrict wholesale/unstable sources of funding and manage higher funding costs. These new standards will have a broad impact across most banks, particularly those centered in commercial and wholesale banking activities. Figure 6.11 provides a simplified overview of how a balance sheet of a universal bank would look under Basel III, based on the new constraints imposed by the Committee, compared to a current structure.

6.3.2 Impact on the risk management framework

The standards and monitoring metrics described in the previous Section complement the BCBS Sound Principles issued in September 2008.

The Sound Principles relate to the following components of a liquidity management framework:

Figure 6.11 Current vs. future balance sheet structure – estimating the impact of Basel III liquidity rules on the balance sheet

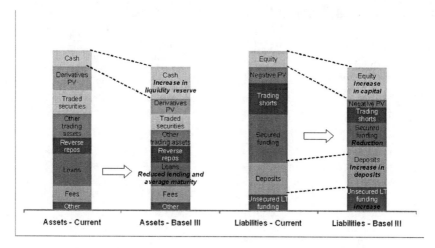

(a) governance: Robust Board and senior management oversight;
(b) risk appetite and limits: the establishment of policies and risk tolerance and associated limits, and the maintenance of a sufficient cushion of high quality liquid assets to meet contingent liquidity needs;
(c) risk measurement: the use of liquidity risk management tools such as comprehensive cash flow forecasting;
(d) stress testing and contingency planning: the development of scenario stress testing and robust and multifaceted contingency funding plans;
(e) FTP: The necessity of allocating liquidity costs, benefits and risks to all significant business activities; and
(f) intra-day risk and collateral management.

Figure 6.12 shows how the Basel III standards and the liquidity management framework interact.

Figure 6.12 Interaction of Basel III standards and liquidity risk management

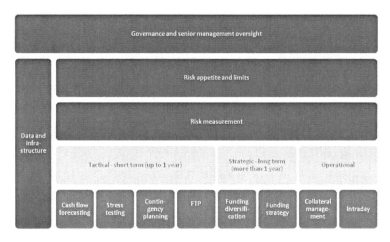

6.3.2.1 *Governance and senior management oversight*

In a number of major banks, which display much larger risk functions compared to treasury teams, it is clear that liquidity and funding have not always been given the same focus as other risks. Very often, liquidity was not considered as a risk per se and was only subject to "light touch" oversight from the risk function.

It is therefore likely that the governance of liquidity risk will evolve towards something closer to "mature" risk classes. In particular, senior reporting lines will be rationalised (between finance, corporate treasury and risk and funding desk) and committee frameworks aligned accordingly (especially ALCO/risk committee responsibilities). The relationship between Treasury and the several other teams involved (e.g. capital management, secured funding desks, cash management and operations, product control and foreign exchange desks) will also be codified, with the Treasurer having much more hands on power over the assets of the business, for example

171

the secured funding desk in an investment bank, which previously operated largely separately. Over recent years, we have also seen a rationalisation of the tactical liquidity functions, with typically one area (usually a repo desk) being responsible for all the short-term funding needs across the institution.

The introduction of the LCR and the NSFR will strengthen the role of the Board and senior management, which will be responsible for managing the business to these ratios and assessing whether any change in strategy, business model and/or funding and business planning is required. For example, Board and senior management will have to make decisions in relation to the funding mix, which are likely to lead to a reduction in the reliance over short-term secured funding and an increase towards more stable sources of funding, such as retail deposits or long-term unsecured funding through issuance of long-term debt, for example.

6.3.2.2 Risk appetite and limits

A bank requires a clear statement of the required shape of the balance sheet to meet liquidity requirements and demands (such as maturities of asset and liability classes); this statement needs to be rolled out via the governance framework described above. Risk appetite and limits are then an expression of the risks to the desired "shape" and provide a means for management to monitor the actual risk profile.

The formalisation of a firm's liquidity risk appetite will be a key part of developing a framework capable of managing the firm's funding and liquidity in a Basel III world. Risk appetite should define the parameters of the liquidity management framework and should be cascaded into a clear limit framework. Furthermore, the scope of limit frameworks governing funding and liquidity will broaden with the implementation of new liquidity constraints and requirements under Basel III. The Basel ratios and monitoring tools are likely to lead to the implementation of additional limits to cover all aspects of liquidity management, including for example funding concentration with limits such as proportion of secured funding versus unsecured funding, maximum exposure to one single repo counter-party or maturity profile for intra-group funding and secured funding.

Boards and senior management will need to take a far more active role in management of funding and liquidity across the organisation and this will require the implementation of clear risk appetite and limits.

6.3.2.3 *Management information and data challenges*

Implementing a robust liquidity governance framework can only be achieved if the relevant committees and senior management receive thorough and frequent reporting on the firm's tactical liquidity position and longer- term funding profile.

As explained in Section 6.2, the Basel ratios and monitoring tools will require firms to provide a wide range of liquidity related data, which is similar in scope to the FSA requirements implemented in the UK in June and October 2010. It is therefore useful to refer to the lessons learnt from this implementation.

One of the key challenges is associated with data and systems: some of the data required for regulatory reporting may not be available and systems may require enhancements to source and store data. For example, identifying unencumbered securities, including those that have re-hypothecation rights, has proved challenging. In relation to the IT infrastructure, one of the key issues is the creation of a central repository, or "golden source" and firms need to decide whether this central repository should be used for liquidity only or for all risks or even for all reporting needs, including financial and risk reporting. In addition, the integrity of the data is key, and reconciliation needs to be performed against various sources, especially for items that are not on balance sheet.

Frequency is another key issue; under the FSA regime, most of the reports are required on a weekly and up to daily basis, but practice shows that daily production is necessary, mainly for control and monitoring reasons.

Given all these challenges, firms have struggled to implement the FSA requirements, with many firms developing tactical solutions incorporating manual intervention before they can move to a strategic solution; this means that firms are also likely to struggle to implement Basel III. However, for most firms which have already implemented the FSA requirements, some benefits have clearly materialised, in the form of a better under- standing of the firm's business model by treasury or regulatory reporting functions, which needed to be strengthened in order to sense-check reporting outputs.

As far as the liquidity ratios are concerned, banks will need to go through a thorough data mapping exercise to map their data to the LCR and NSFR categories. They will also need to build asso- ciated models to calculate the ratios on a daily basis (a minimum 100 per cent LCR should be maintained on a continuous basis by firms). One of the broader implications of the Basel III framework is that banks will need to manage capital, funding and liquidity in a single integrated approach and this will require the develop- ment of simulation tools that allow them to understand the impact of all the Basel III measures taken together, including the liquidity standards, the capital ratio and the leverage ratio.

6.3.2.4 Stress testing

The impact of the financial crisis in highlighting the importance of liquidity has already led to significant evolution of banks' stress testing frameworks and this has been further catalysed by regulatory scrutiny and specific requirements arising from regulatory regimes such as in the UK, that have already imple- mented onerous new requirements. The main areas of develop- ment as a result of these factors have been in:

(a) developing a wider range of more evolved stress scenarios;
(b) developing more detailed and transparent assumptions covering a broader range of risk drivers;
(c) introducing several dimensions to stress testing such as cross-currency, intra-group and before and after manage- ment actions;
(d) aligning internal stress testing scenarios, models and assumptions with regulator-defined frameworks;

(e) developing the systems and data capabilities to allow more frequent and more complex stress tests; and

(f) better linkage with other risk types, in particular, credit, market and operational risk.

The Basel III assumptions will introduce another set of assumptions and parameters with which the above developments need to align, but the impact of introducing a global standard is likely to lead to convergence in approaches to liquidity stress testing as the framework is rolled out.

6.3.2.5 *Implications for business planning, funding and liquidity forecasting and FTP*

Until recently, business planning and forecasting has been conducted in a market environment based on growth without the significant liquidity or funding constraints brought on by the financial crisis. Business planning was largely divorced from capital and liquidity planning – this is changing. Given the focus on liquidity risk management as a result of the severe financial crisis of 2008, there is a need for business planning to incorporate funding and liquidity forecasts into the planning cycle.

Firms will need to achieve a more accurate and granular view of performance incorporating the costs of capital, funding and liquidity in order to measure true profitability and thereby ensure that the firm's scarce resources are deployed appropriately. Pressure on remuneration and related regulation (e.g. Remuneration Policy Statements) are adding further impetus to this, as firms are pushed to align remuneration to risk measures.

This is directly linked to the issue of cost/benefit allocation and funds transfer pricing ("FTP"). As seen during the crisis, the implications of not getting the FTP right can lead to oversized derivatives books and mispriced liquidity costs. From a regulatory perspective, a poor FTP framework could result in increased quantitative requirements, such as higher liquidity reserve requirements or restrictive funding profiles. The EBA Guidelines on Liquidity Cost Benefit Allocation recommend that the FTP process should attribute the costs, benefits and risks to business lines, in a granular, consistent and transparent manner across the firm. The FTP system should be automated to ensure responsiveness and linked to stress testing process and off-balance sheet analysis. In addition, the FTP process should not be based only on blended historical and/or budgeted funding costs.

With the introduction of the Basel III ratios, and especially the NSFR, an additional constraint is being introduced in relation to how the cost of liquidity is allocated to the business and how funding planning is developed. An effective FTP framework should be based on the following principles:

(a) The FTP framework should reflect the lowest available funding rate in a risk-adjusted sense, with an acceptable level of transparency to the business.
(b) Capital should be allocated in relation to the risks incurred due to the particular funding mechanisms chosen.

Under Basel III, firms will have to navigate between their own internal assumptions and the NSFR assumptions. For example, if a firm has a low NSFR and a high LCR, it may choose to charge business units a higher cost of funding for short-term funding than the one dictated by internal liquidity management in order to increase its longer-term funding pools. Such an arbitrage is likely to be challenging when communicating the FTP methodology to the business, which is key to ensure its buy-in. This might lead the business to question the robustness and fairness of the FTP framework.

6.3.2.6 *Implications for day-to-day cash and collateral management and intra-day liquidity*

Collateral Management

The Sound Principles state that effective collateral management requires a bank to be in a position to meet a range of collateral needs, including longer-term structural, short-term and intra-day considerations. In addition, a bank should have sufficient collateral to meet expected and unexpected borrowing needs and potential increases in margin requirements over different timeframes, depending upon the bank's funding profile.

In practice, this means that firms should consider the quality of the collateral being received and determine whether or not that collateral can meet either the 30-day LCR requirement or one year NSFR requirement. The quality of the collateral is typically based on the following factors:

(a) counterparty delivering the collateral (e.g. the relationship the Firm has with the counterparty, the reputation that counterparty has in the marketplace);
(b) counterparty collateral agreement which governs the terms of the collateral;
(c) the type of collateral being pledged, including the currency in which collateral is; and
(d) the type of transaction that the collateral is being held for (e.g. derivative, repo, internal Firm, stock loan).

Firms should also consider the type of collateral the Firm is posting and to whom (e.g. external counterparty, central banks, internal counterparty).

Collateral management has been identified by the FSA in December 2010 as one of the areas where firms need to do more effort in order to implement a robust risk management framework. Many firms still struggle to assess how much collateral is available to central treasury at any point in time. This leaves firms exposed to movements of collateral in cash or securities, in relation to secured transactions and derivatives.

Intra-day liquidity risk

Intra-day is not explicitly captured in the Basel III package (although the Committee is currently examining whether and how this should be taken into account as part of the LCR) but is part of the Sound Principles. As such, it is a key component of a robust liquidity management framework. As an example of how Sound Principles can be applied, the FSA liquidity regime requires firms to monitor their intra-day liquidity position and have processes in place to monitor their intra-day payment flows in real time. However, it is fair to say that, across the banking industry, there is still a lot to do in relation to intra-day management of liquidity. In practice, significant industry-wide effort is needed before firms will be able to comply with the requirements, such as systems and data management improvements, effort from lending agents to make intra-day information more transparent, potential implementation of committed intra-day liquidity lines between firms.

Firms should also consider the effect of a stress on intra-day movements as part of their intra-day liquidity risk management. Liquidity requirements are primarily driven by micro and macro events occurring within the market environment and within the firm – so-called idiosyncratic and systemic events. These events primarily occur over a period of time and are generally captured in a firm's liquidity stress testing models. However, firms must also account for intra-day movements under various levels of stress. Corporate actions, IPOs, companies going into bankruptcy or administration, are some examples of intra-day events that can impact the amount of funding and liquidity a firm needs to operate intra-day. This is another area where the FSA has identified weaknesses across the industry in December 2010.

Under the FSA regime, there is a clear distinction between the firms that are direct participants in a clearing or settlement system and those that are not. The latter in particular do not appear to have grasped the full extent of intra-day risk on their liquidity management as they tend to consider that their nominated agent would ensure that payments and settlement obligations are made on a timely basis. This is not true and these firms need to be proactive to understand how much is at risk, at what point in time, but also how their agents effectively manage their payments. In the draft Dear CEO letter published in December 2010, the FSA states the following:

> "As a minimum, we would expect a firm to have contingent procedures in place to deal with an unexpected reduction in a daylight limit and also an operational failure of their agent. At the point of failure due to a lack of liquidity, history has demonstrated that intra-day payment failure could be the tipping point".

6.3.3   Conclusion

The Basel III ratios and monitoring metrics should be considered together with the Sound Principles as they form a complementary package of measures that constitute a quantitative and qualitative liquidity management framework. It is, however, interesting to note that the Basel III ratios have an impact on how liquidity is managed, and that firms will have to arbitrage between managing to internal and/or regulatory requirements. This is in addition to the challenge of implementing robust liquidity management framework, especially in relation to stress testing, collateral and intra-day management and cost allocation, which was emphasised through the difficult implementation of the various enhanced liquidity regime since 2008.

Chapter 7

Leverage

Fernando de la Mora

7.1 Introduction

The introduction of a leverage ratio requirement to the Basel banking regulations is expected to play an increasingly important role in the management of risk at banks. This Chapter provides an overview of the leverage ratio under the Basel III framework and discusses the proposed approach to the measures of capital and exposure used in calculating the ratio.

In the banking industry, "leverage" is usually thought of as the amplification of returns on investment often through the use of borrowed funds, derivatives or assets with embedded leverage. Leverage allows banks and financial entities to increase the potential gains (or losses) on a trade or investment beyond what would be feasible through a direct investment of an entity's own funds. When banks are exposed to a change in the value of a position by more than the amount that they paid for it, they face a risk that ultimately their capital may be unable to absorb the losses.

Embedded leverage refers to positions or securities that are themselves leveraged. These pose particular challenges for banks since valuing these positions and measuring their risk exposures is often very difficult. Most structured credit products have high levels of embedded leverage, resulting in an overall exposure to loss that is often many multiples of the direct investment in the underlying portfolio.

A leverage ratio is a simple non risk weighted measure of assets to capital. A key challenge for regulators in introducing a leverage ratio is the differences in how certain assets are measured (valued) under US GAAP and IFRS. As a result, leverage ratios based on accounting values would not be comparable across different accounting regimes.

This Chapter begins with a description of what financial leverage is, the risks associated with it and some of its impacts during the crisis. The Chapter then discusses the Basel Committee's response and concludes with some thoughts on the practical implications for banks of implementing this new measure.

7.2   Background

7.2.1   *The role of financial leverage*

The Basel Committee has identified the build-up of excessive leverage leading up to 2007 as one of the principal reasons for the financial crisis. In many cases, banks that were building up excessive leverage were also showing strong regulatory capital ratios, thus masking the coming storm. Some banks' leverage ratios were as high as 33 to 1 (and in some cases higher); meaning for every \$33 in assets, there was only \$1 in equity capital to cover losses. This meant that even a small drop in asset values was enough to wipe out the capital of these banks.[1] This development was accompanied by erosion of the quality of the capital base and liquidity buffers of banks.

Interestingly, two countries with large international banking systems, the US and Canada,[2] had deployed leverage ratios as part of their banking regulatory framework even before the crisis. However, the banking systems in the two countries had quite different experiences during the crisis. In April 2008, Switzerland announced the introduction of a leverage ratio that will become effective in 2013.[3] It is important to keep in mind that the Basel III leverage ratios propose using the new more

---

[1]   *Financial Crisis Inquiry Report*, Preface
[2]   *The Leverage Ratio*, Note Number 11, World Bank & IFC, December 2009, 2
[3]   *www.finma.ch/e/aktuell/Documents/referat_zuberbuehler_mk_20090331_e.pdf*

restrictive Tier 1 capital definition for calculations purposes. As a result, the existing US and Canadian ratios are not comparable to the proposed Basel III leverage ratio. Further, differences in accounting measure of assets under US GAAP and IFRS make the use of accounting values of assets in a leverage ratio intended as a globally consistent measure, very challenging. For instance, unlike US GAAP, IFRS does not allow for netting of derivative exposures. This means that, for example, the US and Canadian leverage ratios are not comparable. Any comparison of leverage ratios globally therefore must recognise these important accounting differences.

When the financial crisis hit, many banks were unable to absorb the write-downs arising from huge off-balance sheet exposures with embedded leverage which had gone largely unnoticed until the crisis put them under the spotlight and balance sheet assets. When banks responded by slamming on the brakes, the sudden deleveraging combined with the interconnectedness of financial institutions further amplified the crisis. Banks lost faith in the solvency of their peer institutions and refused to lend to each other. This vicious cycle was soon transmitted to other parts of the economy, which stagnated due to the reduced supply of credit and availability of capital.

7.2.2 Financial leverage and return on equity

Financial leverage can have a significant impact on a bank's return on equity ("RoE"), a closely-watched measure of a bank's efficiency. RoE can be decomposed into three elements: profit margin, asset turnover and financial leverage. The way in which raising debt increases RoE is not intuitively obvious. One way to think about it is that if a bank adds debt, its assets increase (because of the cash inflows from the debt issuance) and so does its total debt. Provided the return on assets is greater than the cost of debt, RoE increases. As Figure 7.1 shows, two companies may have the same RoE, but this can result from very different strategies. In Figure 7.1, Bank B's RoE is the same as Bank A's, even though Bank B has lower profit margin and asset turnover. Bank B generates the same RoE as Bank A, but with higher risk through its greater leverage.

Figure 7.1 Different strategies can lead to the same RoE

	Profit margin (profit/net income)	X	Asset turnover (net income/ assets)	X	Financial leverage (assets/ equity)	=	Return on equity (profit/ equity)
Bank A	6%	X	0.5	X	4	=	12%
Bank B	3%	X	0.4	X	10	=	12%

7.2.3 Risks of leverage-driven growth

Does it matter if a bank's high RoE comes from high debt and not operating efficiency? If a bank has a steadily growing business, it might not matter that much. Judicious use of debt can boost profitability without undue risk. But if the bank's business is cyclical or volatile, too much leverage can become an issue. The problem with debt is that it creates additional fixed costs in the form of interest payments. The bank has to make those interest payments every year, regardless of its profitability. When a bank increases debt, it also increases fixed costs as a percentage of total costs. When revenue is increasing, this makes for a great strategy since any additional revenue, once fixed costs are covered, fall straight to the bottom line. When revenue is dropping, however, the fixed cost of debt pushes earnings even lower. If a volatile business suffers large losses, its equity may not be sufficient to absorb those losses and may jeopardise the existence of the business. Not surprisingly, debt is often referred to as leverage: it "levers" earnings, making strong earnings stronger and weak earnings weaker. Earnings of cyclical or volatile businesses with a lot of leverage become even more volatile.

Higher leverage poses risks to banks regardless of their size. The example in Figure 7.2 below shows that within a group of banks, each with the same level of regulatory capital and equal shares in a pool of assets (say, uninsured mortgages), the loss of capital due to a deterioration in the pool assets will be proportional to the assets held which depends on the leverage ratio; the higher the leverage, the greater the threat of loss of capital.

In Figure 7.2, regulatory capital and the percentage loss suffered (5 per cent) in a pool of assets is the same for all three banks.

Figure 7.2 Risk associated with leverage ratios

	Bank A (low)	Bank B (medium)	Bank C (high)
Leverage (as a multiple of regulatory capital)	15X	20x	30X
Regulatory capital	100	100	100
Pool assets allowed at full value	1,500	2,000	3,000
Loss of 5% of assets	75	100	150
Regulatory capital after loss	25	0	(50)
Revised pool assets allowed at full value	375	0	(1,500)

However, it is Bank C which suffers the most as a result of its high leverage and, assuming that it held other assets would be forced to deleverage its balance sheet.

7.2.4 Crisis in the making

Leverage at all the big US investment banks increased significantly in the run up to the crisis. For instance, from 2004–07, the top five investment banks (including Lehman Brothers which is not shown in the diagram) all considerably increased their financial leverage (see Figure 7.3), which amplified their exposure to a financial crisis. These five institutions reported over $4.1 trillion

Figure 7.3: Gross Leverage Ratio (Y axis shows assets as a multiple of equity – US GAAP); SNL Financial Data

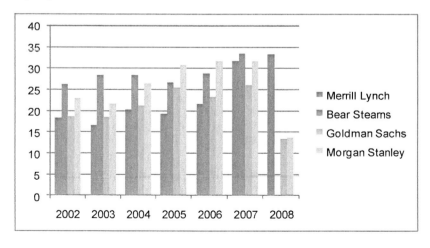

in debt for fiscal year 2007, about 30 per cent of USA nominal GDP for 2007. While Lehman Brothers was liquidated, Bear Stearns and Merrill Lynch were sold at fire-sale prices. Even renowned investment banking houses that survived as independent institutions such as Goldman Sachs and Morgan Stanley were forced to become commercial banks, subjecting themselves to more stringent regulation. With the exception of Lehman, all these companies also received US Government support.

Some experts have blamed the build-up of this leverage on decisions taken by the Securities and Exchange Commission ("SEC") to loosen the so-called net capital rule for the major broker-dealers. The net capital rule regulates the ability of broker dealers in the US to meet their financial obligations to customers and creditors. The rule requires banks to value their securities at market prices and to apply a haircut (discount) based on each security's risk characteristics. The haircut values of securities are used to compute the liquidation value of a bank's assets to establish whether the broker-dealer holds enough liquid assets to pay all its non-subordinated liabilities and still retain a "cushion" of required liquid assets (i.e. the "net capital" requirement) to ensure payment of all obligations owed to customers if there is a delay in liquidating the assets.

This rule was relaxed significantly in April 2004 when the SEC permitted the largest broker-dealers (net capital in excess of $5 billion) to apply for exemptions to the haircut rule. Upon receiving approval, big banks such as Bear Stearns, Morgan Stanley, Goldman Sachs and Lehman Brothers were allowed to use internal models to compute the haircuts on their securities based on international standards used by commercial banks. Many commentators and media reports have subsequently blamed the subsequent build-up of leverage in the system on this change in the net capital provision. Financial reports filed by the banks do show a steady increase in leverage between 2004 and 2008. At Bear Stearns, for instance, the gross leverage ratio defined by US GAAP as total assets divided by total stockholders' equity, rose to 33 in 2007 from approximately 28 in 2004.[4]

---

[4] SNL data compiled by PwC

7.3   Basel response

7.3.1   Basel guidelines

To prevent future build-up of excessive leverage, the Basel Committee has responded by introducing a simple leverage ratio consisting of a capital and exposure measure to act as a supplement ("backstop") to the more elaborate risk-based ratios under Basel III.

The ratio is as follows:

Leverage ratio = Total capital / Total (on- and off-balance sheet) exposure

The ratio is designed to serve two objectives (see para 152):

(a)   prevent the crippling effects of a sharp deleveraging during times of crisis by restraining excessive build up of leverage in the banking sector in the first place[5]; and
(b)   safeguard against model risk and measurement errors by supplementing the risk-based measure with a simple yet robust and transparent measure of risk. This will provide an additional layer of protection to bank capital management. The measure is expected to be applied uniformly across jurisdictions with adjustments for any accounting differences.

The Basel Committee in its final guidance document issued in December 2010 provided some additional details about the

Figure 7.4 Leverage ratio implementation timeline

	2011	2012	2013	2014	2015	2016	2017	2018	a/o Jan 1 2019
Leverage Ratio		Supervisory monitoring	Parallel run 1 Jan 2013 – 1 Jan 2017 Disclosure starts 1 Jan 2015					Migration to Pillar 1	

---

[5]   BIS *Basel III: A global regulatory framework for more resilient banks and banking systems* (December 2010), 60

leverage ratio, which would serve as the basis for testing during the parallel run period. The Committee has divided the transition period into two periods as shown in the timeline above. Supervisory monitoring period commenced 1 January 2011. The supervisory monitoring process will track the underlying components of the agreed definition and the resulting ratio. The parallel run period begins on 1 January 2013 and runs until 1 January 2017. During this period, the behaviour of the leverage ratio and its components relative to the risk-based requirement will be monitored. Disclosure of Banks' leverage ratio and components will start 1 January 2015.[6]

The leverage ratio tested during the parallel run will be the average of the monthly leverage ratio over the quarter based on the definitions of capital (the capital measure) and total exposure (the exposure measure) – see Figure 7.5. Additionally, the Basel Committee will test a minimum Tier 1 leverage ratio of 3 per cent during the parallel run period from 1 January 2013 to 1 January 2017. Based on the results of the parallel run period, any final adjustments would be carried out in the first half of 2017, with a view to migrating to a Pillar 1 treatment in January 2018.[7]

Figure 7.5 Basel III leverage ratio at a glance

Issue	Proposal	Additional Option for Impact Assessment
Definition of capital	Tier 1 capital predominant form of capital	Total regulatory capital
Exposure measurement; adjustments and provisions	Exposure measures follow accounting treatment (i.e., net of provisions and other valuation adjustments)	
Cash and cash-like instruments	Include cash and cash-like instruments	
Capital measure netting	Consistency between the capital and exposure measure. Items deducted from the capital measure are also deducted from the exposure measure.	

---

[6] BIS Press Release Annex, July 26, 2010, 3
[7] BIS *Basel III: A global regulatory framework for more resilient banks and banking systems* (December 2010

On balance sheet netting	Do not reduce exposure for physical or financial collateral, and do not allow on-balance-sheet netting	
Off-balance sheet items	Include the identified OBS items with a 100% credit conversion factor (CCF). Written credit protection is included at notional value. *For off-balance-sheet (OBS) items, use uniform credit conversion factor (CCFs), with a 10% CCF for unconditionally cancellable OBS commitments (subject to further review to ensure that the 10% CCF is appropriately conservative based on historical experience).*	Apply a lower (positive) CCF for unconditionally cancellable commitments or Basel II standardized CCFs
Securitization	Use accounting data	Accounting on-balance-sheet exposure plus underlying loan portfolio of securitizations that have been derecognized
Other derivatives the current exposure method (excluding credit derivatives)	Two options should be assessed for measuring potential exposure. The options are to ignore potential exposure or use other derivatives, the current exposure method. *For all derivatives (including credit derivates), apply Basel II netting plus a simple measure of potential future exposurebased on the standardized factors of the current exposure method. This ensures that all derivatives are converted in a consistent manner to a "loan equivalent" amount.*	
Repurchase agreements and securities finance	Do not allow any netting of repo and reverse repo positions	Use Basel II netting for repo style transactions

7.3.2 Capital measure

The capital measure will be based on the Tier 1 capital as defined in the final guidance document. Please refer to Chapter 3 (Defining capital) for a detailed description of eligible Tier 1 capital. There is emphasis on ensuring that capital and exposure measures in the leverage ratio are consistent. Items that do not contribute to leverage and are deducted completely from capital will also be deducted from the measure of exposure. This means that deductions from Tier 1 capital will also be deducted from the exposure measure.

Further, deductions are required for significant investments in the capital of banks and in financial and insurance entities that are outside the scope of regulatory consolidation (to the extent that they exceed certain thresholds). To ensure that the capital and exposure are measured consistently for the purposes of the leverage ratio, the assets of such entities included in the accounting consolidation should be excluded from the exposure measure in proportion to the capital that is excluded, as described in Section 3.5.

7.3.3 Exposure measure

The exposure measure will follow the accounting measure of exposure. In general, for on-balance sheet items, banks should include items using their accounting balance sheet for the purposes of the leverage ratio. On-balance sheet, non-derivative exposures will be calculated net of specific provisions and valuation adjustments (such as credit valuation adjustments). Purchased physical or financial collateral, guarantees or credit risk mitigation won't be allowed to reduce on-balance sheet exposures. Netting of loans and deposits is also not allowed.

For securitisation, repurchase agreements and derivative instruments, banks should use accounting measures of exposure and the Basel II regulatory netting rules. Treatment of derivatives will be similar: banks should use accounting measure of exposure plus an add-on for potential future exposure calculated according to the *Current Exposure Method* under the Basel II framework. Basel II netting rules will also apply to the treatment of derivatives. This will ensure that all derivatives are converted in a consistent manner to a loan equivalent amount.

Off-balance-sheet items, such as unused commitments and letters of credit, will be weighted at 100 per cent. For off-balance sheet items, the Basel Committee will use 10 per cent uniform credit conversion factors (vs. 100 per cent originally suggested in the December 2009 documents), with a 10 per cent CCF for unconditionally cancellable OBS commitments. This will be subject to further review during the parallel run to ensure that the 10 per cent CCF is appropriately conservative based on historical experience.

7.3.4 Accounting considerations

The Basel Committee proposals are being considered at the same time that the accounting setting bodies are considering significant changes to accounting standards that will affect asset values as reported in banks' financial statements. Additionally, the current and proposed guidance under US GAAP and IFRS differs significantly and consequently will impact institutions implementing the Basel III requirements in different ways. Without coordination, the accounting changes could result in unintended consequences to the regulatory capital levels and capital ratios of banks.

Critics of the leverage ratio have pointed out that technical differences between US and IFRS will make it very difficult to achieve uniformity.[8] Studies have suggested that the two different accounting regimes could show total assets on the balance sheet that differ by as much as 100 per cent, so that a fixed leverage ratio could require twice as much capital in one country as another. This highlights the fact that to be useful, there will have to be an approach that adjusts the leverage ratio for these accounting differences.

The most efficient approach would be for banks to address both regulatory and accounting changes through a single process.

---

[8] *Basel III, the Banks, and the Economy*, Brookings Institution, July 23, 2010

Ideally, the Basel Committee and accounting standard-setters would coordinate the timing of the mandatory adoption of their standards. In addition, they would eliminate or minimise the effect of any inconsistencies in their guidance except where necessary to reflect different objectives and audiences (for example, approaches to valuations and provisions). However, whether this coordination will occur is uncertain given that the views of standard setters differ regarding what role US GAAP or IFRS should play in the prudential regulation of banking entities. For more details please see Chapter 8 – Accounting considerations.

7.4 Conclusion

7.4.1 Limitations of the leverage ratio

The US, despite having a leverage ratio in place, was at the centre of the global financial crisis. So how did policy makers miss the warning signs? Perhaps one explanation is that decades of financial innovation has changed the financial landscape by giving rise to exotic credit risk transfer instruments such as structured credit products. One of the reasons the leverage ratio in the US did little to give a heads-up on the crisis is because the bulk of the leverage that banks were taking on was through off-balance sheet arrangements and embedded leverage.

A World Bank/IFC paper on leverage ratio found that banks were increasingly funding a growing amount of long-term assets with short-term liabilities through off-balance sheet vehicles exposing themselves to significant liquidity risk.[9] The proposed leverage ratio will also be limited in its effectiveness since it does not distinguish bank assets by their riskiness, say between a high credit quality government loan and equity tranches of a CDO. This was one of the reasons banks were able to build up risky balance sheets and expanded their off-balance sheet activities rapidly despite the existing a leverage ratio in the US.

---

[9] World Bank/IFC: *Crisis Response: The leverage ratio*, December 2009

7.4.2 Impact on banks

Banks both big and small are likely to be constrained by the leverage ratio. Even if a bank has the minimum ratios of 7 per cent Common Equity and 10 per cent total capital, these may not constrain asset growth. However, leverage may now prove to be the constraining factor since few countries had leverage restrictions prior to Basel III. The leverage ratio is likely to impact those banks that have a low risk-weighted assets ("RWA") to assets ratio, for example mortgage banks. The illustration in Figure 7.6 below shows three banks with the identical leverage ratios and levels of assets. Bank A, which has the lowest credit risk, becomes the most constrained bank. An unintended consequence of the leverage ratio could be that banks seek out assets that have higher credit risk, provided the returns on those assets cover the cost of the additional regulatory capital.

The December 2010 Basel Committee quantitative impact study found that the average leverage ratio was 2.8 per cent[10] and 3.8 per cent for, respectively, Group 1[11] and Group 2 banks, indi-

Figure 7.6 Impact of RWA to asset ratio

	Bank A (low credit risk)	Bank B (medium credit risk)	Bank C (high credit risk)
Leverage	30x	30x	30x
Accounting value of assets	1,000	1,000	1,000
RWA to asset ratio	30%	50%	70%
RWA	300	500	700
Common Equity Tier 1 capital at 10 per cent of RWA	30	50	70
Asset value allowed to be held	1,000	1,500	2,100

---

[10] Generally, when a bank is referred to as having more leverage, or being more leveraged, this refers to a multiple of exposures to capital (i.e. 50 times) as opposed to a ratio (i.e. 2.0 per cent). Therefore, a bank with a high level of leverage will have a low leverage ratio.

[11] Group 1 banks have Tier 1 capital in excess of 3 billion, are well diversified, and are internationally active. All other banks are considered Group 2 banks.

cating that, in aggregate, large banks are considerably more leveraged than smaller banks.[12] The study also found that 42 per cent of the Group 1 banks and 20 per cent of the Group 2 banks in the sample would have been constrained by a 3 per cent leverage ratio as of 31 December 2009 assuming the new definition of Tier 1 capital was already in place.

One area of high impact is likely to be trade finance activities, which often requires banks to represent their clients through letters of credit and other commitments. Trade finance commitments now run foul of the leverage ratio; they now count in full against that threshold, an approximately fivefold increase over today's capital ratio requirements. These activities are also penalised by the new liquidity rules which are designed to set aside reserves for contingent liquidity risk in off-balance-sheet liquidity exposures such as letters of credit and trade guarantees.

In addition, the leverage ratio is likely to disadvantage banks whose assets have a low risk-weighting and generate proportionately low RWA – for example mortgage banks. Despite being low risk from a credit standpoint, the leverage ratio, because it is risk neutral, may become a binding constraint and require such banks to hold more Common Equity than the new minimum of 7 per cent of RWA.

Further, given the complicated nature of the interconnections between front and back office systems at most major banks, the need to capture granular balance sheet information (for example in relation to off-balance sheet items) to calculate business line leverage ratios could require major investments in systems upgrades, human resources and other operational functions.

7.4.3 The future outlook

A leverage ratio can be a useful regulatory tool but it, by itself, cannot get the job done. One of the lessons of the financial crisis

---

[12] BIS *Results of the comprehensive quantitative impact study* (December 2010), 14

was that the leverage ratio did not adequately reflect the trends in financial innovation because significant leverage was held through economic and embedded leverage, which is not recorded on the balance sheet.

This ratio is likely to rove controversial for some time. As mentioned earlier, US and Canadian banks have been operating under a leverage ratio for some time and are better prepared to deal with it than their counterparts in other countries. European banks have bigger balance sheets than US banks, but with more emphasis on lower-risk assets. Adding a leverage ratio may force them to operate more like US banks in their asset allocations.

If a consistent leverage ratio is implemented alongside other prudential tools or measures, it can provide a comprehensive picture of the build-up of leverage in individual banks or banking groups as well as in the financial system. Indeed the rate of change in the leverage ratio is likely to be a good indicator of increasing leverage risk. As the financial crisis showed, both banks and regulators need to be cognisant of the intrinsic limitations and weaknesses of the leverage ratio. The Basel Committee expects that: the Basel III leverage ratio III will capture these risks adequately; be a useful policy tool that should be relatively easy to implement; and, that it will act as a backstop to more risk-sensitive capital requirements.

Chapter 8

Accounting Considerations

Simon Gealy and Addison Everett

8.1 Introduction

The Basel Committee's changes to its regulatory framework, affecting the application of Basel II and introducing the Basel III guidance, come at a time when accounting standard-setters are deliberating revisions to accounting guidance that will fundamentally change accounting for banks in a number of key areas. Like the changes to the Basel regulatory framework, the work of accounting standard-setters – in the areas where the drive for change is most intense – has been motivated largely by a perceived need to address deficiencies in the current guidance that were highlighted by the global financial crisis.

Historically, there has always been a tension between the regulatory objective of providing adequate provisions and capital to ensure the solvency of banks against expected and unexpected loss and that of financial accounting to present the performance and financial position of banks based on current circumstances. Many observers, in this regard, have expressed an aspiration that regulatory accounting and financial accounting should converge to a greater degree to simplify financial reporting for banks and eliminate sometimes confusing inconsistencies in the information provided to a bank's constituents. The two frameworks have different goals, so full convergence will not be possible. However, in the near-term the job of implementing regulatory and accounting changes can be made easier to the extent that the Basel Committee and accounting standard-setters coordinate development of implementation guidance and refinements to the respective standards.

The International Accounting Standards Board ("IASB") and the Financial Accounting Standards Board ("FASB") are working jointly on more than a dozen joint projects designed to improve both International Financial Reporting Standards ("IFRS") and US Generally Accepted Accounting Principles ("US GAAP"). Through the completion of these projects, the boards intend to issue new accounting standards aimed at improving the relevance of financial reporting for investors and other constituents, while also facilitating convergence between IFRS and US GAAP. These objectives are viewed by many observers as imperatives for promoting the continued globalisation of business and expansion of cross-border investment.

The interaction of the Basel III guidance with both current and proposed accounting standards in the eight areas listed below has the potential to impact directly banks' application of the Basel regulatory framework:

(1)   financial instruments – loan loss provisions and classification and measurement of financial instruments;
(2)   consolidation and de-recognition of financial instruments;
(3)   balance sheet offsetting;
(4)   financial instruments – classification and measurement;
(5)   fair value measurement – credit value adjustments;
(6)   goodwill and acquired intangibles;
(7)   post-employment benefits; and
(8)   deferred tax assets.

Much of the guidance is the subject of current deliberation and exposure for public comment and the Boards expect to issue the new accounting standards from the middle of 2011 onwards. Even a cursory summary of current guidance and the status of proposed guidance, which itself has been the subject of entire books, is beyond the scope of this Chapter. It is assumed that the reader possesses a working knowledge of this guidance.

While fundamentally affecting the current accounting policies applied by banks, current and proposed accounting guidance in the following four areas is less likely to have a significant direct impact on banks' application of the Basel regulatory framework:

(1) revenue recognition;
(2) financial instruments – hedging;
(3) leases; and
(4) financial instruments with characteristics of debt and equity.

Proposed accounting guidance in other areas that is currently the subject of IASB and FASB standard-setting projects is largely related to fundamental changes to the presentation of financial statements. This is not likely to have any direct impact on the application of the Basel regulatory framework by banks. Further, proposed guidance related to the accounting for insurance contracts will likely affect the application of insurance regulatory frameworks by insurers, including insurance subsidiaries of banks.

Surprisingly perhaps, while hedging is generally an area in which banks expend significant effort – in terms of business, risk management and accounting processes – the direct impact on the application of the Basel regulatory framework should not be significant, assuming, conforming changes are made to Basel III to reflect expected changes in hedge accounting guidance.

As this Guide goes to press, both standard-setters have requested views from constituents on the effective dates of the new standards in light of concerns expressed regarding implementation challenges. The effective dates of the new accounting standards certainly have the potential to impact the timing and reliability of banks' financial reporting processes, as well as the ability of qualified staff to implement this accounting guidance and Basel III.

The first part of this Chapter provides an assessment of the interaction of Basel III with the current and proposed accounting guidance in those areas likely to have the most direct impact on banks' application of the Basel regulatory framework. The second part addresses the operational challenges, including examples encountered in practice and potential solutions.

8.2 Interaction of Basel III with current and proposed accounting guidance

8.2.1 Financial Instruments – loan loss provisions

Under current IFRS and US GAAP, loan loss provisions ("LLPs") must be recognised when losses are incurred as of the balance sheet date. This incurred loss principle will change under the proposed guidance, which the IASB and FASB ("the Boards") have indicated that they expect to be issued during the second half of 2012. Under these proposed accounting standards, as currently exposed, loan loss provisions will be required to cover expected losses. For the "good book" these will be built-up over the expected life of a loan and may be subject to a minimum floor of expected losses over the "foreseeable future" or 12 months. This contrasts with the 12 month timeframe used in the Basal regulatory framework. The loan loss provision for loans in the "bad book" will be based on the full expected loss."

Basel III advocates a change in accounting standards towards an expected loss approach in order to ensure that accounting for loan loss provisions becomes more forward-looking, which is precisely what the Boards are proposing. This represents a fundamental change to the current accounting guidance, which aligns it more closely with the corresponding guidance in the Basel regulatory framework. In this regard, banks may be in a position to leverage more efficiently the processes and information used to estimate credit losses under the proposed accounting guidance and the Basel regulatory framework. Notwithstanding this partial convergence, however, banks will still need to manage differences between these two sets of guidance. In fact, the amount of this difference will continue to impact Common Equity Tier 1 ("CET1") capital under Basel III. An example which looks at how to manage this difference is included in Section 8.3. See also Chapter 3 – Defining capital.

8.2.2 Consolidation and de-recognition of financial instruments

One of the more significant deficiencies in current accounting guidance highlighted by the global financial crisis was the

200

existence of off-balance sheet positions in Special Purpose Investment Vehicles ("SIVs") that exposed many institutions to unexpected potential and actual losses which arose when they elected to bail out the SIVs that they managed. Regulators, through their application of the Basel regulatory framework, and accounting standard-setters are now moving in the same direction to capture more of these risks on the balance sheet, and to require more transparent qualitative disclosure, in order to provide a comprehensive description of the risks associated with off-balance entities. At the same time disclosures around the de-recognition of financial assets have been strengthened. The impact of the more significant elements of the new and proposed regulatory and accounting guidance is summarised below.

Under Basel III, minority interests in non-bank subsidiaries will not be included in CET1 capital. The effect of this treatment will be exacerbated by expected changes to the current IFRS and US GAAP accounting guidance for consolidation, which may result in more minority interests being recognised on or consolidated onto to banks' balance sheets. Specifically, the proposed accounting guidance around the assessment of *de facto* control, principal-agent relationships and potential voting rights may result in the consolidation of more entities having non-controlling interests which will be accounted for as minority interests.

As under Basel II, Basel III requires that the aggregate amount of unconsolidated investments by banks in banking, insurance and other financial services entities where the bank owns more than 10 per cent of the common shares of the entity per cent be deducted from Tier 1 and Tier 2 capital. The deduction would be calculated under the "corresponding deduction approach" whereby a deduction would be applied to the same component of capital for which the capital would qualify if it was issued by the investing bank. For example, an investment in preference shares issued by another bank or institution would have to be deducted from the investing bank's Additional Tier 1 Capital. (There is a threshold deduction for investment in common equity of these entities, under which only the excess aggregate investment over 15 per cent – or 10 per cent in respect of any single investment – of the investing bank's CET1 – after deductions is deducted from CET1; the balance can be treated as a risk-weighted asset at 250 per cent).

Beyond the obvious capital impact, this guidance will complicate the task of monitoring capital sufficiency, as investments may move on and off the balance sheet more frequently and, perhaps, unexpectedly, as circumstances change. This Basel III requirement is likely to discourage banks from investing in newly-issued bank and insurance company capital securities. As a result, entities may be forced to establish limits on exposures to these types of investments.

In addition, asset risk weightings for securitisations and re-securitisations have increased significantly under Basel III. Consequently, there will need for more strategic thinking around the capital implications of new structures and the use of securitisations as a funding source.

8.2.3 Balance sheet offsetting

Basel III has introduced a leverage ratio requirement, which will be calculated by comparing regulatory common equity with assets. There are currently significant differences in the respective balance sheet offsetting requirements of IFRS and US GAAP. Perhaps most significantly, derivative positions, including the related collateral, that are subject to ISDA[1] Master Netting Agreements, may be offset on the balance sheet under US GAAP but not IFRS. Basel III requires banks to use Basel netting rules. At present there is little opportunity for capital arbitrage, as both the Basel regulatory framework and the corresponding US bank regulations provide for generally similar offsetting treatment of these derivatives positions in the calculation of bank leverage ratios. However, many observers believe that this same net treatment is most appropriate for financial reporting purposes, as it reflects the true credit risk to which a bank is exposed and is the basis on which changes to collateral are determined. Notwithstanding this, the Boards have proposed a gross model similar to current IFRS

---

[1] Inernational Swaps and Derivatives Association

which will significantly increase total assets reported by US GAAP banks.

Basel III has also introduced changes that affect balance sheet offsetting, referred to as netting in the Basel Regulatory framework, related to the application of margining, re-margining and collateral requirements for counterparty credit risk in connection with repo-style, derivative and securities financing transactions. Specifically, additional levels of granularity are required for determining margining thresholds and re-margining periods. Collateral haircuts may also require more analysis of margin and collateral positions. Implementation of these requirements may necessitate extensive changes to existing reports, processes and systems.

8.2.4 *Financial instruments – classification and measurement*

IFRS 9 *Financial Instruments: Classification and Measurement* (together with the proposed guidance on Impairment and Hedging, referred to as "IFRS 9"), with limited exceptions, classifies financial assets as being accounted for at either amortised cost or fair value through the profit and loss account. Various proposals by the FASB relating to changes in its corresponding guidance appear to provide for potentially different relative levels of financial assets to be accounted for at amortised cost and fair value (either through profit and loss or other comprehensive income). In their latest proposal the FASB has proposed a three-bucket model (preserving the "fair value through OCI" category) in contrast to the two-bucket IASB model outlined above. To the extent that this fundamental difference in asset values is not reconciled by the IASB and FASB, there could be potentially significant levels of incomparability between the regulatory leverage ratios reported by banks reporting under IFRS and US GAAP. This is an example of an area in which the Basel Committee and accounting standard-setters must work together to ensure that the intended regulatory and accounting objectives are met.

To the extent either the IFRS or US GAAP guidance requires relatively more financial instruments to be accounted for at fair value, many observers believe that this will exacerbate the pro-cyclical characteristics that have been the subject of some of the most withering criticism of the current accounting standards in the aftermath of the global financial crisis. Despite this, the guidance currently proposed by both the IASB and FASB unquestionably improves the transparency around the fair values and risks of financial instruments and indeed this may have been crucial to the speed with which regulators acted to avert an even deeper economic crisis.

Unlike the current Basel II guidance, Basel III does not require unrealised gains and losses on equity securities to be accounted for as available-for-sale to be eliminated from shareholder reserves in the calculation of CET1 capital. As noted above IFRS 9 eliminated available-for-sale accounting for financial assets. However, in limited circumstances, IFRS 9 permits equity securities not held for trading to be accounted for at fair value through OCI. Presumably, though, the related shareholder reserves will be subject to the same capital treatment as those related equity securities accounted for as available-for-sale under the current guidance. In these circumstances the corresponding impact on reserves would be eliminated.

For the purposes of the leverage ratio, Basel III also imposes a credit conversion factor ("CCF") of 100 per cent on all non-cancellable and conditionally cancellable off-balance sheet exposures, that include commitments, direct credit substitutes, acceptances, standby letters of credit, trade letters of credit, failed transactions and unsettled securities. Unconditionally cancellable commitments will be subject to a 10 per cent CCF. The accounting for some of these items is inconsistent between IFRS and US GAAP and could create potentially significant incomparability in the leverage ratios of banks reporting under the respective accounting frameworks.

8.2.5 *Fair value measurement – credit value adjustments*

Basel III moves beyond the treatment of counterparty credit risk under Basel II and has established requirements to recognise the effect on fair value not only of a counterparty default, but also the valuation effects of changes in counterparty credit spreads, as discussed in more detail in Chapter 5 – Counterparty credit risk.

Credit value adjustments ("CVA") are included in the measurement of the fair value of financial instruments under current IFRS and US GAAP guidance. While neither IFRS nor US GAAP prescribes a specific methodology for calculating CVA, Basel III specifies both "advanced" and "standardised" approaches (see Chapter 5 for details). The Basel III approach is intended to provide outputs that reflect severely stressed scenarios. The resulting CVA is then included in risk-weighted assets ("RWA"). Many observers expect that CVA calculated using stressed scenarios, reflecting events and circumstances experienced during the global financial crisis will result in dramatically higher adjustments to RWA relative to the existing Basel II levels for these exposures. Further, the use of this approach to calculate stressed CVA may create or increase differences between CVA used by banks for financial reporting and those used in the application of the Basel regulatory framework. Among other things, this could require changes to processes and systems, as well as additional controls over data quality for this data-intensive calculation.

8.2.6 Goodwill and acquired intangibles

The purchase price allocation is a fundamental element of acquisition accounting. Among other things, establishing the value of goodwill and acquired intangibles is part of the purchase price allocation. Like Basel II, Basel III requires a 100 per cent deduction from capital for all goodwill and acquired intangibles, with the notable exception of mortgage servicing rights which are considered in Section 8.3.4. The use of contingent consideration in an acquisition may also affect RWA. These provisions highlight the need for additional planning around potential acquisitions to manage the impact on regulatory capital.

8.2.7 Post-employment benefits

Basel III emphasises that a pension liability (i.e. deficit) determined under a bank's selected accounting framework must not be excluded from (i.e. increase) CET1 capital. Proposed changes to the IFRS guidance related to accounting for defined benefits pension plans, which is required to be adopted by 2013, eliminates the so-called corridor approach, that currently permits the deferral of actuarial losses beyond a specified threshold without recognition in the financial statements. As many banks apply the corridor approach to deferring actuarial losses, adopting this new IFRS guidance could decrease CET1 capital for these banks. Further, the effect of this accounting could introduce additional volatility into the level of CET1 capital. If a bank has a pension asset (surplus), however, Basel III generally requires that the amount be deducted from (i.e. reduce) CET1 capital, as defined benefit plan sponsors often do not have unrestricted access to defined benefit plan surpluses. Where they do, regulatory approval is required to include the amount in (i.e. increase) CET1 capital.

8.2.8 *Deferred tax assets*

The treatment of deferred tax assets is discussed in Chapter 13 – Taxation.

8.3 Practical implementation considerations

8.3.1 *Overview*

Irrespective of whether US GAAP and IFRS converge, differences in the treatment of assets and liabilities between Basel III and both accounting frameworks will persist for the foreseeable future. Accordingly, the development of solutions to mitigate the issues identified in Section 8.2 is a worthwhile exercise. The relative scarcity of capital globally, together with the restrictions placed by Basel III on what qualifies as regulatory capital, highlights the importance of managing the accounting, regulatory and management reporting processes in an integrated manner. Examples of practical considerations include:

a) *Alignment of data*
    In order to improve their understanding of the interactions between accounting and regulatory rules, many banks are

beginning to use the same data and models for both purposes and modify the related output to best suit the accounting or regulatory capital need at hand. This approach also tends to add significantly to the quality of the control environment and the efficiency of preparation which, among other things, frees finance staff to perform more granular analysis and more effectively interpret model output.

b) *Internal and external communication*
The principle of "one version of the truth" is often cited as a basis for the use of common systems and processes in the preparation of management and external reporting information. This applies equally to the interaction between accounting and regulatory reporting and underlines the need for constant collaboration and communication between the finance, risk and regulatory departments. The discipline of disclosing the interaction and differences between accounting and regulatory reporting frameworks can significantly enhance the perceived quality of a bank's management, particularly if supported with appropriate qualitative disclosure to external stakeholders (see also Chapter 12 – Disclosures and Pillar 3).

8.3.2 Loan loss provisions

In order to understand the impact of the loan loss provision on CET1 capital, banks need to reconcile the differences between accounting LLP calculations and the Basel III expected loss calculations. The 2010 Loan Loss Provisioning Survey conducted by PricewaterhouseCoopers ("2010 LLP Survey") indicated that many of the banks included in the survey use their current Basel II expected loss models as the starting point for calculating the so-called "incurred but not reported" ("IBNR") provisions required under the current IFRS guidance for Impairment International Accounting Standard No.39 *Financial Instruments: Recognition and Measurement* (IAS 39).[2]

---

[2] The Basel II models are based on probability of default ("PD"), loss given default ("LGD") and exposure at default ("EAD").

The principal benefits of such an approach are the following:

(a) better aligning capital planning with the financial results of the bank;
(b) deeper portfolio segmentation used in the LLP calculations from the current PD models;
(c) single validation process at the PD/LGD/EAD level;
(d) reduced system and process requirements (i.e. one model instead of two);
(e) reduced risk of errors using one process and model;
(f) alignment of pricing decisions, capital requirements, regulatory reporting, accounting and performance evaluation; and
(g) more effective and consistent communication on risk management (regulatory reporting, management reporting, financial statements, external communication).

The 2010 LLP Survey found that the most significant challenges arising from this approach are as follows:

(a) understanding the theoretical differences between Basel II, IFRS and US GAAP;
(b) achieving appropriate levels of collaboration between finance and risk departments in data quality, data capture and data management;
(c) determining Basel II through-the-cycle (TTC) and the corresponding IAS 39 point-in-time (PIT) adjustments; and
(d) adjusting for the inherent data driven conservatism level in the Basel II models.

Figure 8.1 below illustrates the adjustments that must be made to the Basel II estimated losses calculations in order for them to be compliant with an IFRS accounting expected loss approach. This can be thought of as the "bridge" between Basel II and the corresponding accounting guidance. Regardless of the outcome of ongoing deliberations related to the proposed IFRS and US GAAP accounting guidance related to loan impairment, as noted in the previous section, it is clear that this guidance will be based on an expected loss concept. This bridge, then, can serve as a starting point for banks to determine how best to leverage their Basel loss estimates as a basis for developing their accounting loss estimates and, perhaps more importantly, manage the capital impact of the difference between these two amounts. Each of the individual adjustments is discussed in more detail below to address implementation issues observed in practice or opportunities to improve efficiency. Please note that we have referred to Basel II at various points as a best guess of how Basel III model calibrations may eventually transpire.

Figure 8.1 Reconciling Basel II and IFRS

PD adjustments		LGD adjustments	
Time horizon			
	Day one loss		Credit derivatives
Basel expected loss	TTC/PIT	Effective interest rate	IFRS impairment
Retail	GDP growth	High rates	
Corporate	Recession	Low rates	
Decreasing conservatism			

8.3.2.1 *Probability of default adjustments:*

a) *Time horizon*

Under Basel II, the PD models are based on a one year time horizon. Under IFRS 9, PDs should be calculated over the lifetime of the portfolios. In addition, PDs over the foreseeable future floor (12 months) would need to be calculated. Any differences with the one year Basel II PD would need to be explained.

b) *Through-the-cycle/point-in-time*

PIT estimates are developed and calculated based on the actual default behaviour of a pool of exposures at a particular point in time. In this respect, PIT estimates tend to be volatile through the economic cycle but lead to a more accurate measure of incurred loss as required by IAS 39. TTC estimates do not tend to change in response to changes in economic conditions; they reflect, instead, long-term trends in PD behaviour thereby providing a stable estimate of expected default over time. Basel models may be built on either basis. However supervisors may require banks to make adjustments to reduce the volatility associated with PIT models (e.g. the UK FSA with its use of variable scalars).

Under current and proposed accounting guidance, PIT PDs are generally more appropriate to calculate estimates of loan losses for accounting purposes.

c)   *Day-one losses*
There is currently a difference between Basel II and IFRS in relation to the recording of day-one losses (losses that are recognised at the time of booking a transaction). In the Basel II expected loss calculation, expected loss is calculated for loans on the day that they are originated. IFRS currently requires that an impairment loss be recognised only if there is objective evidence of impairment as a result of a past event that occurred after initial recognition. Accordingly, IFRS does not allow reduction of the carrying amount of a loan on initial recognition through the recognition of an immediate impairment loss. This difference still exists in the related guidance proposed by the IASB and FASB, but is the subject of ongoing deliberation around the convergence of IFRS and US GAAP: recognition of such losses may in fact reflect the commercial reality.

d)   *Probability of default floor*
In the Basel II model, a PD is assigned using a rating category based on the long-run average of one-year default rates for borrowers in each respective grade; a minimum PD floor of 0.03 per cent for all exposures except for sovereign exposures. This inherent conservatism is not permitted in the accounting frameworks and will usually require adjustment to reflect the nature of the risk taken.

8.3.2.2   *Loss given default adjustments:*

a)   *Effective interest rate*
Under Basel II, LGD is defined as the economic loss expected on a defaulted credit facility. This is a broader and more inclusive concept than that in IFRS or US GAAP

accounting measures of loss. Economic loss incorporates discounting effects and funding costs (the mark-to-market loss of value of the defaulted loan and collateral), plus all direct and indirect costs of workout and collections, net of recoveries (including late fees and interest). Further, under IFRS, non-cash transactions such as late payment charges or indirect costs such as the overheads of a collections department are not eligible to form part of the impairment loss calculation.

b) *Downturn adjustment (including LGD floor)*
The Basel II framework is designed to create a conservative estimate of capital requirements. Under this framework, banks are required to use LGD estimates that are based on a conservative view of historical experience and that are appropriate during economic downturns.

In addition to the downturn adjustment, Basel II models include an LGD floor for retail exposures secured by residential property. The level of the floor is set at a minimum of 10 per cent. The impact of the floor would need to be reversed if the Basel models were to be used for accounting purposes.

c) *Credit derivatives*
Basel II models consider the recovery value of any credit derivatives used to hedge credit risk on a defaulted loan as one of the credit risk mitigating factors. Basel II then includes its value in determining LGD[3]. However, the current and proposed accounting guidance require all derivatives (including credit derivatives) to be recorded on the balance sheet at fair value. If the Basel II estimated loss is used as a basis for the IFRS provisioning calculation, the value of the credit derivatives would be double-counted in the IFRS financial statements: adjustment is therefore required.

d) *Inherent conservatism*
Basel models have a level of inherent conservatism which can, on occasion, result in a materially-inflated amount of expected loss relative to accounting provisions. Banks might look at the following in mitigating the impact of this conservatism:

---

[3] Banks using the IRB approach may also choose to adjust PD.

(i)   improving the quality of customer data – where data is missing, banks usually use default values which often reflect averages or the worst case scenarios;

(ii) enhancing controls over rating integrity; and

(iii) disaggregating segmentation in order to allocate data to more precisely reflect the drivers of credit risk.

8.3.3   Pension deficits

As noted above, deficits for defined benefit pension schemes will potentially introduce significant levels of volatility into CET1 capital levels and banks may wish to manage this carefully. One way to reduce the volatility of pension deficits is to reduce the risks in either the assets or benefit obligations of the pension plan. This, for example, could involve implementing portfolio hedging strategies to reduce volatility in portfolio performance, exploring transactions to transfer pension liabilities and risk to third parties, and offering "buy-outs" to retired employees.

Also, as part of pension scheme funding decisions, banks may consider replacing the cash commitments within pension deficit recovery plans with assets of a higher risk-weighting than cash. If structured properly, there could be benefits under Basel III, and insurance levies that must be paid in certain territories such as the UK could be reduced. Banks can replace cash contributions required to fund a pension deficit by transferring ownership of an asset to the pension scheme, immediately reducing the cash required to meet the deficit recovery plan.

If the assets used in a pension scheme attract a higher risk weighting than cash then the Basel III capital requirements will be reduced provided that the assets are treated as plan assets under the IFRS accounting guidance. In theory, assets attracting the highest risk weighting, or assets which are deducted from capital resources, could be used.

Subject to any relevant regulations within a specific jurisdiction, there are many ways a bank can replace cash payments to the pension scheme, including:

212

(a) direct contribution of company assets to the pension scheme;
(b) establishing an investment fund to hold company assets for the pension trustees or supervisory board that they can use if there is a pension deficit at the end of the recovery plan; and
(c) contribution of a company bond, backed by separately held assets, which would provide coupon payments to the scheme and capital at the end of the bond term.

While it is straightforward to value securities traded in active markets, a professional opinion may be required to value other assets. The value placed on an asset may need to be reduced to take account of any time delay likely to happen between the contingent event occurring and the trustees or supervisory board receiving the asset.

In most jurisdictions, if bank management wishes to use assets other than cash to fund the obligations of the plan, they will need to propose a funding strategy formally to the plan trustees, bank supervisory board or other group exercising fiduciary oversight of the plan. Among other things, this proposal would need to address the mechanisms that would be established to ensure that the plan's cash benefits would be funded as they become payable. The five steps below, outline the broad actions that a bank would need to undertake in order to substitute other assets for cash contributions to a pension plan:

(1) Review the current pension scheme cash demands under existing deficit recovery plans and those expected at future valuation dates.
(2) Consider the possibility of substituting a non-cash asset for a cash payment with the trustees or supervisory board as an alternative recovery plan contribution.
(3) Identify company assets which could be used; considering that the value, and ultimately cash proceeds, must ensure to the benefit of the plan even in the event of the bankruptcy of the bank. Among others, these assets typically include:

(i)   minority investments, joint ventures and subsidiaries;
(ii) high RWA (such as asset-backed securities); and
(iii) real property.

(4) When designing a structure to contribute a non-cash asset in place of cash to satisfy a pension contribution obligation, banks need to:

    (i) satisfy the trustees or supervisory board that the alternative non-cash assets is of equal value to the cash they would otherwise would have received;

    (ii) review the capital impact of the transaction under both the minimum Pillar 1 and Pillar 2 requirements;

    (iii) determine whether the desired accounting impact is achieved;

    (iv) consider whether potential access to any surplus created is required;

    (v) review the tax impact and whether there is a current or deferred tax deduction; and

    (vi) ensure relevant legal requirements are met, especially in relation to any self-investment rules.

(5) Implementing the structure will require some or all of the following components:

    (i) agreement with the pension scheme trustees or supervisory board;

    (ii) accounting analysis;

    (iii) tax analysis and sign-off from the appropriate tax authorities;

    (iv) due diligence on the assets including legal review and independent valuation; and

    (v) consultation with regulatory bodies (such as, in the UK, the FSA, the Pensions Regulator and the Pension Protection Fund); and

    (vi) formal legal documentation.

8.3.4 Threshold deductions

The Basel III rules require 100 per cent deduction from common equity for all acquired intangibles; except for mortgage servicing rights ("MSR"). However, this requirement may be relaxed under certain circumstances. The Basel III rules provide that partial offset is permitted up to a threshold of 15 per cent of CET1 capital (prior to taking these deductions) for the aggregate of MSR, significant investments (i.e. greater than 10 per cent) in non-consolidated financial institutions and deferred tax assets arising from timing differences. Further, none of these individual elements may constitute more than 10 per cent of CET1 capital. Achieving this offset in practice will be challenging given the different elements of the calculation and the overall limits under the Basel III rules. See also Chapter 3 – Defining capital.

As discussed in more detail in Chapter 13 – Taxation, Basel III rules disallow many deferred tax assets (such as those arising from historic trading losses) but some deferred tax assets, arising from timing differences, are potentially allowable subject to the operation of the limits set out in this Section.

Any decisions that might affect these individual elements would need to be considered such as:

8.3.4.1 *Changes in investments in non-consolidated financial institutions*

Certain of these investments may be in listed entities; in which case the fair value may change daily, if they are treated as available for sale. Significant rises in share prices may result in no increase in CET1 if the increase takes the total of the three elements above 15 per cent of adjusted CET1. Significant declines in share prices may not reduce CET1 if the entity is no longer at the 15 per cent limit; but it may affect CET1 if there are off-setting movements in deferred tax, other financial institutions investments, acquired MSRs etc.

8.3.4.2 *Changes in asset carrying values, asset tax bases or tax rates*

As discussed in more detail in Chapter 13, Basel III rules disallow many deferred tax assets (such as those arising from historic trading losses) but some deferred tax assets, arising from timing differences, are potentially allowable subject to the operation of the limits set out in this section. Deferred tax balances are principally dependent on three variables – the accounting carrying value of the asset or liability, the related tax basis and the tax rate to be applied. Currently, the tax rates used in many jurisdictions are changing as Governments seek to rebuild public finances after the global financial crisis and, once they become substantively enacted (i.e. typically, when they pass into law) deferred tax assets need to be recalculated. Many other tax laws are also changing. Among other things, these will affect when tax is payable and the non-deductibility of previously deductible expenses, which will affect the tax basis of certain assets. The tax basis of assets also varies through the passage of time, receipt of cash flows, tax depreciation and other factors. This change, combined with changes in the recorded value of assets for accounting purposes, makes deferred tax balances quite volatile. Few calculate deferred tax accurately on a daily basis; for many it is a complicated annual chore. However, it could now impact CET1 capital in a material way, which means that it may need to become something which is monitored and managed on a more frequent basis.

8.3.4.3 Additional purchases of MSR

This might be easier to track for many banks but consideration of the purchase of additional MSR would need to include an assessment of whether the purchase would raise the aggregate MSR balance over 10 per cent of CET1 and whether it would, together with investments in non-consolidated investments in financial institutions and deferred tax assets, total more than 15 per cent CET1. Breeching either of these limits would have an immediate impact on Tier 1 capital. However, amortisation would reduce the exposure over time and might lead to the ability to increase the deduction for deferred tax assets or non-consolidated investments in financial institutions.

Intuitively, some banks might be tempted conclude that they would not breech either limit. Given the potentially significant impact on CET1, though, a rigorous quantitative analysis should be performed to determine the gap between its current positions and the 10 per cent and 15 per cent limits. Further, this information should be considered and updated with respect to current business and capital plans. As the Basel III requirements in this area will be phased in from 2014 to 2018, most banks should have sufficient time to perform this analysis, but starting early will provide the most flexibility for planning.

8.3.5 Credit value adjustments

While most data input to either the prescribed calculation or internal market risk models are likely to be available, as they may be used already for existing financial accounting CVA or VaR calculations, entities will need to ensure that market risk systems are sufficiently scalable to produce the CVA output based on new assumptions and stress scenarios.

Additionally, finance, regulatory and accounting policy teams will need to understand the key differences between the current CVA methodologies applied under the relevant accounting guidance and that proposed under Basel III. This will include evaluating how the results differ, and how the difference between financial accounting and regulatory models can be attributed to key drivers or assumptions, which may also serve as a basis for enhanced transparency around counterparty credit risk in Pillar 3 disclosures.

As discussed in Chapter 5, various risk-weightings will be applied to different types of counterparties in calculating RWA. While the assumptions related to "systemically-important" financial intermediaries with over $100bn of assets are currently proposed to be weighted at 125 per cent, those related to central counterparties ("CCP") are currently proposed to be weighted at 2 per cent. It is therefore assumed that banks will have an incentive to move their OTC derivative portfolios to these platforms.

However, there are complications that may arise from such a transfer. Operationally, a great deal of planning will be required to assess whether to migrate trades to a new counterparty and identify potential downstream impacts beyond the regulatory and financial reporting effects. This process could include activities such as the identification of relevant population, evaluation (on a portfolio or other basis) of the expected capital benefits against the costs of transferring to and utilising a CCP and exploration of potential changes to legal structure of trades as a result of migration.

Banks will also need to address discrepancies between valuation techniques applied to their fair value book and the mark-to-market value applied by a CCP. This would be especially relevant for a CCP, such as London Clearing House ("LCH"), which has moved to an overnight index swap discounting methodology for collateralised trades – this is currently out-of-step with many of the banks with which LCH does business. If a bank decided that it should rely on the fair values produced by the CCP, enhanced disclosures regarding CCP valuation methodologies would then be required to provide the bank's financial statement users with greater transparency over how the numbers are calculated and, the effect of the use of this external vendor on the fair value hierarchy under either IFRS or US GAAP.

8.4 Conclusion

The impact on banks of the significant changes for banks arising from the new accounting and regulatory capital rules make it more imperative than ever that banks manage compliance with the two sets of requirements on a unified basis. The opportunities for improved efficiency and control are somewhat self-evident, but decisions related to the determination and implementation of new accounting policies will impact regulatory capital. This impact could result in a sub-optimal allocation of capital at a time when it is increasingly constrained. The potential economic savings from effectively managing the relationship between accounting and regulatory requirements justifies significant effort and resources being devoted to this endeavour sooner rather than later.

Chapter 9

Role of Pillar 2

Chris Matten

9.1　Introduction

Basel III has remained relatively silent on Pillar 2. In the final package released in December 2010, there is only a single reference incorporating the July 2009 enhancements to Basel II by reference. These enhancements did not make any actual changes to Pillar 2, but merely strengthened the emphasis on the Supervisory Review and Evaluation Process ("SREP"). No changes have been announced to the part of Pillar 2 that affects banks most directly, namely the requirement under Principle 1 to have a process for assessing their overall capital adequacy in relation to their risk profile and a strategy for maintaining their capital levels (the Internal Capital Adequacy Assessment Process, or "ICAAP").

Since there are no changes to Principle 1 under Basel III, this Chapter will mainly summarise the key elements of Pillar 2 and then assess the potential impact of Basel III. The key issue is what role management's Internal Capital Assessment ("ICA") still has to play in a regime with fixed one-size-fits-all capital buffers. The changed guidelines for the SREP will also be reviewed.

On balance, the lack of emphasis on Pillar 2 in the Basel III Framework is regrettable, as a proper application of Pillar 2 would not only act to prevent future crises, or at least minimise their impact, but arguably it could also have prevented the global financial crisis in the first place. This is because of the requirement for banks to assess all of their material risks and consider how much capital to hold against them, and to manage their capital using a forward-looking capital stress test of suffi-cient severity. Unfortunately, given the newness of the concept, the fact that it was still in the process of being implemented when the crisis struck, and the very uneven level of implemen-tation which was by no means uniform across the jurisdictions which had implemented it, there was only limited opportunity to assess how effective it could have been.

In particular, the adoption of one-size fits all capital buffers (the capital conservation buffer and the counter-cyclical capital buffer) in Pillar 1, could potentially have been better handled within the framework of Pillar 2 (by all means with fixed, even punitive buffers, for those banks which cannot meet the requirements of Pillar 2 properly). That said, Pillar 2 is likely in practice to have a key role to play as discussed below, and one must not forget the overall emphasis on risk management under Pillar 2, a point to which we will return towards the end of this Chapter.

9.2 The role of Pillar 2 under Basel II

Essentially, the key responsibilities for a bank under Pillar 2 come under Principle 1, which states that "Banks should have a process for assessing their overall capital adequacy in relation to their risk profile and a strategy for maintaining their capital levels". The process which a bank should typically follow to meet the requirements of Principle 1 is:

(1) Assess the strategy of the organisation and *set a risk appetite* which is commensurate with the strategy. This places some constraints and parameters within which risk can be taken.
(2) Compare this with the organisation's ability to absorb this level of risk, by way of a *statement of risk-bearing capability*. Where this is not consistent with risk appetite, either one, or both, will need to be amended, e.g., by cutting back on risk or increasing the capacity to absorb risk, such as increasing capital.
(3) Do an *assessment of material risks*. This involves putting aside Pillar 1 risk measures for the time being and recon-sidering all risks which the organisation could face. One

should first ask if they are *material* (if not, the bank still needs to document the assessment). Then, for those risks which are material, how are they *managed*? Thirdly, which of these risks can be *measured*, and if so, how? (some risks, such as reputational risk, are clearly material and need to be managed, but it is hard to measure them until they come home to roost). Finally, how are risks *mitigated*? Capital, it should be remembered, is not always the most appropriate mitigant – reputational risk, again, is a good example, as is liquidity risk.

(4) From this, the bank can assess which risks are material and need to be mitigated by capital, and can perform a *preliminary Internal Capital Assessment* ("ICA"), based on the risk profile at a point in time. This can be done using a combination of regulatory capital rules, economic capital models, stress tests, single point analyses or simply management's judgement. The approach used for each risk will depend on the materiality of the risk and the tools and information available to the bank.

(5) Next, the bank should prepare a *forward-looking capital plan*, taking into account both the supply (availability) and demand (requirements) for capital. This is typically conducted over a 3–5 year horizon, but as noted in Chapter 3 the 10-year transition plan under Basel III probably requires extension of the capital plan over the full transition period, albeit at a strategic level. Capital plans, even under a business-as-usual scenario, often imply a capital buffer to accommodate: (a) future growth; (b) volatility in the supply and demand for capital; and (c) uncertainty in the planning process.

(6) Then, the bank should subject the capital plan to a *capital stress test*, taking into account reasonably severe, but not critical, possible events. The initial guidance from some supervisors was a "1 in 25" year event i.e., a reasonably severe economic downturn, as the cycle runs typically for about eight years. However, as a consequence of the financial crisis of 2007/9 these supervisors have pulled back from the "1 in 25" guidance and have adopted differing views as to the severity of the capital stress test scenarios. The outcome of the stress test is an indication of the capital buffer, over and above that determined under step 5,

which needs to be held today so that the bank would be able to weather the stress scenario without breaching its minimum capital ratios. Note that "minimum" in this case does not necessarily mean legal minimum, but the level of capital the bank would need to maintain in order to avoid supervisory intervention and/or loss of market confidence.

(7) Finally, the bank is able to set its *final Internal Capital Assessment* at that point in time, being a combination of the preliminary ICA and the buffer implied by the capital planning and stress testing.

Principles 2, 3 and 4 of Pillar 2 relate to how the supervisors assess and react to this. In particular, they should be able to set a higher capital requirement than the minimum required under Pillar 1, taking both macro (economic) and micro (institution-specific) factors into account, to the extent that the bank has not already done so in steps 5 and 6 above.

It would seem from this that Pillar 2, if done properly, acts as a very powerful tool to mitigate the impact of financial crises and provide greater resilience to the system. Indeed, this is one of the main reasons that it was introduced into Basel II in the first place. Many of the banks that weathered the storm of 2008/09 well had taken these principles to heart and included them in their management practices. It is also noteworthy that in those countries where Pillar 2 was well-embedded in the regulatory framework, such as Canada and Australia, the financial crisis passed with barely a ripple, and even in those countries which were affected, such as the UK and USA, many banks still weathered the storm well and without government assistance.

However, the Committee has decided to include two fixed capital buffers (see also Chapter 10 – Procyclicality for more details) into Pillar 1, thereby both confusing the roles of Pillars 1 and 2 and potentially undermining the importance and effectiveness of Pillar 2. In the author's view, the two capital buffers would be better incorporated into a Pillar 2 stress test buffer as described in steps 5–7 above.

9.3   Impact of Basel III on Pillar 2

There are therefore two areas in which Basel III has an impact on Pillar 2: capital planning/stress testing, and the interaction between the regulatory capital buffers with the ICA. As will be seen, these are closely related.

9.3.1   Capital planning and stress testing

In essence, the two capital buffers are a capital conservation buffer and a countercyclical buffer.

The capital conservation buffer is intended to build up in good times to enable a more resilient banking sector to weather a downturn (or even another crisis). Although the transition rules indicate that the buffer must be fully in place by the end of 2018, it is not clear from the Basel III framework document how, or even whether, this buffer can be eroded in adverse conditions. However, there have been some indications in speeches and discussions that this is indeed intended to be a buffer and could be relaxed in severe circumstances.

The counter-cyclical capital buffer is a macro-level buffer which would result in a buffer of up to 2.5 per cent of risk-weighted assets being added to a bank's capital requirements, based on a country-specific assessment of credit expansion by the national authorities in that country. It would seem that it is intended that this buffer is unlikely to be used very often, but as the decision when to require remains with national supervisors we will have to wait and see.

The problems encountered in capital planning are more fully explained in Chapter 3. Briefly, these problems arise because it is not clear to what extent the capital conservation is permanent, or when banks can expect the counter-cyclical capital buffer to apply.

In a sense, what these buffers are doing is taking a "fixed" portion of the buffer which management would want to hold anyway and transferring it to Pillar 1, leaving the residual buffer in Pillar 2. Of course, if management believes that the "fixed" buffers are greater than the overall buffer they would require, they would just have to live with an imposed higher ICA, as discussed further below.

9.3.2 Interaction of regulatory capital buffers with the ICA

This is really just the other side of the coin from the capital planning buffers. To the extent that a portion of the Pillar 2 buffers have been transferred from Pillar 2 to Pillar 1, there is no overall change in the ICA.

However, one must remember that the purpose of the ICA is to demonstrate that a bank would not fall below its minimum required capital, and thus by implication it raises the overall bar. Management will still need to demonstrate that it can meet these minimum requirements even in a reasonable stress scenario, so the Pillar 2 buffer could be seen as a buffer on top of the (higher) minimum capital requirements, thereby raising the ICA. On the other hand, the buffers under Basel III can be eroded when it is necessary to do so, although the bank would in such circumstances be subject to restrictions on the amount of distributions (dividends, share buy-backs and discretionary bonuses) it could make. Therefore, the extent to which a bank treats the Basel III capital buffers as part of its "minimum" capital will be a function of the degree of its appetite to breach the buffers and suffer the restrictions on distributions. A bank will, of course, also need to consider how its capital ratios will be viewed by the market relative to its peers. Some commentators view seven percent as "the new minimum" for Common Equity Tier 1 ("CET1").

Under Basel II (if Pillar 2 had been applied properly), each individual bank would have to take the factors which now give rise to the two Basel III capital buffers into account when determining its own target capital ratios, and these would be part of the bank's own capital buffers (subject to supervisory review and approval). Under Basel III, part of this burden is taken from the bank and moved to Pillar 1 – using a one-size fits all approach.

To give a simple example, let us consider a bank that has a minimum (legally required) Tier 1 ratio of 4 per cent under

Basel II. In its ICAAP, the bank will consider the future growth needs of the bank (but to keep the example simple we will assume that the bank can fund all future growth out of future profits, keeping its capital ratios stable). The bank will also need to determine, as part of its capital stress tests, how much additional capital it needs to hold today to ensure that, in a downturn, it could still meet the 4 per cent minimum. Let us assume that the bank determines this to be an additional 3 per cent of Tier 1, and thus it sets an internal target today of 7 per cent minimum Tier 1 (and such a target would have been quite typical in the years before the global financial crisis). To keep the example simple, we will further assume that the bank has no non-core equity in its Tier 1 and we will also ignore the changes in the deductions in capital between Basel II and Basel III, so for the purposes of this simplified illustration Tier 1 under Basel II is comparable with CET1 under Basel III.

Under Basel III, the minimum CET1 requirement (before any buffers) is 4.5 per cent. This would imply that our bank would have to increase its own target ratio to 7.5 per cent, such that it could maintain a minimum CET1 ratio of 4.5 per cent even in a downturn. So far, so good, but what if the capital conservation buffer is regarded as "permanent"? If this is the case, then the bank now has to hold a minimum CET1 capital of 7 per cent at all times, implying now that it must today hold around 10 per cent so as to be sure that it never breaches the 7 per cent minimum. This is illustrated in the Figure below.

Figure 9.1 Example of capital ratios including buffers

	Under Basel II	Under Basel III mimima (CET1)	Under Basel III with a 'permanent' capital conservation buffer
Minimum Tier 1	4%	4.5%	7%
Pillar 2 buffer	3%	3%	3%
Target Tier 1 ratio today	7%	7.5%	10%

If, however, the capital conservation buffer is not "permanent" and can be released in times of crisis, then the internal buffer that the bank would need to hold would be the higher of its own estimate (3 per cent in this example) and the capital conservation buffer of 2.5 per cent.

The same is true of the counter-cyclical capital buffer, but at least in this case the Basel Committee is clearly of the view that this will only be imposed in times of over-expansion and released in time of contraction. The question therefore is: to what extent does this need to be included in the bank's own forward-looking capital plans and stress tests? The logical response would be that the imposition, and release, of the buffer is only required to the extent that the bank's own scenarios include a credit bubble and subsequent contraction.

Staying with the same example as above, let us assume that the capital conservation buffer is indeed permanent, and the bank has to maintain a minimum 7 per cent CET1 ratio at all times. Let us also assume a forward-looking stress test where there is initially a credit expansion followed by a crash, and the effect of the crash is to wipe three percentage points off the bank's CET1 ratio. The capital stress test would therefore look like this:

Figure 9.2 Example of capital buffers under stress

	Now	Credit bubble occurs	Crash occurs	Endpoint
Available CET1	10%	10%	7%	7%
Required CET1	7%	9.5%	7%	7%
Surplus	3%	0.5%	–	–

Clearly, in this simple example, the bank only just manages to maintain its minimum capital ratio when the crash occurs, and in practice a bank would wish to add a further buffer on top to ensure that it maintains a margin of error and degree of flexibility.

The same process would need to be followed for the other key capital ratios (Tier 1 and Total Capital).

The important aspect to note here is that Basel III does not remove the need for an ICA, but it has the following consequences:

(a) the ICA will be higher than before, as the minimum capital requirements have gone up substantially, unless the capital planning buffer under the bank's own estimate is equal to the Basel III capital buffer;
(b) with the counter-cyclical capital buffer the bank's own target ratios will need to flex over time; but
(c) this may be offset by a lower buffer under Pillar 2.

In effect, what we see is a partial transfer of buffers from Pillar 2 (the bank's own estimate of its capital stress test buffer) to Pillar 1 (the Basel III capital buffers).

9.4 Implications for economic capital

Many sophisticated banks had based their ICAs on economic capital models, and indeed they were encouraged (even mandated in some cases, such as Australia) to do so by their national regulators. This is now being called fundamentally into question by Basel III. Indeed, one could argue that regulatory capital has now become the binding constraint and will stay that way, rendering economic capital models obsolete from the perspective of capital adequacy assessment.

The reason for this is that the output of a typical economic capital model was broadly consistent with prudent capital ratios under Basel II. Empirical evidence shows that these models, at a 99.97 per cent confidence level or similar, would typically imply that a bank's prudent Tier 1 ratio would be around 6 per cent and total capital around 10 per cent. Such levels would struggle to meet the new capital requirements under Basel III (see Chapter 3), even without the imposition of the capital conservation buffer and counter-cyclical capital buffer, of up to 2.5 per cent each. These boost the minimum ratios for Common Equity, Tier 1 and Total capital by these amounts, leaving potential ratios for these at 9.5 per cent, 11 per cent and 13 per cent, respectively.

Banks cannot simply increase the confidence levels of their economic capital models accordingly, as the very high confidence levels already imply bankruptcy only once every 2,000–3,000 years or so, whereas the Basel Committee has clearly concluded that the risks are far higher than that.

These models have also been discredited by the financial crisis in a number of ways:

(a) the extremely high confidence levels implied a level of safety which clearly was not even close to reality in some cases;

(b) the models in some cases assumed a "diversification benefit" across risk classes which was based on a correlation (itself only an average measure of time) which proved unfounded;

(c) the models did not incorporate feedback loops i.e., they were predicated on a single event, and did not anticipate how an event in one risk class (market risk, say) could lead to further problems in credit, in turn leading back to further problems in market risk and then onto liquidity risk, which is not a function of economic capital models;

(d) the models merely determined "loss", not when (and in which order) losses would occur and how they would be accounted for; and

(e) the models tended to focus only the overall total level of capital and not on the intermediate break points (a distinction the Basel Committee calls "going concern" vs "gone concern").

So what is to be done – should we abolish economic capital altogether? In the author's view, this would be throwing the baby out with the bathwater.

First, it should be noted that these criticisms relate to using overall economic capital models to set overall capital levels. There is clearly still a role for these models to play in understanding and managing risk within the organisation.

Secondly, it should be noted that all banks have a view as to what their *economic capital is,* as distinguished from *economic capital models*. Economic capital in our definition is simply, "management's best estimate of the capital required to operate prudently but efficiently". This is entirely consistent with Principle 1 of Pillar 2.

This assessment of economic capital can be arrived at by a number of different ways, as noted above: a combination of regulatory capital rules, economic capital models, stress tests, single point analyses or simply management's judgment. The approach used for each risk will depend on the materiality of the risk and the tools and information available to the bank. There is no need to adopt the same approach for all risk classes. For example, a bank might have a sophisticated credit portfolio model (economic capital model) for credit default risk and counterparty credit risk, but it might use some simple stress tests or scenarios to assess country risk.

Thirdly, all of the problems listed in items (a)-(d) above can be solved by combining capital stress tests with economic capital models. The latter tend to be very good when it comes to measuring outcomes 1–2 standard deviations from the mean, as we have a wealth of data, but are not so good when it comes to modelling out the full tail of the distribution, where there is little, if any, data.

One solution is to split the loss distribution into two components: a "fixed" component equal to the minimum capital requirements under Basel III, which we can consider to equate to "gone concern" capital, and a variable component based on the EC model which we can use to assess the buffer to be held above the 'fixed' component. In doing this, the parts of the EC model which are used are the narrower deviations around the mean, equivalent to the bank's appetite for breaching the Basel III minima, such as 1 in 25 years. By "minima" in this case we mean the Basel III minimum ratios including the 2.5 per cent capital conservation buffer (see Chapter 3).

Of course, there are still some major questions which need to be answered, such as whether the capital conservation buffer is fixed for all time, or whether it can be used to absorb losses in adverse conditions i.e., is it part of "going concern" or "gone concern" capital? The attitude of individual supervisors will be critical in this respect, as making the buffer fixed could be a part of a national supervisor's own approach to "superequivalence" (i.e. being more strict than the Basel III minima).

In the authors' view, we should not regard the tipping point between "going concern" and "gone concern" (see Chapter 3) as the point where the supervisors decide whether to rescue the bank or let it go under (the Committee approach), but rather the point at which management considers it is no longer able to operate as an independent entity with the confidence of the markets and its counterparties to continue to do business as usual. Conceptually, this is no different to the Committee's view; it simply moves the tipping point closer to the mean of the loss distribution.

Figure 9.3 attempts to reconcile the competing views of Basel III and Economic Capital Models:

Figure 9.3 Basel III and economic capital

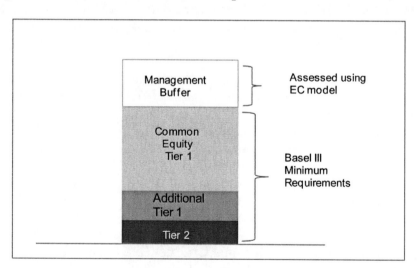

So under this approach a bank would establish a fixed minimum capital level based on Basel III rules, and then use its economic capital model (at a much lower confidence level) to determine the level of buffer that management wishes to hold.

9.4.1 An alternative approach

A number of banks have decided that economic capital models are not the way to go, and have instead moved to a more integrated form of macro-economic modelling linked directly to capital planning and stress testing.

Under this approach, banks first build a financial model which incorporates P&L, balance sheet, risk-weighted assets and capital. Note that these are the basic building blocks of any capital planning and stress testing approach. The model is then populated with the expected (i.e. budgeted or forecast) outcome for the modelling horizon, typically one to three years.

The second step is then to construct a set of macro-economic factors and (this is the difficult bit) determine how these will impact the various components of the financial model. Once this is done and the model properly calibrated and tested, the bank can run as many simulations and scenarios as it likes, and by looking at the resulting capital ratios determine how much of a capital buffer it needs to hold today so as never to go below the required minima.

However, it should be noted that mapping the macro-economic factors to drivers of the financial numbers is not a trivial task, and experience in the few such models that have been attempted so far indicate that it takes a team of skilled economists and financial modellers up to a year, even for a bank with a relatively simple business model operating in a single country.

9.5 Importance of risk management – strengthening the SREP

In their July 2009 paper, "Enhancements to the Basel II framework", the Committee identified the need to strengthen the effectiveness of the supervisory review and evaluation process ("SREP"). The paper also emphasises certain aspects of the bank's own ICAAP, notably:

(a) A careful analysis of capital instruments and their potential performance during times of stress, including their ability to absorb losses and support ongoing business operations.

(b) The ICAAP should address both short- and long-term needs and consider the prudence of building excess capital over benign periods of the credit cycle and also to withstand a severe and prolonged market downturn.

The first of these points is new, and recognises that different components of capital have different loss-absorption characteristics, and the order in which losses are deducted from the different components is highly relevant, a nuance that was largely overlooked in the Basel I and II regimes.

The second point was already included in Basel II, but it emphasises the importance of capital planning and stress testing, a key aspect of an effective ICAAP which were not highlighted sufficiently strongly in Basel II.

Part II of the Committee's guidance is addressed to supervisors, and provides some more detailed guidance than that provided in Basel II, but as this is relatively straightforward and easy to read and understand the guidance is not repeated here.

Of greater relevance to banks, and to the theme of this Guide, is the specific guidance provided in Part III on stress testing (III F – paras 75–83). Paragraph 79 makes it explicit that banks must conduct a forward-looking capital stress test (something that was only implied by para.743 (N.B. paragraph references are to the consolidated version issued in June 2006), in that a bank should, "assess its future capital requirements based on the bank's reported risk profile and make necessary adjustments to the bank's strategic plan accordingly"). This had already been interpreted by a number of supervisors around the world, but no means all, to mean a forward-looking capital stress test, and is now explicitly required. Perhaps understandably, no guidance is given on these stress tests; it will be up to individual banks, in dialogue with their supervisors, to determine the appropriate level of severity.

More generally, there are two links between the emphasis on better risk management and capital adequacy. First, and the main focus of the Committee, is that better risk management should reduce the probability and/or severity of losses, thus reducing the likelihood that a bank will breach its capital adequacy requirements. Secondly, risk management itself influences the level of capital required in the first place, as there is a direct link between risk profile and RWA (the more advanced the approach taken under Basel II, the stronger the link), and with expensive capital likely to become subject to tighter controls and rationing, risk management has an important role to play in managing the demand for capital.

9.6 Conclusion

One of the key components of a bank's ICAAP, namely forward-looking capital planning and stress testing, has taken on greater importance, for three reasons. First, the quantum of new capital involved under Basel III increases the cost of doing business.

Secondly, the uncertainty surrounding the mechanics of the two capital buffers, as explained more fully in Chapter 3, means that, while it has always been challenging enough to forecast future capital supply and demand, it has become even more difficult if the actual minimum capital ratios to be required in the future are subject to a degree of variability.

Thirdly, the Committee itself has put a greater emphasis on the importance of capital planning, making it an explicit requirement under Pillar 2.

For all these reasons, it will be more important than ever to have robust processes in place to forecast capital supply (i.e. availability) as well as demand (i.e. requirements), and to allocate that capital more effectively to the businesses and transactions which provide the more attractive returns. Banks will no longer be able to allow the balance sheet to grow and only afterwards work out how much capital is required – capital management will have to be pro-active and will act as a binding constraint on how much, and what type, of new business is put on the balance sheet.

It should also be noted that the new regime is going to be a challenge for supervisors as well. There are aspects of the regime that are still not clear (such as the exact operation of the capital conservation buffer) and supervisors will need to get themselves familiar with the full range of techniques of managing capital. As this discipline involves an understanding of risk, accounting, economics and the operation of the capital markets, this is clearly a challenge. They will also need to be able to understand how a bank's capital ratios will be managed through the Basel III transition phase, and to be able to assess the credibility of banks' plans which require expert skill and judgment.

Further, the industry remains concerned that there is a tendency towards "superequivalence", that is supervisors setting national mimima that are greater than the Basel III minimum ratios. This was explicitly encouraged by the G20 Summit in Seoul in November 2010, where the Summit Document stated at para.9:

> "We are committed to take action at the national and international level to raise standards, and ensure that our national authorities implement global standards developed to date, consistently, in a way that ensures . . . ., a race to the top".
> (The Summit Document follows the Summit Declaration and can be found at *www.g20.org/Documents2010/11/seoulsummit_declaration.pdf*)

While it is, of course, understood that the various accords and frameworks issued by the Committee are minimum standards, it is important to recognise that there is already enough of a challenge in meeting the Basel III requirements as they stand: supervisors should be cautious in imposing even tougher requirements even before banks and supervisors have become used to operating under the new regime.

Finally, a fundamental building block for strengthened supervision is greater consistency in approaches adopted by supervisors around the world. In the author's view greater consistency in the approach for Pillar 2, against the background of more detailed guidance on the supervisory approaches for Pillar 2, would be an important step in this direction.

Chapter 10

Procyclicality

Monika Mars

10.1 Introduction

Procyclicality can be defined as feedback mechanisms that amplify "normal" business cycle fluctuations. For example, the banking sector's response to the business cycle could include a reduction in lending as the credit quality of borrowers deteriorates in line with economic circumstances or the demand for credit slows as investment opportunities reduce. In this context, procyclicality is characterised by actions, requirements, or conditions that incite behaviour beyond this natural response, and which could lead to a reduction in lending despite demand for loans at appropriate pricing, and to "fire sale" asset reductions at prices below fundamental values, potentially leading to downward spirals in value that affect other holders of similar assets. These responses, in turn, would then result in a further weakening of economic activity.

The issue of procyclicality has been the subject of intense debate since the introduction of the more risk sensitive Basel II capital framework, which has elements that are frequently referred to as "procyclical". Specifically, minimum capital requirements under Pillar 1 of the Framework will increase during economic downturns (as credit quality decreases and default probabilities rise) and decrease during economic booms. However, the actual extent of these procyclical effects, and whether they exceed "acceptable" levels, remains subject to further analysis and observation by supervisors.

During the financial crisis, capital adequacy and accounting rules combined to create a procyclical deleveraging of banks' balance sheets with the resultant negative effects on the "real" economy. Mark-to-market accounting rules forced write-downs in assets, in both the trading and banking books, significantly reducing banks' own funds available to back risk-weighted assets ("RWA"). At the same time, RWA increased through drawdowns on off-balance sheet facilities (e.g. liquidity lines backing securitisation facilities) and the deterioration of borrowers' credit quality.

However, in the early stages of the crisis, the effect of a reduction in available own funds far outweighed the actual increase of RWA, as – in particular – the increase in credit risk capital requirements under the Internal Ratings Based ("IRB") approach, only materialised later in the crisis, when defaults of companies and private individuals started to increase.

This Chapter discusses how banks currently address cyclicality of capital requirements in their risk management practices before outlining the specific guidance included in the Basel III package to address the issue of procyclicality.

10.2   Managing procyclicality

Managing through economic cycles is a primary responsibility of a firm's senior management. Stakeholders, including shareholders, creditors, supervisors and society, expect firms to survive economic downturns as well as to prosper in benign periods. Regardless of regulatory requirements requiring the build-up of capital buffers or provisions in good times for use in bad times, banks – depending to a degree on their individual risk appetites – should have essentially the same goals, with a particular focus on building resources in good times in order to ensure survival in reasonably foreseeable bad times. In particular, senior management is responsible for understanding and successfully managing both risk and capital – and crucially, the relationship between the two – across the complete economic cycle.

10.2.1   Risk management

The tools of risk management include modelling, use of historical data and scenario analysis. As a result, assumptions and data underlying the models can potentially influence or exacerbate procyclicality. If sufficient attention is not given to the interpretation of model outcomes, risk models and capital calculations that are highly sensitive and reflective of current economic conditions may encourage firms to take on excessive risk in upturns when returns are healthy and the apparent downside risk is low.

When economic downturns occur, prudent risk management dictates that appropriate measures should be taken to respond to the increasing risk in the portfolio, possibly including a measured reduction in risk-taking, as well as any needed build-up of capital buffers. However, directly opposed to the situation during boom times, relatively sensitive risk models and capital calculations may without due attention encourage firms to respond in an excessive fashion to the downturn, inducing excessive conservatism that unduly restrains economic activity in the broader economy.

In their internal risk management approaches, banks will use a variety of measures for different applications. These need to address two – potentially conflicting – objectives:

1. For the purposes of day-to-day risk management, banks need risk-sensitive measures that provide an accurate picture of how the risk profiles of transactions, portfolios, and customers are changing in response to underlying changes in economic conditions. These measures can by their nature be relatively volatile and as such contribute to a degree of sensitivity and variability of risk (and resulting capital) measures.
2. For the purposes of more strategic risk and capital management decisions, alternative measures of risk (and capital) that are less sensitive to change in current conditions and that are relatively more stable across the economic cycle are often preferred. These measures will show less volatility over an economic cycle, hence permitting more orderly planning; however, at any point in the cycle, they may, taken alone, over- or underestimate the current risk in the portfolio.

The right balance between the application of the various tools and overlaying expert judgment on the outcomes of the models allow senior management to manage risk and capital success-fully throughout an economic cycle.

10.2.2 Capital planning buffers in Pillar 2

In addition to internal risk management practices, regulatory requirements already exist to ensure that banks determine the necessity and size of a so-called capital planning buffer, which is a Pillar 2 tool in a number of jurisdictions (including the UK and the Netherlands). This buffer is implied under the require-ments of Pillar 2 in the Basel II framework but was not made explicit, and, as a result, has not been implemented consistently across jurisdictions. However, the BCBS's enhancements to Pillar 2 announced in July 2009 now make this a specific requirement, and these enhancements are incorporated into Basel III by reference.

The objective of the capital planning buffer is to ensure firms have sufficient capital to absorb losses and/or to cover increasing capital requirements in adverse circumstances that are outside the firm's normal and direct control (i.e. driven by developments in the economic environment). Banks have to estimate the capital planning buffer as part of their ICAAP process, by applying a stress scenario to their forward-looking capital plan and determining the size of the buffer they would need to hold in order to enable them to withstand this stress without breaching their internal and/or external capital targets. A more detailed description of this process is contained in Chapter 9 of this book.

The combination of internal risk management objectives and existing regulatory requirements already today provides a framework in which banks need to address the issue of cyclical capital requirements and devise effective strategies and tools to manage their risks and capital across economic cycles.

10.3 Basel III proposals to address procyclicality

In the Basel III reform package, the Basel Committee has intro-duced a number of new and explicit measures to address the perceived procyclical behaviour of the financial sector before and during the financial crisis and to make the banking sector as a whole more resilient to shocks.

These cover four broad objectives:

(1) dampening any excess cyclicality of the minimum capital requirement;
(2) promoting more forward-looking provisioning practices;
(3) conserving capital to build buffers in "good times" that can be used in stressed circumstances; and
(4) protecting the banking sector from periods of excess credit growth.

Each of these is outlined in more detail in the Sections that follow.

10.3.1   Cyclicality of the minimum requirement

One of the primary objectives of the Basel II framework was to make regulatory capital requirements more risk sensitive. However, this greater risk sensitivity automatically introduces an element of increased cyclicality of capital requirements over time. As a result, a number of safeguards designed to avoid any excess cyclicality of the minimum capital requirement were included in the final Basel II framework. These included, for example, the requirement to use long-term data series for the estimation of default probabilities ("PD") or the use of downturn loss given default ("LGD") estimates in the IRB approaches for credit risk, as well as the requirement to conduct stress tests that consider downward migrations in the quality of credit portfolios.

Cyclicality of the minimum requirement, however, is not limited to the IRB approaches for credit risk. Downward migrations in external ratings and changes in the level of past-due loans will also create a certain amount of cyclicality under the Standardised Approach for credit risk. Similarly, the Internal Models Approach ("IMA") for market risk will generate higher capital requirements when data from stressed time periods is used. With respect to market risk, the Basel Committee introduced additional capital requirements based on stressed VaR in its July 2009 amendment to the trading book rules (for a detailed discussion of the amendments to the trading book rules see Chapter 4.). While the primary objective of this measure was to increase the capital requirements for market risk so that these better reflected the actual risks in banks' trading portfolios, a secondary objective was to decrease the cyclicality of the minimum requirements at the same time.

In its original proposals in December 2009, the Committee contemplated introducing further measures to reduce the cyclicality of minimum capital requirements specifically for the IRB approach to credit risk. Two approaches were analysed as part of the comprehensive Quantitative Impact Study ("QIS"), namely the use of:

(a) the highest average PD estimate applied by a bank historically to each of its exposure classes as a proxy for a downturn PD; and
(b) an average of historic PD estimates for each exposure class.

Both of these approaches were heavily criticised by banks and other respondents to the consultation, both for conceptual and practical reasons. At a practical level, the method would potentially penalise banks with longer (better) data histories vis-à-vis their competitors. Conceptually it would remove a great degree of risk sensitivity from the framework and in addition remove incentives to improve risk management practices by "locking-in" worst-case PDs, regardless of whether the bank had taken any actions as a result of the events that caused the historic losses. This would also create issues with the "use test" as banks would be unlikely to use such "downturn PDs" in day-to-day risk management applications.

Ultimately, the Committee decided not to include any specific additional measures in the Basel III package, albeit without providing any comment on why the original proposals were withdrawn. Instead, the Committee pointed to "alternative" measures that supervisors can take to achieve a better balance between risk sensitivity and stability of capital requirements. In particular, it mentions the Committee of European Banking Supervisors' ("CEBS") position paper on a countercyclical

242

capital buffer from July 2009, in which CEBS declares a clear preference for the use of the Pillar 2 process to address the issue of procyclicality.

The Committee has also put in place a comprehensive data collection initiative to assess the impact of the Basel II framework over the credit cycle. In December 2009 it concluded that it was still too early to opine on whether the Basel II framework was proving to be more cyclical than expected. No further update on this statement was provided with the release of the final Basel III framework, however, the Committee still gives itself an option to consider additional measures (which could, for example, include the use of downturn PDs) to dampen cyclicality should the cyclicality of the minimum requirement be greater than supervisors deem appropriate at any point in the future.

10.3.2 *Forward looking provisioning*

Under current international accounting rules, provisions for loan losses can only be established in line with the so-called "incurred loss" approach, i.e., provisions are only allowed for exposures where an objective impairment trigger has already been identified. This approach is inherently more procyclical than an "expected loss" method, which would allow banks to establish provisions in a more forward-looking manner. Under the incurred loss model, provisions will tend to be low during benign periods of economic activity and as such the available stock of provisions is likely to be at its lowest just before an economic downturn. As a result, the accounting rules for provisioning are considered to have been a contributing factor to the financial crisis, as banks had insufficient levels of provisions available to cover the losses that they suffered.

The Basel Committee does not have direct decision-making powers over accounting rules, which are set by the Accounting Standard Setters, the most important of which are the International Accounting Standards Board ("IASB") and the Federal Accounting Standards Board ("FASB") for IFRS and US GAAP accounting rules respectively. However, the Basel Committee is actively promoting a change to more forward-looking provisioning practices and supports activities underway in this regard at the standard setters. Specifically, the Committee has publicly communicated a set of high-level principles that should be considered by the IASB when replacing the current IAS 39 accounting standard ("Guiding principles for the replacement of IAS 39", Basel Committee on Banking Supervision, August 2009).

The main principles related to provisioning and impairment are outlined below:

(a) Loan loss provisioning should be robust and based on sound methodologies that reflect expected credit losses in the banks' existing loan portfolio over the life of the portfolio. The accounting model [. . .] should allow early identification and recognition of losses by incorporating a broader range of available credit information than presently included in the incurred loss model and should result in an earlier identification of credit losses.
(b) The provisioning approach should allow for the exercise of professional judgment while using leading economic indicators, changes in underwriting standards and collection practices, and other relevant information when estimating provisions or allowances. Judgment related to these provisions should be well evidenced.
(c) The new standard should allow for provisions for groups of loans with similar risk characteristics.
(d) The new standard should utilise approaches that draw from relevant information in banks' internal risk management and capital adequacy systems when possible.
(e) The approach should encourage provisioning to address credit losses across the entire range of bank internal credit grades for loan portfolios.
(f) The new standard should apply the same impairment approach to all financial assets measured using amortised cost.

The current status of the proposed changes to accounting standards is discussed in more detail in Chapter 8 of this book.

In addition, the Basel Committee is updating its 2006 guidance on provisioning, "Sound Credit Risk Assessment and Valuation for Loans", to be in line with a move to an expected loss approach to provisioning.

The Basel Committee is also addressing perceived disincentives for sound provisioning under the current capital adequacy rules in the revision of the capital definition. Under Basel II, any excess of expected loss over existing provisions needs to be deducted 50 per cent from Tier 1 and 50 per cent from Tier 2 capital. Under Basel III, these deductions will be 100 per cent from Tier 1 capital. Increased provisions reduce retained earnings and therefore common equity Tier 1 capital; under the Basel III rules, this would also be the case for any shortfalls of provisions over expected losses, thus eliminating any capital incentive to under-provision.

The ultimate impact of the changes outlined above cannot be estimated at this stage, as they are highly dependent on developments outside of the supervisors' influence, i.e., the final outcome of ongoing discussions about accounting standards. The move to an expected loss-based provisioning model for accounting standards should bring the prudential concept of expected loss and the accounting concepts of provisions closer together; however, it is unlikely that the "expected loss" definition adopted by accounting standard setters will completely match the prudential definition employed by supervisors. Depending on the level of divergence, this may necessitate the continued operation of two separate methodologies, data and systems infrastructures, to address accounting and prudential calculations respectively.

10.3.3   *Capital conservation buffer*

10.3.3.1   *Introduction*

The capital conservation framework is designed to promote the conservation of capital and the build-up of adequate buffers by financial institutions that can, in theory, be drawn upon in periods of stress. This is to counteract behaviour observed at the onset of the financial crisis, where institutions continued to make distributions in the form of dividends, share buybacks and discretionary bonus payments although their own financial condition and the outlook for the overall sector were deteriorating. While it was perhaps in the interest of individual institutions to continue making distributions in order to avoid signalling weakness and to protect the franchise, collectively their actions made not only the institutions in question but the sector as a whole less prepared to weather the crisis.

The introduction of the capital conservation buffer is designed to ensure that banks build up capital buffers during "good times" that can be drawn upon in periods of stress, as losses are incurred. The framework also addresses the need to rebuild the buffers after the stress period. One way of accomplishing this is by temporarily reducing discretionary distributions of earnings, e.g., by reducing dividends and staff bonus payments. The Committee acknowledges that banks may also choose to raise additional capital from the market rather than conserving internally generated funds to meet the conservation buffer requirement; the balance of the options should be part of the discussions with supervisors as part of the capital planning process under Pillar 2.

The Committee also outlines what it deems to be "unacceptable behaviour" by banks that have depleted their capital buffers, namely to use future predictions of recovery for maintaining generous distributions to shareholders, other capital providers and employees and to continue making distributions in order to signal financial strength to the market. In order to address this, the framework reduces management's flexibility with respect to capital management actions by imposing capital distribution constraints when capital levels breach certain threshold levels.

The capital conservation framework aims to ensure that sufficient capital is available in individual institutions and the sector as a whole to support ongoing business activities of banks in periods of stress, thus avoiding the damaging deleveraging that took place during the financial crisis. As such, it is an additional element that should help reduce procyclicality.

However, a note of caution is needed here, in that the Committee has not made it clear under what circumstances the buffer can be released, and there are concerns that it could become a permanent addition to the capital ratios. Some supervisors have, in recent speeches and discussions, indicated that they would allow the buffer to be drawn down in a crisis, but attitudes are still developing and there is a risk of a lack of consistency. In addition, the market may come to regard the buffer as effectively permanent.

10.3.3.2 Mechanics of the approach

A capital conservation buffer of 2.5 per cent comprised of Common Equity Tier 1 ("CET1") is established above the minimum regulatory requirement, raising the total minimum CET1 requirement to 7 per cent (4.5 per cent CET1 plus 2.5 per cent conservation buffer). However, where banks do not have sufficient additional Tier 1 and Tier 2 funds to meet the 6 per cent Tier 1 and 8 per cent Total capital minimum requirements, any additional CET1 must first be used to satisfy these requirements before being available to contribute to the capital conservation buffer. Capital distribution constraints will be imposed on banks when capital levels drop under this minimum level. It should be noted that the constraints only relate to distributions and do not restrict the operation of the bank in other ways.

The Figure below shows the minimum capital conservation ratios a bank must meet at various levels of the CET1 capital ratios.

Figure 10.1 Minimum capital conservation ratios

Individual bank minimum capital conservation standards	
Common Equity Tier 1 Ratio	Minimum Capital Conservation Ratios (expressed as a percentage of earnings)
4.5% - 5.125%	100%
>5.125% - 5.75%	80%
>5.75% - 6.375%	60%
>6.375% - 7.0%	40%
> 7.0%	0%

Source: "A global regulatory framework for more resilient banking systems" December 2010.

For example, a bank with a CET1 capital ratio between 5.125 per cent and 5.75 per cent is required to conserve 80 per cent of its earnings in the subsequent financial year. If the bank wants to make payments in excess of the constraints imposed by this regime, it would have the option of raising capital in the private sector equal to at least the amount above the constraint which it wishes to distribute. The CET1 ratio includes amounts used to meet the 4.5 per cent minimum CET 1 requirement, but excludes any additional CET 1 needed to meet the 6 per cent Tier 1 and 8 per cent Total Capital requirements. For example, a bank with 8 per cent CET1 and no Additional Tier 1 or Tier 2 capital would meet all minimum capital requirements, but would have a zero conservation buffer and therefore be subject to the 100 per cent constraint on capital distributions.

For the purposes of the framework, distributions and earnings are defined as follows:

(a) **Distributions**: Included in the definition are dividends and share buybacks, discretionary payments on other Tier 1 instruments and discretionary bonus payments to staff.
(b) **Earnings**: These are defined as distributable profits prior to the deduction of elements subject to the restriction on distributions. Earnings are calculated after tax under the assumption that none of the distributable items were paid, i.e., the tax impact of the distributions needs to be reversed out. Banks with a CET1 ratio of less than 7 per cent and making a loss would be restricted from making any distributions, regardless of where they operate within the range of the conservation buffer.

The framework is aimed to be applied at a consolidated level, i.e., restrictions would be imposed on distributions out of the consolidated group. However, national supervisors have the option of applying the regime at the solo level to conserve resources in specific parts of the group.

Although it must be possible for banks to draw down the conservation buffer during periods of stress, banks should not choose in normal times to operate in the buffer range for competitive reasons. Supervisors are therefore given the discretion to impose time limits on banks operating within the buffer range on a case-by-case basis and should ensure that measures to rebuild buffers over an appropriate timeframe form an essential part of banks' capital plans.

The capital conservation buffer requirement will be phased in between 1 January 2016 and year end 2018 and will become fully effective as of 1 January 2019. During the transition period, the buffer requirement will start at 0.625 per cent of RWA in 2016 with a further 0.625 per cent added in each subsequent year to reach the full 2.5 per cent in 2019. National supervisors do, however, have the discretion to impose shorter transition periods and are encouraged by the Committee to do so where appropriate.

10.3.3.3 Implications

The capital conservation buffer regime raises a number of issues for financial institutions. Although the concept of building up capital buffers in good times that can be drawn down in periods of stress is widely accepted, the actual implementation using distribution restrictions is less welcome. This effectively takes away bank management's autonomy (and responsibility) for capital management decisions, by limiting the payment of dividends and mandating the retention of profits when certain threshold values are not met. Some commentators have gone so far as to call the buffers "a massive and unacceptable interference in contractual agreements between banks and investors" (Association of German Banks, "Response to BCBS Consultation on Countercyclical Buffer").

In order to maintain their autonomy over capital management decisions, banks will, therefore, always need to operate above the top level of the range, making a CET1 ratio of 7 per cent (i.e. including the capital conservation buffer) the de-facto new minimum capital requirement. In addition, market participants can be expected to take a similar view and penalise banks that are likely to face disbursement restrictions. This market pressure, added to the internal objective of maintaining autonomy over capital management decisions, could also make drawing down of the buffer in periods of stress much more difficult, as a drawdown would send negative signals to the market and could lead to a drop in confidence by investors in the institution. It is, therefore, not clear to what extent the mechanism will actually work as intended, i.e., supply additional capital for periods of stress.

The operation of the buffer regime will also require banks to implement additional operational and financial processes. In particular, "pro-forma" tax calculations will need to be undertaken to determine the correct "earnings" for the buffer calculations. This could be a complex exercise, particularly in banking groups with operations in multiple jurisdictions and tax regimes (for a more detailed discussion of tax implications of the Basel III proposals see Chapter 13).

On a similar note, solo application of the buffer regime could engender the need to consider a revision of group structures in order to minimise the potential effect of trapped capital in individual entities/subsidiaries and/or jurisdictions. As group structure is frequently related to tax considerations, there could be compounding effects from the need to derive earnings before discretionary disbursements (and the related tax effects) and the solo application of the buffer regime.

Banks also have to deal with an additional level of uncertainty in their capital planning processes, as it is not clear at this stage which jurisdictions might choose to apply a solo buffer regime, nor is it known which countries will accelerate the implementation of the buffer regime.

Finally, banks need to consider the interaction of the capital conservation buffer with their current capital planning buffers under the ICAAP process in Pillar 2. Capital planning buffers will vary between institutions as a function of the underlying volatility of the risk profile (and resultant capital requirements) inherent in the banks' businesses. The level of volatility will also be dependent on the Pillar 1 approaches used by the institutions, as those banks using IRB approaches to credit risk will see much higher volatility – and as a result require higher capital planning buffers – of their minimum capital requirements over an economic cycle than institutions using the

Standardised Approach. In this regard, the use of a uniform 2.5 per cent buffer across all types of institutions represents an unwelcome departure from the bank-specific capital planning buffer to a mechanistic "one-size-fits-all" approach.

10.3.4   Countercyclical capital buffer

10.3.4.1   Introduction

The countercyclical buffer regime aims to ensure that capital requirements for the banking sector take into account the macro-economic environment in which banks operate. As such, it is a macro-prudential tool to be employed by individual national supervisors to address the issue of excessive credit growth in individual jurisdictions. The measures are designed to ensure banks build up additional capital defences in such situations in order to be more resilient to a system-wide stress.

The Basel Committee completed a separate consultation on the concept of the countercyclical buffer, which elicited an overwhelmingly negative response from the banking community, academics and other market participants. Criticism was levelled both at shortcomings in the proposed methodology as well as operational difficulties. Respondents criticised the buffer for being too blunt an instrument and too complicated to calculate. They also pointed out that the mechanism unfairly penalised responsible banks as well as those having contributed to the build-up of excess credit in the system, while not addressing the issue of the unregulated shadow banking system, which might have contributed to the credit growth as well. Some commentators called the proposals beyond the remit of prudential supervision, i.e., indicating that credit bubbles should better be addressed by monetary rather than prudential policy.

A number of respondents agreed with the general concept of a countercyclical buffer; however, they urged the Committee to undertake further analysis of the options available (and the likely impact of the proposals) before finalising the buffer proposal. Even supervisors expressed some doubts about the regime, commenting that experts had not demonstrated an ability to forecast turning points in the cycle, an ability that would be crucial for the regime to operate as designed.

In light of the widespread negative response on the basis of carefully-considered constructive criticism it is perhaps surprising that the original proposal was maintained almost unchanged in the final documents.

The countercyclical buffer regime consists of three elements:

(1) National authorities will assess whether credit growth in a particular market is excessive and could lead to the build up of system-wide risk. Based on this assessment a countercyclical buffer requirement will be introduced. This requirement will be released when system-wide risk either crystallises or dissipates.
(2) Banks will categorise their credit exposures to private sector counterparties on a geographic basis and calculate a bank-specific countercyclical capital requirement based on the country-specific requirements set by national authorities.
(3) The countercyclical buffer requirement for an individual bank will extend the size of the capital conservation buffer. Banks will, therefore, also be subject to distribution restrictions if they do not meet the countercyclical buffer requirement.

10.3.4.2   National buffer requirements

The countercyclical buffer requirement will be determined by an authority to be designated in each Basel Committee member jurisdiction. This can be the Central Bank or another authority charged with the responsibility for macro-prudential supervision. When the authority judges that credit growth is excessive and leads to the build-up of system-wide risk, it will consider putting in place a countercyclical buffer requirement of between zero and 2.5 per cent of risk weighted assets. It should, however, also consider other macro-prudential tools at its disposal (for a discussion of macro-prudential supervision more broadly please refer to Chapter 19.).

The Basel Committee has set out the principles to be followed by national authorities in making decisions on countercyclical buffers in a separate guidance document ("Guidance for national authorities operating the countercyclical capital buffer", Basel Committee on Banking Supervision, December 2010). The decision to implement or raise a countercyclical buffer requirement will be announced up to 12 months in advance of the implementation date in order to give banks sufficient time to adjust to the new buffer level. Decisions to decrease the level of the countercyclical buffer will take effect immediately. In order to ensure transparency, national authorities of the G20 will have to publish their buffer decisions as well as all buffers actually in place on the BIS website.

10.3.4.3   Bank-specific countercyclical buffer requirements

The buffer to be applied by an individual bank will reflect the geographic composition of its credit exposures. The buffer must be met with Common Equity Tier 1 capital in order to avoid distribution restrictions.

Banks must allocate their credit exposures – which include all private sector credit exposures that attract a credit risk capital charge or the risk-weighted equivalent trading book capital charges for specific risk, IRC and securitisation – to individual countries and calculate the countercyclical buffer requirement as a weighted average of the buffers in force in the relevant jurisdictions. The weights are derived from the proportion of the credit risk charge applicable in each jurisdiction and the total credit risk charge for private sector credit exposures.

For the trading book capital charges, banks are asked to work with their supervisors to agree on an approach to translate the charges to risk weights for individual instruments that could be allocated to individual geographic locations. The Committee acknowledges that it may not always be possible to break down charges in this way, as the trading book charges tend to be calculated on a portfolio rather than individual instrument basis. In this case, an allocation mechanism for the portfolio charge based on the EAD contribution of exposures in individual jurisdictions should be used.

The buffer needs to be calculated and publicly disclosed with at least the same frequency as the minimum capital requirements.

10.4.3.2   Mechanics of the approach

The countercyclical buffer requirement is implemented as an extension to the capital conservation buffer discussed in the previous section. The Figure below sets out the conservation ratios for various levels of the CET1 capital ratio in the case that a bank is subject to a 2.5 per cent capital conservation buffer.

Figure 10.2 Minimum conservation buffers when countercyclical buffer applies

Individual bank minimum capital conservation standards, when a bank is subject to a 2.5% countercyclical requirement	
Common Equity Tier 1 Ratio (including other fully loss absorbing capital)	Minimum Capital Conservation Ratios (expressed as a percentage of earnings)
4.5% - 5.75%	100%
>5.75% - 7.0%	80%
>7.0% - 8.25%	60%
>8.25% - 9.5%	40%
> 9.5%	0%

Source: "A global regulatory framework for more resilient banking systems" December 2010.

For buffers other than 2.5 per cent, the relevant buffer ranges are calculated based on quartile ranges of the total buffer, e.g., for CET1 ratios within the first quartile of the buffer, a 100 per cent distribution restriction applies, while for CET1 ratios above the top of the buffer there are no restrictions.

The countercyclical buffer regime is phased in according to the same timeline as that used for the capital conservation buffer, starting on 1 January 2006 and becoming fully operational as of

1 January 2019. During the transition period, the buffer requirement will start at a maximum of 0.625 per cent of RWA in 2016 with a further 0.625 per cent added in each subsequent year to reach its final maximum of 2.5 per cent in 2019. National supervisors have the discretion to accelerate the build-up of the buffer during the transition period in case their jurisdictions are experiencing excessive credit growth during this period.

10.3.4.5 *Implications*

The countercyclical buffer regime will require banks to implement additional data and systems capabilities in order to classify their exposures to individual countries and determine the appropriate buffers to be applied to the exposures. This is likely to require significant investments, in particular by the largest global financial institutions.

The allocation mechanism is not specified by the Basel Committee as the text only talks about "exposures in a jurisdiction" or the "geographic location" of counterparties. In practice, banks operate a number of internal classifications for allocating exposures to countries, using for example the physical location of the counterparty, the booking location of the exposure, but also a concept called "country of risk", which takes into account the contractual and collateral arrangements for the exposures in question. This mechanism is frequently used to determine the utilisation of country limits.

The required allocation of trading book exposures to individual jurisdictions creates an even more difficult operational problem. As the composition of the trading portfolios changes very quickly, banks are likely to be required to create data and systems infrastructures that allow them to recalculate the allocation in short intervals, potentially daily.

Aside from the cost involved in upgrading data and systems, the lack of concrete guidance from regulators and the differences in actual allocation mechanisms, there is a potential for creating an unequal playing field or even stimulating regulatory arbitrage.

From a capital planning perspective, the countercyclical buffer regime introduces an additional layer of complexity, particularly for globally active institutions. On the one hand, they would have to plan their exposures on a country-by-country basis, including the composition of their trading book, in order to be able to forecast the capital requirements due to the buffer. In addition, the buffer will only be announced up to 12 months in advance of it being implemented; this creates issues for all planning horizons over 12 months as banks would likely have to incorporate additional "levels of conservatism" in their planning to account for the potential introduction of buffers in certain jurisdictions.

10.4   Conclusion

The Basel Committee set out a package of four separate measures to address procyclicality in its initial consultation on the Basel III framework in December 2009. In the final framework issued in December 2010, only two of these measures – the capital conservation buffer and the countercyclical buffer – have been finalised (although some technical aspects remain to be fully specified), while the other two – measures to address the cyclicality of the minimum requirement and forward looking provisioning – still face an uncertain future. It is, therefore, too early to judge whether the current package will meet the objectives the Basel Committee originally set out for itself.

While the measures aimed at limiting the cyclicality of the minimum requirement and the anticipated changes to provisioning practices represent changes to Pillar 1 of the Basel II framework, the capital conservation buffer and the countercyclical buffer fall firmly into Pillar 2 territory, albeit replacing the current principles-based Pillar 2 approach with a rules-based, Pillar 1-type approach for parts of the framework.

One of the biggest unknowns as a result of the publication of the Basel III rules is the actual future of Pillar 2 in its current form. The impact on the Pillar 2 regime is also not going to be uniform across jurisdictions, as different supervisors have chosen different ways of implementing Pillar 2 in their respective countries. In particular, not all supervisors operate a process by which each bank is given an individual capital requirement in excess of the Pillar 1 minimum. This approach has been used for a long time in the UK as well as the Netherlands; however, a number of European countries are not operating a regime with differentiated quantitative requirements but use a more qualitative approach to Pillar 2. As a result, the impact of the new buffer regimes on the existing Pillar 2 framework will differ.

Chapter 9 includes a detailed consideration of the implications for Pillar 2, addressing in particular the challenges of setting individual capital targets under the ICAAP, addressing capital planning and stress testing as well as the role of economic capital in banks' internal management processes.

Chapter 11

Stress Testing

Fernando de la Mora, Richard Barfield and Pramit Mitra

11.1 Introduction

11.1.1 *Chapter outline*

Stress testing is an evolving discipline that is playing an increasingly important role in the management of risk at banks and in supervisors' assessments of capital and liquidity buffers. This Chapter discusses the background to stress testing, lessons learnt from the crisis and the implications of the new Basel regulations.

The Chapter provides an overview of the Basel III guidelines that affect stress testing, and also considers the key elements for effective stress testing including governance, methodologies, infrastructure, outputs and actions (such as contingency plans). This Chapter focuses mainly on the capital aspects of stress testing but the principles may be applied to other risks such as liquidity.

11.1.2 *Background*

"Stress testing" is usually used to describe approaches that assess how businesses are likely to perform under a range of severe but plausible downside scenarios. The term has its origins in stress tests used by engineers to test the resilience of buildings and bridges under extreme physical conditions.

Stress testing is considered by the banking industry as an indispensible tool to prepare for and reduce the impact of crisis events. It is an extension of simpler and widespread "what if" thinking but is more structured and sophisticated – and, as a result, more insightful. From a regulatory perspective, since 1996, the Basel Accord has required large international banks and non-bank financial institutions to incorporate stress tests as part of their internal models for the calculation of capital requirements for market risk. Indeed, Basel II made the presence of robust stress testing methodologies a requirement for supervisory validation of advanced Pillar 1 credit risk models and for many supervisors stress testing forms a key input to their review of banks' capital plans under Pillar 2. For many in the industry stress testing is seen primarily as a tool to inform capital and liquidity levels (both for internal and regulatory purposes).

Stress testing is also now an important tool for international bodies such as the International Monetary Fund ("IMF") and the World Bank, who have used macroeconomic stress tests extensively as part of the Financial Sector Assessment Program ("FSAP"). Likewise, supervisory authorities and central banks in many OECD countries have used stress testing to assess the resilience of their financial systems.

For some banks, stress testing is much more than just a regulatory exercise performed by the risk management department to fulfill regulatory requirements. There is an emerging trend for stress tests to be used to examine both upside and downside scenarios and to consider events which are more plausible than, say, a 1 in 200 year capital stress (a concept that many business managers find hard to grasp). By considering upsides and more probable events, stress tests provide insights that can aid the achievement of business goals, fine-tune the business model and inform risk-reward decisions.

11.1.3 Crisis lessons and implications for stress testing

The financial crisis revealed a number of shortcomings in banks' risk management approaches, particularly in the areas of risk measurement coverage, stress testing and monitoring of wrong-way risk. The crisis also exposed the limitations of economic capital models that failed to capture the severity and fat-tail nature of the crisis events. Businesses also failed to use stress testing as an effective tool to measure their capital and liquidity resources and make required course corrections. As a result, supervisory interest in stress testing has increased significantly.

One of the lessons learned from the crisis was that enhanced disclosure can (if conducted and communicated in the right way) promote market confidence. At the beginning of 2009, the results of the Supervisory Capital Assessment Program ("SCAP") in the United States were regarded by many as doing a lot to calm markets by sharing publically the details of the stressed capital adequacy of the 19 largest banks supervised by the New York Federal Reserve and, where needed, the associated remediation plans.

Public supervisory stress tests are likely to feature over the coming years. The Committee of European Banking Supervisors ran a public stress test for 91 institutions in the summer of 2010. In the US, "SCAP 2" was run at the end of 2010 and in the first part of 2011, prior to supervisory approval of the banks dividend payout plans. The European Banking Authority ("EBA"), the successor of Committee of European Banking supervisors, is also running public stress tests in the first half of 2011.

Stress testing also forms a very important component of the new global liquidity risk standard. Basel III requires comprehensive cash flow forecasting, limits and liquidity scenario stress testing. Liquidity requirements are specified in the form of two new measures – the Liquidity Coverage Ratio and the Net Stable Funding Ratio – with specific stress parameters.

At a more micro level, an area of particular concern for regulators has been stress testing of counterparty credit risk ("CCR"). Stress testing of CCR is particularly difficult to develop and understand given the multiplicity of trading counterparties. The Basel Committee found that stress testing in the area of

CCR was not comprehensive, infrequent and often ad hoc. As a result, the Committee has made detailed recommendations that include stress testing and scenario analysis to identify hidden wrong-way risk factors linked to the creditworthiness of counterparties.

Under Basel II.5, trading book rules have been updated to capture the credit risk of complex trading activities through the introduction of a stressed value-at-risk ("sVaR") requirement, which the Basel Committee believes will help dampen the cyclicality of the minimum regulatory capital requirements for market risk.

Reverse-stress testing is an interesting development. This is a concept developed by the UK FSA. Its principal aim is to encourage management to think about extreme events and scenarios that could cause their bank to fail. When done well, reverse-stress testing provides new insights into the risks to which the institution might be exposed and the interactions between different risk types (for example liquidity, market and credit risk).

In the U.S, the Federal Reserve's *Interagency Policy Statement on Funding and Liquidity Risk Management*, issued in March 2010, recommends regular stress testing as a way to understand a financial organisation's current exposure and vulnerability to extreme risks. According to the document:

> "Institutions should conduct stress tests regularly for a variety of institution-specific and market-wide events across multiple time horizons . . . Stress test outcomes should be used to identify and quantify sources of potential liquidity strain and to analyze possible impacts on the institution's cash flows, liquidity position, profitability, and solvency".

However, it is important to recognise that stress testing is not a panacea. It is a tool that needs to be used carefully to get the best value out of it. It can also be dangerous if it is misapplied.

11.2 Basel III guidelines

11.2.1 Capital buffers

The procyclical amplification of financial shocks across the financial system and the wider economy has been one of the most destabilising elements of the financial crisis. In its response, the Basel Committee has proposed a series of measures – in addition to a leverage ratio – to address procyclicality and create additional shock absorbers in the financial system under the new Basel III rules. These measures are designed to dampen excess cyclicality, promote forward-looking provisioning, conserve capital to be available during periods of stress, and protect the banking sector from periods of excess credit growth (PwC, The new Basel III framework – Navigating changes in bank capital management, (October 2010)).

The idea behind the conservation buffer is to create a cushion in good times that can absorb shocks in periods of stress. The framework envisages capital distribution constraints when capital levels fall within a specified range above minimum requirements, with the constraints increasing the closer a bank's capital levels get to the minimum. There will be two types of buffer:

(a) The *capital conservation buffer* should be available to absorb banking sector losses conditional on a plausibly severe stressed financial and economic environment.
(b) The *countercyclical buffer* would extend the capital conservation range during periods of excess credit growth, or other indicators deemed appropriate by supervisors for their national contexts.

The capital conservation buffer above the regulatory minimum requirement of 4.5 per cent is calibrated at 2.5 per cent and is to be met with common equity, after the application of deductions. A countercyclical buffer within a range of 0 per cent to 2.5 per cent of common equity or other fully loss-absorbing capital will be implemented according to national circumstances.

The purpose of the countercyclical buffer is to achieve the broader macro-prudential goal of protecting the banking sector from periods of excess aggregate credit growth. For any given country, this buffer will be in effect only when there is excess credit growth that results in a system-wide build-up of risk. The countercyclical buffer, when in effect, would be introduced as an extension of the conservation buffer range.

Chapter 3 (Defining capital), Chapter 9 (Role of Pillar 2) and Chapter 10 (Procyclicality) explore these topics in more detail.

11.2.2 Counterparty credit risk

One of the key areas of focus under stress testing in Basel III is counterparty credit exposures. To this end, the Basel Committee has raised several questions about CCR stress testing practices – their effectiveness in modeling a rapidly deteriorating credit environment like that witnessed during the 2007 financial crisis. The Basel Committee points out that "stress testing of counterparty credit risk was not comprehensive; was run infrequently, sometimes on an ad hoc basis; and, in many banks, provided inadequate coverage of counterparties or the associated risks" (Basel Committee, *Strengthening the resilience of banking sector* (December 2009)).

Stress testing assumes an even greater importance as banks move to the advanced approaches to assessing credit risk for counterparties (such as Expected Positive Exposure). Stress testing is perhaps the most important tool available to risk managers to check the robustness of the assumptions behind their internal models. For counterparty risk specifically, the Basel Committee advises that stress testing should identify the risk factors positively correlated with counterparty credit-worthiness. Qualitative factors such as complete capture of a particular trade, using multifactor stress testing scenarios, and quantification of collateral concentrations, are also made more explicit under Basel III.

Further, such testing should also address the possibility of severe shocks occurring when relationships between these risk factors change. Risk factors should be classified by product, by industry, by region, and other categories used in the industry. Senior management and the appropriate risk committees are expected to review and discuss regularly the results of these stresses and back tests.

The Basel Committee has made numerous recommendations/ enhancements for stress testing counterparty risk under Basel III (Basel Committee, *Strengthening the resilience of banking sector* (December 2009)). Key issues as stated by the Basel Committee are as follows:

(a) use complete trade capture and exposure aggregation across all forms of counterparty credit risk – not just OTC derivatives;
(b) frequent (at least monthly) stress testing of key market risk factors, such as interest rates, FX, commodity prices, equities, for all counterparties to identify outsize concentrations;
(c) frequent (at least quarterly) stress testing with multifactor scenarios and material non-directional risks (yield curve exposure, basis risk):

  (i) multifactor stress scenarios should include, at the minimum, circumstances involving severe market disruptions/events, a severe liquidity crunch and the unwinding of a major financial institution.

(d) the scenarios used in the stress test should be severe enough to capture historical events such as the recent financial crisis but also scenarios of less severity;
(e) since markets swings also impact creditworthiness, banks should also conduct frequent (at least quarterly) stress tests involving joint movement of exposures and counterparty creditworthiness;
(f) exposure stress testing—including single factor, multifactor and material non-directional risks—and joint stressing of exposure and creditworthiness should be performed at the counterparty-specific, counterparty group (e.g. industry and region), and aggregate firm-wide CCR levels;
(g) stress test results should be integrated into regular reports to risk committees and senior management; and

(h) perhaps most importantly, senior management must ensure that the results of the stress tests are incorporated in the firm's risk framework and culture.

11.2.3   Market risk – stressed VaR

One of the key lessons of the crisis has been the need to strengthen the risk coverage of the capital framework. The Basel Committee concluded that failure to capture major on- and off-balance sheet risks, as well as derivative-related exposures, was a major contributor to the financial crisis.

As a response, it introduced a stressed value-at-risk ("sVaR") capital requirement in Basel III, based on a 10-day 99 per cent confidence basis, but with inputs taken from times of significant financial stress relevant to the firm's portfolio. As a result, in addition to the current requirement of between three to four times the 10-day 99 per cent VaR, three times the 10-day 99 per cent sVaR will be required.

Model inputs will have to be calibrated to historical data from a continuous 12-month period of significant financial stress. Using the financial crisis of 2007–2009 as an illustration, this would be equivalent to a VaR measure calculated over a dataset that included 2008 and 2009. On a daily basis, a bank will be required to meet the capital requirement expressed as the higher of its latest sVaR number and an average of sVaR numbers calculated over the preceding 60 business days multiplied by the multiplication factor. Data sets will have to be updated every month reassessed whenever a material change in market prices takes place. Risk factors incorporated in pricing models will have to be included in VaR calculations and omissions must be justified.

See Chapter 4 – Trading book and securitisation for more details.

11.2.4   Liquidity risk

Liquidity risk management has been a focus of Basel III. The Basel Committee's *Principles for Sound Liquidity Risk*

Management and Supervision has laid out a strong liquidity risk framework, starting from the top of the organisation. As part of this framework, banks will need to establish their liquidity risk appetite, with special emphasis on intra-day liquidity positions and funding risk supported by robust stress testing.

Basel III has also introduced quantitative standards for funding liquidity. The two proposed measures are a 30-day Liquidity Coverage Ratio designed to ensure short-term resilience to liquidity disruptions and a longer-term structural liquidity ratio to address liquidity mismatches and promote the use of stable funding sources. Furthermore, the Committee proposes a set of monitoring metrics to assist supervisors in the analysis of bank-specific and system-wide liquidity risk trends.

The 30-day Liquidity Coverage Ratio requirement is designed to ensure that banks have sufficient high-quality liquid resources to survive an acute stress scenario lasting for one month. This ratio identifies the amount of unencumbered, high-quality liquid assets an institution holds that can be used to offset the net cash outflows it would encounter under a short-term stress scenario specified by supervisors, including both specific and systemic shocks.

The scenario envisions:

(a) a significant downgrade (three-notch) of the institution's credit rating;
(b) a partial loss of retail deposits;
(c) loss of unsecured wholesale funding;
(d) a significant increase in secured funding haircuts; and
(e) increases in derivative collateral calls and substantial calls on contractual and non-contractual off-balance sheet exposures, including committed credit and liquidity facilities.

The critical area of stress testing liquidity risk is discussed in more detail in Chapter 6 – Liquidity and funding. The remainder of this Chapter focuses on the capital aspects of stress testing.

11.3 Key features of effective stress testing

11.3.1 Overview

With the growth in the importance of stress testing, all banks need to be clear on what constitutes effective stress testing. Approaches will vary depending on the nature, scale and complexity of the organisation, but the main building blocks are common to all banks.

A stress test, according to the Basel Accord, is an evaluation of a bank's financial position under a severe but plausible scenario to assist in decision-making within the bank (Basel Committee, *Principles for sound stress testing practices and supervision* (May 2009)) When properly conducted and used, stress testing can provide useful information to all levels of decision-makers about the risks embedded in a portfolio. For instance, at the trading level, stress testing can reveal risks associated with a product or position. Managers can also obtain an aggregated view of risks across asset and exposure classes. A common application is to use stress test results to compare the stressed risk profile with the risk appetite (either at group level or within a business unit) to provide a key risk input to strategic decisions.

Stress testing is built into Basel II. For example, in the US, the final Basel II rules issued by the US Federal Reserve ("Fed") in December 2007 require a bank to periodically stress test its advanced credit risk systems. The Fed requires banks to use stress testing analysis to understand how economic cycles, especially downturns, affect risk-based capital requirements, including migration across rating grades. Stress testing analysis consists of defining stress scenarios and then assessing the effects of the scenarios on key performance measures, including risk-based capital requirements.

The Fed further elaborated on the above definition of stress testing in July 2008 by requiring banks to use the ICAAP to address the potential impact of broader market or systemic events, which could cause risk to rise beyond the bank's chosen risk-tolerance levels, and to have appropriate contingency plans.

The Fed's approach is very similar to that required in other countries that have adopted Basel II. These approaches require banks to take a forward view, typically three to five years, develop a base case capital plan and stress it to determine what level of capital buffer it needs to hold today to safeguard the firm against plausible but severe future stress events.

However, these stress tests are not expected to be regulatory exercises but to be embedded in a firm's risk and capital management systems. In this way, stress testing, including scenario analysis and sensitivity analysis, is intended to provide an additional quantitative perspective that a bank should use regularly to complement other quantitative risk measures (PwC, *Comprehensive stress tests*, (March 2009)).

Figure 11.1 Timeline of stress testing process and activities

The five principal steps in a stress testing process are summarised in the figure below.

1. Plan the stress testing process. Articulate the characteristics of capital stress test process such as objectives, roles and responsibilities, scope, timing, resources and frequency. As part of this step, the engagement of senior management should be planned carefully.
2. Design base and stressed scenarios with business relevant factors. The scenarios selected should be plausible, exceptional, sufficiently severe, relevant and forward-looking. They should also be developed and challenged with senior management input.
3. Assess the likely impact of scenarios on business results. This will be done using various methodologies and tools developed by business lines or risk areas. The impact is assessed with and without mitigation actions (these are

sometimes referred to as "net" and "gross" stress tests respectively).

4. Coordinate group function and business line stress testing activities and resources, data gathering and validation, modeling and risk analysis, and resolution of issues that arise from the stress testing process.

5. Create management reports that draw out the insights from stress tests, present stressed capital positions, as well as key vulnerabilities and risk limit breaches. Recommend mitigating management actions based on stress testing findings.

As the reader can see, stress testing is a very broad topic. To make the analysis of stress testing manageable, it is helpful to divide stress testing into five elements:

(1) Objectives;
(2) Governance;
(3) Methodologies;
(4) Process, infrastructure and capabilities; and
(5) Outputs and actions.

The Sections below discuss each of these in turn.

11.3.2 Objectives

Whatever the stress test, it is essential to be clear on its specific objectives and what the results will be used for.

Stress tests vary from holistic, group-wide macroeconomic scenarios that cover all material risk types, businesses and geographies to sensitivity analyses on, say, interest rate or currency movements in a particular sub-portfolio. Objectives may vary from evaluating a supervisor-determined stress (for example SCAP or EBA), determining a capital buffer for Pillar 2 in the ICAAP, evaluating the credit risk sensitivity to an economic downturn of an AIRB credit risk model etc.

In the summer of 2010, there was media confusion over the purpose of the CEBS stress tests. The purpose was to assess the impact of a plausible but severe economic downturn on the capital adequacy of European banks. However, the media confused this with the idea that the stress test should be to assess what could bring the European financial system crashing down – for example through a series of sovereign defaults.

Stress test results may be used internally or externally, with different implications for stress test model design and the communication of the results. For external use the model has to be carefully communicated to the target audience. If it is mainly used for internal purposes, the model structure and the way results are used have to reflect the (risk) management culture of the organisation (Drehmann, *Stress Tests: Objectives, Challenges and Modelling Choices*, (2008)).

Stress testing takes up a reasonable amount of scarce senior management time. It is therefore important to be clear on the business and risk management benefits that a bank wishes to gain from it. These will vary from firm to firm and will depend on the context in which the stress tests are being run. Benefits and objectives may include:

(a) form an enterprise-wide, cross-functional view of risks;
(b) help drive strategic decisions and business realignment in light of stress testing results;
(c) provide senior management with a coherent structure and tool to assess risks holistically;
(d) help formulate contingency plans vetted by both senior management and business lines;
(e) enhance the capital planning process and reduce the financial cost of future crises;
(f) promote a constructive dialogue among risk, finance and business functions through the overall stress testing process and governance controls; and
(g) understand model risk by testing the model outside the normal operating environment.

11.3.3 Governance

As with any bank-wide process, effective stress testing requires clarity on roles and responsibilities and strong governance arrangements. Stress testing involves a wide range of functions and skills (for example: finance, treasury, economics, strategy, credit risk, market risk and front office etc.). As can be imagined, in a large international bank stress testing can become a very complex process to manage.

The Basel Committee has stressed the importance of board and senior management involvement in stress testing. Firms approach this in different ways, often to allow sufficient focus and board member time, the board role will be delegated to the board risk committee. At the executive level, it is also common for multi-disciplinary stress testing forums to be used to debate scenarios, interpret results etc. This allows senior management to add greater value through its subsequent involvement.

Basel Committee recommendations on governance:

- Form an integral part of the overall governance, including ICAAP, and feed into strategic decision making process on business, capital and liquidity decisions.

- The board has ultimate responsibility with senior management leading the implementation.

Post-crisis, a key challenge for banks is to ensure that stress tests are appropriately severe. Pre-crisis, most banks applied only moderate scenarios, either in terms of severity or the degree of interaction across portfolios or risk types (Basel Committee, *Principles for sound stress testing practices and supervision* (May 2009)). For stress testing to be effective, it is important to create an environment where extreme or innovative scenarios are not rejected by the board, senior management or business unit heads.

A key pre-condition for an effective stress test is appropriate board and senior management involvement. This is critical in ensuring the appropriate use of stress testing in banks' risk governance and capital planning. The involvement should include:

(a) setting stress testing objectives;
(b) defining scenarios;
(c) discussing the results of stress tests;
(d) assessing potential actions; and
(e) decision-making.

Several of the banks that fared well during the financial crisis had extensive senior management involvement in development, monitoring and responding to stress testing results. Less effective processes were characterised by compartmentalisation in silos of the bank and insufficient debate or confrontation of the assumptions behind the cost, risk and speed of new capital raising, hedging and selling the bank's positions. At some banks, stress testing is still performed mainly as an isolated exercise by the risk function with little interaction with business units. The consequence is that there is little wider ownership for the assumptions or the results.

Some recommendations from Basel committee "Principles for sound stress testing practices and supervision" on the use of stress testing and governance are as follows:

(a) Make stress testing an integral part of the overall governance, including ICAAP, and feeding it into strategic decision-making process on business, capital and liquidity decisions.
(b) Make the board ultimately responsible for the use of stress testing results with senior management leading the implementation.
(c) Take views from across the organisation and over a broad range of perspectives and techniques. Ensure that opinions of all relevant experts are taken into account, in particular for firm-wide stress tests, organise periodic dialogue among these experts, challenge their opinions, check them for consistency and decide on the design and the implementation of the stress tests, ensuring an adequate balance between usefulness, accuracy, comprehensiveness and tractability.
(d) Have written policies and procedures and appropriate documentation.
(e) Ensure a suitably robust infrastructure with flexible capability.
(f) Regularly maintain, update and validate the framework.

11.3.4   *Methodologies*

There is a wide range of methodologies available. The choice of which to apply depends on a bank's decisions on stress testing scope and risk coverage which are likely to cover:

(a)   business units;
(b)   geography;
(c)   products, customer segments;
(d)   material risks; and
(e)   risk factors.

The range of methodologies provides management with a selection of tools to apply depending on the objectives of the stress test. The type of stress test methodology to apply can cover:

(a)   sensitivity analysis;
(b)   scenarios;
(c)   group-wide vs. business/portfolio specific; and
(d)   reverse-stress tests.

Sensitivity analysis can be undertaken more easily than scenario analysis and allow quick analysis of potential vulnerability to risk factor changes (e.g. what happens to market risk if interest rates move by 100bp?). Sensitivity analyses can be used, for example, to:

(a)   test the impact on financial positions by movement of one particular risk factor, such as PD/LGD/EAD or an underlying driver (such as employment);
(b)   create a starting point and building block for more sophisticated scenario analysis;
(c)   identify key risk drivers as an important step to build relevant scenarios; and
(d)   provide useful risk monitoring stress tests to be included in regular management information.

Scenario analyses are more sophisticated and test the impact of simultaneous movements in a number of risk factors (for example, what happens in an economic downturn if interest rates, unemployment and house prices all move at the same time?). Scenarios are more time-consuming and complex to design and execute but are likely to be more valuable and insightful than sensitivity analysis.

There are two principal ways of developing scenarios:

(a) **Macroeconomic stress test**: develop scenarios around macroeconomic changes and the impacts on all material risks throughout an economic cycle including impact on overall capital adequacy. It is based on forward-looking, plausible, and relevant economic downturn scenarios that broadly impact a bank's business.
(b) **Event-driven stress test**: develop scenarios around a particular systemic risk event (such as a global liquidity crisis) or to test portfolio-specific vulnerabilities (such as the impact of commodity price shocks on a trading port-folio).

Macroeconomic and event scenarios can be developed using historic data or hypothetical data (e.g. a re-run of the Russian debt crisis or a future hypothetical event such as accelerated climate change). Experience has shown that most banks do both and create future scenarios using a combination of historic and hypothetical data. A key challenge is to ensure that the assump-tions in macroeconomic stress tests are internally consistent and coherent.

Firms also use a combination of top-down and bottom-up scenarios. A top-down approach is usually used for a group-wide macro-economic scenario or for a board-requested scenario such as, "what happens if a specific sovereign-default occurs?" It is increasingly common for regulators to specify the parameters for a group-wide stress test to enable them to rank order banks under a given stress scenario.

Alternatively, as part of the development of scenarios, business units and risk experts will often be asked to provide their bottom-up input to the design of scenarios or the selection of events to be stress tested.

Basel Committee recommendations

Methodology and scenario selection:

- Deliver a complete and comprehensive firm-wide risk picture.
- Create forward looking scenarios which take into account interaction and feedback effects.
- Expert judgment should have appropriate weight realising the limitation of statistical models.
- Use severe events that are particularly damaging to the bank or test the viability of the bank (reverse stress tests).
- Take account of simultaneous pressures in funding and asset markets.

Other areas of focus:

- Risk mitigation techniques should be challenged.
- Securitised products, pipeline exposures, high leverage counterparties, off balance-sheet.
- Exposures and reputational risk should be examined thoroughly.

Reverse-stress tests do not require pre-defined scenario analysis. Instead the question to answer is "what event or combination of events could cause the bank to fail?" The purpose of reverse-stress testing is to force management to think about unusual risks that could be terminally damaging to the business. The process opens the debate to a much wider range of potential events than would normally be considered. This allows management then to identify, for example, emerging risks, new dependencies between risks and, where appropriate, actions to take or data to be monitored.

Having developed a scenario, one then needs to link it to risks and risk factors to establish the qualitative and quantitative impacts of the stress. The analytical approach is shown in Figure 11.2 below:

The process of developing the quantification of impacts runs something like this:

(a) Identify macroeconomic drivers that are most relevant to the bank's risk profile and risk inventory.
(b) Formulate business drivers (e.g. product type, levels of delinquency, LTV, FICO scores).
(c) Identify risk area-specific inputs (e.g. interest rates, market events, liquidity conditions).
(d) Establish business and financial performance metrics linked to risk drivers (e.g. margins, asset growth rates).
(e) Develop financial projections for the income statement and balance sheet which are consistent with these assumptions.

Figure 11.3 shows how the qualitative impacts of two different scenarios (in this case "stag-flation" and a "long freeze followed by depression") are evaluated by considering their impact. In this illustration, the risk types are taken from a bank's risk inventory to illustrate qualitative assessment of potential risks under stressed scenarios.

Figure 11.2 Stress testing framework schematic view

One of the major benefits of scenario stress tests is that management can consider the dependencies and interactions between risk types to create a holistic picture of the risk profile of the institution. This requires management to examine the correlations between risk types under stressed circumstances. One of the important lessons from the crisis is that these can behave quite differently under extreme stress than they have historically. For example, it was accepted wisdom in 2006 that house prices in different regions of the US were not correlated. Similarly, market, credit and liquidity risk in relation to trading portfolios were not considered

Figure 11.3 Illustrative qualitative potential stressed scenarios

Risk type	Bearish Case – Stag-Deflation	Long Freeze and Depression
Collateral Concentration Risk	Both residential and commercial real estate loans may experience high defaults – a level that matches highest historical level. Default correlations increase among all types of collateral.	The real estate defaults drag the bank into negative earnings for an extended period and strain the bank's capital position. Default correlations increase among all types of collateral. Significant shrink in balance sheet ensues.
Counterparty Credit Risk	The bank experience defaults from one or more major counterparties.	Widespread counterparty defaults and wrong-way risk.
Liquidity Risk	The bank may experience a 1-level downgrade in its credit rating and funding costs increase. It still maintains stable core deposits.	May experience a 2-level downgrade and extreme difficulty in wholesale funding. Funding from BTMU or the government is needed.
Mis-Match Risk	Rate curve shifts down more on the long end shrinking the NIM.	The bank may have to offer high deposit rates to attract deposits and may not be able to raise lending rates due to decreased loan demand.
Legal Risk	Increase in foreclosures and collection activities cause increases in lawsuits and legal expenses.	Further increase in litigation costs due to downsizing, reduced staff level and disrupted operational controls.
Pension Funding Risk	Pension fund investment reduction in value creates gaps in pensions funding. Additional contributions need to be made to pension funds, which reduce earnings.	Besides declines in the value of pension funds, the bank is unable to make contributions due to earnings difficulty. The bank may reduce or remove pension benefits.
Equity Risk	Bank equity holding value experiences 30% drop.	Bank equity holding value experiences 50% drop.

together – however, they proved to be closely intertwined with devastating effects.

As part of the methodology, risk managers should check whether quantitative approaches work as originally intended. For instance, they should check that relationships continue to move as expected when extreme inputs are used. If the analysis shows that a certain model is unsound then management should consider rethinking the model or modifying appropriate parameters. Finally, assessment of sensitivity and scenario analysis should be conducted frequently, since models' relationships among variables may change over time.

Using a level of granularity appropriate to the purpose of the stress test, stress testing programmes should examine the effect of shocks across all relevant risk factors, taking into account interrelations among them.

11.3.5   *Process, infrastructure and capabilities*

Figure 11.4 below summarises the steps in a typical stress testing process to assess the impact of macroeconomic stress on capital.

Figure 11.4 Illustrative comprehensive stress test implementation steps

Issue	Implementation steps
Inventory risk exposures subject to stress testing	• Assess current stress testing approaches and define approach for each asset exposure. • Formulate risk drivers such as product type, levels of delinquency, LTV, FICO, that will be used by category. • Establish business and financial performance metrics linked to risk drivers (e.g. margins, asset growth rates).
Model linkage of economic scenarios to loss factors	• Review proposed scenarios and compare with current stress testing being conducted. • Based on proposed economic downturn scenarios and macro variables identify risk factors impacted. • Apply methodologies and tools developed by business lines or risk areas to model impact of scenarios in loss projections. • Aggregate loss estimates by portfolio.
Project net income, balance sheet and loss events under base and severe scenarios	• Link macroeconomic drivers to business drivers that directly affect various line items on the bank's income statement and balance sheet. • Explore the effects of economic scenarios on the bank's portfolio by modeling loss estimates over the next two years. • Aggregate income and balance sheet financial projections including impact of loss events. • Assess the impact on overall capital adequacy and quality ratios. • Evaluate funding / liquidity management strategies.
Evaluate capital management actions and strategies	• Ensure the bank has robust capital management plans to meet its capital requirements through both scenarios • Provide basis for contingent capital planning when capital adequacy is in question under the adverse scenario. • Evaluate capital management actions such as capital raising, preservation or repayment strategies. • Establish ongoing stress test process and evaluate disclosure requirements.

Processes and infrastructure are key areas for development, particularly as the need to execute stress tests on a firm-wide basis faster to meet supervisory expectations grows. However, there is a trade-off between speed and robustness. In most banks the wide-ranging consultations needed to develop robust scenarios, to interpret results and agree mitigating actions should not be rushed.

The capabilities of stress testing teams at the centre and the business units need to be appropriately broad and deep. Often resourcing will require part-time input from many people around the business usually coordinated by the risk team. For stress testing to be effective, procedures and processes need to be well-documented, communicated and understood.

In many firms additional investment is needed in the systems infrastructure used to support stress testing. In large institutions the data that needs to be processed iteratively requires significant computing power.

11.3.6 Outputs and actions

Stress tests are complex to develop and require careful interpretation. It is very important to recognise that stress tests are built on a wide range of assumptions and judgments, which means that the output can only ever be an indicative estimate of the likely outcome of a combination of circumstances that, in reality, is never likely to be seen in practice.

This also means that the results of stress tests need to be communicated very carefully. Most banks, for example, are quite happy to describe their stress testing processes to external stakeholders but are wary of disclosing quantitative results. In addition, it is often necessary to make appropriate investments in the education of the board and senior management.

Communication of results needs to be tailored for the audiences that receive it – different content and emphasis is likely to be required for: board, risk committee, risk and finance, business units and external stakeholders (regulators, investors and ratings agencies).

Effective stress tests will provide:

(a) impact of scenarios estimated in terms of multiple key performance indicators, including profitability, Common Equity Tier 1 ratio, Risk-Weighted Assets and loss rates;
(b) commentary on stress testing detailing context and limitation; and
(c) results sufficient to agree credible mitigating management actions and develop contingency plans.

In terms of actions, results can be used to:

(a) Assist in setting risk appetite/tolerance and setting and refining exposure limits.
(b) Assist with pricing, strategy and capital/liquidity assessment (ICAAP / ILAA).
(c) Develop flexible contingency and recovery plans.
(d) Allow review and challenge of processes, scenarios and strategy.

Contingency planning and mitigating actions are priority areas of supervisory focus. This will require advance planning on how banks will respond to periods of stress and corresponding actions summarised in Figure 11.5 below (PwC, *Comprehensive stress tests*, (March 2009)).

Figure 11.5 shows a variety of escalating mitigating actions which could be deployed depending on the severity and the speed of the stress event. The speed of stress is important because some management actions will take longer than others to have an impact. For example, a dividend cut will have a much more rapid impact than tightening credit approvals and increasing pricing.

If management actions are required and approved, then a separate set of assumptions will need to be run through the model to assess the net impact.

Figure 11.5 Capital adequacy and contingency planning illustration

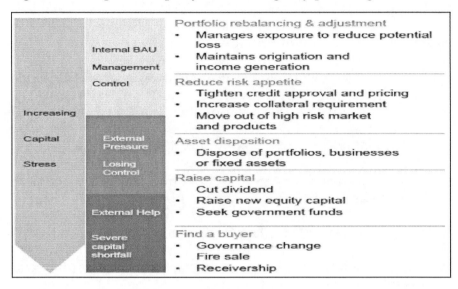

By comparing different stress test scenarios, senior management can formulate a capital position throughout the stressed planning cycle as shown in Figure 11.6 below. This chart also illustrates the trigger levels for certain types of action (see the right hand panel).

Figure 11.6 Capital position planning

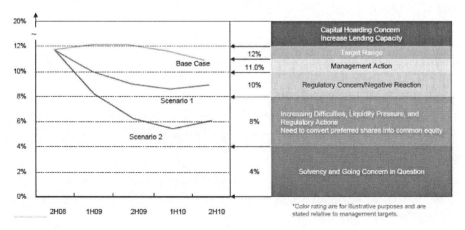

11.4 Conclusion

Stress testing is a critical component in creating strengthened risk management frameworks in firms. It provides valuable insights to the board, risk committee, management and supervisors alike. The specific areas that require attention vary from institution to institution, but clarity is needed over objectives, governance, methodology, processes, infrastructure and the capabilities required to deliver stress tests.

In assessing where a given bank's approach compares with leading industry practice, a useful checklist of the top ten characteristics of leading practice in stress testing is as follows:

1. Governance is critical
2. Wide range of functions are involved
3. Relevant and valuable to the business
4. Uses a family of approaches
5. Combines group-wide coherent and business/portfolio specific stresses
6. Considers a range of severities and likelihoods
7. Integrated in business processes such as planning
8. Flexible and responsive
9. Focus on actions not analysis
10. Management judgement remains paramount

The real value of stress tests comes from the insights that they generate and the actions that are taken as a result – not the numbers themselves.

Chapter 12

Disclosures and Pillar 3

Christophe Cadiou

12.1 Introduction

The original objective of Pillar 3 was to improve market discipline through effective public disclosure to complement the Pillar 1 and Pillar 2 requirements[1]. At the time, the Pillar 3 requirements represented a significant increase in the amount of information made publicly available by banks around capital structure, capital adequacy, risk management and risk measurement.

Prior to the recent global financial crisis, other extensive risk disclosure frameworks were developed by accounting standard-setters and securities regulators. In particular, the International Accounting Standards Board ("IASB"), the US Financial Accounting Standards Board ("FASB") and the US Securities and Exchange Commission ("SEC") considerably expanded the scope of risk disclosures in financial statements and securities filings. Events arising from the global financial crisis, however, highlighted significant shortcomings in both the existing risk disclosure framework and its application. These shortcomings were especially acute in the areas of securitisation, fair value of financial instruments, loan commitments and liquidity risk.

The subsequent further requirements from the Basel Committee on additional disclosure are extensive and concentrated in three areas of recently issued guidance:

---

[1] See Chapter 1 – Introduction, for an overview of the three Pillars of Basel II

(a) enhancements to Pillar 3 market risk and securitisation disclosures in July 2009[2];
(b) additional disclosures accompanying the Basel III framework published in December 2010[3]; and
(c) a consultative document on remuneration disclosures published in December 2010[4].

Bank regulators, securities regulators and accounting standard-setters have, to some extent, tried to coordinate their efforts around risk disclosures and develop a more coherent framework. As a result, a number of disclosures found in Pillar 3 resemble those required by the IASB, FASB or SEC. However, there are some notable differences between these frameworks, which make the production of risk disclosures a complex process for any bank, and their interpretation by market participants difficult. These differences are further discussed later in this chapter in Section 12.3, along with implementation challenges and solutions we have observed from working with banks globally on their risk disclosures.

In terms of the extent to which banks have complied with the risk disclosure requirements, a report published in June 2010 by the Committee of European Banking Supervisors ("CEBS")[5] notes that the quality of 2009 disclosures by European banks has improved in comparison with those of 2008, but that some areas for improvement still exist. Notably, the delay between the publication of the annual report and the release of Pillar 3 disclosures is cited as an impediment to the effectiveness of market discipline. In terms of the content of Pillar 3 disclosures, the CEBS report also highlights potential improvements and suggested best practices (see Appendix III for details). We have separately conducted an analysis of certain selected banks' risk disclosures over the past three

---

[2] Banking Committee on Banking Supervision, *Enhancements to the Basel II framework*
[3] Banking Committee on Banking Supervision, *Basel III: a global regulatory framework for more resilient banks and banking systems*
[4] Banking Committee on Banking Supervision, *Consultative document, Pillar 3 disclosure requirements for remuneration*
[5] CEBS, *Follow-up of banks' transparency in their 2009 Pillar 3 reports*

years, which highlights certain trends regarding the volume, location, timeliness and overall relevance of these disclosures. Appendix I provides more details on this analysis.

Disclosure is not the same as transparency. Most banks have primarily taken a compliance approach to risk disclosures, rather than attempting to use transparency as a competitive advantage. To some extent, the July 2009 revisions to the guiding principles of Pillar 3 ("Guiding Principles") will force the issue, by requiring banks to make disclosures that reflect their real risk profile as markets evolve, in addition to the minimum requirements contained in the prescribed Pillar 3 tables. This new requirement, which has become effective as of 31 December 2010, stresses the banks' responsibility towards market participants to provide complete and transparent information about their risk profile. This should push banks to be more strategic in their approach to risk disclosures and make the disclosures focus on the desired outcome of increasing transparency. The response from market participants to disclosures and their demand for particular types of information will, of course, be key factors in shaping developments

In particular, investors and regulators will want to know on a timely basis the progress the banks are making towards compliance with Basel III and its impact on their profitability and business model. To that end, clear communication with market participants beyond the strict requirements of Pillar 3 and other mandated disclosure frameworks will be critical in the period leading up to the Basel III effective date.

The following Sections provide a more detailed discussion on key aspects of risk disclosures:

(a) an overview of the current and future risk disclosure requirements contained in Pillar 3 and other rules (Section 12.2);
(b) practical implementation challenges facing banks in the production of risk disclosures (Section 12.3); and
(c) lessons learned from the financial crisis, and best practices that emerged from a review of recently published risk disclosures (Section 12.4).

12.2   Overview of risk disclosure requirements

12.2.1   Basel II Pillar 3 overarching requirements and considerations

Figure 12.1 Basel II Pillar 3 requirements

Aspect	Basel II requirement
Disclosure policy	Pillar 3 presents a set of qualitative and quantitative disclosure requirements that should allow market participants to meaningfully assess a bank's capital structure, capital adequacy, and risk. Each bank should document its approach to Pillar 3 disclosures and the process to produce these disclosures in a board-approved disclosure policy document. This policy document should address, at a minimum: • The frequency of disclosures; • Their location; and • The verification process. The disclosure policy is generally not part of the required public disclosures made under Pillar 3, although it is mandated or recommended in some countries (e.g., UK, Belgium and Denmark). At a minimum, bank regulators in most countries will ask to review the disclosure policy.
Frequency	Pillar 3 disclosures are required on a semi-annual basis, except for certain general qualitative disclosures that can be disclosed annually. Information on capital adequacy (Tier 1 capital, total capital, and total required capital) is required quarterly. Due to the volatility of certain risk types, banks are expected to disclose quarterly information that is likely to become obsolete. More generally, banks are expected to publish material information as and when it arises. For those banks subject to the Capital Requirements Directive in Europe, the frequency for all information is annual in principle, but institutions are expected to determine whether more frequent disclosure of certain information types is appropriate, and certain member states (e.g. Spain, Italy) have imposed more frequent disclosures.

Materiality, proprietary and confidential information	Basel II recognised that there is certain information that banks should not be expected to disclose. When the disclosure of certain information would undermine an entity's competitive position, and reduce the value of an entity's investment in certain products, then such information is regarded as proprietary. Similarly, certain information regarding counterparties will be confidential. The BCBS has stated that where the disclosure of proprietary or confidential information could jeopardise the position of the bank, the information does not need to be disclosed provided the bank makes general disclosures on the subject matter and explains why the information has been omitted. All material information should be disclosed. Information is considered material if its omission or misstatement could change or influence the assessment or decision of a user relying on that information for the purpose of making economic decisions, e.g. an investor deciding to buy/sell shares in a financial institution. Banks have discretion not to disclose information that it determines to be immaterial in light of these principles.
Location of disclosures	Given the volume of disclosures required under Pillar 3, it would not necessarily be practicable for banks to include all these disclosures as part of its financial statements or the accompanying securities filings. As a result, the location of Pillar 3 disclosures is not mandated. Some bank regulators have opted to mandate a specific location; in most cases, the bank's website; others have decided not to prescribe the location of the Pillar 3 disclosures. When a choice is given by the regulators, some banks have opted to put the disclosures only on their website, while others are including the Pillar 3 disclosures in their annual reports as part of an integrated risk management report. There are pros and cons to both approaches, but presenting an integrated risk management report is likely to provide greater transparency to market participants.
Verification process	Basel II states that the disclosures under Pillar 3 must be validated. This does not, however, constitute a requirement that they be subject to an external audit. Some regulators (e.g., Germany) have imposed a review of the Pillar 3 disclosures by external auditors; others have required a formal review by internal audit, while a large majority of countries have not imposed any specific requirements.

	Absent any requirement from their national regulators, banks have to determine how the validation process should work. In these circumstances, often an internal audit review of the disclosures is performed to meet the validation requirements.
Enforcement	The key mechanism by which supervisors can ensure appropriate disclosure is through the inclusion of disclosure requirements as a condition for the approval of the more advanced approaches for Pillar 1. Banks seeking to calculate regulatory capital through a more risk-sensitive capital allocation approach have to disclose information about that approach in order to qualify for the more advanced methodology. Failure to disclose this information is regarded as a failure to comply with the minimum standards.

12.2.2 Detailed Basel II Pillar 3 requirements

The Pillar 3 disclosures contained in Basel II consist of a set of qualitative and quantitative disclosures organised around four broad areas, which are further described below.

Changes introduced by Basel III are discussed in Section 12.2.3.

The precise format of the disclosures is not specified in the Accord, and only a limited number of countries have opted to prescribe specific templates. Accordingly, banks can typically choose the order and format in which they make the disclosures, as long as the requirements are met.

The Pillar 3 disclosures, especially as they relate to credit risk, are very comprehensive and require banks to provide a large amount of data. Due to the fact that some banks present their Pillar 3 disclosures as part of an integrated set of risk management disclosures, it is difficult to isolate precisely for those banks the amount of data specific to Pillar 3 requirements. For those banks that present a separate all-inclusive set of Pillar 3 disclosures, the number of pages and the volume of information depend on various factors, including, for instance, the approach taken by the bank on credit risk (IRB approaches require a number of additional disclosures compared to the Standardised Approach).

Some examples illustrating the volume of information presented for each component of Pillar 3 disclosures are listed in Figure 12.2 below for three selected IRB banks. In all three cases, more than 50 per cent of the disclosures relate to credit risk, which is by far the most extensive requirement contained in Pillar 3.

Figure 12.2 Examples of Pillar 3 disclosure volumes

	Number of pages		
Topic	Nordea	NAB	BBVA
Scope of application	1	5	11
Capital structure and adequacy	12	9	5
Credit risk, including securitisations	24	39	35
Market risk	7	3	3
Operational risk	3	2	1
Equities	1	2	3
Interest rate in the banking book	2	2	2
Other	15*	9**	8***
Total	**64**	**74**	**68**

* Disclosures on liquidity risk, derivatives, and appendices with a general description of the regulatory environment
** Disclosures on liquidity risk, and introduction on risk management objectives and organisation
*** Disclosures on risk management objectives and organisation, including internal controls

12.2.2.1   *Scope of application of the capital adequacy framework*

Pillar 3 requirements apply at the highest consolidated level of the banking group to which the Accord applies. Disclosures pertaining to individual banking entities within the group are not required, except for Total and Tier 1 capital that should be disclosed for significant risk subsidiaries where appropriate. Specific information on corporate governance and consolidation is required, such as the identity of the top corporate entity in the group and how its subsidiaries are consolidated for accounting and regulatory purposes. Specific information is also required on the capital treatment of insurance subsidiaries, and other subsidiaries not included in consolidation.

12.2.2.2 *Capital structure*

Capital structure refers to the capital that is issued by institutions and the form that it takes. Institutions are required to disclose the break-down of the components of Tier 1 capital and also total Tier 2 and Tier 3 capital (abolished by Basel III). Qualitative information on the terms and conditions of all capital instruments will also be required, particularly with respect to hybrid capital instruments.

12.2.2.3 *Capital adequacy*

The disclosure requirements for capital adequacy consist of a break-down of the capital requirements for each risk type, and for each approach adopted. For credit risk, banks are also required to disclose capital requirements for separate portfolios. In addition, banks are asked to provide a summary discussion of the bank's approach to assessing its current and future capital adequacy.

12.2.2.4 *Assessment and management of key risks*

Pillar 3 requires information on the key risks that constitute the basis of Pillar 1 minimum capital requirements: credit risk, market risk, equity risk in the banking book and operational risk. In addition, disclosures pertaining to securitisations are also required; these were further expanded following the recent financial crisis (see below on Pillar 3 disclosure changes introduced by Basel III). The only Pillar 2 type risk which is included in Pillar 3 quantitative disclosures is interest rate risk in the banking book. There are no quantitative disclosures required for strategic risk, reputational risk, concentration risk or liquidity risk, but a general qualitative disclosure requirement applies to each of these risks.

12.2.2.4.1 *Credit risk*

The disclosures for credit risk are the most burdensome of the disclosures in Pillar 3, reflecting the increased discretion afforded to banks in calculating the capital charge for this risk. Banks must disclose not only their aggregate position, but also the position held under the different approaches to credit risk that they use. In disclosing specific information on the approaches applied, the aim is to enable the market to differentiate across banks and across jurisdictions. This way, the process of market discipline is enhanced and competitive concerns regarding the consistent application of Basel II by different supervisory authorities, and associated level playing field considerations, should be to some extent mitigated.

Credit risk disclosures are further broken-down into four categories:

1) General credit risk disclosures across all banks

Banks must provide a discussion of their risk management policies, information on key definitions such as "past-due" and "impaired" and a discussion of the loan loss allowance methodology. Credit risk exposures should be disclosed, disaggregated by geographic distribution, industry or counterparty type and residual contractual maturity, together with an analysis of impaired loans similarly categorised. Banks must disclose for each portfolio the approach taken for credit risk under Pillar 1, and where banks have partly adopted either of the IRB approaches, they must disclose their plans for full migration, along with the actual exposures covered by each approach.

2) Disclosures for portfolios subject to the Standardised Approach and supervisory risk weights in the Internal Ratings Based ("IRB") approaches

For those banks under the Standardised Approach, the names of the rating agencies used should be provided. A description of the process used to transfer public issue ratings into comparable assets in the banking book is required, and also the alignment of the agency's scale to the bank's risk buckets, where this is different from the supervisory standard. Exposure amounts after risk mitigation for all risk buckets should also be disclosed (both Standardised and Foundation IRB).

3) Disclosures for portfolios subject to IRB approaches

As noted previously, a key element of the Accord is the increased sensitivity of the capital adequacy framework for credit risk, where banks use internally generated parameters to arrive at minimum capital requirements. The disclosure requirements for portfolios subject to IRB approaches correspondingly reflect this information set and are designed to allow market participants to assess the quality of individual institutions' portfolios.

Information is thus required on the risk assessment process, such as total exposures for each portfolio category across a sufficient number of probability of default ("PD") grades to allow for a meaningful differentiation of risk, and exposure weighted-average risk-weight for each of those buckets. Historical information on the default outcomes on these portfolios is also required, to allow for a comparison of estimates with actual experience and give an indication of the reliability of the bank's estimation process. Disclosures are also required over a longer time horizon (ideally 10 years) that should capture longer-term trends in asset quality and the bank's ability to assess credit risk accurately through different phases of the credit cycle.

Given the complexity of the input variables into the IRB approaches, the scale of these disclosures is potentially very significant. For example, a bank with five broad credit portfolios, each with ten PD grades, will require 50 information points in a given year, multiplied by up to 10 years of required historical information. For banks that have adopted the Advanced IRB approach, this is further compounded by the addition of loss given default ("LGD") and exposure at default ("EAD") parameters.

These quantitative disclosures are supplemented by a qualitative discussion that provides background information on the assumptions underlying the application of the IRB framework, the use of the IRB estimates as part of the bank's risk and performance management, and the means for validating the results of the IRB models.

4) Credit risk mitigation

Where credit risk mitigation techniques have been employed to reduce minimum capital requirements, disclosures are required on the exposures covered by these techniques (e.g. collateral, guarantees and credit derivatives), along with general qualitative information on the types of credit risk mitigation employed and related policies and procedures.

12.2.2.4.2 *Securitisation*

It is generally considered that, prior to the issuance of Pillar 3 requirements, the level of required disclosures on banks' securitisation activities was insufficient to assess the full impact of securitisation transactions on the originating banks' risk profiles[6]. As a result, extensive disclosures were added under Pillar 3, to provide a description of the role played by the bank in the securitisation process, the bank's objectives with respect to these activities, and the accounting policies for securitisations. Quantitative disclosures include a break-down of total outstanding exposures securitised by the bank and subject to the securitisation framework, together with the amount of impaired assets and losses recognized by the bank on these exposures. A break-down of securitisation exposures retained or purchased by exposure type is also required, with the associated capital charges or deductions.

Quantitative disclosures were also to allow market participants to gain an understanding of the bank's exposure to securitisations, the approach followed for capital treatment, and the related capital charge.

The recent financial crisis highlighted further deficiencies in the information provided by banks on securitisations in Pillar 3. As a result, the BCBS decided to revise Pillar 3 disclosures in six areas, which are further discussed below (see "Pillar 3 disclosure changes introduced by Basel III" below).

---

[6] Standard and Poors, *Securitisation plays increasing role in European bank analysis* (2004)

12.2.2.4.3   Market risk

For market risk under the standardised approach, banks must disclose the capital requirements for interest rate risk, equity position risk, foreign exchange risk, and commodity risk. For those banks using the internal models approach ("IMA") for trading portfolios, a description of the statistical approach employed must be provided for each portfolio, with information on the scope of acceptance by the regulator. Various value-at-risk ("VaR") measures are also required with a comparison of these measures against actual outcomes (including an analysis of "outliers" in back-testing results).

12.2.2.4.4   Operational risk

In keeping with the explicit introduction of operational risk into the capital adequacy framework, disclosures on operational risk have also been introduced in Pillar 3. In addition to the general qualitative discussion of the approach followed by the institution for operational risk, institutions that choose to use the Advanced Measurement Approach ("AMA") under Basel II must describe their modelling approach, including any relevant internal and external factors considered. A description of the use of insurance, where relevant, is also required.

12.2.2.4.5   Equity risk in the banking book

Banks must disclose the holding objectives for banking book equity positions and the valuation process used to account for these positions. Quantitative disclosures are also required to help market participants understand the value recorded for these investments in the financial statements, along with indicators as to the liquidity of these positions (i.e. publicly traded or privately held). After Pillar 3 was issued, the accounting standard-setters (IASB and FASB) further expanded disclosures around fair value measurement of financial assets, which are bringing further insights into the valuation risk in these equity portfolios.

12.2.2.4.6 *Interest rate risk in the banking book*

Banks must report the nature of interest rate risk arising in the banking book, including any behavioural assumptions pertaining to prepayments. The sensitivity of earnings to upward and downward movements in interest rates is also required.

12.2.3 **Recent Pillar 3 disclosure changes**

The profound changes in the capital framework introduced since 2009, culminating with the final Basel III rules published in December 2010, have been accompanied by an equally daunting increase in disclosure requirements, concentrated in three areas of recently issued guidance:

(a) enhancements to Pillar 3 market risk and securitisation disclosures in July 2009[7];
(b) additional disclosures accompanying the Basel III framework published in December 2010[8]; and
(c) a consultative document on remuneration disclosures published in December 2010[9].

12.2.3.1 *Market risk and securitisation disclosures*

The financial crisis highlighted inadequacies in banks' risk disclosures, in particular with respect to market risk, securitisation exposures and sponsored off-balance sheet vehicles. In July 2009, the Basel Committee issued new Pillar 3 disclosures requirements, which banks have to comply with by December 2011. These new requirements include the following:

(a) Market risk

(i) Additional qualitative disclosures in relation to methodologies used and the risks measured through

---

[7] Banking Committee on Banking Supervision, *Enhancements to the Basel II framework*
[8] Banking Committee on Banking Supervision, *Basel III: a global regulatory framework for more resilient banks and banking systems*
[9] Banking Committee on Banking Supervision, *Consultative document, Pillar 3 disclosure requirements for remuneration*

the use of internal models for the incremental capital risk charge and the comprehensive risk capital charge.

(ii) Additional quantitative disclosures for trading portfolios under the IMA: stressed VaR values and high/mean/low incremental and comprehensive capital risk charge.

(b) Securitisations

(i) Securitisation exposures in the trading book – quantitative disclosures similar to those already required for the banking book.

(ii) Sponsorship of off-balance sheet vehicles – disclosure of the nature of risks other than credit risk inherent in the securitised assets, list of all SPEs for which the bank acts as a sponsor, and disclosure of quantitative tables on off-balance sheet exposures separately from on-balance sheet exposures.

(iii) Internal Assessment Approach ("IAA") and other Asset-Backed Commercial Paper ("ABCP") liquidity facilities – qualitative discussion of the IAA process, and breakdown of quantitative disclosures on the banking and trading books.

(iv) Resecuritisation exposures – description of processes in place to monitor changes in the credit and market risk of securitisation exposures and mitigate those risks, separate disclosure of the valuation of securitisation and resecuritisation exposures, and aggregate amount of resecuritisation exposures retained or purchased.

(v) Valuation of securitisation exposures – disclosure of key assumptions for valuing positions.

(vi) Pipeline and warehousing risk with regard to securitisation exposures – detailed disclosure of accounting policies for securitisation activities, and quantitative break-down by exposure type of outstanding exposures intended to be securitised.

(vii) Other – explanation of changes in the quantitative data from period to period.

12.2.3.2   *Basel III disclosures*

In conjunction with the final Basel III rules published in December 2010, a new set of disclosure requirements was introduced to improve further transparency of regulatory capital and improve market discipline. More detailed Pillar 3 requirements will be issued by the Basel Committee in 2011 and are expected to be implemented by the end of 2011 (except as noted below for the leverage ratio), but the main features of these new requirements are already known:

(a) reconciliation of all regulatory capital elements back to the balance sheet in the audited financial statements;
(b) disclosure of all regulatory adjustments;
(c) disclosure of the items not fully deducted from Common Equity Tier 1 in accordance with paras 87 and 88 of Basel III (e.g. investments in common shares of unconsolidated financial institutions, mortgage servicing rights ("MSRs"), deferred tax assets ("DTAs") arising from temporary differences);
(d) description of all limits and minima, identifying the positive and negative elements of capital to which the limits and minima apply;
(e) description of the main features of capital instruments issued, with the full terms and conditions of those instruments being made available on the banks' websites;
(f) disclosure of the specific components of capital that are benefiting from transitional provisions;
(g) disclosure of countercyclical buffer requirements with at least the same frequency as the minimum capital requirements; and
(h) disclosure of the leverage ratio and its components (starting January 1, 2015).

Beyond these mandatory disclosures, it will be important for banks to have a clear communication strategy around the impact of and transition to the new capital framework. Most large financial institutions started communicating on the capital impact of expected Basel III rules in their analysts' packs and press releases for the third quarter of 2010. Disclosures generally included an assessment of the quantitative impact of the new rules on RWA and capital ratios, with varying levels of detailed explanations to support these estimates. These institutions also generally disclosed their planned actions to mitigate the capital impact of Basel III, and their plans (or lack thereof) with respect to raising additional capital. Interestingly, only few institutions at this stage provide comprehensive comments on the impact of the introduction of the leverage and liquidity requirements contained in Basel III.

12.2.3.3   *Remuneration disclosures*

The Basel Committee published in December 2010 a consultative document on remuneration disclosures, the comments on which are due by end of February 2011. These proposed Pillar 3 disclosures follow the supplemental Pillar 2 guidance that was issued in July 2009, and stressed the need for sound compensation practices within banks:

> "Firms must disclose clear, comprehensive and timely information about their compensation practices to facilitate constructive engagement by all stakeholders, including in particular shareholders."

The consultative paper proposes that banks disclose qualitative and quantitative information about their remuneration practices and policies on an annual basis at a minimum. Some banks may be exempt from this requirement based on materiality principles similar to those that apply to other Pillar 3 disclosures.

The proposed requirements are extensive, and include the following:

(a) Qualitative
   (i)   information regarding the bodies that oversee remuneration;
   (ii) discussion of the design and structure of the remuneration process;

    (iii) measures used to take into account current and future risks in the remuneration process;

    (iv) description of the way the bank links the organisation's and the individual's performance to levels of remuneration;

    (v) ways by which the bank adjusts compensation to take into account long-term performance; and

    (vi) description of the various forms of variable remuneration used by the bank.

(b) Quantitative

    (i) number of meetings held by the main body overseeing remuneration;

    (ii) adjustments to compensation based on current and future risks;

    (iii) statistical data on various elements of compensation (fixed and variable compensation, guaranteed bonuses, sign-on awards, severance payments etc.);

    (iv) total amount and breakdown of deferred compensation; and

    (v) breakdown of total value of remuneration awards and expenses.

Whilst most banks are subject to some form of existing disclosure requirements around compensation imposed by securities regulators, the Basel Committee proposal is by far the most extensive remuneration disclosure framework. As banks start thinking through the implementation of these new requirements, it will be important that they consider the consistency of messages on remuneration made in annual reports and other public disclosures.

More importantly, the new Pillar 3 disclosure requirements on remuneration reinforce measures that have been taken recently around the world by regulators on this topic (e.g. clawback provisions on incentive compensation in the Dodd-Frank Act in the United States) that are causing banks to take a hard look at their compensation strategies across the board (see Chapter 14 – Reward).

12.2.4 Financial statement risk disclosures

Unlike Pillar 3 disclosures, risk disclosures in financial statements are not governed by a single set of standards; rather, they are defined by the IASB for IFRS reporters, the FASB for US GAAP reporters or other national standard setters for entities reporting under another set of accounting standards. For banks listed in the US, the SEC has also established a set of risk disclosures to be made in filings outside of the financial statements. There are some differences in the requirements of standard-setters or securities regulators, hence the following description starts with the most prevalent framework, IFRS 7, *Financial instruments: disclosures*, as it applies or will apply in the near future to most banks around the world. SEC rules are also referred to in the discussion below, as they apply to all US-registered banks.

IFRS 7 was issued by the IASB in 2005 in response to the lack of a comprehensive framework for disclosures of risks associated with financial instruments. It was adopted by most banks for the year ended 31 December 2007.

The main requirements contained in IFRS 7 are summarised in Figure 12.3 below.

Figure 12.3 IFRS 7 requirements summary

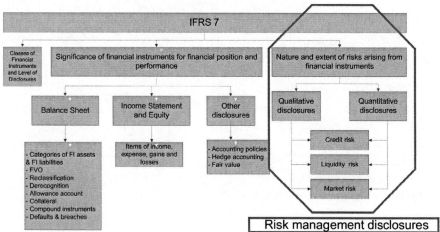

302

Risk management disclosures contained in IFRS 7 focus on risks arising from financial instruments (which includes loans), and require qualitative and quantitative disclosures. The aim of the standard was for reporting entities to present risks "through the eyes of management", and accordingly it is largely principles based rather than prescriptive. Its requirements – as it relates to risk management – are articulated around two main components:

(a) Qualitative disclosures require an entity to provide an analysis of the types of risks that it is exposed to, including its objectives, policies and processes for managing those risks, and how the risks are measured.

(b) Quantitative disclosures are required for each risk arising from financial instruments, and should be based upon data provided internally to key management personnel. This is where the standard takes a principles-based approach, as it requires entities to report the information they use internally to help them identify and manage their financial instruments exposures. That being said, IFRS 7 defines some minimum disclosures around the following risks:

(i) credit risk – information about the maximum exposure to credit risk at the end of the reporting period, collateral and other security held against this risk, and information about the quality of financial assets subject to credit risk, with a special emphasis on past due or impaired assets;

(ii) liquidity risk – maturity analysis of financial liabilities by remaining contractual maturity, and a description of how the entity manages the related liquidity risk; and

(iii) market risk – a sensitivity analysis for each type of market risk that the entity is exposed to; this can show how profit or loss would be affected by changes in relevant risk variables, or leverage from sensitivity analyses prepared for other purposes, such as value-at-risk for instance.

In addition to the above requirements, *IAS 1, Presentation of financial statements*, requires certain disclosures that enables users of its financial statements to evaluate the entity's objectives, policies and processes for managing capital:

(a) qualitative information: objectives, policies and processes for managing capital;
(b) summary quantitative data: what the entity regards as capital; and
(c) compliance with any externally imposed capital requirements.

Entities subject to SEC reporting are subject to certain regulatory disclosures guidance in the form of Financial Reporting Releases ("FRR"), SEC speeches and other SEC communications, such as the "Dear CFO letters". Generally, this guidance is more prescriptive than the principles-based approach under IFRS 7, and targets specific areas where the SEC considers additional disclosure is needed to provide users of the financial statements or filings with a transparent view of the risks faced by the entity.

For instance, in reaction to the residential mortgage crisis in the US, the SEC sent a "Dear CFO letter" in August 2009 asking banks to enhance their disclosures on higher-risk loans (e.g. ARM products, junior line mortgages, high loan-to-value ratio mortgages, etc.) to allow users of the financial statements to understand better the nature of the risks associated with the banks' loan portfolios; this letter includes a number of very specific disclosure requirements. Earlier, in December 2007, the SEC had requested additional disclosures on exposures to commercial paper conduits, SIVs, CDOs, or other similar entities, including categories and ratings, write-downs or downgrades and weighted-average life of related assets.

As is the case for Pillar 3, the financial crisis has highlighted the shortcomings of the financial statement disclosure framework. This is especially true in relation to securitisations and other structured finance activities, for which there is no comprehensive disclosure framework under IFRS. In its April 2008 report, the Financial Stability Forum ("FSF", now the Financial Stability Board) recommended that the IASB improve the accounting and disclosure standards for

off-balance sheet vehicles. In response, the IASB has accelerated its consolidation project, which focuses on tightening up
the definition of control and improving disclosure requirements for entities that remain off-balance sheet. The final standard is expected to come out during 2011. The IASB also
issued in October 2010 amendments to IFRS 7 as part of its
comprehensive review of off-balance sheet activities. The
amendments will allow users of financial statements to
improve their understanding of transfer transactions of financial assets (for example, securitisations), including understanding the possible effects of any risks that may remain with
the entity that transferred the assets.

The FASB has been equally active in setting new disclosure rules:

(a) In December 2008, the FASB issued the FASB Staff Position
    paper ("FSP")[10] requiring additional disclosures by public
    companies about their involvement with variable interest
    entities ("VIEs") and their continuing involvement with
    transferred assets, to improve transparency about these
    transactions.
(b) In June 2009, the FASB completed a project that amended and
    improved US GAAP to address reporting issues in standards
    for consolidation of variable interest entities (and related
    disclosures) highlighted by the recent financial crisis[11].
(c) In July 2010, the FASB published new disclosure require-
    ments for finance receivables and the allowance for credit
    losses to address concerns about the sufficiency of credit
    risk disclosures[12].

Further, new disclosure requirements are likely to follow from
the full scale revision of financial instrument accounting
currently being developed jointly by the IASB and the FASB.

The combination of all these new financial and regulatory
disclosure requirements will present a significant challenge for

---

[10] FSP No.140–4 and FIN 46(R)-8, *Disclosures by Public Entities (Enterprises) about Transfers of Financial Assets and Interests in Variable Interest Entities*
[11] FASB Statement No.167, *Amendments to FASB Interpretation No.46(R)*
[12] Accounting Standards Update ("ASU") 2010–20, *Disclosures about the Credit Quality of Financing Receivables and the Allowance for Credit Losses*

banks. Even though there are some common trends between the new Pillar 3 disclosures and the improvements to financial reporting disclosures introduced by standard-setters (e.g. focus on securitisation activities), the objectives of each regulator are different, and hence so are the requirements. Section 12.3 below further elaborates on the practical challenges of producing Pillar 3 disclosures and the need for a well coordinated approach between financial and regulatory reporting. With the amount of change on the horizon on both sides, this is more than ever an absolute necessity.

The scope and content of financial statements risk disclosures is different from the requirements in Pillar 3, as illustrated in Figure 12.4 below. However, there are significant areas of overlap, and it is therefore important to understand the financial statement risk disclosure requirements in order to manage the synergies and interactions between the financial statements and regulatory disclosures. Section 12.3 below further discusses the implementation challenges associated with managing the overlaps between Pillar 3 and financial statements disclosures.

Figure 12.4 IFRS 7 – Pillar 3 content comparison

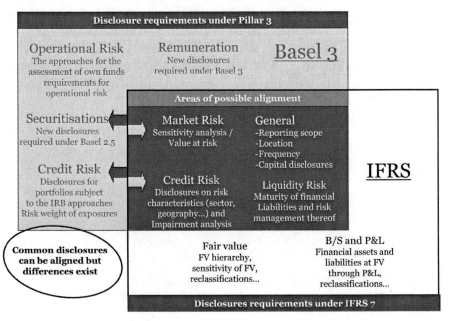

12.3 Practical implementation challenges

Pillar 3 disclosures have been in effect in many jurisdictions since 2007-2008, including inter alia the EU, Japan and Australia. However, many banks around the world are yet to publish their first set of Pillar 3 disclosures. This is true, among others, of the US banks and banks in less developed countries where the implementation of Basel II is still in progress. The following summarises some of the implementation challenges and lessons learned from the preparation of Pillar 3 disclosures by financial institutions that have already reported.

12.3.1 *Establishing a strong governance structure early is critical*

The first challenge that banks face when preparing for Pillar 3 disclosures is to establish a governance structure around the disclosure process. Due to the multiplicity of organisational units involved, one of the key risks associated with the production of Pillar 3 disclosures is the lack of ownership of the entire process, and/or the late involvement of key stakeholders. Typically, successful Pillar 3 implementation projects are sponsored by the CFO and will involve the following organisational units at the very beginning to make sure that all inputs are considered and that responsibilities are defined:

(a) Board of directors (must approve the formal disclosure policy)
(b) Finance and accounting (generally has primary responsibility for financial and regulatory reporting)
(c) Risk management (usually owns most of the data that needs to be disclosed under Pillar 3)
(d) IT (responsible for the design and maintenance of the data collection solution)
(e) Internal/external auditors (may be required by local regulators to validate Pillar 3 disclosures)
(f) External communication and investor relations (define the overall communication strategy around risk management and ensure consistency of messages between all aspects of market reporting)

This last area is going to be especially critical as banks communicate on the impact of the adoption of new Basel III rules to market participants. Recently, there has been an increased focus on capital and risk management in press releases, investor packs and communication to rating agencies in response to the profound impact of the new capital rules on the ability of banks to maintain existing profitability levels.

12.3.2 Pillar 3 presents significant data and process challenges

Once the governance structure is established, the next challenge is around data availability and quality. A methodical approach to sourcing the data for Pillar 3 disclosures is therefore key to ensure that data gaps are identified and resolved early in the process. A good practical tip is to start by making a comprehensive inventory of all required disclosures, and work back towards data availability. In most cases, roughly 80 per cent of Pillar 3 disclosures should be available from data accumulated for Pillar 1, but not all banks consider Pillar 3 requirements when preparing for Pillar 1. As a result, data is often not organised to be easily retrieved and presented for public disclosure. Additionally, certain disclosures come from non-Pillar 1 sources such as accounting records for items like period-end and average gross credit exposures, changes in the allowance for loan losses, or the amount of impaired loans.

Data quality is also a major issue to address. Historically, the risk data that was used in the risk management process was for internal use only, and may not have been of "auditable" quality – after all, data that is 90 or 95 per cent accurate may be fine for risk measurement and management information purposes. Risk data also often includes judgments and assumptions in a way that financial data does not. Pillar 3 raises the bar considerably in respect of the quality of risk data.

Pillar 3 requires that appropriate internal controls over the production of disclosures be in place. Additionally, banks must have an independent validation process. In some cases, regulators (for example, in Germany) have imposed that the validation be performed by external auditors (even for disclosures made outside of the financial statements). In other cases, the validation process can be internal, as is the case for model validation under Pillar 1. In jurisdictions that do not require an external validation of Pillar 3 disclosures, the independent validation process is often placed under the responsibility of internal audit. For banks subject to SEC requirements, Sarbanes-Oxley requirements apply to disclosures made in the financial statements but not to Pillar 3 (unless these are included in the financial statements). Some banks are, however, voluntarily adapting their Sarbanes Oxley processes to cover Pillar 3.

12.3.3   *Banks should establish a coherent disclosure and communications strategy around risk management*

This is probably the most strategic issue that banks need to consider, as Pillar 3 considerably increases the volume of public disclosure around risk management, in particular in the areas of credit and operational risk.

Figure 12.4 above highlights the considerable overlaps between the requirements of IFRS 7 and Pillar 3. In particular, regarding credit and market risk, most of the qualitative disclosures can and should be aligned. Similarly, there are a considerable number of quantitative disclosures that overlap, such as the analyses of credit risk exposures and value-at-risk measures. There are differences, however, between the two disclosure frameworks. For instance, Pillar 3 does not cover liquidity risk and IFRS 7 does not address operational risk or remuneration.

In order to present a coherent and credible picture to the financial markets, there needs to be consistency between the IFRS risk and capital management disclosures and the corresponding Pillar 3 presentation. Banks need to review the consistency of Pillar 3 and other risk management disclosures with other public disclosures such as segment reporting and remuneration as well as any strategy presentations they may have made. This is key in meeting regulators', analysts' and investors' demands for more consistent and insightful information about risk and capital management. While a more transparent approach to disclosure will probably open banks to greater scrutiny, it will benefit those who can demonstrate strengths in these areas.

Experience suggests that risk management and accounting teams do not always communicate effectively. In the context of Pillar 3 and IFRS 7 reporting, failure to do so potentially increases the cost of complying with these requirements and, worse still, the information presented could be inconsistent. Whatever the source, disclosures should be consistent and reflect the views of management. It is therefore essential that a uniform message be delivered from the CEO's presentation to investors all the way to the accounting footnotes, along with Pillar 3 disclosures. This requires a concerted effort between all parties involved, which further emphasises the need for a strong governance structure as highlighted above. It also requires senior management to know and understand these disclosures.

A further issue that needs to be considered by the investor relations department is that the level of sophistication that the bank has been able to achieve under the Basel framework is immediately visible. Under Basel 1988, all banks were subject to the same set of rules, and the only numbers of interest to outside parties were the capital adequacy ratios themselves. Basel II allows a range of different approaches to be adopted, with increasing levels of sophistication. Under the Pillar 3 disclosures, it is apparent which approach an individual bank has adopted.

Also, Pillar 3 significantly increases the level of detail that is disclosed and that can be used by investors, analysts and rating agencies to compare and analyse each bank's risks. For instance, Pillar 3 disclosures provide an opportunity for analysts and others to benchmark key data (e.g. Probability of Defaults or PDs) for each bank against its peer group.

The workload associated with explaining the increasingly complex Basel numbers should also not be underestimated, especially in the early years, where banks may also be operating a mixture of approaches during a transition period to the more advanced levels. Investors and analysts are often inclined to draw conclusions based on an incomplete understanding of the numbers. For instance, for banks adopting the IRB approaches there is a strong element of pro-cyclicality in the RWA calculation – in an economic downturn, one would expect customers to be downgraded and/or probabilities of default to increase. This would result in an increase in RWA relative to the balance sheet volumes, which could lead to incorrect conclusions being made about the quality of the loan portfolio. In addition, banks need to be clear in their communication of the changes from Basel II to Basel III.

Furthermore, the Tier 1 capital and capital adequacy ratio goals, that under the current rules have been comparable between banks, will now depend on the Basel II approach that has been chosen. For instance, how do you compare a Tier 1 ratio goal of 7 per cent for a Standardised Approach bank versus an IRB bank?

12.3.4 Suggested steps towards implementation

Examples of successful Pillar 3 implementations have included the following elements:

(a) Establish a project structure under a strong senior sponsor (e.g. CFO) and appropriate governance
(b) Make key Pillar 3 policy decisions, such as the location of disclosures, their frequency, the scope, definition of materiality, etc. (As part of this, determine which information should be communicated in the audited annual report and which should be communicated through other mediums such as the website)
(c) Determine internal and external requirements for disclosure additional to Basel II and Basel III
(d) Define a communication strategy and involve the investor relations team at an early stage
(e) Analyse the overlaps between Pillar 3 disclosures and other publicly-disclosed risk and capital management information (e.g. IFRS 7)
(f) Design disclosure templates that meet the requirements of Pillar 3 and other public disclosure requirements
(g) Source required data from existing systems; identify data gaps and put in place remediation actions

(h) Define an IT architecture for data gathering, aggregation and reporting
(i) Establish a control and validation process around Pillar 3 and risk disclosure production
(j) Produce and validate disclosures

12.4   Conclusion – the future of risk management disclosures

The global financial crisis has highlighted that transparency is a key element in building and maintaining market confidence. With the recent market conditions, new emphasis has been placed by investors and regulators on the risks to which banks are exposed. In this environment, the quality of a bank's risk disclosures is under tremendous scrutiny. However, in the early days of the financial crisis, public disclosures by financial institutions did not always make clear the type and magnitude of risks associated with their on and off-balance sheet exposures. This was highlighted in the Financial Stability Forum's April 2008 report:

> "A lack of adequate and consistent disclosure of risk exposures and valuations continues to have a corrosive effect on confidence".

Regulators and accounting standard-setters have responded to the crisis by enhancing the disclosure requirements, and banks have demonstrated an increased focus on the volume, quality and timeliness of information provided to the markets. However, much remains to be done to achieve better quality, comparability and transparency of disclosures to meet the basic demands of market participants. Risk disclosures are still all too often prepared with a strict compliance view, located in different media (annual report, separate Pillar 3 report, investor packs etc.), and fail therefore to give a comprehensive and clear view of the bank's risk profile.

Looking forward, as banks start making progress towards the implementation of new disclosure requirements contained in the recent Basel Committee enhancements, several challenges will arise. The more obvious will be to produce the extensive new disclosures around market risk, securitisations and remuneration, and to ensure that these are consistent with the other disclosures produced for accounting or securities regulation purposes.

Beyond this, the most fundamental impact of the changes to Pillar 3 will be the shift from a rules-based approach where disclosures requirements are driven by regulators, to a principles-based approach where banks are primarily responsible for ensuring that they provide market participants with relevant and timely information. This is likely to push banks to re-think the way they approach disclosures, from a mere compliance exercise, to more of a competitive differentiator that enables them to engage effectively with their audiences on risk and capital issues.

Last but not least, the changes introduced by Basel III will challenge banks to provide clear communication around the new concepts embedded in the Basel framework, such as leverage and liquidity, (as well as the impact of the new rules on the banks' business models and profitability). As banks start to explain the impact of Basel III in their communications with investors, some significant differences are already noticeable in the quality and transparency of disclosures made. Some banks have already provided detailed quantitative analyses and mitigation plans, while others have yet to communicate clearly their plans to face the new requirements and to preserve profitability.

Chapter 13

Taxation

Matthew Barling and Anne-Marie Stomeo

13.1 Introduction

In addition to other areas of regulatory reform, the fallout from the financial crisis has led to significant global developments in policy for taxing banks. It would appear that the consensus view amongst supra-national bodies such as the International Monetary Fund ("IMF") and the Organisation for Economic Cooperation and Development ("OECD") is that whilst tax was not a cause of the financial crisis, it was a relevant factor and therefore a tax-related response is required. This view appears in part to be driven by the perceived bias in tax regimes towards leverage and in particular towards the use of debt funding rather than equity funding. This arises from the general principle that interest payments are usually tax deductible while dividends are not. This has led these organisations to consider the role of tax in influencing the behaviour of financial institutions, a concept which has also been picked up by a number of national governments, particularly within the EU.

The first part of this Chapter focuses on the changes in policy for taxing banks. The second part of the Chapter explores the tax implications of other aspects of the wider regulatory reform and in particular those relating to the Basel III capital and liquidity requirements.

13.2 The taxation environment for banks

The post-crisis political environment has accelerated and contributed significantly to a change in policy for taxing banks.

Both national governments and supra-national bodies, most significantly the OECD and IMF, have undertaken studies into the role of tax in contributing to the crisis and how a tax-related response to the crisis may be developed. There have been some arguments to suggest that this has been driven by the political view that tax policy can and should be used to support financial stability.

Broadly, two policy strands have emerged. The first strand, "tackling tax avoidance", focuses on protecting revenues from tax planning undertaken or facilitated by banks. The focus of the second strand is that the financial sector should make a "fair and substantial contribution" towards paying for government interventions, repairing the banking system, reducing risks from the banking system and funding resolution.

13.2.1 Tackling tax avoidance

The focus on protecting revenues from tax planning undertaken or facilitated by banks is a continuation of the work commenced by the OECD Forum on Tax Administration's "Study into the Role of Tax Intermediaries" (2008) which set out its conclusions on the role that tax intermediaries (including banks and financial institutions) play in the operation of tax systems (specifically in relation to unacceptable tax minimisation arrangements). This work has since led to additional studies including the report "Building Transparent Tax Compliance by Banks", OECD 2009, and more recently "A Framework for a Voluntary Code of Conduct for Banks and Revenue Bodies", OECD 2010. The underlying theme can also be linked to the concept of the banking sector making a "fair and substantial contribution" in the wider sense in that the intention is to encourage banks not to engage in tax planning which could result in them paying less than their "fair share" of tax.

13.2.1.1 Banking code of practice

This work has resulted in the publication of a framework for a voluntary Code of Practice for banks and revenue authorities, published by the OECD in 2010, which is in the same vein as the voluntary Code of Practice for banks which has been introduced and implemented in the UK. Although the success of such codes in combating tax planning undertaken or facilitated by banks may be uncertain, there is a clear indication of the direction in which tax policy in this respect is moving.

The OECD published Code of Practice seeks to focus on four main areas:

(1) meeting compliance obligations;
(2) ensuring there are appropriate governance and controls over tax within the organisation;
(3) an expectation that banks will not engage in "aggressive" tax planning; and
(4) enhancing relationships with fiscal authorities.

In the UK, the Code was first proposed in the summer of 2009, and full-scale adoption of the Code was encouraged by HM Treasury in late 2010. This was accompanied by a press release from HM Treasury naming the top tier banks who had signed up to the Code.

The experience in the UK has shown that while many banks already have a tax strategy and associated governance in place, and seek to have transparent relationships with tax authorities, the key challenge in implementing such a code is in defining what "aggressive" tax planning means in practice. In practical terms, the introduction of the Code in the UK has served to increase communication between the banks affected and their contacts at Her Majesty's Revenue and Customs ("HMRC"). In many cases, banks have entered into further agreements with HMRC setting out their interpretation of the Code and how that impacts their business and relationship with HMRC.

13.2.1.2 *Bank losses*

Many banks suffered very significant losses during the financial crisis. The scale of these losses has been a cause for concern for governments and tax authorities both in terms of the potential impact on future tax revenues from the banking sector and through the creation of wider tax risks (e.g. uncertainty, potential for tax avoidance, etc).

In 2010, the OECD released a report entitled, "Addressing Tax Risks Involving Bank Losses", the focus of which was very much on real rather than artificial losses and understanding the risks to business (e.g. in terms of gaining certainty) as well as the risks to governments (e.g. in terms of tax revenue and tax compliance) posed by the losses.

The report in particular recognises the potential for banks to engage in tax planning, on a national and international basis, and recommends that fiscal authorities communicate on a regular basis to combat the risk of loss of tax revenue as a result of such planning. In line with the recommendations of the OECD Code of Practice for Banks, the report recommends that banks continue to work with fiscal authorities in an open and transparent manner.

13.2.2 *A fair and substantial contribution from the financial sector*

The principal concept emerging from the work following the financial crisis is that the financial sector should make a "fair and substantial contribution" to society in recognition of the support it has enjoyed during the crisis (and will continue to enjoy going forward) and the risks that it poses to financial stability. At the request of the G20, the IMF made a number of recommendations in its interim report, "A Fair and Substantial Contribution by the Financial Sector" (April 2010), as to how these goals could be achieved. The principal recommendations, which are discussed in more detail below, included a suggestion for two new global taxes to be introduced: a "Financial Stability Contribution" ("FSC") (or "bank levy") and a "Financial Activities Tax" ("FAT"). It is notable that the IMF report recommended that these apply to all financial institutions and not just banks.

The G20 meeting in Toronto in June 2010 considered the IMF report, but was unable to reach a consensus on a globally-standardised approach to the proposed new taxes. Countries which had not needed to inject public money into the banking sector during the financial crisis (such as Canada, Australia and Japan) were clear in their position that they would not seek to increase financial sector taxation, which they considered unwarranted. Some commentators also questioned whether taxation was an appropriate tool for seeking to achieve financial stability and whether this should instead be dealt with entirely through regulatory measures.

13.2.2.1 Bank levies

Since April 2010, a number of jurisdictions have adopted or proposed to adopt various forms of bank levy on a unilateral basis. As early as January 2010, President Obama announced his intention to introduce a Financial Crisis Responsibility Fee in the US. The UK, France and Germany announced their intentions to introduce a levy in a joint statement in June 2010. Bank Levies are an entirely new form of tax applicable to the banking sector and therefore one of the most significant developments in taxation in recent years. While the European territories that have announced their intentions around the introduction of a levy have produced detailed legislation intended to apply from 1 January 2011 onwards, the US has, to date, not followed President Obama's announcement with any detailed legislation, although some aspects of the design of the fee have been included in the Presidential Budget in February 2011.

The IMF proposed the FSC as a mechanism to cover the net fiscal costs of direct public support to financial institutions as well as a mechanism for reducing excessive risk taking. Bank levies are intended to be a balance sheet-based form of taxation, in many cases using liabilities (excluding equity capital and some other "insured" liabilities such as certain types of retail deposits) as a measure of riskiness and systemic importance. The IMF report discussed a number of uses for the funds ultimately raised from such levies, either as general taxation receipts, or to form a resolution fund which could be drawn down to support the industry at times of stress in the system.

Experience to date has demonstrated a wide range of interpretations of the initial IMF proposals by national governments This has resulted in the scope of the levy, design of the levy base, use of the levy proceeds, and even the administration of the levy itself, differing across all the countries which have introduced a levy. The IMF proposed a universal levy approach, which focused on discouraging risky funding and achieving a close linkage with a resolution mechanism (possibly in the form of a resolution fund), to provide support to the financial sector in the event of a future financial crisis. In reality a fragmented approach has been adopted across numerous jurisdictions. It appears that differing overall objectives in individual states, as well as the need to raise revenue to shore up budget deficits, have shaped the development of national levy policies.

The IMF proposed that a FSC should apply to all financial institutions initially, with some further calibration of the scope of the levy at a later date to penalise the most risky behaviour. However, with one or two minor exceptions, the vast majority of territories that have introduced levies have focused on the banking sector.

Many of the mainland European territories which have announced levies, (e.g. France, Germany, Portugal and Austria) have limited the scope of the levy to the global activities of those banks that are regulated by their home authority, providing an exemption for other EEA banks that operate through branches in their territory under EU "passporting" rights. This contrasts with the UK position, where all institutions operating in the UK (and, in the case of UK-headquartered groups, their global business operations) including those operating through branches in the UK are within the scope of the levy (if their chargeable liabilities for levy purposes exceed £20bn).

The design of each levy differs greatly, with Germany in particular focusing not only on taxing the liabilities of the bank, but also the notional value of derivatives outstanding. The UK levy permits the netting of certain derivative assets and liabilities in arriving at the balance sheet position, while other levies do not.

Divergence of levy design across territories creates a challenge for revenue authorities and banks in managing exposures to double taxation on a global basis. The associated cost of levies (in some cases estimated to be up to 5 per cent – 10 per cent of profits) will no doubt become a key consideration in deciding where and how banks will do business.

Banks will also need to understand the impact of particular activities or product lines on the overall bank levy liability and consider how this should be taken into account for the purposes of measuring the profitability of each business line. For example, there may be low margin businesses which are balance sheet intensive that have a more significant impact on levy liability than other activities such as retail deposit-taking or advisory business. The approach to allocation of levy costs across the various business lines is therefore likely to be crucial in enabling management to assess the contribution of each business to the bank's overall profitability. Similarly, the allocation of levy costs may also be used as a mechanism to encourage behavioural change within the business line itself (e.g. by encouraging business lines to change the scale and/or term of their funding arrangements).

13.2.2.2   *Financial Activities Tax*

The IMF also proposed the introduction of a FAT, intended to be a tax on excess returns, with profits and/or remuneration forming the tax base. The focus on "excess" returns underlines the objective of a FAT as a mechanism for influencing behaviour and reducing risk taking incentives.

Certain territories have already had a form of FAT in place, either as a central part of the tax regime, such as the Danish tax on financial services remuneration, or as a one-off tax responding to public backlash towards "excessive" banking bonuses, such as the UK Bank Payroll Tax introduced in 2009 and the Irish super tax on bonuses introduced in 2011. The EU Commission confirmed in a report in October 2010 that it would undertake a further study to review the potential benefits of introducing a FAT with the goal of targeting excessive risk taking and introducing greater stability into the European banking markets. The Commission's findings are expected to be published in spring / summer 2011.

13.2.2.3   *Financial Transactions Tax or Tobin Tax*

A global Financial Transactions Tax ("FTT"), known commonly as a Tobin Tax (named after the economist James Tobin who first proposed a similar tax in 1972) is also being considered as a potential tax-related response to the financial crisis. The October 2010 EU Commission report referred to above also discusses the merits of introducing an FTT. However, the Commission recognises that such a tax would need to be introduced on a globally coordinated basis in order to meet their objectives around revenue raising and efficiencies. The EU has confirmed its intention to hold further discussions on the potential introduction of an FTT at the G20 level. As at the time of writing the European Parliament had voted to support the introduction of an FTT at an EU level, although it is unclear how it would be adopted or supported in individual member states.

13.3   Tax implications of Basel III proposals

In addition to the changes in the wider tax landscape for banks, the Basel III proposals will also have significant tax-related implications for banking groups. More specifically, the Basel III proposals in relation to the treatment of deferred tax assets for regulatory capital purposes, the changes in the definition of Tier 1 and Tier 2 capital instruments and the new liquidity regime will require particular attention from a tax perspective. Each of these areas is discussed in turn below.

13.3.1   *Definition of capital – deferred tax assets*

Under the Basel III standards, deferred tax assets ("DTAs") receive limited recognition as Common Equity Tier 1 ("CET1") capital. This is a significant difference from the Basel II standard under which net DTAs, as a component of retained earnings or reserves and therefore common equity, received full recognition as CET1 capital. The new standards put an increased importance on the calculation and categorisation of DTAs. See also Chapter 3 – Definition of capital.

The required regulatory adjustments to CET1 capital contain two distinct provisions in relation to DTAs. In order to apply these provisions, it is first necessary to categorise DTAs between those relating to tax losses, and those relating to timing differences.

DTAs that "rely on future profitability of the bank" (para.69 "Basel III: a global regulatory framework for more resilient banks and banking systems" December 2010) are to be deducted in full, net of deferred tax liabilities where the relevant assets and liabilities relate to taxes levied by the same taxation authority and offsetting is permitted by the relevant taxation authority (these netting provisions are in line with the netting requirements under International Financial Reporting Standards)

Their deduction from CET1 capital is proposed to be phased in from 2014 to 2018 (i.e. 20 per cent in 2014, 40 per cent in 2015, 60 per cent in 2016, 80 per cent in 2017, and a 100 per cent deduction in 2018 and subsequent years).

DTAs that arise from "other timing differences" (para.87 "Basel III: a global regulatory framework for more resilient banks and banking systems" December 2010) can count towards CET1 capital, subject to certain restrictions:

(a) recognition is capped at 10 per cent of the bank's common equity (after the application of regulatory adjustments);

(b) as at 1 January 2013, a further deduction must be taken for the amount by which the aggregate of significant investments in the common shares of unconsolidated financial institutions, mortgage servicing rights, and DTAs from other timing differences exceeds 15 per cent of the common equity component of Tier 1 (as calculated prior to the deduction of these items but after the application of all other regulatory adjustments applied in the calculation of CET1); and

(c) as at 1 January 2018, the basis of the 15 per cent limit is amended such that the amount of the three items that remains recognised after the application of all regulatory adjustments must not exceed 15 per cent of the CET1 capital, calculated after all regulatory adjustments.

13.3.1.1   DTAs in context

Not only does this change in treatment represent a significant shift from the current Basel II standard in relation to DTAs, it comes at a time when, for many institutions, DTAs arising from losses are a more significant proportion of their capital base than in previous years. The losses and write-downs incurred by banks during the financial crisis have given rise to very significant tax losses and the majority of tax regimes allow for these carried forward losses to reduce future taxable profits. The related DTAs can therefore represent a significant asset for an institution.

The justification for the DTAs deductions under Basel III appears to be that the DTAs relating to losses are not considered to be loss absorbing in a "gone concern" scenario. The Committee discusses "gone concern" as, "including situations when the public sector steps in to recapitalise a bank that would otherwise have failed".

The distinction drawn between losses and timing differences and the differing treatment that arises brings with it a number of challenges, not least defining how to distinguish between the two. The definition of "timing differences" remains to be determined. We would expect definitions to be in line with accounting requirements (e.g. all temporary differences under IFRS), however, some jurisdictions may distinguish between different types of timing difference.

13.3.1.2   Challenges and response

The creation and reversal of timing differences over time will need to be more closely measured and modelled than the current position in order for banks to understand and plan their capital needs going forward. This in itself presents a challenge around the collection of accurate data from across the group, anticipating the potential impact of future changes in tax law (and significantly accounting standards) and appreciating the impact of different GAAPs on deferred tax balances. While it is expected that tax departments would already have processes in place to collect and analyse this information, these changes will likely place a greater spotlight on these activities, and perhaps even open up the analysis to a new audience.

The effective management of DTA positions is expected to become a renewed focus for group tax departments and the wider institution. This activity is likely to fall into three main categories:

(a) seeking opportunities to accelerate the utilisation of existing DTA;
(b) seeking opportunities to convert losses into timing differences; and
(c) seeking opportunities to maximise the availability of netting.

The changes to the recognition of DTAs for regulatory capital purposes will not have a direct impact on the effective tax rate position of a banking group as this will be dependent upon the recognition of DTAs for accounting purposes which will not be affected by the Basel III changes. However, actions taken by an institution in order to manage its DTA position for regulatory capital purposes could also have an effective tax rate impact (e.g. if a restructuring is effected such that taxable profits arise in a higher tax jurisdiction in order to protect a DTA located in that territory).

The relevance of each opportunity will depend on the particular facts at play in each institution and the relevant tax regime.

13.3.2 Definition of capital – changes to nature of Tier 1 and Tier 2 capital instruments

The phasing out of existing qualifying capital instruments and the changes to the permitted CET1 and Tier 2 instruments give rise to particular tax considerations in relation to:

(a) the relevant tax considerations that arise in retiring existing debt, in particular existing innovative capital instruments and subordinated debt;

(b) the tax attributes and implications of new capital instruments; and

(c) the overall impact on the cash tax position of banks, not just from a corporate tax perspective but also given the introduction of new bank taxes, (e.g. bank levies, FAT, etc).

13.3.2.1 *Phasing out of non-core Tier 1 or Tier 2 capital instruments*

Non-core Tier 1 and Tier 2 instruments to be phased out during the transition phases will include a range of instruments from hybrid capital through to subordinated debt. Given the recent crisis of confidence in the banking systems, it is common for publicly-traded debt instruments issued by banks to trade at a discount (in some cases quite a significant discount) to par value. This in itself creates opportunities and risks from a tax perspective for institutions seeking to restructure their capital. In some territories, and depending on accounting standards, the redemption or repurchase of own debt at a discount can give rise to a significant gain which can deliver a significant capital benefit. This benefit can be further enhanced in circumstances where the gain on the redemption/repurchase is not subject to tax which may depend on the manner in which the transaction is undertaken. Accordingly, careful consideration of the structuring of any such redemption/repurchase transaction may deliver a significant additional capital benefit.

13.3.2.2 *Replacement non-core Tier 1 and Tier 2 capital instruments*

In recent years, many financial institutions have issued hybrid capital instruments (commonly known as "Innovative" Tier I instruments) which have been structured in order to achieve debt characterisation from a tax perspective such that any related interest/coupons payable in connection with the instruments are tax deductible. Under the new Basel III capital definitions, many of these instruments may no longer qualify as Tier 1 capital instruments and will therefore be replaced with common equity. The retirement of hybrid capital instruments of this type and their replacement with common equity may result in an increase in the effective tax rate of financial institutions as a result of a reduction in the overall level of tax deductible funding costs.

13.3.2.2.1 *Debt versus equity classification*

The new standard introduces a number of terms which mostly apply to new capital instruments being issued, which have been addressed and dealt with in other parts of this book. These requirements, such as permanence, flexibility of payments, and, importantly, loss absorption, will have a significant impact on the characterisation for tax purposes (i.e. as debt or equity) of the instruments in question. Given the nature of these requirements, it is likely to be more difficult to structure instruments which qualify as Tier 1 capital in a tax deductible form.

With regard to Tier 2 capital instruments, the EU Capital Requirements Directive II introduces some of these requirements for issuances after 1 January 2011, including, in particular, a condition requiring the write-down of the instrument on the occurrence of a trigger event where any compensation paid to the instrument holders as a result of the write-down would be settled immediately in the form of common stock. In the UK, the FSA has issued guidance on the interpretation of the Directive and therefore the requirements for UK issuers.

In particular, the Basel III consultative document issued in August 2010 notes in respect of Tier 2 issuances that, "as the proposal retains the essential debt characteristics of the relevant instrument and does not give the holder equity risk outside of a failure situation, it should be viewed as traditional convertible debt by investors, accountants, or tax authorities".

The intention here may be interpreted as being that replacement Tier 2 capital instruments should be treated as debt for accounting and tax purposes. Classification as debt would potentially secure a tax deduction for interest payable. However this will depend on the relevant accounting rules and tax laws, and their application to the particular characteristics of any given instrument.

In addition, consideration would need to be given to the tax treatment of any accounting gains that could arise on the write-down or conversion of these instruments. It is conceivable that a write-down following a trigger event could give rise to a significant taxable profit. Although such a write-down would only occur at a time of considerable financial stress, when it might be expected that considerable tax losses could be available to offset the related taxable profit arising, this may not always be the case. For example, the position could easily be complicated where the location of losses in the group structure is such that they could not be offset for tax purposes against any gains arising on the write-down of the capital instrument.

Therefore, it will be crucial that a full analysis of the impact of any new instruments be carried out, considering not just the tax attributes in a business as usual environment, but also considering the tax implications in a stress scenario.

13.3.2.2.2   Interaction with bank levies

The tax attributes of replacement debt will also be relevant in the context of bank levies. Many territories where levies have been introduced only exclude Tier 1 capital from the tax base of the levy. Therefore Tier 2 instruments could suffer an incremental levy cost, for example in Germany that would represent up to 4bps of levy charge per annum.

13.3.2.2.3   The investor's tax perspective

Clearly, issuers must ensure that any instruments they issue will appear attractive to outside investors. As regards the relevant tax attributes, again the question of the classification as either debt or equity will be crucial. This classification will then drive what, if any, withholding taxes would be levied on the coupons paid out on such instruments and may impact on the taxation treatment of any income and related gains (or losses) arising in the hands of the investor.

For some territories, the question of stamp duties or transfer taxes will also be relevant. For example in the UK, stamp duty is levied on the transfer of chargeable securities, broadly defined as UK equities or in some cases instruments that may be converted into UK equities. The question therefore arises as to whether replacement Tier 1 and Tier 2 instruments, carrying the conversion features discussed, would be considered chargeable securities for these purposes. See Chapter 16 – Stakeholder Perspectives for a wider discussion of investor perspectives.

13.3.3   *Overall impact on cash tax paid*

We noted above that the increase in capital requirements is likely to have a significant impact on bank's cash tax paid, particularly given the common use of hybrid capital instruments. These additional cash tax costs may arise in a variety of ways including:

(a) one-off cash tax impact of retiring existing capital instruments which no longer meet the revised capital standards;
(b) reduction in the quantum of tax deductible interest expense due to the restructuring of debt as equity like instruments;
(c) potential tax costs on conversion of instruments to common equity; and
(d) the overall impact of new financial sector taxation on a balance sheet basis.

Any appraisal of the costs arising from the replacement of existing funding and the raising of new funding will need to be carried out on a post-tax basis, given the potential material nature of one-off tax costs, as well as incremental tax costs and the impact of tax on the attractiveness of the instruments to investors.

Intra-group funding arrangements may also need to be restructured in order to meet local country regulatory capital requirements. There may also be opportunities for banking groups to structure their intra-group funding arrangements in order to mitigate the impact on the group's effective tax rate of the Basel III capital changes applicable to external capital instruments issued by the group.

13.3.4 Basel III liquidity requirements

The recent financial and economic crisis has had a significant impact on the traditional banking business model and has resulted in banks holding a larger proportion of longer term liquidity to support their activities. Basel III introduces a global liquidity standard for the first time; see Chapter 6 – Liquidity and Funding. These stringent regulatory liquidity requirements raise new questions about who should bear the cost of holding liquidity buffers and what the appropriate arm's length pricing should be for internal funding arrangements (including addressing the impact of moving from a shorter-term funding model to a longer-term funding model). These questions fall into two broad categories; first, how should costs associated with holding adequate liquidity be borne by the members of a group, and, secondly, whether and how sources of stable funding (e.g. customer deposits) should be rewarded.

"Negative carry" is a term used to describe situations where the cost of funding an asset exceeds the return generated by that asset. Where a liquidity buffer is held in a specific location, the return generated on high quality liquid assets in that location may be too low to cover the cost of holding the liquidity buffer (which may represent longer term and less liquid liabilities). This raises a number of questions, specifically from a transfer pricing and arm's length perspective, including how to determine where in a global organisation the assets are held (or attributed to) that require such a liquidity buffer and how the cost of such liabilities should be disseminated to the relevant locations.

In establishing a transfer pricing methodology for negative carry (associated with holding liquidity buffers) to be borne by the members of a group on an arm's length basis, a bank will need to consider several factors. For example, the choice of methodology may depend on whether the organisation is structured as a group of legal entities or as a single entity with foreign branches. In the former case, consideration should be given as to what level of liquidity buffer should be held by each separate legal entity within the group and what the cost of that liquidity buffer would be (taking into account the assets held by each entity and their stand-alone credit rating). In the latter case, branch attribution requirements could result in assets and funding costs being allocated to different parts of the bank based on a detailed understanding of which locations are carrying out the activities that give rise to such assets and liabilities.

Complex modelling may also be required to determine the liquidity buffer requirements associated with various types of assets held by branches and legal entities within a group. It will also be crucial for banks to consider whether locations receiving liquidity buffer charges will be able to deduct them for corporate tax purposes.

The second aspect deals with identifying whether a liquidity premium, or some form of reward, should be allocated or attributed to locations and/or business that have access to stable sources of funding (e.g. retail customer deposits) that may reduce the overall level of liquidity risk within a bank. This is equally challenging as it may be difficult to observe directly the actual stability (or term) of such liquidity and the benefit that a bank gains from holding such sources of stable funding.

Similar questions have been raised in the context of understanding the way in which the cost of bank levies should be allocated/attributed across a bank where there is a variety of different businesses contributing to and providing relief from (e.g. covered deposits) a levy from a group perspective.

13.4 Conclusions

The financial crisis has prompted a re-assessment of the relationship between the financial sector – banks in particular – and wider society and whether there is an appropriate sharing of risks and rewards between them. The basis on which financial institutions, and the transactions they undertake, are subject to tax is emerging as a central element in this re-assessment. The policy decisions taken over the coming months and years in this area are likely to have far-reaching and long-term consequences for the sector. Alongside this, the regulatory reforms under

Basel III will also have significant tax consequences for banks and will require a tax-related response as banks try to improve their post-tax return on equity in the Basel III world.

Overall, the changes to the general tax environment coupled with the impact of the regulatory reform are likely to mean the following:

(a) The overall tax burden on the financial sector in many countries is likely to increase as a result of new taxes and new restrictions on the scope for tax planning.

(b) Banks will need to take action to manage their deferred tax asset positions actively as the regulatory capital haircuts applied to these under Basel III comes into effect.

(c) The effective tax rate of banks and other financial institutions may increase as a result of a reduction in the level of tax-deductible funding costs by virtue of the regulatory capital reforms under Basel III.

(d) The tax position of banks and other financial institutions is likely to be subject to close scrutiny from a number of groups including governments, tax authorities and the media.

All of the above mean that taxation will continue to have a high profile for banks and other financial institutions.

Chapter 14

Reward

Tom Gosling

14.1 Introduction

Remuneration has been one of the most high profile and comment-worthy fields of regulatory intervention over the last two years. This Chapter does not address the detailed aspects of each of the many regulatory codes that have emerged. Rather, it draws out the key themes that are common across the regulatory developments and discusses some of the practical responses and approaches that need to be considered by firms. The Chapter begins by considering the forces for change in the remuneration area. It then provides commentary and practical considerations under the headings of risk adjustment, compensation design, governance and disclosure.

14.2 Forces for change

Regulators, although moving at different speeds, are increasingly aligned in their recognition of the importance of remuneration as an issue of relevance to financial stability. There has been active dialogue on the issue, in large part through the auspices of the Financial Stability Board and G20.

Governments are also becoming increasingly involved in the remuneration debate in the sector. This involvement is taking two main forms:

(1) Remuneration conditions for firms participating in various government support programmes, which may be industry wide for general access programmes, or negotiated on a

firm-by-firm basis where firm-specific support is put in place.

(2) General reviews of governance and remuneration in financial services, such as the Walker Review in the UK, and the Treasury Department review in the US.

When PwC carried out a major study over the late spring and summer of 2008 into the role of remuneration in the financial crisis, there were some who thought that the whole remuneration issue was going to go away. The biggest barrier to change was first mover disadvantage. Regulators were identified as a force for change by only 13 per cent of respondents, ranked seventh out of 10 such forces.

The widespread involvement of governments in providing capital to the industry has significantly reduced the argument of first mover disadvantage. Change is now well underway. And few today would identify regulators as anything other than a major force for change.

Economics also has its role to play. As banks have grappled with impairment losses and higher capital requirements, levels of return on equity that were once considered normal have now become aspirational. This has led firms to look harder at ensuring they are getting value for money from compensation, and capital and cost pressures have been a significant driver behind the increased use of deferral programmes and the search for innovative deferral instruments.

14.2.1 An embarrassment of riches

But as regulation has developed, the fragile international consensus on reform has started to fracture. Within the G20, very different approaches have been taken, from the rules-based approach in Europe implemented via CRD3, through the principles-led firm-by-firm approach in the US, to some territories where very little seems to have happened at all. "Not our problem" is the reaction of some territories to what they perceive as an over-zealous Anglo-Saxon reaction to an issue that they feel never really affected them. What emerges from the US in the spring of 2011 will be critical in shaping the global picture. To date, US regulators have not been keen to follow the more prescriptive lead of their European counterparts. Draft rules released around the time of writing would apply strict deferral rules only to a couple of dozen senior officers in US firms, requiring 50 per cent deferral of bonus. This compares with rules covering typically 100 to 250 executives in Europe, with a requirement to defer 60 per cent of bonus for the highest earners, with only 20 per cent of bonus available to take immediately as cash. Europe's position as an outlier therefore seems assured. Banks are likely to cry foul and bring increasing pressure on politicians to ensure a level playing field.

The lack of level playing field is dangerous to efforts for continued reform, but the common elements globally are sufficient for the industry to be convinced that change will be enduring. Common themes are finding their way into the Basel III texts on remuneration, and through the European Directives applying to all sectors of financial services (see for example emerging developments in relation to Solvency II).

The four pillars of governance, risk adjustment, deferral and disclosure have taken strong root, and it does appear that they will persist as themes in regulation globally, even if the rigour of implementation will continue to vary.

14.2.2   *What are the key issues to consider?*

There is much congruence between the principles emerging from regulators and governments globally. Financial firms themselves have also recognised the need for change. Central to the debate is for banks to demonstrate to regulators that remuneration is structured so as not to encourage excessive risk taking. The four key issues for financial services firms to consider are:

(1) **Incorporation of risk into performance measures** – how can management ensure that bonus outcomes adequately capture the risk assumed in generating profits in a given year?
(2) **Design of compensation** – how should compensation be used in order align executives with appropriate risk-taking?

(3) **Remuneration governance** – what changes are required to the governance of remuneration to ensure conflicts of interest are managed, and alignment with the firm's risk-appetite can be demonstrated?

(4) **Disclosure of remuneration** – what information is required by regulators, investors, and the public to make informed decisions about banking remuneration?

Regulators, and in some cases governments, are applying significant scrutiny and challenge to these areas and will continue to do so over the coming months and years. It is imperative for firms to devise a sufficient, yet proportionate, response to this challenge.

It is not the purpose of this Chapter to provide a record of the approaches taken by different territories to regulation. Instead the focus is on the common themes and principles that apply across all main interpretations and the implications for firms.

In all of this, it is important to recognise that the underlying aim of the regulations is to ensure that compensation plays an appropriate role in ensuring the entirety of a firm's operations are consistent with and supportive of sound risk management.

Changes to compensation are important. But there is a danger in adopting an isolated reward design solution, which generates the appearance of progress, but with little by way of underlying change. For the outcome to be successful, compensation changes must be viewed in the context of the firm's wider enterprise risk management approach. Equally, compensation must be aligned with how the firm is actually run and performance measured. Alignment is the watch-word.

The process should ideally start with a coherent articulation of risk strategy, profile and appetite. This then cascades into the supporting processes, information, infrastructure and reward systems to support strong business performance and capital management. As Chapter 17 – Implications for risk management, discusses, any future approach to compensation should be integrated within a multi-disciplinary approach. As well as addressing the technical aspects of risk management, growing attention is being paid by firms to the question of risk culture – how to define it, measure it and influence it, in which task compensation is just one lever for change.

Delivering and embedding such a model constitutes a major change programme. It often requires commitment to delivering a sustainable change in the culture of the organisation, which is difficult to achieve. This wider requirement should not delay implementation of the specifics. However, the importance of a coherent approach – and the limitation of any specific initiatives taken in isolation – should not be underestimated. As ever, no single initiative will provide the answer. Success is driven by a coherent set of mutually-reinforcing actions, undertaken within the context of strong leadership and a vision for the organisation.

But practitioners know that, especially in banking, compensation is important in its own right. Commentators observe that compensation did not cause the credit crunch – but it did add fuel to the fire. From regulators' points of view, practices in compensation are a highly visible indicator of the quality of governance throughout the firm – those that got compensation wrong were more likely to have got other things wrong as well. We can expect regulators to take a sustained interest in this area for the foreseeable future. So change must be real, not just apparent.

14.3 Incorporating risk into performance measures

14.3.1 Developing practice

Prior to the financial crisis, risk-adjusted measures had not been widely used in remuneration in the sector, although change is coming. The PwC survey of summer 2008, "Financial Services Briefing: Reward New Paradigm?" showed that only 30 per cent of firms used a risk-adjusted measure, but two-thirds of the remaining firms were evaluating or implementing such measures. The situation is already substantially different, with most firms now using risk-adjusted metrics as part of the bonus funding process, and where robust risk measures do not exist for particular risk categories, they are looking to supplement them by a mix of quantitative and qualitative risk commentary.

Banks require a structured, yet discretionary, approach to incorporation of risk into the remuneration process. The figure below describes a framework that PwC has used with a number of clients.

Figure 14.1 Incorporating risk into the remuneration process

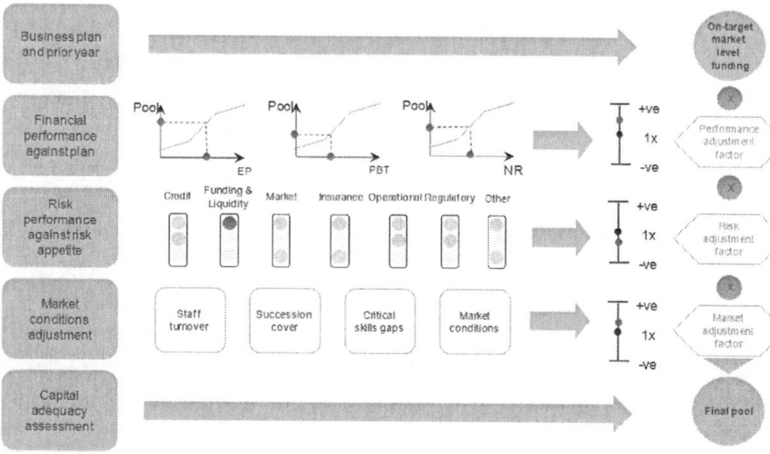

This approach provides a structured framework by which compensation can be viewed through performance, risk and other relevant lenses. All major banks have reviewed their approach to bonus funding in light of regulatory intervention. In almost all cases the result of this review has been more input from control functions into the bonus process, and in particular risk information.

The use of detailed risk-adjusted performance in determining remuneration in the banking industry has only become widespread during 2010, in response to regulatory pressure. Although the FSA Remuneration Code and Financial Stability Board Implementation Standards both referred to risk-adjustment in 2009, the regulatory focus last year was on remuneration structures and, in particular, deferral. This year, the focus of both the FSA and firms has shifted towards risk adjustment in determining the performance on which bonuses are based, and the role played by the risk function in the remuneration process.

14.3.2 Risk-adjusted measures

As risk-adjustment has gained prominence as a concept, the role of economic profit in bonus funding has also increased, encouraged by the endorsement of regulators. However, in the authors' experience, only a small minority of banks use economic profit in a formulaic way to determine bonus pool outcomes. Instead, economic profit and year-on-year developments and performance against plan have gained prominence as just one of the factors in a triangulation process for determining bonuses. Other factors include financial performance information, qualitative and quantitative risk metrics, non-financial factors and assessment of market competitiveness of pay.

Most organisations tend to make relatively few risk adjustments to economic profit for bonus purposes. Instead, organisations have tended to drive the economic profit definition off economic capital models. Many banks have used economic capital for a number of years. In these banks, performance measurement incorporates risk directly in a more sophisticated way and more broadly than using regulatory capital based on risk-weighted assets ("RWA") (which cover market, credit and operational risk only). This means that banks that use economic capital tend to apply fewer risk adjustments than those banks that use regulatory capital. For remuneration purposes, complementary risk metrics are used to provide Remuneration Committee insight into any risks not adequately covered by the economic capital model.

Those banks that use an economic capital definition of economic profit also tend to use complementary measures that reflect a regulatory capital perspective. Since the crisis, for many firms, regulatory rather than economic capital has become the key constraint (it tends to be higher than economic capital). A number of cases have consequently been seen where economic profit definitions have moved to RWA-based definitions (in addition measures such as return on risk weighted assets ("RoRWA") may be used as a key performance metric).

The inherent shortcomings in a single metric to determine bonus funding, combined with the extraordinary circumstances of the last two years, mean that the focus in banks has been on ensuring that senior management and the Remuneration Committee have a range of metrics and perspectives on risk that enable them to make an informed judgment about bonus funding – rather than a series of line item adjustments to economic profit to derive a single performance statistic to drive bonus funding.

Regulators are not just concerned about the lack of risk-adjusted measures in bonus plans for the front-office. They are also concerned about the incentives for board directors. Through our discussions with regulators it is clear that there is a view that the combinations of earnings per share ("EPS"), return on equity ("RoE"), and relative total shareholder return ("TSR"), which have been widely used at board level, have incentivised the pursuit of growth and leverage in a market upswing.

For example, relative TSR (which compares the total return achieved by holding the shares of a bank with that achieved by a peer group of companies) is a measure widely supported by institutional shareholders over the last decade. But it has arguably encouraged a "strategic herd mentality". Firms seeking to outperform in an upswing arguably have an incentive to achieve this by taking the greatest risk. This is illustrated below in a UK context, where three of the four greatest potential beneficiaries from relative TSR plans in the period 2001–2006 subsequently failed.

Figure 14.2 UK bank TSR quartiles 2001–2006

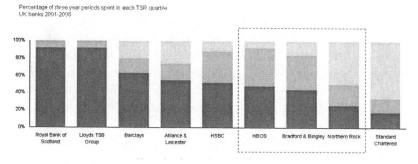

It is becoming clear that regulators will expect a more robust linkage between performance measures and risk than has historically been present in many firms.

The panacea would be a risk-adjusted form of TSR. Our research work has analysed a number of approaches to this. Classical risk measures based on volatility – Jensen's Alpha, Sharpe Ratio, Information Ratio – which adjust TSR for risk-based on volatility or beta measures are one approach that has been proposed. However, our research shows that these measures would have had little meaningful impact on historic outcomes, and it is not clear that the volatility-based risk measures are reliable or relevant to banking challenges.

One approach we have developed which we believe has merit for consideration is to look at risk-adjusted TSR by comparing TSR rank with market-measured risk rank, measured through relative credit default swap ("CDS") spreads over the performance period.

Figure 14.3 Risk-adjusting TSR using CDS spreads

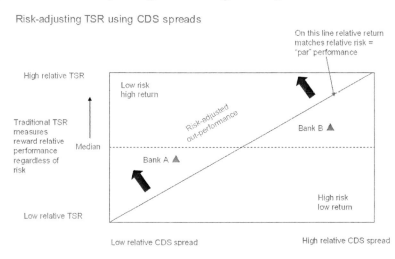

Under a conventional TSR measure, Bank A is below median and does not vest, Bank B is above median and does – however Bank A has produced relative performance in excess of its relative risk whereas Bank B has performed below its relative risk – i.e., Bank A has out-performed on a risk-adjusted basis.

Given the difficulty of separating the impact on CDS spreads from new risks taken by current management, versus development of risks inherited from previous management, this type of measure is more likely to be successful once the crisis is firmly behind us.

14.3.3   The perfect is the enemy of the good

One of the reasons why risk-adjusted measures such as economic profit ("EP") are not as widely used in compensation as might be expected (for most of this Guide we use EP as a shorthand for risk-adjusted measures based on economic capital models, of which there are many variants) is that they can be perceived as complex, given the number of adjustments sometimes recommended.

There will always be reasons why an EP measure is imperfect. There may be a particular risk it does not account for. It may be "too complex". There may be uncertainty over what the right cost of capital is or what capital should be allocated to a particular business. Different businesses have different costs of capital, and so on. The result has been the continued widespread use of simplistic revenue or asset measures.

However, firms are realising that an initial EP implementation may not be perfect, but it is an important input to decision making. And it is generally better to start simple, get something implemented, and then work with it and improve it, rather than to seek the perfect manifestation of EP first time round.

At the opposite end of the spectrum lies the view that within EP lies the answer to risk management. This view may be paraphrased thus, "if we get the right risk-adjusted EP measure, and tie it to compensation, then we'll get the right behaviour". This has been the view of some regulators. However, practitioners generally observe that rigidly formulaic constructions tend to lead to unintended consequences.

Moreover, the limitations of these models are well-documented and will not be repeated here. But in general, the assumptions on which they are based are most likely to break down in a crisis situation, which is when regulators need them to influence behaviour most. Many of these models will be enhanced using the data from the current crisis. But as ever, there is the concern that calibrating models to the past means we fix the problem we have just had, rather than the one we are about to have.

14.3.4 The importance of pragmatism

Commentators note that the most resilient firms had in place a range of defences against excessive risk taking. This often includes sophisticated risk-adjusted measures cascaded to a granular level, with regular, timely reporting to inform management understanding of the profile of risks across the firm.

Given model limitations, leading firms use stress testing to assess how the firm might respond to future unfamiliar events. Managers are challenged to identify the risks that have not been captured in the models and to consider the linkages between risk types. Qualitative and non-financial measures of risk need to be incorporated into bonus pool funding and performance management. Individual performance management needs to be robust enough to ensure that these measures bite at the right level.

Firms that have not yet done so need to start taking steps towards a more sophisticated – yet pragmatic – approach, backed up by sound judgment and appropriate discretion, in line with the practices of leading firms. So what is required? A check-list of suggested actions is given below, and discussed in more detail in subsequent paragraphs:

(a) Explicit, qualitative risk-based oversight of bonus-pool determination should be introduced, based on a dashboard of financial and non-financial risk measures.
(b) Risk-adjusted measures should be cascaded to at least divisional level, as a primary influence on pool determination

for senior management and risk takers, with focus on business areas with greatest complexity or long-tail risks.

(c) Risk-adjusted measure definitions should be reviewed to ensure key risks captured, and where they are not captured, introduce robust qualitative measures and controls.

(d) Definitions of capital used in risk-adjusted measures should be reviewed and clarified, and stress-testing incorporated to capture hard-to-quantify risks and correlation breakdowns within risk-adjusted measures used for reward.

14.3.5 Qualitative overview and non-financial measures

Explicit, qualitative risk-based oversight of bonus-pool determination should be introduced, based on a dashboard of financial and non-financial risk measures.

In the authors' experience, the easiest way to bring risk factors into remuneration decisions is to introduce an explicit consideration of risk, on a qualitative basis, into bonus pool determination. The Remuneration Committee, or for divisions an appropriate internal governing body, would consider the group risk report and other risk indicators as part of the determination of the proposed bonus pool allocations. The chief risk officer (or divisional risk officer as appropriate) should be asked for their view and to provide context to these discussions. A discretionary judgment is required as to the extent to which bonus pools are justified in the context of risks taken, compliance with the firm's risk appetite policy, and resolution of problem risk areas. Particular attention should be given to risks that are not captured in any risk-adjusted metrics used, and to the future potential profit impact of risks assumed today.

What is crucial is getting the right information in the right place at the right time. A number of firms have found it helpful to produce a formal "dashboard" framework comprising qualitative and non-financial risk factors to inform discretionary bonus discussions. Information on bonus outcomes should be correlated with qualitative views of earnings quality and adherence to risk appetite. Even where sophisticated risk-adjusted measures are used, this qualitative oversight is vital. EP should also not be blindly measured at the end of the period without reference to the risk appetite that was articulated and mandated at the period start.

A number of firms have introduced a range of non-financial measures explicitly into a balanced scorecard which determines either a proportion of the bonus or a modifier to it. The impact must be material, and must be shown to bite even for outstanding financial performers. The balanced scorecard would include aspects around:

(a) People (such as engagement or succession management).
(b) Risk (such as compliance, ex-post assessments of risk, problem resolution, process).
(c) Customers (satisfaction and retention).
(d) Key operational metrics.

The use of a balanced scorecard requires evidence to be provided during the performance management discussion, and therefore ensures that appropriate factors are taken into account in the performance management process. At the same time, this provides an audit trail to support any required process review.

14.3.6 Cascade of economic profit and its limitations

Risk-adjusted measures should be cascaded to at least divisional level, as a primary influence on pool determination for senior management and risk takers, with focus on business areas with greatest complexity or long-tail risks.

The most appropriate risk-adjusted measures depend on the nature of business undertaken. Detailed work is required in each circumstance. The most common measures are likely to be variants on EP, risk-adjusted return on capital, VaR etc. Selection and definition of risk-adjusted metrics could form a publication in its own right. To make the measurement meaningful, and to create shared accountability amongst managers, risk-adjusted measures should be cascaded to at least divisional level.

Cascading the metrics below divisional level is desirable but is not a trivial exercise. Significant work is required on cost allocation models, supporting management information infrastructure, etc. It is important not to forget that cost allocation (e.g. of shared branch costs) often requires subjective judgements to be made. In many firms, the reliability of economic capital models decays significantly below divisional level would not be of sufficient reliability to form the basis for compensation.

The more granular the allocation level, the greater will be the need for discretion, and for a rounded scorecard view of performance, in order to avoid unintended consequences and gaming. But, undoubtedly, using more granular risk and capital information as a driver of compensation should act as a disincentive for building up excessively risky positions.

Of course, the approach adopted must be proportionate. Greater focus, transparency and sophistication are required in higher-risk, more complex areas.

Risk-adjusted measure definitions should be reviewed to ensure key risks captured, and where they are not captured introduce robust qualitative measures and controls.

It is important to be explicit about which risks are captured by any given risk-adjusted measure. Based on what is seen in the industry, Figure 14.4 below shows a summary of the key risk areas and whether they are commonly taken into account or not.

Where risks are identified that are not within the measure, then these should be priority areas for a qualitative overview.

Definitions of capital used in risk-adjusted measures should be reviewed and clarified, and stress-testing incorporated to capture hard-to-quantify risks and correlation breakdowns within risk-adjusted measures used for reward.

346

Figure 14.4 Risk-adjustment by risk type

	Risk area	Comments
Commonly included	Market	• Typically based on capital asset pricing model (CAPM) and VaR • Can be supplemented by stress testing
	Credit	• Consider through-the-cycle approaches to avoid pro-cyclicality
	Credit concentration	• Reflected in sophisticated credit risk models • Stressed correlations should be considered
	Financial leverage	• Often included in historic CAPM cost of equity • Consider adjustment for strategies that increase or decrease leverage
	Operational	• Typically follows regulatory requirements which involve arbitrary calculations linked to income, which can be a poor indicator of risk assumed • Supplement with qualitative overlays
Commonly excluded	Liquidity	• Can be handled through liquidity gap analyses or by pricing for liquidity risk through the funds transfer pricing or stress testing
	Business risk	• Most commonly assessed through stress-testing
	Reputation risk	• Difficult to quantify

Primary definitions of capital include:

(a) **Invested capital**: Shareholders' equity including goodwill, being the capital on which a cost-of equity return is required to generate an economic profit for shareholders.
(b) **Regulatory capital**: The minimum capital that must be held by the firm in order to meet regulatory requirements.
(c) **Economic capital**: Allocated to businesses in proportion to the risks run, on a modelled basis, and used to set economic profit targets and determine, e.g., pricing decisions. Stress testing can be used to create capital estimates for hard-to-quantify risks.

In practice, firms have to manage to all of these capital requirements in order to meet the needs of different stakeholders. Economic profit formulations vary as to which of these capital definitions determines the capital charge. It is important to recognise how definitions differ.

In principle, economic capital models can be superior for compensation purposes, largely because of the scope of risk classes covered, and superior recognition of risk-diversification. However, when they are used for compensation, governance over economic capital models needs to be strong and effective. However, in the current environment, many firms have found regulatory capital to be the key financial constraint. As a result, economic profit formulations based on regulatory rather than economic capital have had greater prominence than might be expected in a period of greater stability.

When considering economic profit generation for bonus pool purposes, most firms resist an entirely formulaic approach. Economic capital definitions will often form the primary basis for bonus pool determination. But economic profit should also be viewed relative to invested capital, regulatory capital and economic capital bases. The capital view of the world which focuses on rare, e.g., 1 in 200 years, events needs to be complemented with an earnings volatility perspective, and stress-tested capital requirements under a range of scenarios.

The financial world is complex. The experience of firms establishing risk-appetite and measurement frameworks suggests that no single view will be sufficient to capture all elements of performance. Again this supports the use of a rigorous discretionary process, taking into account a wide range of information, rather than a simplistic formulaic assessment.

14.4   Design of compensation

All of the major pronouncements on reform of compensation in the financial services industry have alighted on the concern that compensation has been too short term, and not aligned with the risk profile of business being undertaken.

There are, of course, many aspects to this. Regulators have asked questions about whether leverage overall is too high. As a result, a number of firms have "rebalanced" compensation, increasing base salaries by as much as 100 per cent with an offsetting reduction in bonus pools. As well as reducing leverage, this can improve employee perception of compensation at a time when bonus pools are highly uncertain.

However, the key issue raised by regulatory intervention has undoubtedly been the use and design of deferred compensation. As a result almost all firms in the banking sector, and many beyond it, are reviewing their deferral policies.

The questions being asked are:

(a) Claw-back, deferral, or both?
(b) How much compensation should be deferred and for what period of time?
(c) Under what circumstances should deferrals be forfeitable?
(d) At what level of the business should deferrals be constructed?
(e) Into what kind of vehicle should deferrals be made?

Key points of guidance, based on practitioner experience, are discussed in more detail below:

(a) Claw-back should be used to cover the ability to reclaim bonus in limited circumstances of misstatement or misconduct. Deferral of bonus should provide the primary ex-post risk-adjustment mechanism to align reward with sustainable performance.
(b) A balance needs to be struck between line of sight in deferral programmes and the unintended consequences of too localised a risk exposure.
(c) The deferral vehicle should be chosen to maximise the behavioural impact of the deferral, which will generally argue for simplicity over complexity.

14.4.1 Claw-back and forfeiture

Claw-back should be used to cover the ability to reclaim bonus in limited circumstances of misstatement or misconduct. Deferral of bonus should provide the primary ex-post risk-adjustment mechanism to align reward with sustainable performance.

Should bonuses be awarded subject to claw-back, or deferred subject to forfeiture, or both? The debate is not merely once of semantics:

(a) Under a **claw-back** arrangement, the bonus is paid, but subject to certain conditions that allow it to be reclaimed within a specified period. The conditions commonly include restatement of earnings, misconduct, actions detrimental to the firm, and in some cases poor performance.
(b) Under a **deferral** arrangement, the payment of bonus is deferred for a period of time, provided no event occurs which causes it to be forfeited. The conditions may be the same as under a claw-back arrangement, but more commonly include performance conditions.

It is much better to be in a position of not paying something to an individual, than taking them to court to reclaim it.

For this reason, deferral arrangements generally allow more flexibility in the terms that give rise to forfeiture. In the authors' experience, creating a practically enforceable claw-back arrangement is very challenging. As a result, claw-back is generally restricted to more extreme events. It is unusual, for example, for claw-back to include conditions relating to firm performance.

Experience has shown that for reasons of flexibility, enforceability, and other technical issues such as taxation:

(a) Claw-back facilities should be introduced for cash bonuses to cover limited circumstances, such as incorrect financial data or financial restatements, whether fraudulent or not (interestingly, the definition under the US legislation is restricted to the circumstance of executives having knowingly engaged in providing inaccurate information relating to financial statements or performance metrics used to calculate their own incentive pay).
(b) Deferral should be used to enable forfeiture in the case of financial or individual performance transpiring to be unsustainable (not through fraud or misdemeanour).

14.4.2 Performance adjustment

The dilemma in designing deferred compensation is as follows:

(a) To maximise alignment with outcomes requires the longest possible deferral, and the greatest flexibility in the conditions relating to its release.
(b) The longer the deferral and the vaguer the conditions, the more it is discounted by individuals and the smaller the influence it has on behaviour.

However, it is also true that because of the tendency of recipients to discount deferred compensation, too small a deferred element renders it meaningless.

There is no exact science to this. However, reviews of emerging regulatory developments and discussions with regulators suggest the following expectation:

(a) For senior management and trading roles exposing the firm to material risk, over half of incentive compensation should be paid in deferred form.
(b) Deferral should be on a phased basis over up to three to five years for the most senior positions and highest risk/longest tail businesses.

A concern of regulators is to influence behaviour in business as usual circumstances, and not just extreme circumstances. The key is how to construct incentives that prevent build up of excessive risk in firms during the normal economic cycle.

A balance needs to be struck between line of sight in deferral programmes and the unintended consequences of too localised a risk exposure.

Clause 19.3.49E of the FSA's proposed Remuneration Code states that:

1. A *firm* should reduce unvested deferred variable *remuneration* when, as a minimum:

a.   there is reasonable evidence of *employee* misbehaviour or material error;

b.   the *firm* or the relevant business unit suffers a material downturn in its financial performance;

c.   the *firm* or the relevant business unit suffers a material failure of risk management.

2.   For performance adjustment purposes, awards of deferred variable *remuneration* made in *shares* or other non-cash instruments should provide the ability for the *firm* to reduce the number of *shares* or other non-cash instruments.

The clause is an evidential provision, rather than guidance, meaning that failure to comply can be taken as enforceable evidence of failure to comply with a handbook rule. This increases the significance of the clause.

The main issue of concern for banks is the interaction between (1)(b) and (2), which requires a performance condition on deferral that goes beyond linkage to the share price, enabling the number of shares to be adjusted. This is emphasised in para.3.96 of the FSA's Consultation Paper, which states that:

> "On share and share-linked deferred awards, although the share price will provide a form of performance adjustment at the firm level, in many cases the link between individual performance and share price performance can be relatively weak (except in certain cases such as the CEO). It is therefore highly desirable for firms to have the ability to reduce the number of shares awarded based on business unit and / or individual performance . . ."

This represents a toughening of the FSA's stance compared to the 2009 review, when they accepted deferral into shares as adequate performance linkage on deferred compensation.

The FSA is urging firms to create a stronger linkage between deferrals and the performance of the business area which generated the bonus deferred. The proposition is that the value of shares is too remote from individual business areas to create accountability and incentive to deliver sustainable performance. In Switzerland, the regulator FINMA has imposed structures requiring a downwards revision of deferred bonus on a divisional basis if a division makes a loss.

However, in certain circumstances increasing the sensitivity of performance adjustment on deferrals can increase the incentive to take risk, by increasing the amount of compensation dependent on a given year's performance.

Example

For example, take a situation where a bonus of typically £1m per annum is paid. In a pure cash bonus model, £1m is at risk on a given year's performance.

Now take a situation where 40 per cent is paid in cash with the remainder vesting in equal tranches over three subsequent years. In a localised variable deferral model, a decline in local business unit performance following award of the bonus causes a corresponding fall in the deferral value.

Under this model, £1.6m becomes at risk on a single year's performance (see figure 14.5). In other words, the incentive to take risk in order to defer a performance decline actually becomes stronger when the deferral is introduced.

Figure 14.5 Deferral and unintended consequences

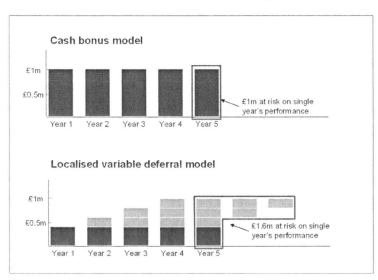

The key issue created by the localised variable deferral model is that, by basing the deferral adjustment on the same performance basis as the bonus assessment, the sensitivity to annual performance is actually increased rather than decreased.

As a result, banks are tending to rely on Remuneration Committee discretion to apply performance adjustment to deferred compensation, based on judgements about group and individual performance, but not on a formulaic basis.

14.4.3   Deferral vehicles

The deferral vehicle should be chosen to maximise the behavioural impact of the deferral, which will generally argue for simplicity over complexity.

There are many different ways to structure deferrals and link them to performance, the most appropriate depending on the circumstances of the firm. However, it must always be borne in mind that compensation objectives are usually best achieved by maximum simplicity.

Figure 14.6 Deferral vehicles

Approach	Advantages	Disadvantages
Shares Deferral into shares	• Alignment with group • For group executive committee shares without performance conditions form a simple and suitable deferral vehicle	• Too remote to have behavioural impact below divisional level • Combining shares with performance conditions adds complexity • Dilution onerous at low prices
Cash Deferral into cash	• Simple • Avoids additional discount for share volatility • No dilution	• No group alignment • No performance alignment
Bonus Bank Deferral into a "bank" whose value fluctuates with performance	• Can be simple • Build-up of bank allows straightforward allocation of "negative" performance • Can provide a return, for example in line with group of divisional RoE	• Can over-smooth reward-performance relationship and so be confusing to participants • Tendency to become over complicated

Divisional Equity Deferral into real or phantom units based on value of division	• Gives sense of ownership stake • Provides upside as well as downside, so more motivational • Tax and accounting advantages for real equity	• More complex • Potentially volatile valuations
"Toxic Assets" Deferral into real or phantom written-down toxic assets	• Sense of moral justice • Provides incentive to maximise recoveries • No dilution	• May create excessive rewards if asset values over-depressed • Only a partial alignment with shareholders • No incentive linkage to future business
Subordinated Debt Deferral into company subordinated debt, perhaps with conversion feature into equity if capital trigger activated	• Aligned to financial strength of firm • Conversion can strengthen capital base in times of stress • Justifies payment of coupon to employees	• Only operates at a group not divisional level • If too complex, perceived value for employees will be adversely impacted

Clarity of purpose of the deferral arrangement is key to ensuring that the right design is chosen.

There has been much recent discussion of the use of contingent convertibles of "cocos" in compensation design. In principle these have a number of attractive properties. They are less risky than shares for the participant, and so can overcome some of the growing concerns about over-exposure through increased levels of share deferral. Yet they still obtain beneficial capital treatment for the bank. However, regulatory clarity about what does and does not count for favourable capital treatment remains uncertain. It may be that the features required (for example the regulator having an option to convert) may be deemed as creating too much uncertainty for an employee compensation instrument. While regulatory clarity is awaited, firms are exploring simpler structures. These include simple cash deferral arrangements that change nature in the event of a trigger event, such as Common Equity Tier 1 capital ratio falling below a prescribed level. If the trigger is activated, then the deferred cash payment may simply be delayed until the capital position of the bank recovers. Alternatively, it may convert to equity. Such structures keep many of the elements of simple cash deferral, while retaining an element of protection for the firm if the bank comes under financial duress. We can expect this to be a field of further exploration and innovation in the coming years.

14.5   Governance of remuneration

14.5.1   *Change is underway*

Perhaps the most profound changes to come out from the current crisis will be changes to governance arrangements. This will extend beyond pay. However, governance in relation to pay is important in its own right. Partly because, as much as the technical design of incentives, it is how pay systems are governed that influence behaviour, but also because how a firm is governed in relation to pay can be an observable signal of how its governance operates more widely.

Changes to remuneration governance are proving to be profound. Pressure in relation to governance is coming from a number of areas including:

(a)   Regulators who have, or will, be putting forward views on good practice in relation to governance.
(b)   Government support programmes, participation in which is likely to involve requirements in relation to remuneration, reporting, and governance.
(c)   Shareholders, who are increasingly focussing on the oversight applied by remuneration committees to pay both at board level and below.
(d)   The "Triangle of Mistrust" between shareholders, remuneration committees, and management, which demands a more transparent and effective governance framework.

For institutions that will be under most scrutiny from the regulator on this issue, there will be a requirement to put in place a framework that enables the <u>demonstration</u> of good governance and independent oversight. The aim must be to achieve this at minimum cost and disruption to the business management processes.

Regulators now require some kind of annual report on remuneration practices throughout the firm, which may even extend to a certification from the remuneration committee chairman that the policies discourage excessive risk taking and are robustly enforced. Such certification requirements are already falling on firms participating in second-round government support programmes in the US. It is likely that this will include an annual interview of the chairman of the remuneration committee at major banks.

These developments represent a significant extension of the remit of remuneration committees. Consideration needs to be given to how certifications of the type likely to be required will be supported. In our view this requires the governance arrangements covering pay more widely to be reviewed.

The remuneration committee's traditional role has been to provide oversight of remuneration of the most senior executive cadre, with reporting accountability to shareholders through the remuneration report. The remit has typically involved oversight of broader remuneration policy, but which, in practice, declines rapidly below executive committee level.

There are now two significant potential changes to this remit. On the one hand both regulators and, for banks receiving state aid, governments, are now potential stakeholders in relation to remuneration practices. Both are likely to have reporting requirements. On the other, the interest of these stakeholders extends far beyond the traditional shareholder interest in executive director remuneration, and into remuneration policy across the firm.

Boards need to consider whether the remuneration committee as currently constituted can effectively fulfil, and be demonstrated to fulfil, this broadened mandate. The authors' view is that the remuneration committee is the correct committee to own the company-wide remuneration issue. Consistency between the approach to issues governing executive and wider management and employee remuneration is vital, and there will be a body of expertise built up in the committee that is relevant to both discussions.

Figure 14.7 Stakeholder roles

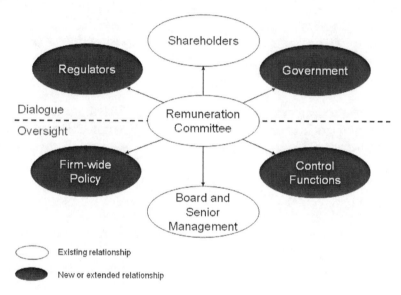

However, the composition of the committee will need to be looked at critically. Depth of sector expertise is more likely to be required of non-executives sitting on a committee dealing explicitly with company-wide remuneration arrangements. Moreover, who attends the committee may require review, including greater involvement from control functions other than human resources (for example risk and finance), when appropriate.

14.5.2 Cascading governance through the firm

A formal – yet pragmatic and workable – governance structure should be adopted to provide appropriate oversight from the remuneration committee down into the divisions and individual bonus determina-

tions. This should encompass an explicit role for control functions, especially risk, and should enable the remuneration committee to demonstrate appropriate oversight of the remuneration process.

In an ideal world, management of remuneration risks would be included within the firm's normal risk management processes and reporting lines. However, recent events have thrust remuneration into the spotlight, and regulators are paying special attention to it. There is an expectation of a separate reporting and assurance process relating to remuneration, in order to satisfy regulatory requirements. Firms need to respond to this pressure.

The rigour and formality of oversight below the remuneration committee therefore needs consideration. This covers both the oversight of divisional decision making, and also the appropriate involvement of group control functions. The risk function rarely has formally defined, or scrutinised, roles in the compensation process. Even the involvement of finance can be desultory and reluctant. Too often the process is disproportionately borne by human resources. Yet the complexity of modern financial services businesses, and the requirement for a deep understanding of the risk implications of remuneration arrangements, means that this is no longer viable.

It is now necessary for the involvement of control functions in remuneration becomes formalised. A number of models may be appropriate, depending on the particular business structure and issues.

Any such model must meet the following criteria:

(a) Creates a direct line of oversight to the remuneration committee.
(b) Defines an explicit role for the control functions, especially risk.
(c) Minimises the disruption to the management of the business on a business as usual basis through the line management structure.
(d) Enables the remuneration committee to provide assurance to regulators and other external parties as required.

(e) Ensures appropriate flows of information.
(f) Provides appropriate checks and balances to manage conflicts of interest.

One such model is shown below, illustrating how a formalised remuneration oversight committee, with representation across the control functions, could add supporting rigour to the normal remuneration process. Note that in this model the left-hand side represents the normal management hierarchy. The remuneration oversight committee sits <u>alongside</u> this process, rather than supplanting it. This is important for ensuring that remuneration remains a legitimate tool of business management. The purpose of the remuneration oversight committee is to review, challenge, and report issues from a risk perspective to the remuneration committee.

Figure 14.8 Remuneration oversight committee model

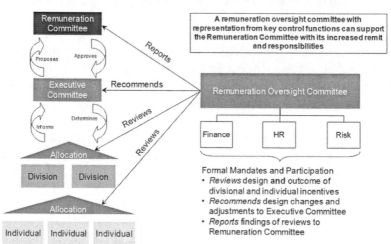

As well as reviewing the design of remuneration plans and processes, the committee would provide independent oversight of divisional incentive outcomes. This might include, for example, a review of bonus hotspots, to ensure that the results delivered accorded with the group centre's qualitative understanding of the quality of those businesses and the risks being run, or an assessment of the extent to which bonus had been achieved at the cost of not meeting the firm's risk appetite.

The Committee would make recommendations to the Executive Committee, and would report to the Remuneration Committee on the reviews it had undertaken and any adjustments recommended. In some cases there would be separate Remuneration Oversight Committees for different divisions or regions. Where a firm already has divisional Remuneration Committees, then the Remuneration Oversight Committee would not operate in addition. Instead the constitution of those divisional Committees would be amended to ensure appropriate risk and control function representation.

Establishing the remit and membership of the Remuneration Oversight Committee is not trivial, and requires careful planning. This is an area where a large number of firms will have to undertake significant changes in order to meet regulatory requirements.

14.5.3 *Managing inputs to the Remuneration Committee*

Robust processes to support the application of discretion need to be developed and documented. The requirements of internal and external advice to the Committee need to be reviewed to ensure that the Committee is obtaining access to appropriate information.

In the emerging governance environment, it will be necessary to have processes that are strong, and seen to be strong. Remuneration processes that are able to sustain board level certification to regulators and governments must be capable of demonstration, and resilient to audit. This will require a review of compensation processes to ensure appropriate recording of evidence and audit trails. Data collection protocols will need to be reviewed.

Data on risk and compensation will need to be cross-referenced in a much more rigorous way than previously to identify any misalignments. This will require consistency in reporting segmentation, timing, and frequency.

Remuneration committees will need to review the advice that they receive both from within and without the business. Few remuneration committees historically received a briefing from the chief risk officer in the context of remuneration decision making. This is now changing. Remuneration committees should have available appropriate data on quantitative and qualitative risk measures when determining bonuses.

At the same time, external advice requirements will need to be reviewed. Advisers will need to be able to help remuneration committees to make decisions that fit their business. Data on what everyone else does will become of more limited value.

Regulators are seeking greater transparency. It is probable that regulators may want some sort of report or certification from the employer as to the suitability of bonus awards, and even if it does not go that far, may subsequently investigate remuneration practices. They are likely to be particularly keen to ensure that robust performance management is in place that means that risks are managed.

Finally, the nature of the discretions held by remuneration committees is becoming more complex. The use of risk adjusted measures and the increased importance of deferred compensation (and the decision of whether to forfeit) create an environment in which judgments made without proper substantiation will be even more likely to be seen as arbitrary, inconsistent, or capricious, and therefore a source of legal risk.

Within this, robustly applied performance management systems and processes will help ensure implementation of the firm's policies, and will be a crucial line of defence against external scrutiny.

14.6   Disclosure of remuneration

14.6.1   Unintended consequences?

Chapter 12 – Disclosure and Pillar 3, deals with disclosure requirements of Basel III so a few short comments only are made here.

CRD3 set out aggregate remuneration disclosures required to be made by covered European firms, and draft disclosure requirements under Basel III have built on these. These rules set out information requirements to help external stakeholders make informed decisions about the risk profile of remuneration within a firm.

Broadly the information required covers remuneration arrangements for senior management and risk takers:

(a) Governance arrangements
(b) Total variable pay pools
(c) Split between cash and deferral
(d) Performance and risk adjustment measures
(e) Performance adjustment of deferred compensation

These rules are now in place in the UK, with the first disclosures from banks imminent. The Basel III Committee is suggesting some extension to the CRD3 requirements. Their proposals require firm-wide disclosure of remuneration and variable pay pools rather than just for senior management and risk takers. Further information on risk adjustment is also required.

In some territories, notably the UK, the political battleground has related to individual disclosures. The Walker Review in the UK recommended banded disclosure for all individuals earning more than £1m. The previous UK Government had published draft legislation adopting this. But concerned about implications for a level playing field, at the time of writing, this had not been implemented. As part of the "Merlin" discussions with the major UK banks, the largest UK banks have committed to voluntary disclosure of the total remuneration of the five highest paid managers below the board. The UK Government has announced the intention to legislate for a similar requirement applying to all banks operating in the UK for next year.

Proponents of greater disclosure argue that only provision of full information will enable proper scrutiny of bonus practices – "sunlight is the best form of antiseptic". However, with any disclosure around pay, care is required to avoid unintended consequences. Individual disclosure in particular can simply provide the information to support upward pressure on pay levels.

It does seem now that the momentum behind unilateral adoption of individual disclosures has abated. The aggregated disclosures already proposed should provide a good starting point for external stakeholders to understand and challenge remuneration practices at firms with which they are involved.

More generally, remuneration reporting will need to move from compliance to communication. Consistency of message will be required in the submissions going to different stakeholders. Increasingly, remuneration reporting will need to explain and justify policies, rather than just present arid facts. There will be a greater need for clarity of expression and the avoidance of remuneration gobbledegook. The focus should be on transparency rather than volumes of information. This will particularly be the case with regulatory submissions.

In addition, with international firms operating in multiple jurisdictions, governance processes will be required to ensure consistency of response to requests for information.

For larger financial institutions, the chair of the remuneration committee should be prepared to meet face to face with regulators and shareholders on a regular basis. Their time commitment is likely to be significantly increased as a result of this new role as spokesperson and advocate for the firm on remuneration matters. The boundary between remuneration reporting and public relations will blur.

It is clear that financial firms will need to make their case on remuneration in a much more compelling, sensitive, and thoughtful way than in the past. Those that succeed in getting their message across will have much greater freedom of action.

14.7 Conclusion

Looking back two years from the early part of 2011 it is remarkable how much the remuneration landscape has changed within banks. The regulatory developments have had teething problems. Lack of a level playing field for regulation and enforcement internationally has been a real problem, particularly for European banks. Regulators have, at times, imposed arbitrary requirements on deferral practices or definitions of risk takers, which have not always led to logical outcomes. But on balance the proposals put forward by regulators have been reasonably balanced and have, overall, had a positive impact on the operation of remuneration policies in banks.

Now that the initial adoption phase is over, it is to be hoped that the emphasis will turn from issues of remuneration structure (deferral and so on) to the questions of governance and, in particular, risk adjustment. It is these dimensions that provide the greatest opportunity for securing enduring behavioural change.

Chapter 15

Recovery and Resolution Planning

Duncan McNab

15.1   Introduction – in peace plan for war

Recovery and Resolution Plans ("RRP") are one of the tools that regulators around the world are using to address the issue of banks that are too big to fail. The expectation is that the risk of a bank failure should be reduced if there is better planning for financial disasters (recovery) or, failing this, that the impact of failures could be reduced if a plan had been prepared to enable an institution to be taken through receivership or bankruptcy in an orderly fashion (resolution).

It is worth clarifying the difference between recovery and resolution upfront. Recovery plans set out how the bank would survive severe stress scenarios and assume that the bank is still functioning as a group. On the other hand, resolution plans describe how a collapsed bank could be wound down in an orderly fashion, returning insured deposits and trust assets to customers quickly and intact and without funding from the tax payer.

In the wake of the Lehman collapse and the near collapse of other firms such as Bear Sterns, Northern Rock and the Icelandic banks, many regulators have asked the questions: "how could the collapse have been avoided?" and "how could such a collapse have been less disruptive to the financial system"?

The answer to the first question is typically that management should have quite radical plans in place to restructure the business over a short time frame. These "financial disaster recovery plans" include actions to generate liquidity and repair the capital position of a bank. Such plans are no protection against the risks of management denial and failure to act, so there also needs to be some form of governance and risk-based trigger framework under which these plans would be invoked.

Whether or not Lehman could have been saved if it had had a recovery plan is a moot point, but the subsequent bank rescues might have been more effective if, in peace, the banks had prepared for war. What is clear is that the Lehman administration itself was initially hampered by the fact that no thought had been given to how such a complex institution would be resolved and very little had been done to facilitate such an outcome should it arise. An RRP could have mitigated some of the biggest challenges of the Lehman collapse, including, for example:

(a) the lock-up of hedge fund assets;
(b) uncertain outcomes from one million pending or failed derivative trades;
(c) ambiguity as to which Lehman legal entity counterparties were exposed;
(d) difficulties in managing the operational and financial inter-dependencies of Lehman affiliates around the world in an insolvency environment; and
(e) the market's inability to predict the timing and value of recoveries from the failed Lehman entities.

If the worst cannot be avoided then the day of bankruptcy should not be the first time that the resolution authorities are consulted. The administrators or other resolution bodies do not want to find themselves planning the resolution in real time based on information that they have to hunt down themselves. The speed with which protected depositors and secured creditors can be repaid is also enhanced by the existence of a resolution action plan and an accompanying business information pack.

As of April 2011, more than 15 banks in the Europe and North America have started to develop some form of RRP in response to a request from their home country regulator. This is primarily at the request of their regulators with the suggestion that there may be capital implications if the plans are not sufficiently robust. The approach has also been linked to the potential capital surcharges for Systemically Important Financial Institutions ("SIFIs"). Systemic importance in this context may apply to a single national jurisdiction or to a global perspective – the so-called Global SIFIS or G-SIFIs.

Many banks that have drafted plans have found that there are business benefits to the process. The detailed understanding of legal entities and their interdependencies that is required during recovery and resolution planning has helped banks identify opportunities for simplification and ultimately cost savings. Recovery planning also makes good sense in an increasingly uncertain economic environment and may protect shareholders from the much worse scenario of resolution.

15.2 International overview

15.2.1 Financial Stability Board

In April 2009 the G20 established the Financial Stability Board ("FSB") to, amongst other things, develop protocols for better cross-border resolution. In Pittsburgh later that year they concluded that SIFIs should develop globally consistent, firm-specific contingency and resolution plans.

Since then, most of the G20 have been running some form of pilot recovery and resolution planning exercise for the globally significant banks under their jurisdiction. The results of these pilots were used to develop the recommendations made by the FSB to the Seoul meeting of the G20 in November 2010. A number of areas were identified that impede effective resolution in globally-complex financial institutions:

(a) transaction booking practices;
(b) intra-group guarantees;

(c) global payments operations;
(d) information technology; and
(e) service level agreements.

In a communiqué after this summit, the FSB made it clear that RRPs will be mandatory for G-SIFIs. Criteria for determining G-SIFI status is expected to be published at the end of 2011. Once these plans have been put in place regulators will assess the resolvability of G-SIFIs against additional criteria that are also being developed during 2011. In the proposals, the regulators have the power to change the legal or operational structure of institutions if they conclude that they cannot be resolved effectively.

In their November report, the FSB highlighted the need to improve national resolution regimes to facilitate cross-border resolution. This would require changes to laws in many countries to permit resolution authorities to share information more freely and to pursue the "global best interest" even if this may not accord with national interests. The plan is that these new laws will enable cross-border crisis management groups to develop a globally-coherent response to the next financial crisis.

A high level of international cooperation is not only important for effective cross border crisis management but it is also essential for the consistency of the regulations that all G-SIFIs will have to follow. The FSB is seeking to achieve this through peer reviews which are being carried out through 2011 and 2012. Early signs are that there is more to do with regard to international cooperation since there seems to be a lack of consistency on certain areas (e.g. whether the emphasis should be on recovery or resolution).

The FSB is also reviewing restructuring mechanisms that would enable a "bail-in". A bail-in is in substance a markedly accelerated receivership process that would enable a troubled bank to recapitalise itself over a very short period – typically, a weekend. The FSB is looking at debt-to-equity conversions, contingent convertible capital and other innovative mechanisms to achieve this. A bail-in is unlikely to be feasible if the loss is too large or uncertain.

15.2.2 European Commission

On 20 October 2010, the European Commission ("EC") published a communication on an "EU framework for Crisis Management in the Financial Sector". Following this, on 6 January 2011, the EC launched a consultation on the technical detail underpinning this framework. The aim of the consultation being to ensure that authorities across the EU have the powers and tools to restructure or resolve all types of financial institutions in a crisis, without European tax payers bearing the burden. A formal legislative proposal on bank recovery and resolution will follow and is expected in June 2011.

In developing its crisis management framework, the EC is primarily concerned with giving effect to seven principles:

1. putting prevention and preparation first;
2. providing credible resolution tools;
3. enabling fast and decisive action;
4. reducing moral hazard;
5. contributing to a smooth resolution of cross-border groups;
6. ensuring legal certainty; and
7. limiting distortions of competition.

The EC has structured its consultation paper so as to cover the technical detail required to create a framework based on these principles. The consultation paper deals specifically with: how current supervisory regimes can be enhanced to improve effectiveness in prevention and preparation; what tools are available to local supervisors in enforcing recovery and resolution; how early intervention measures may be used to address developing problems; how group resolution should work (this includes proposed multilateral and firm-specific agreements between jurisdictions); and how bank resolution should be funded.

Following this first step, the EC will examine the need for harmonisation of European bank insolvency legislation and will look to review and potentially consult upon changes to European insolvency regimes by the end of 2012. By 2014, depending on the substantive rules in place as a result of the earlier reviews, the EC will consider taking a third step by seeking to create an integrated resolution regime possibly based on a single European Resolution Authority.

15.2.3 *UK*

Since the publication by the Treasury of a 163 page report on "Establishing Resolution Arrangements for Investment Banks" in December 2009, the UK has been taking a lead role in developing proposals for RRPs. A number of banks, assessed to be of systemic importance on a global basis, were asked to submit RRPs to the FSA in 2010. The FSA has provided the banks with an information request that includes a number of templates and pro-formas with the objective of achieving consistency and comparability in the plans. The bank submissions were received during October and, as at January 2011, the FSA is analysing the responses.

In the meantime, the Financial Services Act 2010 has come into force legally compelling the FSA to bring in some form of RRP requirement for all licensed deposit-takers in the UK.

A consultation paper detailing the actual requirements is expected to be published during 2011, followed by new requirements of all deposit-taking institutions for 2012.

15.2.4 *US*

Too big to fail regulation in the US has been dominated by the Dodd-Frank Act. In addition to existing powers over banks, Dodd-Frank has given the Federal Reserve ("FED") and the Federal Deposit Insurance Corporation ("FDIC") special powers to resolve non-bank financial companies that are determined to be systemically important.

Whilst the details of the Dodd-Frank Act were being finalised, a number of regulators in the US pushed ahead with recovery plan pilots. The FED and the Office of the Comptroller of the Currency ("OCC") requested initial recovery plans from a number of globally active, interconnected banks. These initial plans were submitted in August 2010 and feedback was provided in college of regulators meetings in November and December of the same year. As of January 2011, the US regulators have requested the pilot banks to submit a second version of their plans sometime during the second quarter of 2011. The FDIC has also published a notice of proposed rulemaking pertaining to resolution planning which describes potential resolution plan requirements.

15.2.5 Other European jurisdictions

15.2.5.1 Switzerland

On 4 November 2009, against the backdrop of the global financial and economic crisis, the Swiss Federal Council established a Commission of Experts to examine the question of limiting the economic risks posed by large companies (the "Commission of Experts"). It was identifie by the Commission of Experts in an interim report released in April 2010, that the two big Swiss banks were the only companies in Switzerland that could be classified as "too big to fail" ("TBTF") and therefore, urgent measures were required to counter the TBTF issue relating to these banks.

In response to this issue, the Commission of Experts released a final report on 30 September 2010 which explores and proposes specific measures. These include measures to ensure that the organisational structure of systemically important banks is resolvable in the event of a crisis. It has been proposed that it is the responsibility of the systemically important bank to organise itself in such a way that it guarantees resolvability in the event of a crisis and that, if it is unable to demonstrate this, then the supervisory body may enforce reorganisational measures.

15.2.5.2 Germany

Towards the end of November 2010, the German Parliament passed a new German Bank Restructuring Act. This was done with the aim of providing enhanced legislative powers to the German regulator ("BaFin") and the German central bank (*Deutsche Bundesbank*) designed to help ailing credit institutions. The legislation became effective on 1 January 2011.

Of the new supervisory powers, the most notable is the regulator's ability to propose losses to debt holders outside of insolvency as part of an early intervention measure. In addition to this, the new legislative tools also provide the powers to transfer all or part of the business to a private sector purchaser and to transfer all or part of the business to a bridge bank or non-bank entity, in which a restructuring fund may own shares.

15.3 Recovery – financial Business Continuity Planning

15.3.1 Introduction

Recovery planning is similar to Business Continuity Planning ("BCP") for a potential financial disaster. This might be a disaster that befalls the specific institution or a market-wide stress. If it is the former then it may also be some combination of the two, since a financial crisis in a G-SIFI is likely to have some impact on the financial markets.

In its simplest form, a recovery plan is a menu of quantified capital and liquidity actions that an institution can feasibly take during a financial crisis. The plan should show that the impact of these actions is far more than is necessary to survive extreme stress scenarios, both idiosyncratic and market wide. The plan should also explain the governance arrangements for execution of the plan, and its maintenance and use.

15.3.2 Writing a recovery plan

Writing a recovery plan can be a cathartic experience for the survivors of the last global financial crisis. To some extent it can be used to tell the story of how the institution successfully responded to those events, identifying lessons learned and enhancements to be made. However, a plan needs to go beyond this to envisage more extreme stress scenarios and more radical potential responses.

In a recovery situation a group still has control of its subsidiaries and is able to move cash around the group, dispose of assets, de-risk businesses, etc. As a result, it is possible to prepare a recovery plan on a centralised basis for the whole group. It is also likely that some components of the recovery plan may already exist (e.g. liquidity crisis plans, ICAAP stress scenarios, M&A protocols for the disposal of businesses, etc.), and it is expected that firms leverage these tools and processes for the development of initial and subsequent plans. Where such processes do exist they need to be critically examined to ensure that they are coherent with the rest of the plan and that they are sufficiently robust in their assumptions and responses.

One likely outcome of the planning process is a list of actions that the bank can take now that will improve the chances of a successful recovery and/or its processes to develop recovery plans. This might include changes that will enable quicker separation of businesses for disposal or enhancements to the decision-making process during a time of crisis.

15.3.3 Governance

There are at least three phases of governance that need to be considered in the recovery planning process:

(a) project governance over the initial drafting and submission;
(b) ongoing governance to ensure that the plans are kept up to date and fit for purpose; and
(c) governance over the invocation of the plans during a crisis period.

In terms of project governance, it is important to demonstrate a level of ownership and involvement in the planning process from the board. Not only is this the regulators' expectation but it is also a practical necessity if the board is to adopt these plans, in haste, in a time of crisis. The drafting of the plan itself will require significant input from a number of functions including strategy, risk, finance, operations, technology, legal and compliance. However, the functions can only achieve so much and strategic decisions on core/non-core businesses or on how portfolios would be de-risked or realised will require engagement with business line management. The optimal project structure will vary from bank to bank but will typically involve a working group or groups reporting to a steering committee.

The ongoing governance of the plan will need to be developed as part of the drafting process. An individual or committee needs to be appointed to adopt the initial plan and then be responsible for ensuring that it is kept up to date for changes in the business or other factors. Other factors can include developments in regulatory requirements for capital or liquidity or changes to the regulations covering RRPs. It is also appropriate to consider at this stage whether the plan should be reviewed by internal or external audit. Some regulators have suggested that an annual certification may be required to ensure that the plan remains relevant.

The governance section of the recovery plan should set out the protocols to invoke the plan and execute recovery actions. There should be a clear articulation of triggers that management monitors to inform it as to when to invoke the plan and assess whether particular actions should be contemplated or taken. In many cases, these triggers will be based on capital or liquidity metrics but they may also include qualitative metrics such as the discovery of a significant fraud. Judging the triggers and establishing a menu of potential recovery actions is one of the most difficult aspects of recovery planning. A balance needs to be struck between setting these out with sufficient clarity and certainty to avoid management denial in a time of crisis and retaining enough flexibility to enable the right response to the specific circumstances being faced.

A number of banks have appointed an individual to act as the Business Recovery Officer ("BRO"). The BRO is typically a member of senior management who has ultimate responsibility for the development and maintenance of the RRP. The BRO will also play a key role in the monitoring of triggers and invoking the plans if necessary. In the context of resolution planning, it has also been suggested by some regulators that the BRO should be locked into a longer notice period with the specific role of helping the resolution authorities for the first three to six months of the resolution.

15.3.4 · Recovery plan contents

Whilst the main body of a recovery plan is a menu of capital and liquidity actions set in the context for various stress scenarios, most plans include other contextual information. As well as the governance over the plan most banks are including background information on the structure and business activities of the group, the methodology adopted to develop the plan and the processes that exist to support the plan. The Figure below shows the typical content of a recovery plan.

Figure 15.1 Recovery plan content

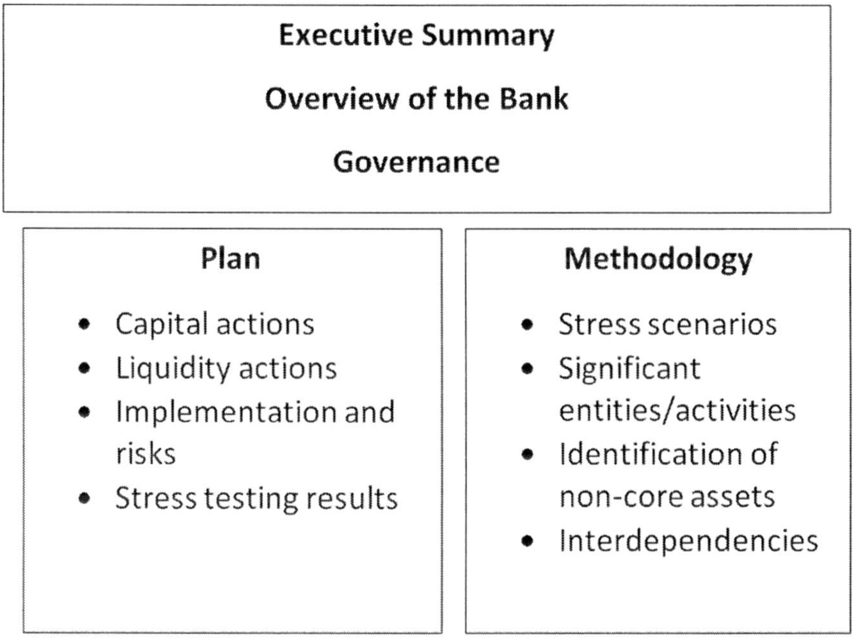

Executive Summary
Overview of the Bank
Governance

Plan	**Methodology**
• Capital actions • Liquidity actions • Implementation and risks • Stress testing results	• Stress scenarios • Significant entities/activities • Identification of non-core assets • Interdependencies

For each action the plan should:

(a) quantify the expected capital and liquidity impacts of the action;
(b) estimate the implementation time frame;
(c) summarise the potential barriers to, and risks of, implementation;
(d) assess the impact on the ongoing franchise;
(e) indicate under what circumstances the action might be most appropriate; and
(f) identify those who would be involved in the implementation of the action.

Some plans estimate the capital and liquidity that would be necessary to survive extreme stress scenarios, both idiosyncratic and market wide. This analysis usually includes an indication of the time frame over which these needs would arise. Whilst it is not possible to specify an action plan for every eventuality, the plan should hopefully demonstrate that there are plausible options available to deal with the example stress scenarios provided in the plan.

15.3.5   Areas of regulatory focus

In the pilots that have been run, certain regulators have requested that specific topics are addressed in the plans. Examples include systemic risk, contagion control and de-risking trading books.

15.3.5.1   Systemic risk

The regulators' primary concern is to ensure the stability of the financial markets. To this end, banks have been requested to summarise their various activities and identify which ones are systemically important. A recovery plan should indicate how continuity in these systemically important activities will be achieved in the event of a crisis.

15.3.5.2   Contagion control

Contagion control is related to systemic risk, although the emphasis is more on how banks can monitor their exposures to other banks and manage their own position if another bank gets into trouble. This may require improvements to credit monitoring systems and an exercise in lessons learned from the last financial crisis.

15.3.5.3   De-risking trading books

One of the fastest ways to reduce capital requirements is to manage down the risk on trading books. This can be pure risk reduction (e.g. through additional hedging transactions) or it can be through asset sales which have the benefit of raising liquidity at the same time. Regulators have asked banks to demonstrate how they would significantly reduce the risk on trading books in a time of market stress and when the bank itself may be a less attractive counterparty.

15.4 Resolution – planning for your own funeral

15.4.1 Introduction

Whilst most banks see the benefits of recovery planning, resolution planning is more controversial. Management is understandably reluctant to expend resources planning for an eventuality when shareholders are likely to be wiped out. However, a number of regulators see this as a critical step that is needed to resolve TBTF – or at least institutions that are too complex and unprepared to fail in an orderly manner without dislocating the financial markets and significant costs to the government.

If a failed bank can be relied upon to return monies to protected depositors and secured creditors and to manage its way through the resolution process without massive disruption to the financial markets, then it matters less if banks fail. Indeed, if effective resolution could be ensured perhaps there would be less need to raise capital and liquidity requirements to avert bank collapses in the first place.

There are other reasons why resolution planning is a less popular process. There is little real world experience of major bank resolution and it is therefore harder to imagine what the hurdles might be and how they should be planned for. Resolution is also something that happens to legal entities in their various legal jurisdictions. Whilst recovery planning can be done by a core team at head office, resolution planning needs to be thought through at legal entity and location level. The dismemberment of a group into legal entities brings into sharp relief the financial and operational interdependencies within the group. The identification of these interdependencies is a critical step to resolution planning but is one that can seem overwhelming.

Finally, there is less clarity over the ownership of a resolution plan in contrast to a recovery plan. Ultimately it is the resolution authority that will finalise and if it comes to it deploy the resolution plan. Where resolution plans have been requested from banks these are being used as a starting point to inform the resolution authorities on how management would approach a resolution. Typically, banks are being asked to identify systemically important activities and to demonstrate how these would be separated from the rest of the business in a resolution scenario, including an analysis of the interdependencies within the bank and how they would be resolved.

15.4.2 Governance

The governance over the resolution planning will have much in common with the recovery plan and may indeed be part of the same RRP process. Project governance will be more elaborate given the need to consider multiple entities in different jurisdictions and the identification of interdependencies will require a broader interaction with the business in particular on the operational side.

The triggers for resolution will be those specified in local insolvency law or by specific regulations. The recent EU proposals provide the regulators with reasonably broad powers to pre-empt technical insolvency and place a bank into resolution when insolvency seems likely.

15.4.3 Plan contents

The actual structure and content of a resolution plan will be driven by the nature of the request from the regulators. Those regulators that have included resolution in their pilots have made it clear that the resolution authorities will ultimately develop the actual resolution plan. They have requested information from the banks to help them identify systemically important entities and the interdependencies that might make their resolution more complex. There have also been requests for separation analysis to demonstrate how certain parts of the business might be separated for sale to a third party, bridge bank etc. The most comprehensive request has come from the Swiss regulators who have asked their G-SIFIs to demonstrate that their systemically important functions will continue in the event of insolvency.

A comprehensive resolution plan will need to be more modular in structure than a recovery plan. There will need to be a central plan that sets out the overall framework and governance structure and more detailed plans for the significant legal entities.

The central plan will need to identify the systemically important functions in the group and the legal entities that enable the functions to operate. The central plan should highlight the major interdependencies in the group and any pre-emptive actions that might be taken to improve the resolvability of the bank.

The legal entity ("LE") plans will need to provide both an action plan for the resolution and a business information pack. Typical contents for the LE plans might include:

Figure 15.2 Resolution plan content

Executive Summary
Overview of LE
Governance

Action Plan LE	**Business Info Pack LE**
Immediate actions	Description of entity, its
Suggested medium	activities and role in group
term plan	Critical people
Managing	Critical processes
interdependencies	Critical IT
Communication plan	Financial information
Implementation	Counterparty information
	Contractual information

15.4.4   Areas of regulatory focus

As mentioned above there has been less consistency in the nature of requirements from regulators around resolution planning. There have been certain common themes however.

15.4.4.1   Interdependencies

The identification of financial and operational interdependencies is the most common theme amongst the regulators. The lessons learned from the Lehman administration suggest that this is an area where some forethought and planning could make a huge difference to the resolvability of a financial institution.

The first step is to identify the dependencies that exist for those entities that are deemed to be systemically important. These can then be analysed to determine how their impact can be mitigated. The mitigation might take the form of simplification, substitution or contractual mechanisms to ensure the orderly resolution of the entity.

15.4.4.2   Complexity

The complexity of global financial institutions conflicts with the need to take quick and decisive action in the early days of their resolution. The availability of properly structured information should enable the resolution authorities to quickly understand the business and how it operates. This should be in sufficient detail to enable them to assess the impact of stress events and to finalise the resolution plan as quickly as possible.

Ideally, the resolution authority will be working with a suggested action plan developed in advance by management. Management is best placed to understand the complexity of the organisation and to propose which actions might be the immediate priority.

15.4.4.3   Trust assets and retail deposits

Regulators are understandably keen to understand how the procedures for the segregation of trust assets will operate during a resolution scenario. These procedures should seek to minimise market volatility, preserve clients' liquidity, maximise recovery value and reduce timing uncertainties.

In a similar vein, they are also seeking to understand how retail customer deposits will be preserved or transferred to another bank or bridge bank. Included within this should be a communication plan designed to avoid panic amongst the customer base.

15.4.4.4   Unwinding trading books and derivative portfolios

In a number of pilots the regulators have sought to understand how the banks would resolve their investment banking activities in a manner that would have minimal impact on the stability of the financial markets.

15.5   Reality check – lessons learned from the pilots

The banks and the regulators are going through an iterative process as the early pilot results have been analysed and comments fed back. As with any new subject matter there was relatively little upfront guidance as to what the content and structure of a plan should be. As a result, there has been some diversity in how the pilots have been run and the resultant plans that have been submitted.

The UK's FSA recognised this as it reviewed the initial submissions from its pilot banks. Their solution was to go back to the banks with a more detailed "Phase 2" information request. Spanning 50 pages, this was much more prescriptive about the process that the banks should go through and the format in which the analysis should be presented.

Each bank has had its own challenges in gathering the data and performing the analysis necessary to complete a plan. The following are some of the more common hurdles that they have had to face:

(a) Achieving board and senior management buy-in to the value of recovery and resolution planning when the specific circumstances that will be faced in a crisis cannot be forecast with any certainty.

(b) Getting the level of detail right; sufficient for the plan to be of real use in the event of a crisis without getting bogged down in an analysis of every entity in the group.

(c) Finding and managing the data requested. Some banks soon recognise that some form of data depository is necessary to consolidate the data and ensure it can be updated effectively.

(d) Analysing interdependencies. It has surprised many banks how little they know about how their legal entities interact with each other, and the extent to which these relationships are formalised.

(e) Creating a framework that is flexible enough to meet changing requirements. The pilots have typically focussed on recovery planning but the expectation is that resolution planning will follow. The regulators have also targeted the home state banks in their pilots but it is inevitable that the larger international banks will have to respond to requests from host regulators in other countries as well.

(f) Addressing concerns over confidentiality. Some aspects of the plans may be either commercially or politically sensitive; accordingly, banks have sought to instil safeguards over plan content, while anticipating that they may be shared amongst the college of regulators.

15.6 Conclusion

RRPs will remain firmly on the regulatory agenda in 2011 and beyond. During the first half of 2011 we can expect to see a series of consultation papers and/or proposed regulations coming out from regulators around the world as they seek to clarify their requirements for RRPs. The requirements will have significant implications for business strategy and business models and financial institutions should analyse and comment on them from both a local and a global perspective. Through the consultation process, banks and regulators alike are hopeful to achieve a greater level of international consistency. By the end of 2012 many banks will have some form of recovery and/or resolution plans in place and will be working with their regulators to refine the plans and their infrastructure to mitigate the risk of failure and facilitate orderly resolution.

Chapter 16

Stakeholder Perspectives

Richard Barfield

16.1   Introduction

The financial crisis, Basel III and related reforms have implications for many stakeholders in the financial system. This
Chapter considers the perspectives of a number of stakeholders
other than banks and regulators. The challenge, as ever, for
bank boards is how to balance the interests of a wide range of
stakeholders whose objectives may not be aligned.

The Chapter first considers the type of stakeholders that fund a
bank's balance sheet (the funding spectrum) and then examines
the implications of Basel III for each main grouping: equity
investors; debt investors; and depositors. The Chapter also
considers borrowers and other bank customers, before covering
government, the taxpayer and rating agencies (where Dodd-
Frank and the European Commission will have a major impact).
It concludes with a discussion of the importance of transparency
in rebuilding trust with all stakeholders.

16.2   The funding spectrum

Banks' funding is provided by many different stakeholders and
covers a spectrum that ranges across:

(a)   retail and commercial deposits, where money may be
      withdrawn in an instant (but is often not), for example:
      retail and commercial current accounts and sight deposits;
(b)   retail and commercial term deposits;
(c)   wholesale (i.e. funding from other banks) short-term and
      long-term funding;

(d) debt, both senior long-term debt and subordinated debt; and

(e) equity funding (which may be in the form of preference shares with guaranteed dividends or ordinary equity).

The risk appetite of funding providers increases across the spectrum – whether they realise it or not. At the low-risk end, the majority of retail deposits are usually insured to a certain level independent of the bank in question. There are 107 countries that have some form of deposit insurance scheme (source: International Association of Deposit Insurers). The level of coverage varies by country (for example in the UK by the Financial Services Compensation Scheme, which insures deposits up to £85,000 per customer per institution; comparable figures for other schemes are $250,000 in the US; JPY 10m in Japan; Rs100,000 in India; and, €100,000 in the EU from 31 December 2011). However, these insurance arrangements usually only apply to retail depositors and perhaps a minority of commercial depositors such as smaller small and medium-sized enterprises ("SME"). At the high-risk end, equity shareholders may potentially lose everything if a bank fails. In between, wholesale debt funding may be provided on a secured or an unsecured basis, depending on whether the bank provides collateral to the funding provider, as well as in deposits (e.g. money market instruments and certificates of deposit). A key aim of regulators post-crisis is also to increase the risk to debt-holders through, for example, "bail-ins" – where part or all of their investment may convert to equity that is loss-absorbing.

Securitisation also plays an important role in bank funding. It allows banks to lend and then package small loans (for example credit card receivables) together in a way that allows the bank to issue securities to investors to finance the lending activity. Securitisations are designed in a way that provides investors with securities that have varying risk profiles. The higher-risk securities have a higher risk of default and provide a higher return. Securitisation played a key role in the financing structures of banks before the crisis but the securitisation markets are currently running at about 20–25 per cent of the pre-crisis levels (for example, in the UK $40bn of residential backed mortgage securities were issued in 2010 compared to $160bn at the peak in 2006). Part of the contraction in the supply of this key source of funding is due to the unfavourable capital treatment that securitisations receive under Basel III (see Chapter 3 – Defining Capital).

Basel III is making fundamental changes to the funding structures of banks. Chapter 6 on liquidity considers the implications of Basel III for liquidity and funding principally at the shorter end of the funding spectrum. At the longer end, equity (shareholders' capital and retained earnings) will become the dominant source of long-term funding with reduced emphasis on subordinated debt and hybrid instruments. The Basel Committee is still interested in stimulating the development of new debt instruments that will, under certain circumstances, for instance in recovery situations, bear losses – known euphemistically as "taking a haircut". There is also enthusiasm from regulators for "contingent capital" which are debt instruments that convert to equity in times of stress (these instruments are discussed below).

16.3   Equity investors

In many ways, the Basel reforms are making equity investors the most important and powerful stakeholder group in relation to the funding of banks. Without their willingness to provide capital, the financial system cannot function. Interestingly, in the rush to reform, there has been practically no discussion of the implications of regulatory changes for returns to equity investors. This is an important issue. If returns fall below the cost of capital or do not provide investors with a sufficient return for the risks that they take, equity investors are likely to move their capital from under-performing banks to those that generate better returns or, failing that, from the banking sector to sectors where returns are more attractive. Alternatively, if banks cannot earn an appropriate return, certain bank business models will no longer be viable, which may lead to break-up and disposals. Within the banking sector those banks that are able to demonstrate more attractive returns (relative to the risks that they take) than their peers should find it easier to attract (and retain) equity funding than their competitors. This, in turn, should translate into reduced equity and debt funding costs as the level of financial leverage reduces.

16.3.1 The equity market view

A key concern for the Basel Committee in developing the long transition period from Basel II to Basel III was to ensure that the vast majority of banks would be able to meet the increased capital requirements from retained earnings without having to go to the market to raise new capital.

At the time of writing (January 2011) the market to book ratio for many larger banks was around parity. This is the ratio of market capitalisation to the book value of equity and is a combined measure of the value creation and growth prospects of a firm. One needs to be careful of reading too much into a single ratio, but a market to book ratio of one implies that the market expects banks to earn the cost of equity, earn no net equity spread (i.e. return on equity will equal cost of equity), require no external capital raisings and that any growth in earnings will be negligible. This implies that, in round numbers, the market would be expecting return on equity of around 10–12 per cent (a typical, current, Capital Asset Pricing Model range for cost of equity for banks) which is significantly lower than pre-crisis levels of around 20 per cent.

Clearly, there are several major uncertainties that remain unresolved – for example, how much additional capital that Systemically Important Financial Institutions will be required to hold. Uncertainty exists over whether some of the large international banks will be broken up or forced to carry additional capital through ring-fencing of certain activities or subsidiarisation (this means leaving universal banks whole but requiring self-sufficient entities to be created for, for example, retail and investment banking activities and for individual countries). These risks mean that, for the next few years, bank share prices for the larger firms are likely to carry a discount for uncertainty until these issues are resolved and the full impact understood.

390

However, on one critical question, the authorities, the banks and investors have, so far, been silent – in a Basel III world, what should an appropriate return on equity be? There is a general expectation that returns will be lower than pre-crisis levels but markets are still uncertain as to where the new level will be. Reduced leverage will have a dampening effect (see Chapter 7). Beyond reducing leverage, there are two principal sets of counterbalancing forces that are likely to have a major influence on the risk of banks – reducing or removing the implicit guarantee of government support leading to an increase in risk counterbalanced by higher capital and liquidity buffers which, everything else being equal, should lead to lower risk. Views differ as to how banks' cost of capital will change. On the one hand, there are academics who argue that – based on the theories of Modigliani and Miller – banks could hold significantly more equity capital at a lower marginal cost of equity. On the other, there are bank CEOs who need to persuade asset managers that their investments are safe, that the bank will deliver on its strategy and that it will earn an attractive return on equity. Irrespective of the theoretical arguments, banks need to form their views on what returns are achievable relative to their appetite for risk and then manage their investor communications strategy accordingly. The results announcements from banks for 2010, given in the first part of 2011, seem to indicate that international banks are targeting returns in the region of 12–15 per cent. For example, HSBC is targeting a return of 12–15 per cent, compared to a previous target of 15–19 per cent; Credit Suisse targets 15 per cent; Barclays 13 per cent. It is important to recognise that the targets being quoted cover a time-frame that is shorter than the transition period to the full implementation of Basel III.

It is interesting to note that despite the increase in bank equity capital levels and reduction in leverage since the crisis, equity beta factors (a principal driver of cost of equity) remain higher than pre-crisis levels and are not falling. Figure 16.1 shows the trend in betas for a selection of large international banks. Pre-crisis, the approximate range was 0.5 to 2.0; post-crisis the approximate range is 1.0 to 2.5. Arguably betas were unrealistically low before the crisis as the markets had mispriced the risk of the sector.

Figure 16.1 Evolution of bank equity betasv

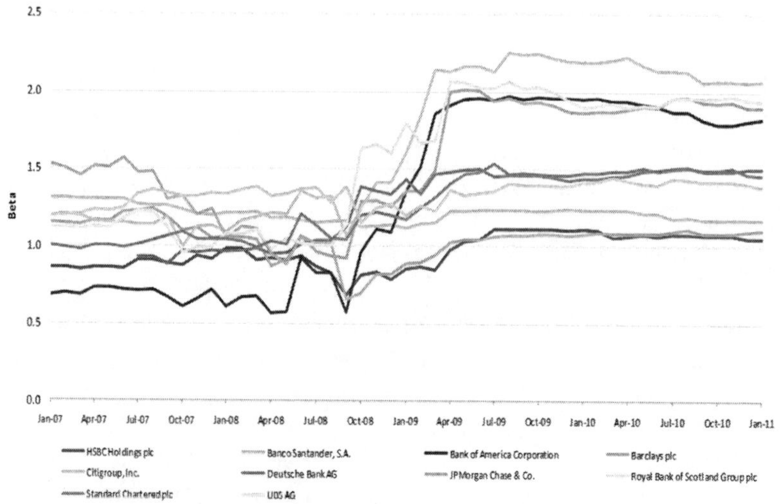

Source: Capital IQ and PwC analysis

16.3.2 *Dividends*

Another key consideration for equity investors is the Basel III conservation ratio. This will constrain management's ability to pay dividends when the Common Equity Tier 1 ratio falls below 7 per cent of RWA. In theory, investors, in aggregate, are indifferent as to whether dividends are paid because when they receive a dividend the net asset value of the bank falls by the amount paid. This means that, overall, the investor is neither better nor worse off with or without a dividend. However, investor preferences for income or capital growth, tax rules and the tax positions of individual investors mean that, in practice, investors are highly sensitive to dividends. In addition, dividends have important signalling power about the future prospects of a business. This means that if dividends are cut due to firm-specific (as opposed to industry-wide) issues, then the share price often falls significantly and takes a long time to recover before investor confidence in the firm is re-established. There would therefore be additional penalties from the market for banks that breach the conservation ratio. To avoid these additional penalties, in practice many firms will be careful to maintain Common Equity Ratios well in excess of the minimum of 7 per cent.

Another group of investors is preference shareholders. The effect of the gradual phasing out of the contribution of preference shares to Tier 1 regulatory capital means that, from the banks' perspective, these become an increasingly expensive source of regulatory capital. For example, if part way through the Basel III transition period only half of the preference share capital counts towards Tier 1, the cost of financing this effectively doubles because the bank needs to pay a coupon on the whole issue. This means that preference shares and other instruments that no longer qualify are very likely to disappear from bank capital structures faster than the timetable dictated by the Basel III transition period. Investors looking for fixed income returns from investments in banks will probably need to look at other debt securities that qualify as Tier 2 capital. However, given the announcement by the Committee in January 2011 that Tier 2 capital will have to be "contingent capital" (see below), the distinction between Additional Tier 1 and Tier 2 becomes blurred and the market for traditional subordinated debt will disappear over the transition period.

Understandably, the transition to new regulatory definitions of what constitutes eligible regulatory is also having an effect of stifling investor appetite for new issues until the precise details have been finalised. The markets for new issues of traditional Tier 1 and Tier 2 capital are effectively closed until these details are clear.

16.4 Debt investors and contingent capital

16.4.1 Debt investors

Senior debt will remain a key feature of banks' funding structures. Debt investors will see a steady supply of such instruments. However, the traditional forms of subordinated debt will gradually disappear. The Basel Committee's announcement on 13 January 2011 requires all new non-senior debt instruments (and Additional Tier 1, like preference shares) to include an equity conversion trigger.

Debt investors have seen an increased supply from banks of medium-term note issuance. This supply is likely to be sustained over the next few years as banks seek to "term-out" their funding structures to reduce their liquidity risks. On the demand side, it is possible that the introduction of Solvency II in Europe will reduce demand from insurance companies for medium-term bank debt, but at this stage the outcome is unclear. Bank treasurers will be monitoring carefully developments and the transition arrangements for Solvency II. As discussed in Chapter 3, Tier 2, Tier 3 and current hybrids will be phased out completely. However, the time pressure to refinance Tier 2 into contingent capital is likely to be less extreme than for Additional Tier 1 capital. This is because the cost of sub-debt – typically 100bps over senior – is likely to be much lower than the cost of contingent capital. Even if Tier 2 is haircut by a large percentage it may still be cheaper for banks to leave the sub-debt outstanding for as long for as possible before it is replaced by contingent capital.

16.4.2 Contingent capital

Contingent capital instruments, sometimes referred to as "CoCos", are debt-like instruments that convert into equity when a firm is in trouble. They will carry a higher coupon because of the higher risk that the investor may potentially lose the investment in the event of a default. Some contingent capital instruments have already been issued for example by Lloyds Banking Group (November 2009) and by Rabobank (March 2010). More recently, Credit Suisse announced in December 2010 that it may raise up to $30 billion in CoCos over the coming years to replace securities that will no longer qualify as available regulatory capital under Basel III. In January 2011 Credit Suisse placed $6.2bn of CoCos with two of its largest investors to replace existing hybrid instruments. The issue was oversubscribed. Although some regulators, such as FINMA in Switzerland, already require contingent capital to form part of a bank's capital structure, a liquid market for these instruments has not yet developed.

Contingent capital instruments may convert to equity when a bank is relatively healthy but experiencing a name-specific stress. As a result of the stress, the bank experiences losses and a key indicator such as its Common Equity Capital Ratio falls below a pre-determined trigger level that causes the CoCo to convert. The additional equity capital allows the bank to weather the storm and recover.

In the event of severe stresses that result in a bank becoming insolvent from a regulatory perspective, the instruments would convert at the point of resolution (i.e. regulatory intervention or administration) and provide additional capital to absorb losses. The idea is that contingent capital would provide additional protection for unsecured creditors such as depositors, which, in turn, would reduce the need for government (i.e. taxpayer) support and reduce the need for a government guarantee to support the institution. The regulators' intention is that contingent capital should stimulate increased market discipline from debt-holders, as they would want to avoid conversion, which exposes them to greater loss. In theory, this should lead debt-holders to exercise greater influence over management and make management more risk-averse. Barclays has announced that it is considering CoCos that could convert back to debt once a stress event has passed – nicknamed the "hokey-cokey CoCo".

Contingent capital is a relatively new idea and it is not yet clear what the market appetite for it will be nor how such instruments will be priced. There are also tax and accounting issues to address. It is worth noting that CoCos provide a particular challenge to the investment management industry. This is because many investment managers only hold mandates for either fixed income or equity investments. CoCos fall between these two stools and until new mandates are issued (or old ones modified), many investment managers have no mandate to buy these products. CoCos are, of course, attractive to some hedge funds because of the high yield and their risk characteristics. It will be interesting to see if other market participants, such as insurance companies, develop new products that provide banks with the option to increase capital requirements under certain circumstances.

Some banks are considering awarding bonuses in the form of contingent capital instruments. This could be a way of using deferred bonus payments to increase available equity in stressed circumstances. Meanwhile the high yield of the CoCo provides cash income to the employee.

An important practical consideration which has not yet been addressed is how trigger ratios will operate. How can investors be sure that triggers will be applied objectively and without political interference? Will their operation require regulators to make a judgment? On what publicly-disclosed numbers would this judgement be based if it takes place outside a bank's normal reporting cycle? Another problem is the conversion ratio – set it too high and the ordinary share-holders will suffer, set it too low and the notes are unattractive to debt investors. Also, does there need to be a floor? Remember that the only time these get converted is in a situation where the ordinary share price will have collapsed. Investors will require confidence in the answers to these sorts of questions before they invest.

Despite the uncertainties, CoCos appear to be coming – banks and investors will continue to watch developments closely. A key development in 2011 will be the FSB's report on SIFIs expected around the end of 2011.

16.5   Depositors and borrowers

16.5.1 Depositors

In general, putting current, low, central bank interest rates aside, the crisis has been good for retail and commercial depositors. The liquidity that they provide is a key component in reducing bank dependency on short-term wholesale funding, which dried up during the crisis. The supply of these deposits is limited, which means that prices have been raised in liquidity-constrained markets such as in the US and Europe, as banks compete fiercely for them. In addition, to increase customer confidence and deposit stickiness, deposit insurance availability has increased – usually funded by the banks through national industry compen-sation schemes. As a result, despite the popular denigration of banks in several countries, many savings product customers are likely to do better in the future than they did in the past.

The drive from banks to adapt their funding structures to meet the Basel III liquidity requirements also means that banks are thinking carefully about product design and how to service better the needs of aging populations in the developed economies. Those banks that have private banking and wealth management activities have an advantage to exploit through their access to growing savings markets. In addition, overcoming the perennial challenge of making cross-selling work can potentially provide opportunities to gain deposits from their borrowing customers. In the UK, off-set mortgages, which are particularly in vogue which can be attractive to borrowers with some cash to spare that they want to keep in reserve rather than to pay down debt.

Another consequence of the new liquidity rules is that banks are keen to increase the stickiness of deposits. This may have unintended consequences for depositors in the medium term. One way to increase stickiness is to cross-sell other products and services. So, for example, a business deposit account customer may be encouraged to borrow, to use money transmission and payment services etc. This may be convenient, but a sticky customer with a range of products with one institution will then be vulnerable to earning less or paying more across the range of products that it holds. As stickiness increases, ease of switching diminishes and competitiveness declines.

16.5.2 Borrowers

Highly-leveraged customers (and governments) were as vulnerable as highly-leveraged banks to the crisis. It was predictable that banks would reduce their appetite for risk and be much more cautious in making lending decisions than they were before the crisis. At the same time, lack of customer confidence and significant cash holdings on corporate balance sheets mean that demand for lending has dropped in many markets, despite central bank interest rates being low.

The cost of lending, though, has increased in real terms and credit spreads have widened (except in some Asian markets where an excess of liquidity has led to the opposite problem – low interest rates and a deposit margin squeeze which is depressing banks' profitability). In part, this is to cover impairments on the existing book (where re-pricing opportunities may be limited) but also to finance the cost of the new liquidity and capital regimes. For example, the new Net Stable Funding Ratio means that longer-term lending will be more expensive and that its supply is likely to be reduced.

Many banks use a loan-to-deposit ratio as a simple indicator of liquidity risk (this simple measure does not pick up the liquidity gaps that arise in the future). There are two ways to reach a target ratio – increase deposits or reduce lending. This means that the liquidity rules may have an effect of reducing the supply of credit to borrowers.

Regulatory capital requirements are driven by RWA. An intended consequence of the new rules is to reduce the level of riskier assets – for example through reducing exposure to counterparty credit risk – while increasing the quantity and quality of capital. However, an unintended consequence is that most banks have put in place initiatives to reduce RWA across the board to make sure that their use of capital is efficient as possible. By-products of RWA-reduction initiatives include reducing the level of undrawn credit facilities for which there are capital charges and reducing undrawn funding lines for which there are contingent liquidity charges. Actions like these reduce financial capacity and the risk appetite of retail and commercial borrowers, which in turn is likely to have detrimental impacts on entrepreneurship and the capacity for economic growth.

An unintended side effect of the desire by regulators to ensure that banks are more liquid and able to fund themselves through onshore customer deposits has been a trapping of a large pool of liquidity in many savings-driven markets, such as those in most Asian countries. These excess savings would normally have been transmitted through the international banking system to markets with a shortage of liquidity, notably Europe and the USA. Instead, they are trapped onshore, leading to low interest rates and, as the banks have loan/deposit ratios of around 70 per cent and have nowhere else to lend the money, to the makings of a property bubble – which is precisely the sort of thing Basel III is meant to prevent!

16.6   Government and the taxpayer

This Section discusses the balance between the wider government interest and the narrower interests of regulators and supervisors; and considers the value of the implicit guarantee of support.

16.6.1 Government

Governments and politicians are interested in being associated with economic growth and an environment of financial stability. This is reflected in the goals of the G20 and the mandate of the Financial Stability Board (see Chapter 1). So while regulators and supervisors are keen to do everything that they can to prevent systemic failure, government has to weigh the potential damage to economic growth of too much risk aversion in the regulation of the banking system. The economic arguments and implications are discussed in detail in Chapter 18.

From the perspective of the overall economy, it clearly makes sense to provide government support when this is a cheaper option than the economic fall-out from bank failure. While banks and governments agree that banks should not receive support to the extent that was required in the crisis, it is also important for the authorities to be proportionate in terms of the safety levels that they want to build into a banking industry whose prime role in the economy is to encourage economic activity by taking risk, whether through maturity transformation, credit risk or other risks.

A simple, high-level view of the proposed regulatory changes seems to indicate that the balance of risk could be going too far in terms of safety. For example, the liquidity rules could mean that a typical universal bank would have to hold, say, 20 per cent of its balance sheet in liquid assets like government securities to safeguard it against a potential once-in-a-hundred-year liquidity event. These assets are held with a "negative carry" (i.e. cost) of around, say, 100bps (the opportunity cost of holding these assets is of course even higher). In addition, the new Basel III capital rules, in terms of definition and RWA, mean that equity capital requirements have more than doubled for the world's larger Group 1 banks (the Basel Committee defines Group 1 banks as those that have Tier 1 capital in excess of €3bn, are well-diversified, and are internationally active) as a whole (results of the quantitative impact study, December 2010, Bank of International Settlements – pages 2 and 10). Based on figures at the end of 2009, RWA increase by 23 per cent and the tighter definition of capital causes a fall of 41 per cent in available regulatory capital: this means these banks in aggregate would have needed to more than double equity capital to maintain their existing ratios. See Figure 16.2.

Figure 16.2 Illustration of Basel III impact on Group 1 banks

	Basel I/II	Basel III	Change
Available capital	10.0	5.9	–41.3%
RWA	100	123	+23.0%
Common Equity Tier 1 ratio	10.0%	4.8%	–52.0%

In simple terms this means that return on equity will more than halve unless the banks respond through increased prices etc. Note that this halving is before the increase in minimum ratios or the impact of the Liquidity Coverage Ratio and the Net Stable Funding Ratio which will reduce return on equity even further. There is a risk of regulatory over-reaction because regulators and supervisors have no incentive to support economic growth. Their key concern is to avoid bank failure and the consequences of failure.

Safety and insurance need to be paid for which diverts resources from elsewhere in the economy. In certain countries politicians are still keen to knock bankers (some three years after the crisis) and by implication the banking industry. However, governments know that they need to make sure that economic growth can be supported by the financial system at an economic cost. From the banking industry's perspective, in some ways, government should be its strongest ally in making sure that a balanced and proportionate solution is found. However, there are also conflicts of interest in, for example, government support for new Basel liquidity rules conflicts with the government need, in many cases, to finance deficits through the issuance of government bonds – the liquid asset that banks are being required to hold.

Another key consideration for governments has been the interconnectedness of the financial system. Because of the dependencies between institutions, the failure of one may cause others to fail. At the time of the crisis, many of these complex linkages were unclear, which meant that governments were forced to take a conservative approach, err on the side of caution, and provide support that may have been unnecessary had there been greater transparency.

Government support was aimed at supporting institutions, not individuals, but it meant that, in many cases, the public perception is that the bank management teams that had taken excessive risks and caused their institutions to teeter towards the edge of the precipice were saved (and paid) by unwilling taxpayers. However, in most cases those management teams have been fired. In some countries, as a result of this support and the apparent cost to the taxpayer, there has been an understandable public outcry at the level of pay in the banking industry. Market forces mean that this is a difficult issue to address – there is no first-mover advantage in reducing pay. However the strength and persistence of public feeling probably means that there will be future changes and interventions, although the precise nature of these remains unclear.

In some countries, a bank tax has been imposed to contribute to the cost of bail-out. Such taxes often end up feeding the general public purse and, like, for example, the provisions that are set aside for the decommissioning of publicly-owned nuclear power stations, are not invested to create a ring-fenced reserve for the purpose in question. Some banks have advocated the creation of such a fund. However, others argue that such a fund encourages risk-taking in the financial services industry.

16.6.2 *Value of the implicit guarantee*

The value of the implicit government guarantee is significant and can be observed in the market. This is because both

Moody's and Fitch provide ratings for banks on a "supported" and a "stand-alone" basis. Comparing funding costs using these two ratings allows one to estimate the cost of the guarantee (note that the ratings themselves involve a high degree of judgment). Using Moody's data and three categories of banks – larger, medium, small – the Bank of England estimated the value of the implicit guarantee as shown in Figure 16.3.

Figure 16.3 Value of implicit guarantee on funding costs – UK banks

	2007	2008	2009
Large	0.4%	0.9%	2.3%
Medium	0.5%	2.5%	0.9%
Small	0.0%	0.5%	0.7%

Source: Bank of England Financial Stability Report, December 2010

As expected, the value of the guarantee increases during a crisis, but, as illustrated by the trend in medium banks, falls back once the market has regained confidence. At 2.3 per cent, in 2009 the value of support in funding costs for the large UK banks terms was significant – the Bank of England estimates its notional pre-tax value at £100bn. Given the uncertainty in 2009 over the risks in Lloyds and RBS, it is not surprising that the value should have been high. (Large in this context means the four larger banks with activities in the UK – Barclays, HSBC, Lloyds, and RBS; medium covers Nationwide and Northern Rock; small covers smaller building societies). However, a high value in the implicit guarantee is not necessarily a bad thing. If it results in lower bank funding costs which in turn translate into lower credit pricing; customers and the economy will benefit. UK banks, of course, are not alone in benefiting from this implicit guarantee which other governments provide to their banks.

16.7   Rating agencies

Rating agencies play an important role in providing independent assessment of the risk of firms and securities. The rapid growth in rating agency fee income in the run-up to the crisis through, for example, services provided to rate Collaterised Debt Obligations ("CDOs"), has led to concerns that objectivity may have been compromised. As a result, new rules and regulations have been devised to ensure that advisory and rating activities are kept separate. In Europe the European Commission is consulting on changes (see below). In the US the Dodd-Frank Act, requires that the US authorities conduct three studies:

(1) Strengthening Credit Rating Independence. The SEC is required to conduct a study of the independence of "nationally rated statistical ratings organizations" (NRSROs) and their impact on credit rating issues. This study will include, among other things, an evaluation of how NRSROs manage conflicts of interest resulting from NRSROs providing other non-credit rating services and the potential impact of a prohibition on NRSROs providing such services.
(2) Alternative Business Models. The Comptroller General of the United States is required to conduct a study of alternative means for compensating NRSROs to create incentives to provide more accurate ratings.
(3) Creation of an Independent Professional Analyst Organisation. The Comptroller General of the United States is required to conduct a study on the feasibility and merits of creating an independent professional organization that would establish independent standards and an ethics code for NRSRO ratings analysts and oversee the profession. This study supplements another portion of the Act, which requires NRSRO employees to be tested for knowledge of the credit rating process or to otherwise meet standards necessary to produce accurate ratings.

In Europe, on 5 November 2010, the European Commission announced a consultation on the role of the rating agencies in the financial system. The scope of the consultation was broad ranging and covered sovereign debt ratings, competition, liability and conflicts of interest. However, the period of consultation was quite short – until 7 January 2011 – indicating the urgency with which the European Commission wishes to deal with these issues. In March 2011 the European Commission identified four key objectives for reform of rating agencies: to reduce the level of concentration; to reduce the overreliance on ratings; to improve the rating process for sovereign debt; and, to deal with conflicts of interest.

Rightly or wrongly, rating agencies are regarded with some suspicion by Congress and the European Commission and are likely to face a long haul to re-establish their reputations. However it is difficult to see how capital markets can function effectively without independent assessment of the relative riskiness of firms and instruments. An individual firm does not have access to the same range of data that an independent agency might have. Indeed the Basel framework relies on these independent judgments to support parameter estimation and risk assessments – for example in the Standardised Approach or the liquidity standards. This requirement remains an unresolved issue in the US – until a solution is found, Dodd-Frank effectively makes the implementation of Basel II impossible. However it is clear that firms are now much more wary of relying on external ratings to the extent that they did in the past and, as a result, are strengthening their own risk analysis capabilities. At the same time, the agencies are grappling with rebuilding their own reputations and responding to the regulatory challenge to raise their standing and professional standards.

Banks are likely to see greater information demands from the agencies and greater challenges from them as they aim to develop more detailed and more effective understanding of the risks that banks run. Fitch is currently in the final stages of introducing a new quantitative tool to analyse bank regulatory capital. Standard and Poor's ("S&P") uses its own measure of risk-adjusted capital and RWA. S&P is also conducting a fundamental review of its rating methodology for banks and consulted with the industry on its approach in the first quarter of 2011.

16.8 Transparency for stakeholders

16.8.1 The need for transparency

Banking is a confidence trick in the best sense of the phrase. For the financial system to operate, it is essential that customers, counterparties and funding providers all have confidence in the institutions with which they deal. Rebuilding trust and confidence remains a priority for all firms affected by the crisis and the industry as a whole. For those firms with state support, re-established confidence on a stand-alone basis is a pre-condition to regaining independence.

The need for greater transparency is seen as central to establishing and maintaining confidence in financial markets. This comes in various guises, for example, greater transparency in derivatives trading through standardised contracts executed on centralised trading platforms to replace opaque trades between banks and their customers – invisible to everyone other than the parties involved. This approach aims to make the volume and nature of derivatives being traded clearer to customers, supervisors and banks. Certain forms of derivatives are likely to be regulated directly. For example while credit default swaps have some of the characteristics of insurance products they are not regulated as such. There are no limits on the number of credit default swaps that can be written on a particular counterparty or instrument. The hidden leverage created by multiple derivative transactions in relation to the same risk creates a multiplier effect that currently remains an unaddressed threat to future financial stability. The same is true of commodity derivatives.

The future of securitisations and asset-backed securities markets also depends on greater transparency of the risk characteristics of the underlying assets. Many mistakes in assessing the risks of asset-backed securities were made, not just in terms of methodology, but also by concentrating on average pool data rather than taking care to understand the granular detail and the behaviour of key segments in these portfolios. There was also insufficient attention devoted to the possibility of the future being different to the past and to the likelihood of increased probability of tail risk. Interestingly, these risks were sometimes misunderstood even when the data was available.

Lack of transparency gives an information advantage to those that have access to data that others do not. This remains an issue that is still to be played out in relation to assets that became toxic during the crisis. This is evidenced by the number of specialist mortgage securities traders and hedge funds that are currently taking advantage of relatively illiquid markets for pre-crisis securities in anticipation of increasing asset values.

Transparency is also related to another important development: the reduction in the level of proprietary trading undertaken by investment banks. By trading on their own account, one part of an investment bank could be directly acting against the interests of the customers of another part of the same institution (and this would be invisible to both sets of customers). The Dodd-Frank Act aims to reduce the level of proprietary risk-taking to a minimal amount but there are definitional and implementation issues that supervisors recognise they will need to monitor carefully. As a by-product, conflicts of interest may also be reduced. Transparency has also been a key challenge within the management processes of many financial institutions. It is clear that many firms had taken on risks that were poorly understood by those assuming them and by the senior management and boards in those firms. At one extreme, there are the anecdotal traders who focus on maximising bonuses with no regard for the welfare of their customers, colleagues or for the organisations for which they work. The argument goes that they have no interest in making sure risks are understood and managed. Indeed they may well have an interest in making sure that the risks are hidden and misunderstood! At the other extreme there are detail-minded CEOs who understand very well the risks in the business and demand the information to understand them better.

16.8.2 *Wider considerations*

Transparency requires more than compliance with current disclosure rules for annual reports. Chapter 12 – Disclosures and Pillar 3, discusses in detail the key enabler of effective disclosure.

There is also a clear imperative for all firms to make sure that they fully understand the risks that they are taking on and to reduce reliance on delegated assessments by third parties such as ratings agencies. Chapter 18 – Implications for Risk Management, discusses some of the remedies that banks are applying to strengthen risk management

A number of the reforms aim to make sure that risks are better accounted for in performance measures and that remuneration takes into account the risks assumed in making profits. The days of bonuses linked simply to revenue or asset growth are numbered. However, banks and supervisors should not underestimate the challenge in making such changes stick nor the relentless effort required to change behaviour and culture. As soon as new rules and regulations are introduced, clever minds look for ways to circumvent them or take on risks, which the rules may have missed – the "side letter" problem. Chapter 14 – Reward, discusses the wide range of changes that are being pursued to better align incentives with risk and align management's goals with those of a wider group of stakeholders.

Some commentators argue that it will take more than stronger risk culture and governance to prevent the worst excesses; radical solutions are needed to address the agency problem – the separation of the interests of management from those of owners and other stakeholders. One option may be to increase greatly the personal liabilities of the directors of financial institutions. In some countries a failure of a firm means "go to jail" for the directors (directly and without passing "go"). A counter-argument is that such an approach would sharply change the risk/reward trade-off and would probably lead to talented managers leaving the industry, thereby reducing the overall quality of management. Others argue for the reintroduction of a partnership culture that was common to many Wall Street and City firms half a century ago.

However, the practical challenge for most firms is how to meet their responsibilities to all stakeholders within the context of the existing legal and ownership structures, despite their imperfections.

16.9 Conclusion

The consequences of Basel III are wide reaching and will affect many stakeholders both through primary impacts and as yet unforeseen secondary effects. These consequences will vary considerably around the world: from the savings of a Chinese entrepreneur to the equity-release mortgage of a pensioner in the UK; from a fixed-income trader moving from an investment bank to a hedge fund; to the corporate treasurer looking for a bespoke derivative; from a European public authority seeking to invest surplus funds to an unemployed electrician in South Africa seeking an overdraft. All are finding the financial world a different place. Even by the end of the transition period the full implications of Basel III for investors, customers, counter-parties and governments are unlikely to have crystallised.

Chapter 17

Implications for Risk Management

Sonja du Plessis

17.1   Introduction

17.1.1   Overview

A principal outcome of the financial crisis was recognition of the need for banks to strengthen risk management significantly. Whilst the Basel Committee's recommendations and guidance focused on aspects such as liquidity monitoring and reporting, counterparty credit and stress testing, the Senior Supervisors Group ("SSG"), the Financial Stability Board and the G20 have recognised the need for a more comprehensive approach to risk management. Most banks have made and are taking active steps to do this – often in an environment of closer scrutiny and challenge from their supervisors.

Strengthening risk management requires many different areas of the firm to be addressed together. It may involve better risk measurement and quantitative analysis, but, more often than not it requires firms to make improvements to the "softer" themes such as governance and incentive structures, and key enablers, such as information technology and infrastructure. Basel concludes that one of the key causes of the financial crisis was the failure of management; it is not just about better tools and processes, it is about making sure people use them and that there are consequences for not doing so. Only by addressing these interrelated components with a coherent programme can banks succeed in implementing sound risk management practices.

This Chapter considers the implications of Basel III and wider reforms for risk management under four main Sections:

1. **Establishing an effective organisational culture that explicitly support good risk management practices**: many practitioners refer to this as a "risk culture". This is probably the most important soft dimension of strengthened risk management and requires being explicit about how much risk the bank is willing to take and what returns to achieve. It requires the support of formal and informal working practices to be able to monitor that risk profile and avoid taking on exposures outside of appetite. Without an explicit risk culture, other initiatives are likely to fail.

2. **Role of the board**: in setting an effective risk culture, the tone from the top and the board's leadership role in governance are key. This Section addresses matters such as board responsibility for oversight of risk and control functions, obligations towards stakeholders, the setting of risk appetite, oversight of senior management and considerations in determining the effectiveness of the board.

3. **Chief risk officer ("CRO")**: this Section discusses the changing role of the CRO, including the impact of reporting lines, the attributes of a successful CRO, the CRO's role in determining adequacy of risk resources, and effectiveness of the risk function.

4. **Integrating risk in the business**: risk management does not operate as a function in isolation – its successful integration with the business is critical to strengthening risk management. This Section discusses the elements of the risk management framework and the factors that are essential for success.

The Chapter concludes with an assessment of the changes that banks are experiencing and the actions that they are likely to take.

17.1.2 Background

There have been a number of important publications since the crisis – notably those from the Senior Supervisors Group ("SSG"), the Basel Committee, the European Commission and, in the UK, the Walker Report.

The SSG published a report that highlighted very succinctly the causes of the financial crises. The report, issued in October 2009 and titled "Risk Management Lessons from the Global Banking Crisis of 2008" ("SSG report") reviews in detail the funding and liquidity issues central to the recent crisis and explores critical areas of risk management practice in need of improvement across the financial services industry.

The SSG report highlighted four main reasons for failures in governance:

a) the unwillingness or inability of boards of directors and senior managers to articulate, measure, and adhere to a level of risk acceptable to the firm;

b) arrangements that favoured risk-takers at the expense of independent risk managers and control personnel;

c) compensation plans that conflicted with the control objectives of the firm; and

d) an inadequate and often fragmented infrastructure that hindered effective risk identification and measurement.

The report concluded that despite firms' recent progress in improving risk management practices, underlying weaknesses in governance, incentive structures, information technology infrastructure and internal controls require substantial work if they are to be addressed properly. Chapter 14 – Reward, discusses incentives and compensation in detail.

A year later, in October 2010, the Basel Committee on Banking Supervision published "Principles for enhancing corporate governance" ("Basel paper"), which addresses sound corporate governance principles and the role of supervision, in an effort to guide enhancement of corporate governance frameworks. The paper is comprehensive and discusses, for example: the role of the board; the qualifications and composition of the board; the importance of an independent risk management function, including a chief risk officer or equivalent; the importance of monitoring risks on an ongoing firm-wide and individual entity basis; the board's oversight of the compensation systems and the board; and senior management's understanding of the bank's operational structure and risks.

In June 2010 the European Commission published a green paper, "Corporate governance in financial institutions and remuneration policies" ("EC green paper"), on a range of options to strengthen corporate governance in EU financial institutions. The EC green paper has been published with the Commission Staff Working Paper, "Corporate Governance in financial institutions: the lessons to be learnt from the current financial crisis and possible steps forward". The subsequent report, based on the consultation's responses, is currently doing the rounds at the European Parliament and it is expected that political agreement on any legislation or regulations arising from this will be reached during the course of 2011. The consultation paper put forward some proposals that were similar in substance to Sir David Walker's, "A review of Corporate Governance in UK Banks and Other Financial Industry entities" published in November 2009. However, others went further particularly around board composition and risk governance. A further consultation paper on corporate governance in listed institutions – covering all industry sectors – is due out in the second quarter of 2011.

It is by no means certain what the landscape will eventually look like. Nevertheless, there are key principles to consider. Firms that are not addressing corporate governance and the wider implications for risk management at the same time as calculating regulatory capital requirements and implementing detailed amended requirements for the quantitative risk types will be challenged when trying to evidence that risk management is embedded in their organisation. Boards, senior management, and most of all, CROs will have to reconsider how they are equipped and supported to fulfil the duties of care that have been placed on them.

17.2 Establishing an explicit risk culture

An explicit risk culture, including a clear statement of a firm's attitude to risk is a vital component of effective risk management. Whether driven by regulation, for example, Basel III or Solvency II, or by changes in firms' risk appetite, culture needs to move from being implicit to being explicit. The failure of boards and management to establish an appropriate risk culture undermines any sound risk operating model and allows for ambiguity and abdication of responsibilities, which, in turn, lead to unmanaged risks and eventually to poor performance. Similarly, if firms' reform agendas to strengthen risk management are to be sustained and change secured, they must be accompanied by creating and maintaining an explicit risk culture.

The efforts of firms, regulators and policymakers are focusing on driving cultural change, principally through compensation, to align better the interests of key risk-takers with those of shareholders and customers. It is doubtful that this alone will drive the step change in culture required in the post-crisis world. Recent experience has shown that transparency over the risks being taken needs to exist across a basic three-phase business management cycle: strategy and planning, business execution, and performance evaluation.

In theory, risk culture is the result of history, leadership, and organisational values, as articulated in firm policy and other communications. Further, it would result in framing the behaviours that underpin management's risk decision-making. However, in most firms, the risk culture is a result of allowable and tolerated behaviours, and practices. Therefore, it is critical for firms to "discover" their actual culture. To start the process of change firms need a candid appraisal of actual culture. This can be difficult to achieve – it is very hard to stand back and form an objective view of the culture of which one is part. However, by focusing on allowable and tolerated behaviours and practices, such an appraisal is possible and may well result in the stark realisation that there are major shortcomings.

Typical examples of sub-optimal behaviours and practices include:

a) Business planning dominated by the pursuit of growth or improved profitability without regard to economic, macro-economic or operational and reputational risks.
b) Entrenched silos with limited willingness to challenge risks, whether within a particular risk class, across business lines or between functions. Organisations that are not set

up to challenge and review risk portfolios across the formalised types of risk, or across functional or divisional silos will find it harder to entrench practices that support effective risk management.

c) The inability of others to challenge high revenue genera-tors with questions on why and how they achieve such high performance, or instances of looking the other way because known "out-of-limit risk taking" resulted in high performance.

In performing a self-appraisal, firms need to analyse their organisation across the broad range of behavioural factors that influence culture. The significance of these factors will vary by firm, business line and function but there are common factors that need to be considered: leadership, governance, motivation, people and infrastructure.

To describe the desired culture and behaviours clearly, there are a few core principles that firms should aim to institutionalise:

a) consideration of risk recognised as an integral part of decision-making;
b) measurement of returns on a risk-adjusted basis;
c) comprehensive understanding of key risks, recognising interactions and impacts across business lines, functions and risk classes;
d) focus on action, not analysis; and
e) clear expectations of the behaviours to be exhibited by senior personnel both within, and outside, the risk function.

The Holy Grail for banks is to have risk management fully embedded in the business. This involves bringing risk informa-tion and insight to bear on every decision an organisation takes, from acquisitions and divestments to new product launches and transaction pricing. It is about taking an implicit consider-ation of risk in the decisions that a bank takes and making that consideration explicit within formal and informal processes. To achieve this transformation, people at all levels of the organisa-tion need to understand their responsibility for risk, and a culture should be promulgated whereby raising risk issues is encouraged and regarded as a strength.

17.3   Role of the board

17.3.1   *Governance*

As one of the four reasons for failure in governance, the SSG report identified the unwillingness (or inability) of boards of directors and senior managers to articulate, measure, and adhere to a level of risk acceptable to the firm. The Basel paper on governance addresses this through a clear articulation of the responsibilities of boards of directors and their interaction with senior management. Board members are charged with "actively carrying out their responsibility for banks, including its business and risk strategy, organisation, financial soundness and governance". In practice, this sets a high hurdle for non-executive directors who are required to have a clear understanding of the business and its strategy, as well as the capability and robustness of risk and control functions.

Whereas governance requirements have been aimed previously mainly at shareholders, the Basel principles have become much more explicit about the board's responsibility towards other stakeholders. The Basel paper clearly point out that "in discharging responsibilities, the board should take into account the legitimate interests of shareholders, depositors and other relevant stakeholders". In practice, this means that boards can no longer be content with understanding only the financial significance of risks to the firm, they also need to think about the potential impact on other stakeholders and the resulting reputational risks to the firm.

Materiality has been used as a concept to highlight issues of significance that would need to be debated at board level for some time. This has mostly been based on financial impact, e.g. losses bigger than x per cent of profit, etc. The focus on financial impact would highlight issues of concern to stakeholders such as shareholders. Broadening the materiality framework to cover the range of stakeholders – including shareholders, customers, employees and regulators – could result in a consistent business-wide approach to escalation of risks, or known issues that could be significant to any of these stakeholders.

An example of such a framework is set out below in Figure 17.1. A framework like this could be used as the basis for a material events escalation policy.

Figure 17.1 Risk impact materiality

Shareholder	Customer	Staff	Rating agencies	Regulator
• Potential event with negative P&L/Economic Profit impact of £xm/£xm respectively • Potential event with negative balance sheet impact of £ym (where y is less than x) • Major impact on perception of competency of management in eyes of shareholders	• Brand – specialist national media interest over one week or any main national interest • General – major impact on over 5 per cent of customer segment	• Unexpected major event affecting staff morale, major loss of staff or loss of key staff	• Potential major deviation from current risk appetite • Major impact on perception of competency of management in eyes of bondholder • Unplanned movement of 1 per cent (in absolute terms) in the capital ratio	• To be referred to the CRO for review and discussion • Potential for fine or enforcement • Potential of major disclosure to regulator • Potential to reduce capital below the buffer • Potential for impact on supervisory rating

17.3.2 Providing oversight for risk and control functions

The principle that boards should provide effective oversight of risk and control functions places an implicit requirement for the heads of control functions, such as the CRO, chief financial officer ("CFO"), chief compliance officer ("CCO"), and chief information officer ("CIO") and head of internal audit to provide the board with a level of assurance that the necessary risk management capability and infrastructure exists within the firm.

This and the three lines of defence are further explored in Section 17.5 on the role of the CRO.

17.3.3 Oversight of senior management

The EC green paper asked for comment on the following proposals for the board's role in risk management:

(a) requiring the board to publish a "risk control declaration" and to set up a procedure for the board to approve new financial products (this already exists in many countries such as the UK, Netherlands and France);

(b) requiring the board to inform supervisory authorities of any material risks of which it is aware; and

(c) requiring an executive report on the adequacy of internal control systems.

Additionally, the Basel paper specifically refers to the need for the board to oversee senior management: in monitoring their actions; regular meetings; questioning and reviewing critically information; setting formal performance standards; and ensuring knowledge and expertise. The Basel paper also points out that "the board should also ensure that the bank's organisational structure facilitates effective decision making and good governance".

The materiality framework can provide a strong basis for delegation of authority as well as escalation of risks. Escalation of risks with an impact beyond the stated materiality level can be stated as the clear responsibility of business management. Delegation policies then can be aligned not to exceed this materiality level. The materiality framework illustrated above was used by the particular organisation to delegate responsibility for risk management by stating that it is the joint responsibility of the particular risk director (e.g. market risk director, credit risk director, etc) and the executive director of the division to escalate issues that exceed these materiality levels to the risk committee and the board. Each of the divisions has a similar framework that stipulates the levels at which risk should be escalated to its divisional board.

17.3.4 Board risk committees in practice

Whereas a number of firms have included risk management oversight as one of an audit committee's oversight duties, this will become increasingly difficult to justify to regulators. Most firms now have a separate risk committee of the board, but often encounter practical difficulties when setting up and managing sub-risk committees to support and challenge the submissions to the board risk committee.

Committee membership case study

Situation: This firm had a board risk committee but encountered difficulty with having a mechanism for reports to the board risk committee to be challenged and overseen by the risk function. The firm therefore used a business risk committee as the vehicle for reporting and reviewing risks across the organisation. It was also where policies and risk appetite statements were recommended for approval by the board risk committee. However, the effectiveness of this business risk committee was under challenge.

Issue: Although the executive directors were members of the committee, most of them delegated attendance to their divisional risk officers. The divisional risk officers attended the meetings where papers were presented to them by their risk colleagues who headed up the various risk disciplines, The committee became a forum where the risk professionals talked to each other about the risk profile of this firm, with little senior management attention and buy-in to the action plans required to address areas outside of risk appetite.

Solution: During a programme to improve risk governance, the executive directors were interviewed about their reasons for non-attendance of this committee. The main reason was the sheer volume of papers and lack of focus of the submissions to the committee. Four key changes were implemented that effected a step change:

Membership was changed to include only senior management (the executive director of each of the divisions, as well as the HR director, CFO, CRO, CIO). Risk directors would attend to present papers, however were not included in the

---

membership of the committee. The CEO took up the chairmanship of the management risk committee.

A materiality framework was debated and approved by senior management to guide the reporting of risk management issues to the committee and ensure that significant issues were debated at senior executive level. This materiality framework covered all key stakeholders and was then used as a guide to cascade to the divisional and individual business units to set their own levels of materiality.

A set of guidelines to the papers were implemented that clearly focused the attention of members on the key issues, including the decisions they were required to take. This helped to reduce the volume of papers significantly, and less material issues were delegated to sub committees to attend to and resolve

All actions that came out of the discussions of the business risk committee were owned by the executive directors around the table.

The CEO requested that these measures be reviewed after a year of operation, and the review at that time concluded that these measures were effective and considerably improved the effectiveness of the business risk committee.

17.3.5 Qualification and commitment of board members

The Basel paper requires board members to have appropriate qualifications and experience to enable them to fulfil their obligations, both on an individual and a collective basis. The EC green paper asks whether recruitment policies should specify the duties and profile of directors and the chairman. Regulators are already exercising much stronger approval mechanisms for the appointment of board members, with rigorous interviews prior to approval of key appointments.

It would be unrealistic to expect non-executives to pick up the intricacies of a business and the strategic direction within the few hours that are often allocated for board meeting preparation. This means that non-executive board members will need to have enough prior experience to understand the business well. Immediately, the pool of available non-executive directors is reduced. In addition, the time required for all board members to discharge their duties appropriately will have to be increased and the remuneration of board members will need to be increased accordingly. A reduction in the pool of non-executive directors may therefore mean that we will see the emergence of "professional" non-executive directors who exclusively devote their time to this duty.

In practice, for many organisations the increased demands will require investment in a training and awareness programme of "up-skilling" existing board members, as well as induction programmes for incoming board members. Non-executives at firms that are prepared to invest in training programmes are likely to be much more confident in interaction with the regulators.

The increased responsibility placed on directors would require greater involvement as well as time commitment. There remains a continuous tension between a high enough level of involvement in the business to gain the required under-standing, and maintaining the degree of independence required by a non- executive board member.

The EC green paper also requested views on whether the number of boards on which a director may sit should be limited, suggesting a cap of three.

In this era of increased personal accountability, it is likely to become increasingly difficult to find candidates for non-executive financial institution directorships who are willing and able to take on this challenging role.

17.3.6 *Effectiveness of the board*

The Basel paper refers to a requirement for the board to assess its effectiveness periodically. The EC green paper asks for views on the compulsory evaluation of the board by an external evaluator, with the results being made available to supervisory authorities and shareholders. While the requirement to assess the board performance, is not new, the implications of the Basel paper are that bank board's should assess its performance in respect of its risk management duties.

17.4 Risk appetite

The board is expected to approve and oversee the implementation of the bank's strategy and risk appetite. The Basel paper states that "under the direction of the board, senior management should ensure that the bank's activities are consistent with the business strategy, risk tolerance/appetite and policies approved by the board."

The board plays a vital oversight role but its ability to challenge management is severely limited if it lacks relevant expertise. The crisis has highlighted the extent to which even experienced bankers were out of touch with practices that had huge ramifications for an organisation's overall exposure, e.g., the role played by structured investment vehicles in funding, or the liquidity puts that allowed investors to sell CDOs back to the issuing bank. There is a big overlap here with the risk identification component of the risk management framework – a bank's oversight functions could have all the expertise in the world, but if they are not getting timely and relevant data, they will be hamstrung. Still, everyone involved in some form of oversight role – not just the board, but also members of the various risk committees – needs to have a more complete understanding of the bank's businesses and their underlying risks.

The SSG report also referred to the lack of articulation, measurement, and adherence to a level of risk acceptable to the firm. It went into some detail about how boards did not understand the risks undertaken by their firms, and how senior management lacked direction regarding the setting of risk appetite in the first place.

Risk appetite is a complicated affair at the heart of risk management and business strategy. Defined well, risk appetite embeds risk metrics and methods into business decisions, reporting and day-to-day business discussions. It sets the boundaries which form a dynamic link between strategy, target setting and risk management.

However, many firms have struggled with the concept of risk appetite and have experienced considerable difficulties in getting their boards to articulate their risk appetite. Boards often struggle with this, because it is difficult to talk about risk appetite without grounding it, or providing some reference framework within which it can be set.

It may be helpful to think about the following concepts when articulating risk appetite:

(a) **Risk capacity**: the maximum risk that the firm can bear influenced by internal and external drivers.
(b) **Risk appetite**: the types and amounts of risk that the bank is able and willing to accept in the pursuit of its business objectives, as established by its executive committee.
(c) **Target risk profile**: a description and quantification of the specific level of risk that the bank plans to run. The target risk profile links the group's risk appetite to strategic ambitions and business performance.
(d) **Actual risk profile**: the point-in-time measure of the specific level of risk the bank is exposed to. MI reporting is designed to measure actual risk profile against the target risk profile.
(e) **Risk limits**: quantifiable maximum exposure amounts that the bank will accept under normal circumstances, linked to risk appetite.
(f) **Risk tolerance**: qualitative statements that provide guidance on the bank's willingness to accept risk. Risk tolerance thresholds are defined with the bank's risk capacity to,

e.g., maintain investment programme; maintain dividend; raise fresh capital as going concern; remain solvent to xx standard.

(g) **Credible risk responses**: the availability of risk responses and the velocity at which they can be executed when risk events emerge helps to bring focus to a firm's desired ability to reduce risks in times of stress.

A clearly articulated risk appetite would reflect the group's risk capacity, business strategy and financial goals. To do so the board will define:

(a) clarity over the risks that the organisation wishes to assume;
(b) explicit articulation of the attitudes to risk of the senior management; and
(c) an agreed basis for consistent communication to different stakeholders.

In our experience, a top-down approach is usually the best way to begin to tackle the problem of defining risk appetite. The top-down view of risk appetite leads typically into an assessment of the desired risk profile and an action plan to achieve it. It is a way to bring in the views of external stakeholders and to create a proactive statement of what management believes its risk appetite should be.

The implication for management is clear: identify the risks that the organisation faces, measure them and articulate the appetite for them. This needs to be done in a comprehensive and balanced way where quantitative measures are combined with qualitative measures, as well as those for which the institution may have zero tolerance. To embed risk appetite effectively in the business requires management to establish limits for each risk type and cascade these to lower levels in the organisation. All limits need to be communicated clearly to business management and the various control and oversight functions.

It is very important that all of the material risks and risk dependencies affecting the bank's businesses be properly

423

accounted for in the overall appetite. As the crisis has shown, if key risks are ignored, organisations can be exposed to life-threatening events. Crucially performance measures and reward must take account of risk in the framework.

The risk appetite framework must also include mechanisms to force the risk profile back within desired parameters and include an early warning system to alert the bank to changes in the underlying risk profile. In addition it is essential to take a multi-dimensional and balanced view of risk appetite and refresh it periodically.

17.5 Chief risk officer

17.5.1 Changing role of the CRO

In the "new world" CROs must have organisational stature and mandate to operate across the totality of the business model. Not only have changes in reporting lines been affected, but there is also much more emphasis on integrated risk management, which will have an impact on raising the profile of the CRO. Although there remains a high emphasis on technical skills, it is also clear that other attributes are increasingly important, such as the ability to influence at a very senior level; establish teams that can properly face-off with the business and support the business in their responsibility for taking and managing risk. In this period of ever-increasing regulatory focus, relationships with regulators are also increasingly important. The EC green paper explores a number of clear proposals regarding the role of the CRO. The Basel paper also focuses on certain aspects which are discussed below in Section 17.5.2.

As an example of supervisory expectations of the CRO, the UK FSA provides a detailed list of features of the CRS's role. Figure 17.2 is drawn from the FSA's Senior Management Arrangements, Systems and Controls sourcebook (SYSC) – Chapter 21 which is effective as of 1 May 2011. We also provide our comments and observations.

Figure 17.2 Features of CRO role

Expectations	Comments and observations
A CRO should:	
1. Be accountable to the firm's governing body for oversight of firm-wide risk management;	The accountability to the firm's governing body has been made explicit, as has the oversight of firm wide risk management. This puts greater emphasis on integrated or enterprise-wide risk management and may see a change in the CRO skill set.
2. Be fully independent of the firm's individual business units;	Independence has not generally been an issue. In fact, having individuals and functions that are empowered to be "objective" yet close enough to the rhythm of ebusiness is critical. In practice, in some cases, an independent risk function may become too removed from the rhythm of the business and contribute to the failure of risk management.
3. Have sufficient authority, stature and resources for the effective execution of his/her duties;	Authority is dealt with in the reporting line, which has been changing. In the past CROs often reported to the CFO, whereas the reporting line has recently been elevated to the CEO. Stature can only be dealt with through the attributes of the CRO (see section 17.5.2) Resources, and the effectiveness of resources, are the subject matter of section 17.5.3.
4. Have unfettered access to any parts of the firm's business capable of having an impact on the firm's risk profile;	There is a need for the CRO to have access data and information across and within the businesses to evaluate aggregate risk (e.g. total exposure to counterparties) to the firm. The ability of the CRO and the risk function to look across silos and asset classes is essential.

5. Ensure that the data used by the firm to assess its risks are fit for purpose in terms of quality, quantity and breadth;	This is important in terms of providing assurance to management around the risk management information that they receive. However it puts an explicit responsibility on the CRO that is very complex to execute. See section 17.5.5 on data and Technology
6. Provide oversight and challenge of the firm's systems and controls in respect of risk management;	It is necessary for the CRO to have authority to cause businesses with common customers or underlying asset classes to conform to fewer core product processing systems in order to standardise and simplify the sources of key risk management information.
7. Provide oversight and validation of the firm's external reporting of risk;	No major changes, although Pillar 3 requirements have become more onerous since 2008.
8. Ensure the adequacy of risk information, risk analysis and risk training provided to members of the firm's governing body;	The requirements of board members to guide risk appetite and strategy has, with this requirement, been effectively delegated to the CRO. This is an additional burden that will require greater investment in defining and articulating risk appetite, and rigorously defining reporting requirements.
9. Report to the firm's governing body on the firm's risk exposures relative to its risk appetites and tolerance, and the extent to which the risks inherent in any proposed business strategy and plans are consistent with the governing body's risk appetite and tolerance.	See 8 above.

17.5.2   Attributes

The Basel paper states that, for the effective execution of his/her responsibilities, a CRO should have sufficient authority, stature and resources.

Authority is generally dealt with in terms of the reporting lines. Increasingly, CROs are reporting to CEOs instead of through other executive directors such as the CFO.

Stature is predominately a matter of attributes of a CRO. Mere technical ability is not enough anymore – it is necessary to have strong influencing skills. A CRO needs to be able to influence management at the most senior level in order to provide appropriate level of challenge and oversight. Risk professionals need to have enough credibility with the business, and sometimes extraordinary influencing skills, to get messages across that the business may not want to hear. There are three key attributes required for getting such messages across:

(1)   technical ability – which can be presumed for someone in the CRO role;
(2)   credibility – which requires a deep understanding of the business, not only the technical risk management requirements;
(3)   backbone – which is all about having the resolve to stand up and challenge when required.

17.5.3   Adequacy of risk resources

The principle that boards should provide effective oversight of risk and control functions places an implicit requirement for CROs, CCOs and heads of internal audit to provide the board with a level of assurance that the necessary risk management capability and infrastructure exist within the firm. In practice, this requires a clear framework against which capability and capacity for risk management can be assessed.

The responsibilities of the CRO could be set out in two main areas:

(1) oversight of the risk profile of the organisation; and
(2) facilitation of risk management in the business by ensuring the availability of the necessary skills and resources.

A defined risk management framework that sets out the basic risk management processes and how they interact can also be used by central risk functions or internal audit departments to assess adequacy of skills and resources in each of the framework components. One approach is to apply four assessment ratings: inadequate, needs improvement, effective and efficient. Adequacy of skills is reviewed on this basis as well as adequacy of tools and supporting technology. For areas that are inadequate or need improvement, action plans are agreed and monitored. The structuring of the agenda of risk committees can also be balanced to address these areas.

17.5.4   Three lines of defence

One of the ways to clarify the way in which the organisational structure impacts risk management, is to have a defined operating model for risk that is well understood by all stakeholders and that reinforces the way in which risk management activity permeates throughout the business. This would start with the articulation of a vision and design principles for risk management that address the risk functionality across the business.

A clearly defined service model helps to identify stakeholders dependent on the risk management activity. Combined with a functional model that specifies interaction with stakeholders it helps to articulate specific roles and responsibilities across the three lines of defence ("3LOD").

Figure 17.3 sets out the principles of the 3LOD model, many banks have found it helpful to articulate for each material risk the specific risk management activity carried out by first line and second line. This helps to set out roles and responsibilities and to clarify delegation and escalation processes.

For example, credit risk is managed on a transactional level by the relationship managers and the sanctioning teams, as well as

Figure 17.3 Three lines of defence

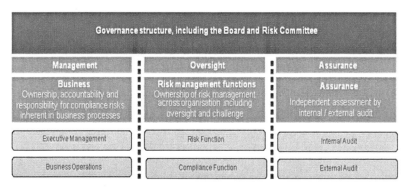

at a portfolio level by the divisional and global credit risk teams. Market risk is managed by dealers, back office confirmation clerks and treasury teams that hedge risks as much as by the specialist functions that would challenge concentrations and model assumptions.

Many areas of operational risk are managed through support functions such as human resources, operations and IT security. Setting out activities clearly helps to identify areas where oversight may be duplicated, for example by HR and finance functions and IT security. This also helps to set out key areas of control for internal audit to focus on.

17.5.5 Embedding risk management in the business

One of the ways to help provide clarity on the way in which risk is managed and mitigated across an organisation is the articulation of a risk management framework that is well understood by all stakeholders and that reinforces the way in which risk management activity permeates throughout the business. This is more than a theoretical exercise, it is about capturing the practical processes and behaviours that enable risk management in terms of a standard framework.

Figure 17.4 Risk management framework

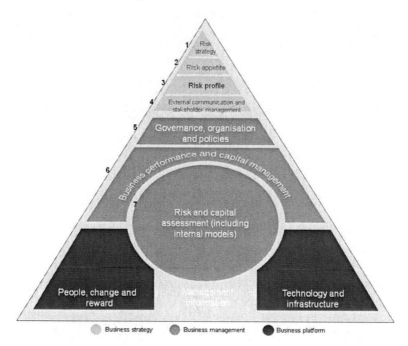

1. Risk strategy

The articulation of a risk management framework starts with a risk strategy that sets the vision and design principles for risk management that address risk functionality across the business. Risk strategy should be closely aligned with the business strategy, placing a risk dimension at the heart of decision-making. Risk is a core consideration when setting strategy, formulating business plans, managing performance and rewarding management success. As discussed earlier according to the Basel paper, the board should approve and oversee the implementation of the risk strategy including risk appetite.

2. Risk appetite

A clearly articulated risk appetite, as discussed in section 17.2 should reflect the group's risk carrying capacity, business strategy and financial goals. Processes and procedures can then be put in place to manage risk on an enterprise-wide basis within defined (hard and soft) boundaries without stifling day-to-day operations.

3. Risk profile

Risk profile refers to the identification and assessment of all (current and emerging; desired and undesired) risks faced by the organisation. Robust processes can then be put in place to aggregate and prioritise risks on an enterprise-wide basis. In the case study discussed below, the ultimate responsibility for ensuring that senior management and the board are aware of the risk profile of the organisation is one of the two main roles of the CRO.

4. External communication and stakeholder management

Section 17.3.1 discussed the responsibility of the board in managing stakeholders, including stakeholders other than shareholders. By articulating a focused external communications strategy as part of the risk management framework, this activity can become embedded within the business processes of an organisation. Such a strategy would be centred on actively managing the organisations stakeholders in order to create value and capture wider business benefits.

5. Governance, organisation and policies

Governance structure is a key aspect of the risk management functionality of an organisation. It helps to clarify senior management accountability and responsibility for "top tier" risks. The effectiveness of risk committees is an important aspect of governance. The practical aspects of running risk committees are discussed in the case studies (below and in Section 17.3.4).

The way in which the organisation is structured also impacts risk management practices. The three lines of defence model is emerging as the industry norm. This is further discussed in Section 17.5.4.

Finally, clear risk management policies and procedures for managing all material risks is essential for embedding risk management in the business.

Case study: risk management organisation

Situation: This bank has had a risk committee for every risk type, and a risk committee for each of its divisions. According to the previous CRO, the FSA commended this organisation for its risk governance, which included independent members on each of the risk committees for the different risk types.

Issue: This complex bank did not have any mechanism whereby risk across the different businesses and risk types could be reviewed. There were spectacular failures in risk management, some of which were clearly attributable to the fact that risk was managed and overseen in silos.

Solution: When the bank was taken over, the risk type committees were incorporated in sub-risk committees which encompassed the whole business, and reported to an executive risk committee, which, in turn, supported the activities of a board level risk committee.

---

6. Business performance and capital management

The management and measurement of business performance on a risk-adjusted basis, considerably enhances the risk management framework of an organisation. This will be dependent on capital allocation practices that are based on a risk/reward trade off. Risk would then be reflected in product design and pricing and post sale portfolio management.

7. Risk and capital assessment (including internal models)

Internal risk and capital models are central to a risk management framework. Models should meet highest quality standards, be appropriately calibrated ("real time") and fully tested and documented. Models should also be subjected to independent scrutiny and validation.

Quantitative risk models are a key component of a risk management framework, and the application of models is highly dependent on the underlying high performance technology platforms. Ongoing development of new technologies provides increasing capacity for computationally intensive models, yet this technology needs to be understood, and models implemented appropriately to take advantage. In addition, the requirements of quantitative modellers responsible for developing, validating and backtesting models are distinct from those of a production environment, yet cannot be considered separately. Indeed, models must be developed with full knowledge of exactly what data is and is not available, and how those models will be implemented and used in practice.

8. People, change and reward

Section 17.2 discusses key issues of an explicit risk culture in some detail. Risk culture can be embedded with balanced score cards, incentives and rewards schemes that are aligned with strategy, risk appetite etc. Another aspect of this element is establishing and monitoring the required level of skill, experience and knowledge exhibited in the majority of the bank's relevant staff. The bank in the case study above identified this as the second key responsibility for the CRO.

9. Management information

The information used for risk management inevitably spans business lines, geographies and management structures, and ranges from consolidated portfolio views down to individual transactions. Having this articulated as part of an organisation's risk management framework, helps to clarify responsibilities for the provision of critical management information.

10. Technology and infrastructure

Most, if not all banks struggle to address the data and technology needs of risk managers. To meet the challenges, risk technology and technologists must tackle fundamental issues outside their direct control, and forge cooperative partnerships with owners of data and systems across the organisation to address issues at source, rather than compensate for them in isolation.

It is important to develop a comprehensive and consistent definition of the data requirements for risk, along with clear ownership and governance models for each data type. This combined with a move towards common views of data across functions, results in improvements in data completeness, timeliness and quality, and ultimately allows risk managers to make better-informed decisions.

Key risk processes including risk reporting and limit management are enabled by technology, such as business intelligence tools and workflow packages. Selecting the right solution can play an important role in process automation and control improvement, and in providing the right information to the right person at the right time.

Implementing Basel III requirements will require a further look at the complex technology and data needs of risk managers. Implementation of the requirements is likely to present many firms with the opportunity to refine and refresh their risk systems requirements.

17.6 Conclusion

Over the last couple of years there have been significant changes in the risk management of firms but there is still a long way to go.

There have been considerable efforts taken to ensure that governance has become more effective and works in practice. At its most tangible, the hours and days devoted by many boards and non-executives to risk management matters has increased greatly. Admittedly this is partially a natural reaction to the extended crisis. In many cases the new CEOs of firms are those that are practiced in the arts of stabilisation, control and restructuring – rather than growth, acquisition and diversification. This means that the executive committee and the board's agendas now devote considerably more time to risk than they did before.

Many CROs are new in role resulting in a considerable loss of experience and skill from those that have moved on. In turn the new CROs have been quick to strengthen their teams where they can and to set higher hurdles in terms of the competencies that they expect from their people. At the highest levels, there has often been a step change in the quality of information reported to senior management and to the board.

The agendas for change are long and extensive. Those firms badly affected by the crisis completed their internal investigations long ago. The resultant remediation plans are extensive and in large banks have resulted in multi-year programmes. These are being pursued with vigour and cover wide-ranging topics such as global liquidity reporting, enhanced stress testing processes, data remediation programmes, and the cascade of risk appetite to limits. However, bringing about sustained and sustainable change is always challenging. In some firms this requires as much effort on the cultural side as it does in terms of improved models and risk technology – without lasting behavioural change, the use of new and improved infrastructure will not be optimised. As discussed earlier in the chapter, these changes often primarily relate to embedding better risk management practices in the business.

Banks also need to develop their responses to the supervisors' new-found obsession with regulated legal entities. This has implications for new governance structures, revised management information and new devolved management responsibilities. In some jurisdictions there may also be the challenge of creating self-standing risk functions in new entities that result from the restructuring of existing institutions.

The implications of Basel III and other reforms for risk management appear far-reaching and long-lasting.

435

Chapter 18

Implications for the Economy

Nick Forrest

18.1   Introduction

Regulators have been required to make far-reaching changes to the international banking regulatory regime, but have needed to limit adverse impact on the wider economy at a time of fragile economic recovery in many countries from the recession of 2008/9. The economic impact of regulatory reform has therefore been critical in guiding regulators on both the calibration and the transition path from Basel II to Basel III and for other reforms.

By understanding the potential economic impact of the reforms, banks can understand what regulators intend through the reforms themselves and potentially identify unintended consequences. Further, understanding of some of the wider impacts of the proposed reforms can guide banks' strategic responses.

How banks respond to reforms, through their lending and pricing decisions, will impact the wider economy. This means that banks, through understanding how their actions impact the economy, can play a crucial role in reducing any adverse economic impact of reforms and help to maximise the stability benefit of reforms. This will be not only of benefit to the wider economy, but also to the banks themselves, who, on balance, also gain from a stable financial system and continued economic growth.

This Chapter sets out the mechanisms by which banking regulations impact the economy. It then assesses the likely impact on banks from the Basel III reforms, and then summarises analysis of the impact from earlier Basel reforms. The Chapter then reviews the potential economic benefits and costs arising from the reforms and considers some of the wider economic impacts not captured in this analysis.

18.1.1 Impact assessment

Regulatory impact assessment using cost-benefit analysis is now standard practice for assessing proposed regulations before implementation, and in many countries (e.g. within the EU) is a formal requirement. It involves comparing costs and benefits of regulatory options at the level of individual institutions (private costs) and overall economic (or social) cost. In the UK, the FSA assesses the likely effects of a proposed regulation on the quantity, quality and variety of services offered/sold, the efficiency of competition, the FSA's direct costs and firms' compliance costs.[1]

Analysis of direct costs and benefits is typically sufficient, but in the case of the proposed Basel III reforms, the possibility of much greater macro-economic effects necessitates using tools that can measure impact on a macro-economic level.

18.1.2 Stability versus growth

At its heart the debate around banking regulatory reform has been about the trade-off between financial stability and economic growth. Various regulatory reforms are intended to promote a more stable financial system, but these reforms are not cost free – they may impact the economy's growth rate, both in the short-term and long-term. Intuitively this feels right, as times of excessive growth have often been associated with financial instability, caused, for example, by excessive credit growth and/or asset bubbles. At the other end of the spectrum, there is evidence that very unstable economies often struggle to grow. So there does appear to be tension between forces for financial stability and forces for economic growth.

---

[1] *www.fsa.gov.uk/pubs/other/mfa_guide.pdf*

However, it is not always as simple as this, as some economic volatility (fluctuations in growth rate) can be compatible with long-run economic growth, as some dynamism can be good for an economy[2]. It is also generally acknowledged that financial market openness brings higher economic growth, but can lead to more volatile outcomes:

> "Over the last two decades most of the fastest growing countries of the developing world have experienced lending booms and financial crises. Countries in which credit growth has been smooth have, by contrast, exhibited the lowest growth rates. It would thus appear that factors that contribute to financial fragility have also been a source of growth, even if they have led to occasional crises."[3]

There are other situations where financial stability and economic growth are more positively linked. For example, decisions to make business investments are more likely in more stable economic environments, as investors typically require a premium for bearing risk. So, in this context, financial stability can reinforce economic growth.

There are also broader social/political considerations as the impact of financial crises tends to vary across different sections of society (e.g. unemployment) and individuals tend to prefer stable and predictable conditions so they can smooth their consumption more easily over time[4]. However, such political considerations are out of the reach of banking regulators, and there may be alternative policy tools to address those particularly hard hit during and following financial crises.

---

[2] In Joseph Schumpeter's work "Capitalism, Socialism and Democracy", he popularised the term *creative destruction*, where successive waves of innovation by entrepreneurs drives long-run economic growth.

[3] A paper by Rancière, Tornell and Westmann (2006) "Decomposing the effects of financial liberalization: Crises vs. Growth" investigates the relative magnitude of the direct positive effect on GDP of financial liberalisation (defined as a formal regulatory change that allows foreign investors to invest in domestic securities) and the indirect negative effect of a higher propensity to crisis. It finds that the magnitude of the direct positive effect is 5–7 times larger than the indirect negative effect.

[4] Krussell, P. & Smith, A. (2002) "Revisiting the welfare effects of eliminating business cycles", Carnegie-Mellon University Working Paper.

So this Section has demonstrated that there need not be a strict trade-off between financial stability and economic growth. Rather, the objective of the G20 and the Financial Stability Board is to promote both financial stability and economic growth. This is likely to be found in a set of banking regulatory reforms which do not pursue financial stability at all costs, but do seek to capture the economic benefits that financial stability brings at appropriate cost.

18.1.3 *Short-term versus long-term*

There are both short-term/transitional and long-term (also termed steady state) costs and benefits. The economic benefits of a more stable financial system will be realised over the longer term, while the cost of reforms has the potential to be far greater in the short-term, as banks adjust to new regulatory requirements. All these effects can be combined into an overall economic impact assessment by discounting all costs and benefits in a common monetary base into a present value, but these short-term and long-term analyses have been typically kept separate. This is because the short-term impacts – or transition impacts – are particularly important given their magnitude and the fragility of economies in some countries into which the reforms will be implemented.

Because of the importance of short-term impact, there have been two key dimensions to the Basel III reforms. First, there has been the overall calibration of reforms, representing the end point for the reforms. Secondly, there has been the implementation timeframe, which does not influence the desired end-point, but does seek to manage the short-term transitional impact. The calibration of reforms affects the long-term economic impact, whereas the transition timeframe affects the short-term economic impact. Simply put, a fast implementation timeframe will have a more rapid, and typically more damaging, short-term economic impact, which is why the Basel Committee has been careful in its selection of implementation time period.

18.1.4   The Macroeconomic Assessment Group ("MAG")

Given the importance of assessing the economic impact of the Basel III reforms, the chairs of the Financial Stability Board and Basel Committee on Banking Supervision established the Macroeconomic Assessment Group ("MAG") and the Long-term Economic Impact Group ("LEI") in February 2010 to coordinate an assessment of the macroeconomic implications of the Basel Committee's proposed reforms. The membership of the MAG comprises macroeconomic modelling experts from central banks and regulators in 15 countries and a number of international institutions. Stephen Cecchetti, Economic Adviser of the Bank for International Settlements ("BIS"), was asked to chair the Group. This group produced its final report in December 2010[5], and some of their results are repeated in this Chapter.

18.2   How banks (and banking regulations) impact the economy

Banking reforms typically depress the returns which banks can earn for their shareholders, either by increasing the amount of capital required for regulatory purposes, or by reducing the profitability of banks (e.g. through costly liquidity requirements). To remain attractive to investors, banks are therefore expected to restore shareholder returns through a range of responses. A number of possible responses are set out in Figure 18.1 below.

The impact of banks on the economy has been well researched because of their crucial role in determining the impact of monetary policy. While this work is centred on the impact of policy changes (e.g. interest rates or more direct market operations), it can still be used to assess economic impact of regulatory changes. This works well for broad changes to the price and availability of credit, but is less suited to identifying more subtle or sub-market impacts.

---

[5]   *www.bis.org/publ/othp12.pdf*

Figure 18.1 Schematic of economic impact

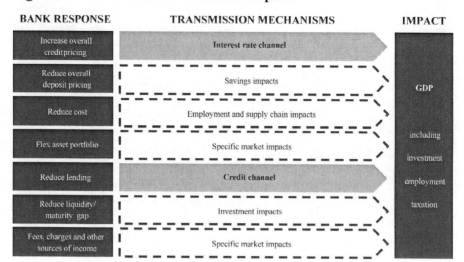

BANK RESPONSE	TRANSMISSION MECHANISMS	IMPACT

18.2.1 Increasing credit pricing

A likely response to the proposed Basel III reforms is that banks will seek to increase credit margins leading to more expensive credit across the banking system. This is consistent with the outcome expected from a competitive market with an industry-wide increase in costs. Understanding the impact of credit pricing can borrow much from the economics of monetary policy. While this is focussed on the policy rate (e.g. base rate) component of credit prices, rather than the bank margin, each contribute to economy-wide credit prices, and so much of the economic thinking of how interest rates impact the economy can be applied here.

The interest rate channel[6] is considered the cornerstone of monetary policy – most macroeconomic models of the economy include the relationship between interest rates, inflation and economic growth in their operation.

As characterised in the description of the interest rate channel, a policy-induced increase in the short-term nominal interest

---

[6] Channels represent an articulation of impact through the economy, generated though conceptual economic thought and supported by empirical evidence.

rate leads first to an increase in longer-term nominal interest rates, as investors expect some lasting impact. These movements in nominal interest rates translate into movements in real interest rates, provided nominal prices are slow to adjust. This means that firms, finding that their real cost of borrowing over all horizons has increased, cut back on their investment expenditures. Likewise, households facing higher real borrowing costs scale back on their purchases, particularly durable goods. Aggregate output and employment subsequently fall.

So if banking reforms force an increase in bank credit pricing, in much the same way there is likely to be a reduction in business investment and consumer expenditure, both dampening economic growth. However, one important mitigating effect is through the likely reaction of policy rates themselves. As higher bank margins increase the economy-wide cost of capital, there will be a negative impact on inflation and growth. In this situation, central banks can hold short-term policy rates lower than they would otherwise be. This means that any headline increase in bank margins may not be fully passed through into increases in absolute credit pricing.

On 16 December 2009, David Miles, a member of the Monetary Policy Committee of the Bank of England, gave a speech at Bloomberg entitled, "The Future Financial Landscape". In discussing the monetary policy implications of the likely more restrictive banking sector regulations, he asserted that:

> "the natural short-term nominal rate – that is the policy rate set by the central bank – consistent with a particular average rate of inflation [may be] a bit lower [than it would be without regulatory change]".

This offsetting effect is not one-for-one, due to the role of non-bank lending and external trade effects, but the Basel Committee's MAG study, which investigated economic impact models with

---

[7] Extracting from the final MAG study, the unweighted mean GDP impact is 0.24 per cent for a 1 percentage point increase in the capital ratio without monetary policy response compared to a GDP 0.11 per cent impact with a monetary policy response. However, it should be noted that at the very low interest rates of 2009–2011, central banks have little downward flexibility, so monetary stimulus to counter increased credit margins would be less effective than at higher base rates.

and without a monetary policy response, suggests that around half of the increase in bank margins could be offset by lower policy rates[7].

In practice, changes to banks' margins are unlikely to be uniform. Margins are likely to rise most in those areas of use of regulatory capital or with fewer alternative sources of finance. This means that the impact on different sectors of the economy will vary. Large businesses with access to a diverse range of capital sources may not experience a marked increase in credit pricing, but more risky areas such as lending to smaller and medium sized businesses, or providing high loan to value mortgages, are more likely to experience a more marked increase in credit pricing.

18.2.2 Deposit pricing

Ordinarily, banks manage their margins on both assets and liabilities, so overall net interest margins can be restored through reducing the deposit rates paid to savers.

The economic impact of such a move is complex. In the short-term some households may be less willing to save, as the incentives to save are reduce. This could increase consumption expenditure and increase GDP, but this could be offset from those households who depend upon savings and who would be more likely to reduce expenditure. However, over the longer term, lower savings levels are likely to reduce investment levels, and so the long-term impact of such a move is likely to be negative.

Under normal circumstances reducing deposit rates would be a strategic option available to banks, but with central bank short-term policy interest rates at near-zero across most OECD countries, and with high demand for customer deposits as banks rebalance funding sources, a strategy of reducing deposit rates is unlikely to be commercially viable for banks. It has not received much attention from regulators or policy makers, but the low rates of saving in western economies are acknowledged as a source of concern and part of the structural rebalancing of the economy following the financial crisis should be towards savings and investment-led growth:

"And now think of where we need to go: an economy based not on consumption and debt but on savings and investment" (British Prime Minister David Cameron speaking at the 2011 Davos World Economic Forum)

18.2.3 Reducing cost

Banks seeking to restore shareholder returns will face increasing cost pressure. Indeed, the operational cost structures for banks are likely to be materially different once they have responded to the post-crisis business environment and regulatory reforms. Such cost pressures have already affected a number of large global banks. By September 2010, almost 45,000 jobs had been lost at RBS and LBG, the two part-state owned UK banks. The macro-economic impact of such job losses tends to be larger because many banking jobs are more highly paid than average salary levels.

Cost reductions at banks not only impact the banks and their employees – they also affect the companies that supply banks. Key examples include computer services and postal services – indeed in the UK, the banking sector is the biggest user of these industries and any reduction in the size of the banking sector would be expected to have a knock-on effect upon these industries. Figure 18.2 lists the largest industries within the UK banking sector supply chain.

Further PwC analysis (using economic multiplier techniques and supply chain data from Figure 18.2) suggests that for every £1 spent by banks in the UK, a further 58 pence is spent in the banking sector supply chain.

However, the impact of operational cost reductions at banks should not be overstated. As an economy rebalances, then much of the economic activity displaced from the banking sector should be restored within other sectors. Provided this does happen, then operational cost reductions are more of a transitional issue than long-term economic issue.

Figure 18.2 UK Banking sector supply chain

	Sector	Supply chain expenditure (£m)
1	Computer services	3 778
2	Other business services	3 053
3	Banking and finance	3 050
4	Market research, management consultancy	2 916
5	Postal and courier services	2 809
6	Telecommunications	2 227
7	Owning and dealing in real estate	1 973
8	Advertising	1 680
9	Auxiliary financial services	1 594
10	Printing and publishing	1 230

Source: ONS Supply and Use Tables, 2004–2007. The Combined Use Matrix for 2007

18.2.4   Changing balance sheet asset mix

Banks will respond to the Basel III reforms with a reappraisal of individual business areas. Those areas that have been particularly targeted by the reforms will be expected to have the biggest falls in profitability and banks would be expected to draw back most heavily from those areas. For example, capital-intensive higher loan-to-value mortgages will now attract higher capital costs, and therefore their price is likely to rise and availability fall, which will have an impact on housing markets. The policy challenges surrounding property markets are outside the scope of this book, but we need to expect that as banks re-balance the mix of assets on their balance sheets, this will impact particular asset markets.

Such reappraisal will be done on a bank-by-bank basis and so is difficult to aggregate across the industry. In Chapter 2 – Strategic context, of this Guide we present how the Basel reforms could impact different areas of the banking industry. This will in turn have economic impacts, but at an individual market level.

446

18.2.5 *Reducing lending*

Reducing otherwise profitable lending is not likely to be the preferred strategy for banks. However, increased capital requirements may force banks to reduce the size of their balance sheets, especially if regulatory requirements are implemented quickly and banks are unable to raise sufficient equity to provide the necessary regulatory capital. Banks may voluntarily reduce lending in some areas where the regulatory requirements make lending less commercially viable. This is most likely at the higher end of the risk spectrum. Some banks may also be constrained in their overall leverage, even though this has been set by the Basel Committee to be more of a backstop to excessive credit growth. For those banks constrained by overall leverage, they will seek to reduce gearing by shedding assets with low returns (on assets), for example residential mortgages. This serves to illustrate how the impact of reforms is likely to differ across banks, depending on which reforms they are constrained by.

The impact of reduced bank lending has also been studied in the context of transmission mechanisms for monetary policies. Collectively known as "credit channels", these were initially viewed as a supplement to the interest rate channel to explain real world outcomes which could not be explained by the interest rate channel alone. However, their roles as distinct channels means they are helpful in assessing how regulatory capital changes could impact the broader economy. There are three broad credit channels which have been described in the academic literature: the balance sheet channel; the bank lending channel; and the bank capital channel.

The *balance sheet channel* suggests that movements in policy interest rates also affect the strength of firms' balance sheets, which in turn drives a wedge between the cost of funds raised externally (for example, through the issuance of imperfectly collateralised debt) and the opportunity cost of internal funds. This increase in the opportunity cost of capital acts to reinforce the interest rate channel through reducing investment incentives. This channel is more relevant in the context of non-financial firms, but could have limited impact at banks.

447

The *bank lending channel* traces a more direct impact of monetary policy on the ability of banks to supply credit, through altering the reserves of banks. It had been somewhat overlooked in the decades prior to the global financial crisis of 2007/8, largely because the availability of finance from capital markets together with banking deregulation had reduced lending constraints within the banking sector. However, the credit crisis has forced a reappraisal, led by Ben Bernanke. His earlier work, with Alan Blinder in 1998[8] set out how constraints in banks' reserves and deposits would limit the supply of loans. This was broadened in 2007, when he suggested that non-bank lenders also face constraints and could be part of the bank lending channel[9].

A *bank capital channel* has been suggested as distinct to the bank lending channel. The bank capital channel does not rely on banks' reserves – rather monetary policy affects bank lending through its impact on bank equity. In a 2009 paper, Skander J. Van den Heuval showed that lending by banks with low levels of regulatory capital has a delayed and then amplified reaction to interest rate shocks, relative to well-capitalised banks[10]. This channel therefore provides the most applicable framework for analysing the consequences of banking regulations for bank lending and broader economic impact.

The existence of these credit channels is therefore key in assessing how changes to banks' capital requirements could impact the broader economy through changes to credit supply.

A further channel described in the academic literature is the *asset price channel*. This suggests that as asset values, both for firms and for banks fall, then financing investment becomes harder. It is therefore a reinforcing channel, but not a direct channel from the perspective of assessing the economic impact of bank regulatory reform.

---

[8] Bernanke and Binder, 1998, *Credit, Money and Aggregate Demand, The American Economic Review*, Vol.78, No. 2

[9] For a fuller explanation of the bank lending channel refer to the BIS Working Paper, No.297: *The bank lending channel revisited*, by Piti Disyatat

[10] Skander J. Van den Heuvel, 2009, *The Bank Capital Channel of Monetary Policy*

18.2.6   Reducing liquidity/maturity gap

A key function of banks is "maturity transformation" – taking short-term deposits and lending over longer terms. This naturally brings liquidity and funding risks which cannot be avoided and which are a focus of the regulatory regime.

Banks seeking to reduce their regulatory capital and liquidity requirements can, as one of many options, shorten the maturity of loans, but this will have an associated economic impact. Such a reduction will impact the ability of businesses to finance longer term projects, and could further dampen business investment, and consequently economic growth. During the financial crisis there was a shortening of the average term of available lending[11].

However, overall availability of credit is likely to be more important than the term of available credit.

18.2.7   Increasing fees, charges and other sources of income

Banks can seek to restore shareholder returns through raising fees and charges (e.g. application fees for loans or monthly fees for banking services) or, more radically, the Basel III regulatory reforms may act a trigger for a reassessment of the business models and charging structures for providing certain financial services.

The challenge for banks in responding in this way is twofold. Firstly, this is likely to involve cross-subsidisation in some form as the increase in regulatory costs could be passed to the pricing of unrelated services or products. This is unlikely to be economically efficient, as users of banking products will not be paying charges relating to their cost of provision[12]. Furthermore, regulatory

---

[11] The UK Department of Business Survey on the access to finance for medium sized businesses showed that the average tenor, or maturity of loans had fallen from 7 years in 2007 to 4.3 years by 2009 and 3.6 years by 2010. The authors caution the robustness of the findings due to low sample sizes. Available at: *www.bis.gov.uk/assets/biscore/enterprise/docs/r/10-p108-results-2010-finance-survey-mid-cap-businesses*

[12] Cross-subsidisation is common place in banking. For example, the main personal current account is often provided below cost to provide a customer relationship capable of profitable sales of additional products and services. This book does not seek to address the complex advantages and disadvantages of cross-subsidisation in banking services.

authorities are in the process of reviewing the fees and charging structures of banks, so an increase in costs of charges unrelated to their direct cost of service is likely incur further regulatory scrutiny.

18.3   Likely response of banks

The previous Section set out the range of possible responses banks can take to the Basel III reforms. Most of the macroeconomic models focus on the overall level of credit pricing and lending supply, rather than some of the more detailed potential responses to asset mix or operational costs.

This Section focuses on these two key determinants – credit pricing and lending supply.

18.3.1   Credit pricing

18.3.1.1   Overall pricing levels

A number of studies have sought to assess the likely rise in credit pricing as a consequence of the Basel III and other banking reforms. Analysts JP Morgan suggested a selection of global banks would need to increase overall credit pricing by 1.23 percentage points to restore returns[13]. The Institute of International Finance found that rates could be higher by 1.32 percentage points following the reforms[14]. Both pieces of work were carried out on the unfinalised proposals and captured broader effects than the Basel III proposals, but give a broad indication of possible increases to credit prices.

The MAG's final report in December was based on the final Basel III proposals and the Basel Committee's Quantitative Impact Study ("QIS") which assessed the impact of the Committee's capital and liquidity proposals on individual banks and the banking industry. The MAG found that:

a)   each 1 percentage point increase in the capital ratio raises loan spreads by 13 basis points; and

---

[13]   J P Morgan, "Too big to fail, Running the Numbers", 17 February 2010
[14]   IIF,"Interim Report on the Cumulative Impact on the Global Economy of Proposed Changes in the Banking Regulatory Framework", June 2010

b) the additional cost of meeting the liquidity standard amounts to around 25 basis points in lending spreads when risk-weighted assets ("RWA") are left unchanged; however, it drops to 14 basis points or less after taking account of the fall in RWA and the corresponding lower regulatory capital needs associated with the higher holdings of low-risk assets.

Assuming that the Basel III proposals, on average, raise the capital ratio by around 4–5 per cent (on a constant Basel II definitional basis – see Chapter 3 – Capital Definition), the increase in credit pricing could be between 0.66 and 0.79 percentage points.

A further piece of work carried out by David Miles, Jing Yang and Gilberto Marcheggiano from the Bank of England suggests that the impact of higher capital ratios could be less substantial than suggested by the studies above[15]. This work finds that the principles of Modigliani and Miller hold to a certain extent for banks. This means that higher levels of capital reduce other funding costs and the cost of equity, so that the overall costs of capital is only slightly increased with higher capital levels. They estimate that if the risk weighted capital ratio doubles to 16.8 per cent, and leverage halves, the impact on the weighted average cost of capital would by a much lower 0.18 percentage points. A study by Anat Admati and colleagues drawing upon the same Modigliani and Miller principles reached a similar conclusion that economic regulators should not be concerned with threats that even substantial in equity requirements will have significant effects on the economy and growth.[16]

18.3.1.2 Differential pricing responses

The impact on credit pricing is likely to vary considerably across asset classes due to different levels of capital intensity, available substitutes and both competitive and market pressures. For example, large corporates have a greater range of alternative finance provides (e.g. capital markets) compared to

---

[15] "Optimal bank capital", Bank of England, External MPC Unit Discussion Paper No.31
[16] Admati, A, DeMarzo, P., Hellwig M, and Pfleiderer P. (2010) "Fallacies, Irrelevant Facts, and Myths in Capital Regulation: Why Bank Equity is Not Expensive". Stanford University Working Paper No.86.

smaller and medium-sized businesses ("SME") This means that banks are likely to have stronger commercial incentives to limit credit price increases for larger corporate and SME could therefore bear the brunt of credit margin increases. However, banks could also decide that they cannot compete for larger corporate lending and cede the business to capital markets.

Setting aside competitive dynamics and focussing solely on the capital intensity of asset classes, it is possible that the average residential mortgage, which typically requires less regulatory capital than other asset classes, could face an increase in credit margins of more like half of the average, whereas SME lending, which requires greater amounts of regulatory capital per loan amount, could experience credit pricing increases of more than 50 per cent of the average increase. At the top end of the scale, unsecured consumer lending may require 3–4 percentage point increases in loan margins to restore product returns.

18.3.2 Lending supply

The impact on lending supply is greatly influenced by the period over which banks are permitted to comply with the reforms. Banks will not de-lever unless they have to (assuming the lending is otherwise profitable). This means that deleveraging will only occur if banks have to shrink the size of their balance sheets and they are unable to raise sufficient fresh equity capital.

Analysts from Credit Suisse reviewed the Basel capital and liquidity proposals in March 2010 and concluded that a rapid implementation could force banks to de-lever by over 10 per cent[17].

18.4   Impact of previous regulatory changes

18.4.1   Basel I

The 1988 Basel accord resulted in a global agreement to a minimum bank capital ratio of 8 per cent of risk weighted assets. It was successful as intended in that it did result a

---

[17]   Credit Suisse, "UK Banks", 9 March 2010

gradual increase in banking capital ratios. A study by Juliusz Jablecki[18] showed that capital ratios in a group of 29 OECD countries over the years 1990–2001 increased significantly from roughly 8.5 to about 12 per cent – a conclusion that was found in a number of comparable studies.

The economic impact of this increase in capital ratio is difficult to quantify and there have been few economic impact studies. One by Hall (1993) presented evidence that from 1990 to 1992 American banks reduced their loans by approximately \$150 billion, and argues that it was largely due to the introduction of the new risk-based capital guidelines. He suggests that:

> "To the extent that a 'credit crunch' has weakened economic activity since 1990, Basel-induced declines in lending may have been a major cause of this credit crunch"[19].

Furthermore Peek and Rosengren (1995) find evidence, at least for banks in New England, that capital regulation (along with lower loan demand overall) contributed to the significant slowdown in credit activity during the 1990–1991 recession. Moreover, their results show that poorly capitalised banks reduced their lending more than their better-capitalised competitors.

However, other economic researchers reached different conclusions. Using time-series, cross-sectional data on US banks, Berger and Udell (1994) found no link between a more stringent regulatory capital regime and the "credit crunch"[20].

The global economic recovery of the 1990s, combined with a reduction in interest rates and further financial market deregulation and financial innovation helped to limit any long-term detrimental economic impact arising from Basel I. So while the long-term economic impact of Basel I was reasonably muted,

---

[18] Juliusz Jablecki, *"The impact of Basel I capital requirements on bank behaviour and the efficacy of monetary policy"*, December 2009

[19] Hall, Brian J. (1993). "How Has the Basle Accord Affected Bank Portfolios?" *Journal of the Japanese and International Economies*, Volume 7, Issue 4, pp 408–440.

[20] Berger, A.N., and Udell, G. (1994), "Did Risk-based Capital Allocate Bank Credit and Cause a "Credit Crunch" in the United States?" *Journal of Money, Credit, and Banking* 26, 585–628.

the more significant impact was the incentive it gave banks for regulatory arbitrage – for example by using securitisation techniques to lower capital requirement, which arguably had a far greater role destabilising the financial system during the most recent financial crisis.

18.4.1   Basel II

As a consequence of the blunt nature of Basel I and the perception that banks were able to circumvent capital requirements, the 1994 Basel II accord sought to fundamentally realign regulatory capital requirements to the risks of holding different asset classes. Basel II did not intend to increase the overall amount of capital held in the banking system.

Because the impact on overall capital requirements was limited, and because the implementation of Basel II was carried out over an extended period (and not completed across all countries), the economic impact was modest. If anything, the Basel II regime provided a stimulus to certain asset classes with low risk weights, which may have had short-term economic benefit, but which may have contributed, in part, to the global financial crisis[21].

18.5   Impact on the broader economy

18.5.1   The cost of crises

As the aim of the banking reforms is to prevent systemic financial crises and increase financial stability, the possible benefit of reforms can be assessed by examining the impact of previous crises.

The cost of a crisis is most often measured in terms of the total output loss it causes. Some financial crises have little impact on the economy, they are contained within the financial sector and do not disrupt the flows of credit around the economy. The failure of Long Term Capital Management in 1988 was such an example.

---

[21] While the Basel II regime can be ascribed as a contributor to the 2008/09 financial crisis, there are a substantial range of other factors that have been identified. A full exposition of the causes, contributors to the crisis is outside the scope of this book, as a number of titles have been written on the topic.

However, other financial crises have far bigger impact, as the recent crisis has shown. Numerous researchers have shown that economic recessions that are associated with a credit crunch, equity falls and housing price falls tend to be deeper and longer recessions[22].

Since economic costs add up over a number of years, a discount rate is used to construct a present value (PV) of the cost of a crisis. The total PV cost of a crisis depends on many factors, but they can be summarised in three main attributes, which are shown in Figure 18.3 below:

Figure 18.3 Illustration of the cost of crises

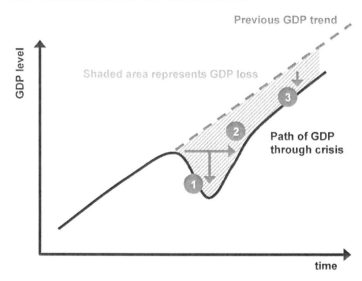

(1) Depth of crisis

When a crisis occurs, economic output drops below its trend level. In a sharp recession, the overall level of output will fall. This can be measured in terms of the maximum deviation of GDP from its pre-recession trend.

---

[22] IMF Working Paper WP/08/274, "What Happens During Recessions, Crunches and Busts? by Stijn Claessens, M. Ayhan Kose, and Marco E. Terrones

(2) Length of crisis

Recovery to the trend growth rate after the initial output drop may be quick (for example in the case of a "V-shaped" recession) but may take many quarters (for a "U-shaped" recession). This can be measured as the length of time to return to the previous trend growth rate, or the time until this rate is exceeded.

(3) Level of "scarring"

If output does not return to its pre-crisis trend (as is shown in the Figure 18.2 above) then scarring is said to occur. Scarring will occur unless there is a "catch-up" period of growth that is higher than the long-run trend rate, reducing the gap between the trend level and the actual GDP. Scarring can be measured either as a percentage of GDP that is lost permanently by the time trend growth resumes, or it can be expressed as a proportion of the depth of the crisis that is permanent.

It is more difficult to estimate the cost of a crisis if there has been a period of strong growth prior to a crisis. This is because the reduction in output can represent the unwinding of unsustainable growth. This means it is difficult, but necessary, to estimate the path of the economy had there not been a crisis, where inevitably a degree of judgment is required.

The impacts of financial crises have been well studied. A number of studies are summarised in Figure 18.4 below:

Figure 18.4 Studies of the impact of financial crises

Study	Empirical findings
Bordo, Eichengreen, Klingebiel, Martinez-Peria, World Bank working paper, 2000	For industrialised countries, banking crises have occurred with an annual frequency of 2–3 per cent, looking at 1880–1939 and 1973–1997. This is roughly equivalent to crises in 1 in 30 to 1 in 50 years.
Hoggarth, Reis and Saporta, Bank of England working paper 2001	For a range of crises in 14 high-income countries, banking crises since the 1970s have cost between 20.7 per cent and 26.0 per cent of GDP on average, depending on the measurement method. The cost of the 1974–1977 crisis for the UK was estimated to be between 26.5 per cent and 31.1 per cent of GDP.

Study	Empirical findings
IMF World Economic Outlook, October 2009, Ch. 4	This study considers 88 banking crises between the 1970s and 2002. On average, the authors found that during the crisis, output drops by around 10 per cent. Output growth resumes at a similar rate to the pre-crisis trend after around three years and output does not typically rebound to its pre-crisis trend, leaving a scarring of 10 per cent after seven years.

Although the authors note a significant level of scarring, the cases they consider diverge considerably. Seven years after a crisis, a quarter of countries are 6 per cent or more ahead of their pre-crisis trend, with a quarter of countries being 26 per cent or further behind. |
| Carmen Reinhart, Kenneth Rogoff, working paper January 2009 | The authors assess a number of systemic crises in developed countries in the 20th century. They find output falls (from peak to trough) by an average of 9.3 per cent. If trend growth were 2.5 per cent, this would imply a maximum gap between trend and actual output of approximately 14 per cent. The duration of output downturn averages 1.9 years.

The authors do not address potential degree of scarring.

The authors note that housing and equity price cycles, along with unemployment, are longer then the output downturn. In addition, they not significant increases in public debt due to bail-outs, a cost which is not included in our methodology. |
| Valerie Cerra and Sweta Chaman Saxena, BIS working paper 2007 | The authors assess a range of events including banking crises using two different datasets. Output falls (from peak to trough) by 11.7–12.7 per cent. If trend growth were 2.5 per cent, this would imply a maximum gap between trend and actual output of approximately 17–19 per cent. The duration of output downturn averages 2.2–2.5 years. The results suggest that scarring can be considerable (close to full amount of the output lost). |
| An assessment of the long-term economic impact of stronger capital and liquidity requirements, prepared by the Basel Committee on Banking Supervision (BCBS), August 2010 | Based upon a cross-country historical empirical analysis, the probability of a banking crisis is 4 per cent to 5 per cent or once every 20 to 25 years. The impact of an average banking crisis is:
– 19 per cent of pre-crisis GDP where a crisis is only temporary
– 164 per cent of pre-crisis GDP where a crisis has permanent effects
– 63 per cent of pre-crisis GDP across all crises
This shows how the results are highly dependent upon the degree of permanent impact of crisis which is assumed. |

457

Figure 18.5 draws upon these studies to show how the estimation of benefits can be very wide, depending upon the assumptions used in the calculation. The first scenario in the table uses the low end of the output impact studies and incorporates the amount of long-term scaring which has, on average, occurred in previous financial crises. The scenarios become progressively more economically damaging with greater scarring levels, a longer time period of analysis and in calculation 4,5 and 6 are based upon the 2008/09 crisis rather than a typical crisis. The figure of £7.4tr in calculation 7 is close to the upper estimate calculated by Andrew Haldane from the Bank of England in his speech, "The $100bn Question" (March 2010).

Figure 18.5 Benefits calculation scenarios

Calculation	Time period of calculation (years)	Impact of crisis on GDP	Permanent Scaring	Frequency of crisis	Impact £bn PV 2010	per cent of 2010 GDP
1	20	30%	Historic	2.5%	£203bn	14%
2	20	30%	Historic	5%	£406bn	28%
3	20	30%	25%	5%	£936bn	64%
4	20	30%	50%	5%	£1.4tr	94%
5	20	Current	100%	Current	£2.2tr	154%
6	40	Current	100%	crisis	£4.4tr	304%
				averted		
7	70	Current	100%		£7.4tr	507%

Source: PwC calculations

This table reveals some important points. First, the assessment of benefits from banking reform is difficult and can deliver wide-ranging estimates. The degree of permanent scarring is a highly sensitive component of the calculation, but the least easy to estimate – can we say that the US economy has not fully recovered from the 1989–91 savings and loans crisis, or the UK economy from the 1973–75 secondary banking crisis? In Japan there is more a more compelling case to suggest the Japanese crisis in the early 1990s still has lasting impact, but this still reveals that it is very difficult to know what track the economy would have taken without the crisis. Would Japan's rising wealth levels and aging population have slowed down its economy, even if there had not been a banking crisis?

Traditional macroeconomic models suggest that in the long-term it is economic fundamentals, such as technology and productivity that determine the size of the economy. Over the longer term, the subsequent impact of financial crises should therefore reduce.

18.5.2   *Potential benefits of greater financial stability*

Translating the assessment of the cost of crises into an economic benefit of reforms requires understanding how much past, present and future reforms contribute to an increase in financial stability. This is clearly made harder because of the range of reforms enacted and still being considered and because of the way reforms interact with each other. Higher capital levels, depositor insurance and resolution plans will *jointly* have a greater likelihood of achieving a more stable financial system than relying on any one reform alone. But the benefit of individual reforms is dependent upon the success of other reforms. For example, if resolution plans (as discussed in Chapter 15) could be created which seamlessly transfer a failing bank into a new institution with no impact on credit flows, or credit pricing, then the benefits to financial stability would be considerable. If this were the case, higher capital ratios would have little additional stability benefit. Furthermore, if all reform proposals are measured with respect to the pre-crisis banking environment, there is danger of double counting stability benefit.

We also cannot assume that the proposed reforms will be entirely successful. There may be unintended consequences which sow the seeds of a future crisis e.g., pushing lending into unregulated sectors. Nor can we predict exactly from where the next crisis will originate, in the same way few foresaw how subprime mortgage securities would trigger the most recent global financial crisis. This suggests a cautious estimate of stability benefits.

In order to quantify how capital levels (and to a certain degree liquidity levels) reduce the likelihood of crises, it is possible to investigate how different capital ratios across countries have contributed to lower frequency and lower impact of financial crisis. FSA economists Matthew Osborne and William Frances used a panel of OCED countries to estimate that:

> "increasing the levels of capital and liquidity by one percentage point would have reduced the probability of a crisis in the UK by more than 6 percentage points, and by smaller amounts in other countries. Increasing regulatory requirements further would have reduced the probability further, but the returns to increased regulatory standards are clearly declining, with the gains falling 5 per cent in the UK for a move from a one point increase to a two point increase, for instance. It is also possible to calculate the effects of increasing capital requirements and liquidity requirements on their own, and it is clear that when they change together they slightly offset each other . . . Changes in capital adequacy alone are at least twice as effective as changes in liquidity alone, especially in the UK."[23]

The MAG used a similar approach to simulate moving from a 10 per cent tangible common equity to risk weighted asset ratio ("TCE/RWA") ratio to a 15 per cent TCE/RWA ratio. In their analysis this reduces the annual probability of a crisis from 1.2 per cent (1 in 83 years) to 0.3 per cent (1 in 333 years) (assuming the Net Stable Funding Ratio is also met). The MAG found that there was no discernable impact from increasing capital and liquidity levels on the severity of a crisis.

18.5.3 Macroeconomic models of economic impact

There are a range of economic modelling approaches that can be used to assess the economic impact of higher credit pricing, or reduced loan supply. They are summarised below:

(a) *Reduced-form empirical approaches* are based on long-run time series data for several macroeconomic variables. They

---

[23] Ray Barrell, E Philip Davis, Tatiana Fic, Dawn Holland, Simon Kirby and Iana Liadze, "Optimal regulation of bank capital and liquidity: how to calibrate new international standards", Financial Services Authority Occasional Paper no.38

are relatively straightforward to estimate in statistical soft-
ware packages, but they require good data on appropriate
macroeconomic variables and banking variables.

(b) *Dynamic stochastic general equilibrium ("DSGE")* models are
complex models that incorporate economic interactions
"from the ground up". The macroeconomic effects in the
model are based on outcome of many microeconomic
outcomes. They are therefore difficult to specify and results
often do not give outputs that are accurate representations
of the real world.

(c) *Semi-structural forecasting models* are a broad class of models
in which macroeconomic linkages are specified by several
individual equations. Each equation may either be empiri-
cally estimated or drawn from economic theory, or a
combination of both. Dynamics and balancing of equilibrium conditions can be included either directly through the
equations or by numerically re-computing the model until
it converges to an equilibrium.

18.5.4 Results obtained from macroeconomic models of economic impact

Given the range of macroeconomic models available, it is
unsurprising that there is a wide range of results obtained.
The chart below summarises the output from a number of
macroeconomic models in terms of the impact of a 1 per cent
reduction in credit on GDP.

One approach which focussed on the interest rate channel
includes the FSA/NIESR which uses NiGEM – an international
macroeconomic model of the UK economy. They estimated that
a 1 percentage point rise in the capital adequacy target reduces
output by at most 0.08 per cent in the long-run. For the US, their
modelling suggests that a rise in the liquid asset ratio target of
1 percentage point reduces output by at most 0.03 per cent in
the long-run[24].

An alternative long-run impact approach was suggested in
Box 7 of the Bank of England's June 2010 Financial Stability

---

[24] Financial Services Authority Occasional Paper no.38

Report[25]. This assessed the incremental costs of higher equity capital, as equity displaces debt funding and, on this basis, estimated a 1 percentage point increase in capital requirements translates into a 0.07 per cent increase in credit margins[26]. The long-run impact of higher bank lending spreads on GDP can be assessed using a simple production function of the economy. In this framework, an increase in non-financial firms' cost of capital reduces their investment and, ultimately, the level of GDP. On the basis of a number of simplifying assumptions, a 7 basis point increase in lending spreads maps into a 0.1 per cent permanent decline in the level of GDP – a result broadly comparable to the FSA/NIESR modelling.

Figure 18.6 Impact on GDP from reduction in credit

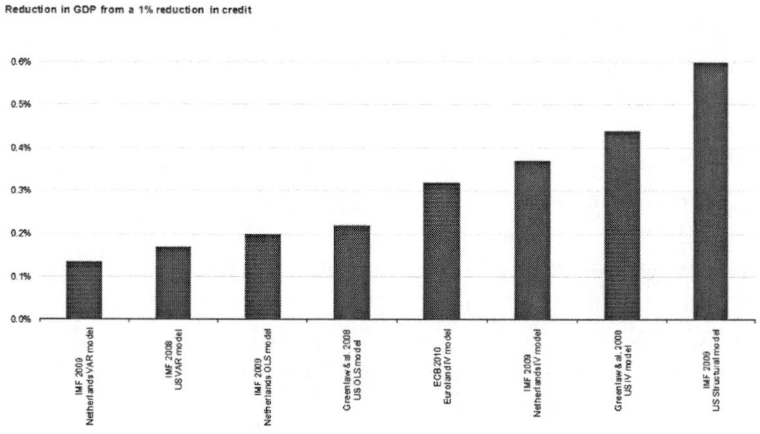

Reduction in GDP from a 1% reduction in credit

The IIF cumulative impact study allows comparison across different territories[27]. It concluded that by 2015, the level of real GDP across the US, Japan and Euro Area in a regime of regulatory reform was projected to be about 3.1 per cent below what it would otherwise be. This amounts to an average of about 0.6 per cent per year, which fades very notably once the period of transition

---

[25] *www.bankofengland.co.uk/publications/fsr/2010/fsr27sec5.pdf*

[26] This analysis made a number of simplifying assumptions, including no impact of lower leverage on the cost of debt or equity and all of the adjustment falls on customer lending rates rather than through lower operating costs, increased non-interest income, or lower retail deposit rates.

[27] IIF,"Interim Report on the Cumulative Impact on the Global Economy of Proposed Changes in the Banking Regulatory Framework", June 2010

is through. For the US, the path of real GDP is projected to be 2.6 per cent lower by 2015; for Japan, the path is 1.9 per cent lower; but for the Euro Area the path is as much as 4.3 per cent lower. The reasons for the higher impact in the Euro area include: (i) a larger impact on required amount of new Tier 1 equity and long-term debt issuance at Euro area banks, which has a larger impact on higher required credit spreads; and (ii) Euro area economies have larger banking systems (relative to the size of the economy) and are more dependent upon debt financing.

Faced with such an array of models the MAG adopted a "metas-tudy" approach. This involved collating studies of economic impact from its partners from around the world. These models were then aggregated and their findings are presented below:

Figure 18.7 Aggregate impact of a 1 percentage point increase in the target capital ratio implemented over eight years, excluding spillover effects: distribution of estimated GDP deviation across selected models (in per cent)

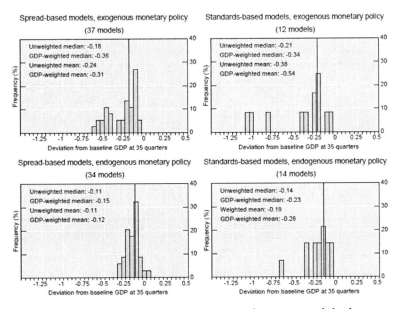

Source: MAG. Note: Distributions are computed across models that meet the specified criteria. The vertical line indicates the unweighted median. The shaded areas indicate the range between the 20th and 80th percentile. Quarters are measured from start of implementation.

463

Averaging these models, the Final MAG Report estimated that:

> "if higher requirements are phased in over eight years, bringing the global common equity capital ratio to a level that would meet the agreed minimum and the capital conservation buffer, this would result in a maximum decline in the level of GDP, relative to baseline forecasts, of 0.22 per cent, with a range of estimates around this point average."[28]

These results contain a number of key findings:

a) spread-based models (higher credit pricing) exhibit smaller economic impacts than standards-based models (which incorporate economic impact through the availability of credit);

b) the most extreme (detrimental) impact is generated through models which restrict the availability of credit (top right diagram). At worst, each one percentage point increase in capital ratio can lead to a 1 per cent deviation from baseline GDP;

c) endogenous models allow monetary policy to respond (e.g. lower interest rates) and therefore mitigate part of the impact on GDP; and

d) the larger impacts were caused by disaggregated (bank-by-bank) models. This reveals the danger in aggregation – while a banking system in aggregate may be well capitalised, there may be some institutions which are not and it is these weaker institutions which contribute to the bulk of adverse economic impact.

The conclusion from the analysis is that banking sector deleveraging is to be avoided. A preferable way of minimising economic cost is to implement reforms over a sufficiently long time period, so that banks are able to continue lending by meeting regulatory capital requirements through retained earnings, or raising fresh capital. In this scenario increased capital and liquidity requirements will translate into a higher credit pricing, but this will minimise economic cost.

---

[28] BIS, "Final report on the assessment of the macroeconomic impact of the transition to stronger capital and liquidity requirements", 17 December 2010. Press Release.

This helps to explain why the Basel committee has proposed an extended implementation timeframe, with full compliance across all areas by 2022.

18.5.5   *Overall impact on the economy from Basel III*

In the previous sections, we have established that the benefits of financial stability can be substantial and that the costs of reform can also be considerable. Given the variation in both the benefits and costs, it is very difficult to bring together a framework to assess any "optimal" capital ratio where the net benefits are maximised.

When combined with the potential benefits which are brought by financial stability, most studies have concluded there are net benefits of increased capital and liquidity requirements. These benefits cover a broad range of capital ratios. The MAG study suggested that net benefits were maximised up to a capital ratio of 14 per cent (6 per cent higher than pre-crisis levels, where the capital ratio is defined as tangible common equity divided by risk weighted assets). The FSA found a similar result in its occasional paper (no. 38) on optimal capital ratios with a range of 2 to 6 percentage point increase in capital and liquidity ratios increasing overall economic welfare. However, these conclusions do come with a number of caveats:

(a) The quantification of economic benefits is highly uncertain, whereas economic costs are more easily assessed. Further, economic costs are concentrated during transition, whereas stability benefits are achieved over the longer term.
(b) The assessment of benefits is particularly dependent in the assumption of lasting impact from crises. Without this assumption, the net benefits of increased capital ratios peak at much lower capital ratios.
(c) These two points above, combined with the overall uncertainty over the estimates of benefits suggests that a cautious approach needs to be adopted by regulators before requiring banks to hold much higher capital levels.

18.6   Conclusions

This Chapter has set out some of the complexities in assessing the overall economic costs and benefits of regulatory reform. The key implications for banks are:

(a)   Banks have a role and a responsibility to help deliver the benefits of financial stability.

(b)   Deleveraging is neither good for banks, nor the economy (albeit in some sectors of the economy it may be essential). In general terms, credit re-pricing leads to lower economic impact than deleveraging.

(c)   Banks should expect lower returns on equity compared to pre-crisis levels, but these should be compensated by a market-wide re-pricing of credit across most asset classes. Banks will need to evaluate how their cost of equity evolves as the reforms are implemented. This will require updating pricing models to reflect updated return requirements. Banks that do not do this are likely to be out-priced by competitors.

(d)   If banks restore original pre-crisis returns, this would suggest higher risks levels returning to the financial sector.

(e)   The reforms could require banks to increase credit margins by as much as 0.66 percentage points to 0.79 percentage points, with the biggest pricing increases being in high-risk lending, such as personal unsecured credit, SME lending and high LTV residential mortgage lending. However, lower policy rates mean that the increases to long-term credit prices to business and retail consumers could be markedly lower. A lower cost of equity (through the Modigliani-Miller effect) could further reduce the requirement to increases the price of credit.

(f)   There will be potential for competitive gains as pricing changes. This is analogous to consumption tax increases, where businesses delay the increase to hold or grow market share.

(g)   Banks should take advantage of the implementation timeframe in order to reduce the economic impact of any unnecessary deleveraging. This may require resisting any shareholder and management pressure to "fix" the regulatory requirements as soon as possible.

(h) Those business areas most directly impacted by the Basel III reforms will need a fuller appraisal. Bank responses in these areas are likely to be more substantial than mere re-pricing. Business models may need to change and certain activities may have to be curtailed.

(i) The overall economic impact is likely to modest – MAG calculates a 0.22 per cent deviation from baseline GDP over an 8 year implementation timeframe. This appears to be a reasonable central case estimate, but risks remain. Any significant deterioration in either the economy or in capital markets could reduce the ability of banks to maintain credit flows and detrimental economic impact would increase significantly.

(j) Regulators have made a case for target regulatory capital ratios significantly higher than the Basel III reforms. This means that the proposed capital and liquidity requirements may only be a step towards even higher capital ratios. Such increases are likely to be focussed on Systemically Important Financial Institutions ("SIFIs").

Chapter 19

Implications for Supervision

Patrick Fell

19.1 Introduction

"Changing the rules alone cannot make the financial system safe. The judgment of banking supervisors is crucial"[1]

Mere rules are not enough. This Chapter looks at the potential effects of the recently published Basel III regulations on the supervision of banks. Before we go into the detail note that one should distinguish the terms regulation and supervision – even regulators (and supervisors – the terms are often used interchangeably) – regularly confuse them:

(a) Regulation, put simply, is the process of developing a set of required practices – in this case to try to ensure that banks are solvent and act prudently as custodians of deposits and as key parts of the financial system. The normal expression of regulation is a rulebook. It will be apparent that the prudential rulebook for banks has expanded exponentially, with the simplicity of the 1988 Basel I approach having been turned into more complex and risk-focused approach that is Basel II/III.

(b) Supervision, by contrast, is the way the authorities ensure the banks are complying with these rules. This typically involves a combination of ongoing off-site surveillance of the bank from the supervisors' offices and periodic on-site inspections. In their supervision, supervisors need to set the words of the rules in the context of their overall supervisory

---

[1] See S. Raihan Zamil, "Judgment Day" IMF Finance & Development, September 2010, Vol. 47, No. 3

objectives, the specific position of the bank as an entity and the position of the market as a whole. Only then can they use their skill, judgment and experience to take appropriate action where needed. Thus supervision should involve much more than a check-box approach to the application of the rulebook.

Regulation and supervision therefore should work hand in hand. However, it could be argued strongly that the problems of the banking sector in recent years show that this has not happened: there has been a combination of ineffective regulation and inconsistent supervision. The regulators have developed and are beginning to implement more granular rules to address each perceived "gap" where a risk has been found that they believe needs to be addressed. However, this appearance of granularity and thus certainty in the rulebook is misleading. In almost all cases the application of the prudential rulebook is heavily reliant upon informed judgment by supervisors. For example, as the IMF paper points out:

(a) exactly what constitutes sound risk management is not clear cut; and
(b) capital adequacy appears to be a quantitative question but in fact is largely a qualitative assessment.

On the first point, those involved in risk control have seen a never-ending game of catch up. It appears as if every year the regulators are getting better at defining good controls. However, while the volume of controls may increase, banks' businesses develop and markets change, making the existing control requirements inevitably inappropriate.

The IMF also points out that capital is also subjective. Even the "formulaic" Pillar 1 is based on major assumptions, for example around the liquidity of assets, and the period over which they will be held, while the subjectivity in Pillar 2 is obvious to all. There never will be a "correct" capital figure, the number is but an estimate by bankers and their supervisors based on limited information and without any of the benefits of hindsight. Supervisors around the world find this a huge challenge and attempt to deal with it by building an architecture of assessments

470

and formulaic buffers, but ultimately it comes down to their judgment.

In practice, therefore, the prudential rules can only ever be an approximation to a system for proper management of risk, and at best represent a lagging indicator of capital needed, that records previous problems. It is up to wise and experienced supervisors to use their experience and judgement to identify the far more relevant upcoming problems.

The supervisors are therefore always inevitably attempting to achieve an ideal that is higher than is likely to be possible. However, they can achieve a lot if the job is done well (and in most cases the job is done well). Putting all this another way, an IMF staff paper states that supervision should be "intrusive, sceptical, proactive, comprehensive, adaptive, and conclusive"[2]. This requires much more than testing mechanical compliance with a rulebook.

19.2   The core principles

The advent of Basel III focuses banks' attention on capital, liquidity, leverage and many other key issues. However, Basel III has come into existence not only to deal with problems at an individual bank level, but also as a result of a perception that supervision of the system as a whole needed to be better. As a result, it brings a whole gamut of challenges to the supervisors; challenges that banks need to understand if they are to get their own responses to Basel III properly calibrated.

The starting point is best summarised by reference to Basel's Core Principles[3]. These are minimum standards for sound supervision and have been used by countries as a benchmark for assessing the quality of their supervisory systems and for identifying future work to be done. Their original development reflected a valid belief in the early 2000's that a global body like

---

[2]   IMF Staff Position Note 10/08 – "The Making of Good Supervision: Learning to Say 'No' ". Jose Viñals and Jonathan Fiechter, with Aditya Narain, Jennifer Elliott, Ian Tower, Pierluigi Bologna, and Michael Hsu
[3]   Core Principles for Effective Banking Supervision – Updated October 2006

Basel should push forward global standards for banking supervision, as well as the more traditional role of promulgating rules applying to the banks themselves.

Basel's 25 principles (2006 version) broadly can be categorised into seven groups:

(1) Objectives, independence, powers, transparency and cooperation (principle 1)
(2) Licensing and structure (principles 2 to 5)
(3) Prudential regulation and requirements (principles 6 to 18)
(4) Methods of ongoing banking supervision (principles 19 to 21)
(5) Accounting and disclosure (principle 22)
(6) Corrective and remedial powers of supervisors (principle 23)
(7) Consolidated and cross-border banking supervision (principles 24 and 25)

The Core Principles have undoubtedly been a valuable tool in bringing up the standards of supervision around the world. However, they are being reviewed at the time of writing to deal with the new challenges and to set up a supervisory framework that complements the new Basel III standards for banks.

This involves looking at the areas where the principles have been shown to be inadequate and at the possible responses by supervisors. For example, in October 2009, the Senior Supervisors Group of the Financial Stability Board ("FSB") reviewed the funding and liquidity issues central to the recent crisis and explored critical areas of risk management practice warranting improvement across the financial services industry.[4] Subsequently, in November 2010 the FSB took on this mantle in the context of looking at systemically important financial institutions ("SIFIs") and raised a series of issues that will set the agenda for supervisors over the coming years. Some of the key points are summarised in Figure 19.1 below[5]:

---

[4] Financial Stability Board Senior Supervisors Group – *Risk Management Lessons from the Global Banking Crisis of 2008*, 21 October 2009. This report was a companion and successor to the first report, *Observations on Risk Management Practices during the Recent Market Turbulence*, issued in March 2008.
[5] Financial Stability Board – *Intensity and Effectiveness of SIFI Supervision; Recommendations for Enhanced Supervision*, 2 November 2010

Figure 19.1 The FSB's challenges to supervisors – key issues

Macro-prudential supervision:

- *Supervisory authorities must have a well developed macro-prudential surveillance approach to identify trends and developments that might negatively impact firms.*
- *The macro-prudential approach should identify the key sources of market and industry information, articulate a regular communication regime with those sources and take into account the expertise of all of its various disciplines (credit, market, operations risk).*
- *The approach to macro-prudential supervision must regularly inform the senior management team within the supervisor and where appropriate should generate senior level communication between firms and the supervisor.*

Supervising SIFIs:

- *The organisational structure of supervisors should reflect the importance of SIFIs, allowing SIFI supervisory team leads direct access to the most senior personnel in the supervisor.*
- *National supervisors should ensure that the assessment criteria for the control environment at SIFIs reflect the fact that there is a "higher bar" for these firms.*
- *Resource allocation by supervisors must consider systemic risks posed by banks and should reflect the fact that, for SIFIs, there is a minimum acceptable level of annual work that should not be breached.*
- *There should be extra focus on consolidated supervision given the importance of these issues for SIFIs. This should address group-wide supervision, assessing the quality of host country supervision, and the supervision of foreign locations.*
- *For SIFIs in particular, complete outsourcing of onsite work to third parties is not an acceptable substitute for work performed by a supervisor's own resources.*

Powers and authority:

- *The macro-prudential approach should be endorsed by all government stakeholders as well as providing for consultation and coordination with those stakeholders.*

Processes and tools:

- *Early intervention should be an element of the supervisor's mandate.*
- *Business model assessment and product-oriented risk analysis are needed. Supervisors should be guided to understand better the risk embedded in the business models of the banks as well as in the design of their product offerings.*
- *There should be greater use of horizontal ["thematic"] reviews and good practice around the use of this valuable supervisory tool.*
- *Consideration should be given to developing expanded guidance to supervisors on how to assess a board and determine board effectiveness better.*
- *There should be greater use of financial analysis and the enhancement of supervisory practices around this.*

Resources:

- *Supervisors should regularly (at least annually; on a rolling basis) take stock of existing skills and projected requirements and review and implement measures that could be taken to bridge any gaps in numbers and/or skill-sets.*

Clearly the supervisors need to do a lot to make these changes real; the following pages look at some of the issues in more detail. Before turning to these issues though, it is worth commenting briefly on the new role of the supervisor.

19.3 Rethinking supervision

The 2006 Principles ("Principle 19") referred to "safety and soundness [of individual banks], and the stability of the banking system", but there are few other mentions of systemic risk. In essence the old regime was much more focused on the micro side of supervision – the individual bank – than the system as a whole. Taking on the new broader systemic role will demand much of the supervisors. All the stakeholders (banks, government, central banks and the wider public) will be relying on their expertise to a greater extent than before. To try to meet those expectations supervisors will have to take leaps of faith; they will need to embrace the new territory of macro supervision and link it to their more familiar micro-prudential homeland.

Effective implementation in this new world will have to be grounded on:

(a) an excellent understanding of the economy and a robust, transparent and generally accepted process for assessing the cycle;
(b) the ability to assess the position of institutions both as individuals and as parts of a broader system; and
(c) courage and contrary thinking – the ability and willingness to lean against the wind.

Of these the second is worthy of early comment. The banking system is a complex web of relationships, with each element within that web interacting with and influencing the other elements. Further, the banking system nests within and inter-acts with the wider (regulated and unregulated) financial system, and beyond that with the wider national and global economy.

The dynamics of the system are thus far more than the sum of the reactions of the individual banks; indeed, results at a systemic level may be counterintuitive to those focusing on individual banks, or even on the financial sector. Supervisors therefore have to develop an approach that places as much emphasis on the interactions and second, third (and so on) order impacts on the system as they have on ticking off the supervision tasks at individual banks.

To put it another way, financial sector supervisors have historically sought more or (sometimes) less successfully to achieve safety by developing and enforcing increasingly detailed rulebooks for individual banks. This has increasingly led to a position where the banker's world is defined by rules, say around systems and controls or capital levels, that try to anticipate what could happen, and stop it. The detailed rulebooks are used to keep the regulatory lid on a market pot, but if that pot is boiling ever faster because of market heat, more weight is needed, with explosive consequences. To stretch the analogy (perhaps too far) often the rulebooks and supervisors focus on one regulated "pot" when another is boiling over unwatched. The supervisors should be looking at the whole stove not just the regulated pot, and the macro-prudential initiative in Basel III is an attempt to achieve this.

As a final note on the area, some banking supervisors have come to believe that detailed rules for individual banks are the way forward – some have described this as a very legal approach. Supervisors perhaps need to think laterally and develop a framework that nudges the system as a whole towards safety with less use of rulebooks and the force of law. Other routes are taken in other industries, for example in energy or telecoms regulators might focus more on market structure and on rates of return to achieve the wider governmental objectives. For banking such a debate has barely started.

19.4   New style supervision – the glide path

The implementation of Basel III is planned to take place over a long period. Clearly implementing Basel III over such a period is fraught with difficulties. The biggest challenge supervisors, governments and central bankers face over the implementation period, and indeed beyond, is to reconcile four very different objectives:

(1) The politicians' (and economists') desire for an extended glide path towards sustainable macro-economic growth: under this view (which has driven the extended implementation period for Basel III) banks need an extended timetable to raise new capital either in the markets or by retaining earnings so as to meet the new requirements without shrinking their balance sheets dramatically and thus triggering an economic downturn. The jury will remain out for many years on whether this is needed, or whether the new requirements can easily be met, for example by retaining earnings in banks, with limited or no new capital issuance, but the risk that tightening capital and liquidity rules will brake economic growth cannot be ignored.

(2) The supervisors' micro-prudential supervision objectives for the safety and soundness of individual banks: from the beginning the supervisors in charge of supervision of individual institutions may find themselves attracted to higher capital ratios, more liquidity in each bank, tougher attitudes to Pillar 2, and aggressive stress tests – this conservatism reflecting the lessons that they have learned from the events of the financial crisis. They may have little to gain from supervisory forbearance in the interests of the common good of the economy. Some countries are clearly heading down this route.

(3) The supervisors' macro-prudential aims and the use of tools to meet them: the new regime demands that banking supervision reflects the economic cycle. For example it will demand that capital buffers are built up counter-cyclically, even during the implementation period. Such attempts to smooth the cycle may easily go directly against micro-prudential objectives. Further, in the implementation period supervisors will need to set individual banks on a "micro" glide path into the countercyclical regime, which may conflict directly with the "macro" glide path towards sustainable growth.

(4) The central bankers' desire for monetary stability: currency flows and stresses have been a feature of the crisis, perhaps creating or exacerbating economic upturns and downturns. Clearly there is a close interaction between monetary conditions and the banking sector: monetary policy and supervision might not always sit happily together.

This is where the mettle of all parties will be tested. It is quite possible that at some point there will be conflict between the various objectives and lively debate between the interested parties. How and/or whether they are reconciled will change the future of banks, the banking sector and possibly the economy. Each country will need to build its own approach and reach its own compromises. In some this could call into question the structure of supervision, with a desire for a joined up approach (say through a unified regulator/central bank) having to be weighed against the need for focus on these very different issues. Ultimately it seems that government will need to pick up the baton for the most difficult decisions.

Stepping away from these big picture concerns, and before we turn to the mechanics of supervision, it should be noted that supervision does not take place in a vacuum – it is not a neat scientific experiment with all unwanted variables removed. Indeed, there is a common (and probably valid) view that regulators are always catching up with the last crisis, and get there just in time to get caught out by the next one.

The supervisors will need to take change into account. For example, in the market and political spheres:

(a) Investors in the capital markets will reach their own decisions on the adequacy of each bank's capital and liquidity. They could be content to see it safely on its regulatory glide path to full Basel III compliance over the extended implementation period, or they could seek certainty, albeit at a cost, in the form of early compliance with the tougher regime. In an environment where disposals and acquisitions of banks' activities are likely, new shareholders and management teams in particular might veer towards getting the bad news out early. The various regulatory stakeholders mentioned above will have different views on what they would prefer.

(b) Over the ten year implementation period banking markets will change and develop. New pressures and problems will emerge and new financing channels for the economy (such as shadow banking, which waxed and waned even over the ten years before Basel III was developed) will arrive on the scene (and possibly depart again).

(c) Finally, regulation is ultimately a political statement: different countries will have different views on their national objectives and the means to get to them. The G20 consensus on objectives, tools and ratios could crack, either dramatically or more subtly by differential implementation, leading to a far more uncertain picture than is intended.

19.5 Key principles for macro-prudential supervision

One has only to look at the major elements of the Basel III accord to identify the challenge supervisors face. They have not previously had to deal with the macro areas that Basel explores, and even where they have done so the intensity of their supervision has been far lower than Basel III demands: they are almost completely untested in the field. This is something that highlights the biggest concern over Basel III – it assumes that the supervisors and governments can think better and faster than the economy and the market, and will push the right levers soon enough to achieve what they want. Only time will tell: it is likely that there will be some successes, but some failures, and when working to remove systemic risk failure is not an outcome that is easily acceptable.

Setting aside such doubts, the authorities will need to put in place a framework through which the new macro-prudential supervision can operate. Some key principles for this are proposed below:

(a) **Have clarity of purpose** – be clear on the aim of each new regulation and requirement, and whether it serves a macro or a micro purpose. There is a great danger that, in regulators' minds, better regulation means more regulation. Better should mean only that.

(b) **Use the right tools for the job** – put simply, designing and calibrating the system as a whole to minimise the danger of another major financial crisis for as long as is possible is not the same thing as regulating each bank with the aim of minimum risk of loss to its own depositors: different approaches are needed. Mixing the tools can result in throwing the book at the problem – layering up standards designed for different purposes. Looked at another way, one could say that regulators risk trying to cover their (understandable) failure to identify the bubble (and manage the resulting systemic risk) by applying tighter regulation to individual banks, as a poorly targeted proxy for systemic assessments and actions.

(c) **Develop a thoroughly thought through twin track approach** – for example micro prudential supervision should be adequate to identify and oversee a bank with an overstretched balance sheet in a "normal" market cycle (accepting for now that such can be defined). Solutions might involve more capital and better controls at that bank. In contrast, a severe property bubble would be identified by macro supervision, may result in systemic risk and thus may require a systemic approach to resolution involving (for example) using tools such as interest rates, minimum loan to value ratios, the tax system, changes to the scope of regulation and (possibly) additional capital requirements.

(d) **Focus first on market-wide macro-economic indicators** – macro supervision demands an approach that:

   (i) is alert to new sources of systemic risk;
   (ii) coordinates an international response when needed; and
   (iii) is separate from national politics but sensitive to national economic needs.

(e) **Develop and regularly revisit a macro-prudential dashboard** – such an approach could be based around agreed key indicators in each market and at different levels (globally and nationally for example). The indicators should be relatively small in number and focused on the specifics of the country. Examples could include:

   (i) overall banking market leverage levels and concentrations;

(ii) banking sector aggregates;

(iii) aggregates for non-bank and unregulated financial institutions;

(iv) key inflation and asset price level data;

(v) specific indicators for commercial and retail property values, affordability and associated lending and affordability of that lending;

(vi) specific indicators for any other assets considered systemically important;

(vii) other relevant systemic risk indicators; and

(viii) stress tests of the indicators.

These should be inputs to a decision process, thus forcing the regulators to take conscious action and articulation of decisions (even if these are "do nothing").

(f) **Focus on the impact of failure, not just the risk** – some firms are systemically important, meaning that their risks need to be considered explicitly in the macro analysis of the industry and the economy; they cannot be dealt with only via the micro as implied above. The issue in overseeing such systemically important firms is more the <u>impact</u> of failure, than the <u>risk</u> of failure and it is that that needs to be addressed. The supervisory objective should be to ensure that when the risk materialises (not if it materialises, since risk cannot be 100% removed even by very intrusive regulation) the impact is manageable. In short, fewer firms should be genuinely systemically important, after the "impact mitigants" come into effect.

In consequence, the mitigants need to be the focus of supervisors' attention, for example:

(i) market structure and avoidance of concentration;

(ii) interconnectedness and large exposures limits;

(iii) clearing arrangements;

(iv) bank resolution regime;

(v) legal clarity on operational and settlement issues; and

(vi) client asset segregation.

(g) **Capital is usually not the answer** – raise capital levels as a final option, not the first – in some cases a capital increase for a group of banks, or in exceptional cases an individual bank, may be needed for such firms to mitigate "their" systemic risk (indeed, for all firms, including non-systemic firms, it may be that the level of capital required should be increased to reflect a previous incorrect assessment of risk). However, capital should be the last port of call, not the first: minimising the impact as described above is likely to be a more effective area for early focus. Raising required capital levels above market norms may be an admission of regulatory failure elsewhere.

(h) **Be aware of market distortions caused by excessive regulation** – regulation not only provides a buffer against failure; it also acts as a barrier to entry to the industry. Hence regulation deprives market users of new choices and the industry of the opportunity to develop new efficiencies. A competitive open market is likely to provide a better and more efficient industry than will supervisory exhortation and compulsion.

(i) **Implement any new regime to reflect the systemic risk now, not historic levels** – the plan is for the new regime to be implemented when economic conditions permit. The structure of the market will flex over this period, and it is possible that institutions that were systemically important will no longer be so. The new regime is primarily intended to deal with systemically important banks, so the regulators need to consider the scope of the regime carefully.

19.6 Will the authorities be able to meet the expectations placed on them?

There is much more to Basel III than macro-prudential supervision, and in other areas it poses supervisors some big challenges.

19.6.1 Supervising SIFIs

Identifying and supervising SIFIs is a major area of focus, given the problems with which they were associated in 2007/8. As a result the FSB published the seminal paper on the subject in

November 2010[6] (referred to also at the beginning of this chapter when challenges for supervisors were listed). The paper points clearly to the need for adequate resourcing of SIFI supervision:

> "The level of supervision applied by national authorities must be commensurate with the potential destabilization risk that such firms pose to their own domestic financial systems, as well as the broader international financial system."

Space does not allow a line by line analysis of this important SIFI paper (the points raised earlier in this Chapter provide a flavour of the analysis), but the big themes laid out in it will undoubtedly form the basis of many supervisory upgrades around the world. Supervision is not just big themes, though. The regulators will also need to consider more detailed points around the scope of application of SIFI supervision. Will the work be entirely at group level or will the position of individual legal entities in different countries be relevant? How focused will supervisors (at head office and/or local subsidiary level) be on requiring SIFIs to change their structure to make it easier to supervise and easier to wind up in the event of default? How will the regime deal with the supervision of branches as against head offices? Many questions remain to be answered, and while some of them demand common policies across the world, in other cases the interpretation will need to be specific for an institution.

19.6.2   Getting the right funding and skills

A (perhaps the) fundamental Basel III debate is around how much society is willing to pay for regulation and whether it will get the safety it expects from it.

Much of this is an economic debate around capital and liquidity ratios, and the costs of crises, but for the supervisors there is a very tangible cash cost issue. Supervisory budgets are already

---

6   Intensity and Effectiveness of SIFI Supervision Recommendations for Enhanced Supervision – 2 November 2010

large and growing and more cost is inevitable. As an example, at the time of writing the UK's FSA operates with a budget of some £500m, but its responsibilities across the financial services sector are already huge and arguably the public is expecting more than it can reasonably deliver, even before the demands of Basel III.

A balance has to be struck between the extra funding needed to supervise Basel III, as expressed through, for example, the government's budget or fees to the industry, and the extra benefits achieved. There is a limit to what can be achieved by any supervisor even with extensive resource and the point of declining marginal returns is difficult to identify and to justify. There thus comes a point where regulators and government have to recognise the limits of what is possible.

As well as the amount of funding its source is also a problem. It has to be provided either by the state (out of general taxation), or by the industry (for example via fees and levies), or a combination of the two. State funding can give government a budget and political challenge, but it means it can oversee regulation more directly. On the other hand, many bankers accept the premise of more regulation of SIFIs, but want it done well and are willing to pay to make sure it is – but such an approach can easily call into question the independence of the regulator. The regulator can try less direct routes, for example require banks to commission and pay for independent long form reports and audits, but while valuable these do not absolve the regulator from responsibility or solve the resource problem.

Supervisory budgets are driven largely by headcount, and the basic resource question for supervisors is therefore how many heads are needed. Here there is no consensus. To quote the FSB on SIFI Supervision [7]:

> "There is a wide range of supervisory resourcing applied by different national authorities to SIFI supervision. Per

---

[7] Financial Stability Board – Intensity and Effectiveness of SIFI Supervision; Recommendations for Enhanced Supervision 2 November 2010

SIFI, it ranges from a low of 14 people, to a high of over 100 which can include the exclusive use of dedicated teams or a mix of dedicated teams and teams that participate in the supervision of all SIFIs and non-SIFIs."

Supervisors around the world need to understand why they operate hugely different resourcing models. There may be different drivers in these models, ranging from differing attitudes to risk, use or otherwise of technology, use of on-site vs. off-site supervision (see below), and use of external experts as against own staff. The position is very far from clear, but a more open discussion on the issue is to be expected now it has been brought to the table.

Turning from numbers to people, supervisors will also need new skills to supervise SIFIs and other complex firms in the way now required. Critically, one of the FSB's proposals (referred to earlier) is that supervisors should be willing and able to challenge the bank's business model. Supervision will thus be riskier as supervisors will need to be able to make good their claim to be able spot weak models well in advance.

It will be difficult to spot problems successfully and totally consistently: few supervisors would claim they have a better pool of management expertise than the industry. There may be some cases where the supervisor can add significantly to management's expertise at, for example, a smaller bank or a mutual bank, but assessing the business models of all banks, particularly the SIFIs, is fraught with challenges and risks to the supervisor if mistakes are made.

Taking up this challenge will mean supervisors having to upskill their staff at all levels. What will be critical will be the supervisors' access to people who have run banks and have the breadth of experience to make a robust case: technical knowledge is not enough to deliver the right result. The implication is that supervision will cost more as senior and experienced people are recruited, which will require supervisors to look to their funding model, whether based on government support or fees from the industry. Such people may not need to be full-time supervisors – the UK FSA for example has used former practitioners ("Senior Advisors") for many years to assist its teams to get a balanced view and to spot the problems that a less experienced individual would not have seen before.

Also, of course, it is not enough to be able to spot a problem; regulators have to be able to do something about it. They will need to have the authority, both legally and in practice, to force through changes to models that management and shareholders judge to be appropriate, but regulators do not. Where this can be based on facts and analysis pushing through changes may be possible, but where it is based on hypothesis and the application of experience it may be that banks will be able to push the regulators back.

Drilling into the detail a little by way of example, the proposed new liquidity regime mandates that supervisors have a far greater knowledge of treasury issues than before, and the net stable funding ratio exacerbates the problem. Supervisory attention in most countries has (surprisingly) focused far more on issues such as reporting, capital and governance than on liquidity. Getting the right skilled treasury resource into place is a major challenge if the supervisors are to ask for the right information and know how to use it when they get it.

Finally, the supervisors will be expected to exercise a lot more judgment in the new world and they will be at far greater risk of getting it wrong, indeed given the scale of the task it is virtually certain they will do so at some point. This mandates a robust QA process over decisions at each supervisor. QA in this context does not just mean tests to make sure the boxes have been ticked (though that may be important), but structured oversight and review of supervisory decisions by individuals experienced in the industry who can compare and contrast across different banks. Some supervisors have had panel processes for many years, staffed by experienced staff members or by former practitioners, but these are expected to become more widespread: supervisors need to be able to defend themselves against allegations of bias and inconsistency, as well as lack of understanding of the industry. Supervisors will be expected to look for senior individuals to fill these roles.

19.6.3   How to organise the resource

In recent years the supervisors have also had to deal with huge change in the industry: to do their job well they have constantly had to evaluate the forces at their command against the growing complexity of banking and its risks. One can perhaps argue that in recent years an increasingly detailed rulebook has been a problem in this process: supervisors have had to be conscious of the risk of building up teams of process-focussed individuals, who check compliance with an overly detailed rulebook, at the expense of using experienced industry experts, who are capable of carrying out wise prudential supervision. Different supervisors have taken different approaches to the issue.

However, the advent of Basel III alters the supervisory requirements further. Supervisors will now need to use experienced individuals once again, for example in order to reach the required views on banks' business plans, but also will need to have in place deep specialists to deal with the technical areas that they now need to consider and to complement the more generalist supervisors; liquidity is an obvious example.

These two pools of resource, generalist supervisors and deep specialists, will need to form an integrated Basel III team carrying out a coherent supervisory programme. To make this work, a move towards matrices is envisaged, with the experts responsible for developing the policy for their particular area, drawing on their detailed knowledge and the experience in the market of the generalist supervisors, and supplementing the generalists at the coal face of supervision when it is appropriate to bring them in. For example, counterparty credit risk specialists are in short supply and need to be used where they give the greatest benefit. Similarly highly experienced supervisors can better spend their time reaching balanced judgments on the overall position of banks than in developing highly technical policy on a specialist area.

The matrix issue goes right through the organisation and its people: management will need to develop appropriate career paths for the different specialists (say economists or modellers), also consider whether they wish to keep generalists or special-ists for the long term or to expect, and maybe prefer, that people who have gained industry and specialist knowledge elsewhere will come into the organisation for just a few years before returning to the industry. Alternatively they might feel that being a professional supervisor in such demanding times demands a whole career, not just a short stint to tick a box on the CV. The advent of Basel III makes it difficult for supervisors to avoid the issues.

19.6.4   Where to deploy the resource

For supervision to be effective it needs to be visible, probably much more so than it was before 2007. A recent IMF Staff Position Note sets out the basis for debate: [8]

> "Good supervision is intrusive. Supervision is premised on an intimate knowledge of the supervised entity. It cannot be outsourced and it cannot rely solely or mainly on offsite analysis. Supervisors in the financial sector should not be viewed as hands-off or distant observers, but rather a pres-ence that is felt continuously, keeping in mind the unique nature of financial supervision."

The financial crisis thus raises questions about the balance between:

(a)   Off-site supervision: for example reviews of new and finan-cial information at the supervisors' offices; and

(b)   On-site supervision: ranging from short supervisory visits through to a permanent on-site presence.

The former includes the analysis of supervisory data gathered through standard reporting forms as well as work to set the bank in the context of wider economic and sectoral developments, and the context provided by similar reviews of its peers.

---

[8]   "The Making of Good Supervision: Learning to Say 'No' " Jose Viñals and Jonathan Fiechter with Aditya Narain, Jennifer Elliott, Ian Tower, Pierluigi Bologna and Michael Hsu

The latter is far more immediate and hands on. It allows detailed inspections of transactions and supporting evidence and observation of governance processes, for example via the following elements:

(a) interviewing management;
(b) inspecting the written policies and procedures and assessing by inspection of records and observation the degree to which they are followed;
(c) evaluating whether the bank's financial statements accurately show the bank's capital and liquidity position;
(d) checking the accuracy of accounting records;
(e) checking the adequacy of internal controls and the audit function;
(f) checking for compliance with laws and regulations; and
(g) summarising the findings and assigning an assessment or rating to the bank.

On-site supervision can, if done well, produce a very useful view of a bank. However, it is resource intensive and many regulators use it sparingly, and complement it with off-site monitoring.

There are clearly many half-way houses, for example off-site work on supervisory returns showing compliance with the rulebook, perhaps supplemented by short on-site visits or special reports by independent third parties (normally accounting firms). Similarly, some supervisors have carried out thematic reviews across particular sectors of the banking industry to identify and assess common themes.

Different national supervisors have historically adopted widely different approaches to on-site supervision. To give three very different examples:

(1) In Germany, the bank supervisor, BaFin, and its prede-cessors have historically relied heavily on detailed on-site reviews by the bank's auditors to supplement its own supervision. BaFin's 2008 annual report[9] explains that they

---

[9] BaFin Annual Report '08 – Chapter V: Supervision of banks and financial services institutions

conduct supervisory audits for three reasons: when the supervised banks request that their internal risk measurement procedures or market risk models be inspected; when the BaFin initiates them itself as part of its random monitoring program or to delve deeper into a bank; and when the BaFin inspects institutions on the basis of a statutory schedule of prescribed intervals. In 2008, for instance, the BaFin conducted 244 special audits, of which 61 were those requested by banks, 20 were prescribed under the law, and 163 were conducted solely at the BaFin's initiative

(2) In the UK, the FSA carries out limited on-site reviews itself through its "ARROW" review process. It also commonly requires banks to commission "Section 166 reports" from independent experts (often the bank's auditors) where essential. Use of this tool was normal in banking supervision by the Bank of England in the years before the FSA was founded in 1997, was then minimal until 2007 but has increased very significantly since then. FSA officials now believe that the approach avoids committing extensive supervisory resource to each bank, and allows the costs to be better allocated to the firm impacted.

(3) In the US, for the Federal Banking Authorities on-site examination is a primary tool of supervision, and the FBAs are mandated to conduct full-scope on-site examinations of banks at least once every year or 18 months. There is a substantial continuous supervision programme at major banks.

Each of these countries, and many other countries, chose the model they did as they felt it would be the best approach for their situation. Much work has been done around the world to develop the best approach for the local situation, but many will now revisit their analyses and conclusions.

This is not just an issue for supervisors in major economies. In 2010 the Financial Stability Institute carried out a study of the priorities of 133 supervisors around the world. This is summarised in Figure 19.2. The study was focused primarily on Basel II, but the results showed that the more basic issue of on/off-site supervision was at the top of the list of concerns across the board (the figures below are in terms of percentages of jurisdictions)[10] :

Figure 19.2 Supervisory priorities

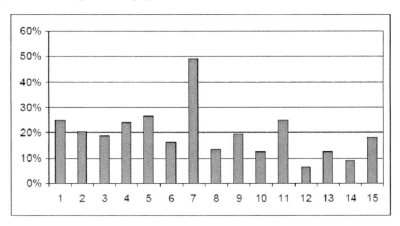

Legend

1 Legal changes	9 Bank Resolution and Crisis Management
2 Quality of capital	10 Accounting and Reporting
3 Macropudential supervision	11 Consolidated and cross-border supervision
4 Credit risk	12 Core principles
5 Liquidity risk	13 Risk management
6 Stress testing	14 AML/CFT
7 On- and off-site supervision	15 Others
8 Corporate governance	

Clearly supervisors will be revisiting the approach they have taken with the benefit of their recent experiences and assessing whether it remains adequate to ensure their supervisory staff have a close enough understanding of the inner workings at banks, and is still relevant in the Basel III world. It would not be surprising to see the supervisors mandating more on-site supervision. Indeed, it is possible that some senior bankers would prefer such supervision, provided it can be properly resourced, so as to make sure their bank is overseen in a way that is appropriate to the risks and the business, not remote and rule based.

---

[10] Financial Stability Institute; Occasional Paper No. 9. 2010 FSI Survey on the Implementation of the New Capital Adequacy Framework August 2010

However, there is a long way to go. To quote Paul Tucker of the Bank of England[11]:

> "A remarkable fact is that although the style of banking supervision varies enormously across the world, almost nothing seems to have been done to get to the bottom of the question of which approaches are the more effective – having an army of on-site examiners, such as for example in the United States; or relying on offsite analysis, which tends to be the pattern in much of Europe."

19.7   The place of the regulator

The financial crisis has not just impacted the principles and processes of regulation. As a result of widespread public and government concern, many countries have rebuilt their regulatory arrangements in a bid to make it more fail-safe, and to address specific weaknesses they have identified. A detailed analysis of all these changes is beyond the scope of this chapter. However, some examples are worthy of note:

•   In the US the formative undertaking to reshape the prudential supervisory and consumer protection apparatus that is the Dodd-Frank Wall Street Reform and Consumer Protection Act, was signed into law by President Obama in July 2010. Its title is briefer than the weight of the volume would lead one to believe:

> "An Act to promote the financial stability of the United States by improving accountability and transparency in the financial system, to end "too big to fail", to protect the American taxpayer by ending bailouts, to protect consumers from abusive financial services practices, and for other purposes."[12]

> Extensive detailed rulemaking over many months if not years is needed to bring the Act into effect.

---

[11] Paul Tucker, Deputy Governor, Financial Stability, Bank of England at the FSB and Korean G20 Presidential Committee Conference, Korea 3 September 2010 "Financial Crisis and G20 Financial Regulatory Reform: An Overview".

[12] Dodd-Frank Wall Street Reform and Consumer Protection Act

Dodd-Frank makes major changes to the allocation of responsibilities among regulators as well as to many other areas of financial regulation. Of particular importance here is the creation of the Financial Stability Oversight Council ("FSOC") and the designation of the Federal Reserve Board as the instrument of oversight for SIFIs, including large banking organisations, certain non-bank financial institutions and financial market utilities. The safety and soundness aspirations of the whole Act can be seen from the purposes of the FSOC:

"(A) to identify risks to the financial stability of the United States that could arise from the material financial distress or failure, or ongoing activities, of large, interconnected bank holding companies or nonbank financial companies, or that could arise outside the financial services marketplace;

(B) to promote market discipline, by eliminating expectations on the part of shareholders, creditors, and counterparties of such companies that the Government will shield them from losses in the event of failure; and

(C) to respond to emerging threats to the stability of the United States financial system."[13]

As its name implies the FSOC has an oversight role over other supervisors; it is mandated to collect information and guide the supervisors based on its view of current and emerging risks. Clearly this significantly tips the balance of power between the government, the supervisors, and the banking industry and will have a major impact on the way banks are supervised and the rules applied.

- In the European Union governments agreed to create pan-EU supervisors for banking (in London), securities (in Paris) and insurance firms (in Frankfurt). However, this was not considered enough, and at a higher level the European Systemic Risk Board is also being set up to oversee the whole European system. The board will be independent of the governments on a day-to-day basis and will monitor

---

[13] Dodd-Frank Wall Street Reform and Consumer Protection Act

markets and send warnings to EU nations on economic and financial risk.

- In the UK, the 1997 single regulator structure and its creation the Financial Services Authority ("FSA") is being unwound, with Bank of England ("BoE") becoming the macro-prudential regulator. Micro-prudential supervision of banks will be undertaken by a new Prudential Regulatory Authority ("PRA") which will be owned by the Bank of England, and a separate regulator will take on consumer financial services regulation. One of the main objectives is to give clarity over responsibility for financial stability, something notably lacking in the previous arrangements.

- Finally, in France, the banking and insurance authorities have been merged to establish the Prudential Supervisory Authority (Autorité de Contrôle Prudentiel or "ACP") with the three aims of improving financial stability, enhancing consumer protection and strengthening international supervisory cooperation.

There are therefore many ongoing changes in the structure of regulation at an international and at a national level. Clearly governments aspire to financial stability, and see restructuring the regulators as a route to that target. While some may claim that this will not achieve all that is hoped the restructuring does perhaps show a new realisation that regulation had become too separated from financial stability. A major part of this is the highlighting of the crucial advantages of a strong institutional link between prudential supervision and the central bank. Put another way, without a core of financial stability all other regulation is irrelevant; the organisational structure needs to be one that keeps regulators as organisations and as individuals focused on that issue before all others.

19.8 International oversight

Much of this book has been about the new international rulebook under Basel III, and this chapter has focused on supervision against that rulebook, which of course is primarily at a national level. However, an international framework of rules demands international oversight to ensure consistency and quality.

It is not enough just to develop new regulations: implementation is all and on this the onus is now with Basel's Standards Implementation Group. This group will conduct follow up and thematic peer reviews at all member countries to ensure that they implement fully all aspects of both Basel II and III. Basel will also be following up by reviewing implementation by banks and supervisors in areas like stress testing and sound liquidity risk management.

Peer reviews are one approach to ensuring effective implementation. Another tool that is of growing importance is the "supervisory college", formerly an obscure niche of in the world of supervision that has now been pushed into the spotlight by the G20 itself and by a paper issued by the Basel Committee setting out eight principles for such colleges.[14]

Supervisory colleges have existed for many years and are multilateral working groups of relevant supervisors formed for the purpose of enhancing effective consolidated supervision of an international banking group and informing decision making. They grew out of informal arrangements between national regulators for the effective supervision of international groups. Major banks with operations in many jurisdictions may face nesting colleges – international, regional (notably within the EU) and possibly national (across different functional regulators such as banking, investment business and insurance).

Despite not being decision-making bodies, the colleges did, for example, enable discussion and planning of supervisory assessments and sharing information about the overall risk assessment of an international banking group. They also enabled better crisis management, a notoriously difficult area. Nevertheless, it is probably fair to say that while the supervisors found the arrangement very useful, they needed more structure to be truly effective and the G20 statements and Basel principles may help to ground them in a more formal international agreement. As

---

[14] Basel Committee – Good Practice Principles on Supervisory Colleges – October 2010

an example, it is difficult for the outsider to anticipate the legal difficulties a supervisor may face in sharing information about a banking group with the supervisors of other parts of the group; they are often constrained by national legislation when they need to have frank debate on an international basis. Basel's eight principles do not solve such complex issues but they do help put them in a framework within which a trusting relationship can be built.

If we turn to the broader supervisory agenda as represented by the Basel Core Principles, there is a way to go. The IMF's Financial Sector Assessment Program ("FSAP") reviews present a comprehensive and in-depth analysis of a country's financial sector. These have shown a picture of the extent of compliance, or rather non-compliance, with the Basel Core Principles so far:

> "Recent assessments of 24 countries ... identified a large incidence of deficiencies in consolidated supervision (CP 24), operational independence (CP 1.2), powers to take corrective action (CP 23) and comprehensive risk management (CP 7). This last principle summarizes the supervisory review process laid out in the Basel II framework, with supervisors required to satisfy themselves that banks have an appropriate and comprehensive risk management process, including board and senior management oversight and encompassing all material risks."[15]

Figure 19.3 below gives a summary of the whole picture.

In response to the challenge shown here, FSB and the IMF are moving forward with reviews to ensure the proper implementation of international standards, particularly as regards globally important SIFIs ("G-SIFIs"). For example, as regards the FSB[16]:

> "Home jurisdictions for global SIFIs (G-SIFIs) should ... subject their G-SIFI policy measures to review by the proposed Peer Review Council ["PRC"]."

---

[15] IMF – "The Making of Good Supervision: Learning to Say 'No' ". Jose Viñals and Jonathan Fiechter with Aditya Narain, Jennifer Elliott, Ian Tower, Pierluigi Bologna, and Michael Hsu
[16] FSB – "Reducing the moral hazard posed by systemically important financial institutions", 20 October 2010

Figure 19.3 Non-compliance with Basel Core Principles

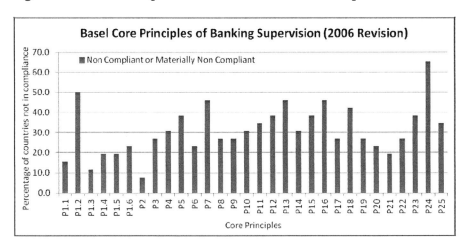

The PRC comprises senior members of the relevant national authorities having G-SIFIs operating as home or host in their jurisdictions and, inter alia, will conduct its initial assessment of national G-SIFI policies by the end of 2012.

The IMF is taking a stronger line also. The agreement in 2010 to make the FSAP mandatory for countries with systemically important financial sectors represents an important step in ensuring that the new standards are implemented and adhered to. As of September 2010, such countries are required to undergo financial stability assessments every five years.

At the same time as all this global work, regional oversight arrangements are being developed. In the EU, the European Systemic Risk Board ("ESRB") was formed on 16 December 2010 to identify and oversee the risks in the market and coordinate with the IMF and FSB. It will issue recommendations to countries or groups of countries and where necessary inform the Council of Ministers of the EU countries. It will be independent of individual governments and will cover both the Euro-zone and countries in the EU but outside the zone. To reflect that, the members elected as first Chair of the ESRB the President of the European Central Bank, Jean-Claude Trichet, and as first Vice-Chair Mervyn King, Governor of the Bank of England.

To summarise on international oversight: international bodies are making efforts to assess the adequacy of the responses of regulators and supervisors in order to drive forward the national implementation of Basel III. The question is whether these assessments will persuade those that are not complying to take action. If compliance with Basel III is as partial as compliance with the Core Principles then implementation progress is likely to be slow. However, there is hope that Basel III will be different – these are not principles that apply to supervisors alone, they are rules that impact banks and there may be pressure from the market on those banks from jurisdictions that do not comply fully. As an example, if may be that having a capital ratio lower than the Basel III levels is seen by the equity and credit markets as signalling weakness, not as an advantage. For international banks and SIFIs, at least, the national regimes are likely to be less important than the global standard. One has to caution though that crises have a habit of fading from the mind, and in due time lower ratios and weaker national regimes may once again be seen to be "realistic" and "commercial".

19.9 Conclusion

The judgment of supervisors is critical to the successful implementation of an enhanced international supervisory structure such as Basel III, as well as to the stability of individual banking organisations and the system as a whole. The international supervisory community, led by the FSB and the IMF is taking up the challenge and putting in place global standards and mechanisms for supervising compliance.

At one level all this promises well. However, the paragraphs above have shown that the national supervisors and international bodies face huge challenges if they are to implement successfully a globally consistent and coherent supervisory framework that is resilient, encourages coordinated vigilance and timely corrective action, while remaining flexible to adapt to evolving markets and institutions. Even the best supervisors will have to make many changes if they are to play their part in the planned improvement in long-term financial stability.

The changes that will be the catalysts for success are as much about people as process. For example, supervisors will need to:

(a) work more closely with other bodies such as fiscal author-
     ities and central banks as well as nurture considerable and
     sustained cooperation between supervisors across sectors
     and jurisdictions;
(b) make sure they have the right people who are able to take
     and implement consistent and reasoned decisions in highly
     subjective areas; and
(c) have the ability, willingness and support to move quickly
     and effectively.

To conclude, Basel III makes supervision a far broader discipline than before with macro-prudential supervision and
recovery and resolution firmly on the agenda as well as more
traditional aspects such as capital, systems and controls.
Supervisors face many challenges as a result, but need to deal
with these in the context of the overall objective. Market crises
will always be with us as the economy changes and develops
but supervising to reduce the frequency and impact of crises is
a realistic aim, and one the Basel III package taken as a whole
seeks to achieve.

Appendix I – Trends in Pillar 3 reporting and risk disclosures

1. Sources of information

The global financial crisis has highlighted the need for more transparent risk disclosures, and these have been the subject of a number of studies by regulators and other stakeholders over the past three years, including among others the following:

- PricewaterhouseCoopers, *Accounting for Change: Transparency in the Midst of Turmoil, a Survey of Banks' 2007 Annual Reports* (August 2008)
- Committee of European Banking Supervisors ("CEBS"), *Report on Banks' Transparency on Activities and Products Affected by the Recent Market Turmoil* (June 2008)
- CEBS, *Assessment of Banks' Pillar 3 Disclosures* (June 2009)
- CEBS, *Follow-up Review of Banks' Transparency in their 2009 Pillar 3 Reports* (June 2010)

In addition to these reports, the observations summarised below are based on an analysis of the Pillar 3 reports and risk management disclosures of 22 banks over the past three years (2007 through 2009). The list of banks surveyed is included in Appendix I.

2. The volume of information provided has increased over the past three years

A review of the Pillar 3 reports and risk management disclosures over the past three years reveals the fact that the volume

501

of risk information provided by banks has increased substantially over the past three years, as illustrated in Figure 4 below.

Overall, the number of pages of risk reports published by banks has increased by 14 percent from 2007 to 2008, and 13 percent from 2008 to 2009. On average, banks' risk management disclosures have increased from 49 to 56 pages over the 2007–2009 period.

In terms of how the volume of disclosures has evolved over the past three years, there is also a significant disparity amongst banks – some have increased the volume of disclosures by more than 60 per cent over the 2007–2009 period, while others have reduced the number of pages by nearly 25 per cent. On the one hand, new requirements imposed by certain regulators or standard-setters as a result of the financial crisis forced a majority of banks to add new disclosures, in particular around areas such as securitisations. On the other hand, some banks aimed at increasing transparency by providing less but more relevant information about their risk profile.

Figure 4 Change in the volume of risk management information year-on-year

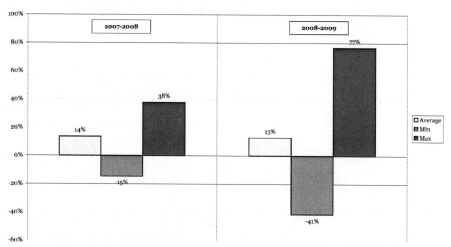

In terms of absolute number of pages again, the range of practices is quite wide, the most comprehensive risk disclosures report included 166 pages in 2009, while some other banks' disclosures include less than 20 pages of information. This difference is driven in part by the relative size and complexity of these institutions' operations, as well as by the approaches taken for Basel II (e.g. IRB approaches for credit risk require substantially more disclosures under Pillar 3 than the Standardised Approach). However, disparity is also driven by the banks' strategy around risk management communication: some banks have used disclosures as a means to provide transparency to market participants on all the risks they are facing, and how they are addressing them; others have opted for a pure compliance approach, where only the minimum required information is provided.

3. There is diversity in practice on the location of risk disclosures

As discussed in Section 12.2, the location of Pillar 3 disclosures is, in most jurisdictions, not mandated by regulators. As a result, practice varies among banks as to whether Pillar 3 disclosures are presented together with related risk management disclosures in the annual report, or as a separate report (see Figure 5 below). No bank amongst the 22 surveyed has changed its approach from 2007 to 2009, but more banks are included in the 2009 sample, hence the shift noted in Figure 5.

The presentation of Pillar 3 disclosures as a separate report has the advantage of gathering all the Pillar 3 information in one place and allows more flexibility for updates when changes arise during the period. On the other hand, the presentation of an all-inclusive risk management report provides market participants with a comprehensive view of the risks facing the bank, risk management strategies and results of these strategies. In addition, as further discussed below, the separate presentation of Pillar 3 disclosures generally results in a time lag between the financial information and other risk-related disclosures provided in the annual report and the supplemental disclosures provided in the Pillar 3 report, which reduces transparency for market participants.

Figure 5 Risk management and Pillar 3 reports presentation

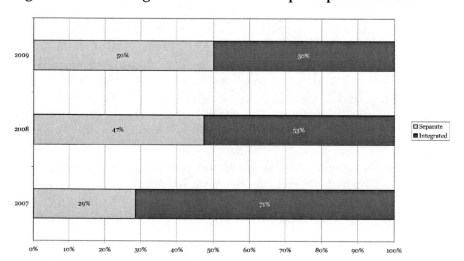

4. Timeliness of risk disclosures has not improved significantly

For the market discipline to function effectively, it is important that market participants have access to information on a timely basis. As illustrated in Figure 6 below, the average timeline of Pillar 3 disclosures publication has not changed significantly between 2007 and 2009, contrary to expectations. On average, banks report their Pillar 3 disclosures roughly 100 days after their fiscal year-end, with a significant disparity between the fastest (33 days in 2009) and the least timely (261 days in 2009).

For those banks that publish their Pillar 3 disclosures as a separate report, there is in some cases a significant delay (up to 131 days) between the publication of the annual report and the Pillar 3 disclosures – see Figure 7 below. On average, however, Pillar 3 disclosures are provided relatively close to the date of the annual report.

Figure 6 Days between year-end Pillar 3 report publication

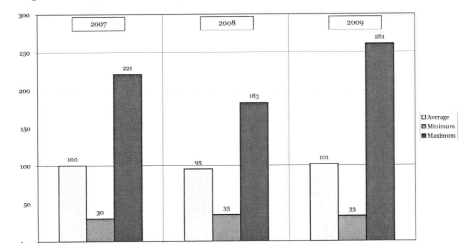

5. The quality of disclosures needs improvement

Pillar 3 and other risk disclosure requirements provide a minimum framework for banks to provide necessary information to market participants in relation to their risk profile. Whilst a few banks went beyond these minimum requirements and presented additional information to provide a full picture of their risk profile to market participants, most institutions limited themselves to a strict compliance exercise by following the letter of the rules.

As new risks arose in the midst of the financial crisis that were not contemplated in the minimum disclosure requirements of the various frameworks, the industry generally failed to provide timely information around those risks. As a result, market participants started questioning the effectiveness of the disclosure requirement frameworks, with a focus in particular on securitisation activities. In its April 2008 report, the FSF noted that while disclosure of structured finance-related risk exposures had improved, "a lack of adequate and consistent disclosure of risk exposures and valuations continues to have a corrosive effect on confidence".

Figure 7 Time lag between annual report and Pillar 3 report publication

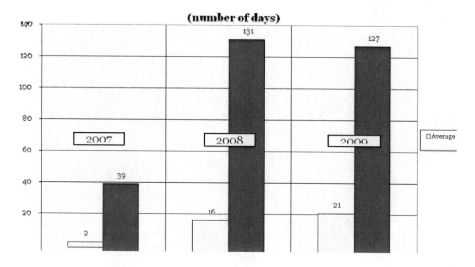

Generally, as noted in the CEBS June 2008 report, banks' disclosures failed to provide comprehensive information on their business model and risk management, and meaningful information on exposures and impacts, with appropriate levels of granularity. The usefulness of disclosures on accounting policies and the presentation of disclosures in general were two other areas where improvements were needed.

Worse, even compliance with the most basic requirements was not observed by all banks. In its June 2009 report on the review of 2008 Pillar 3 disclosures, the CEBS notes "some areas in which disclosures could be enhanced":

- the composition and characteristics of own funds;
- the back-testing information for credit risk and market risk;
- the quantitative information on credit risk mitigations and counterparty credit risk; and
- the granularity of information on securitisations."

In its June 2010 report on the review of 2009 Pillar 3 disclosures, the CEBS observed that "some items of information (both qualitative and quantitative) required by the CRD are not provided by all credit institutions". The list of those items repeated the first three areas listed in the June 2009 report. As it relates to disclosures on securitisations, the CEBS notes that "banks' information on securitisation has been generally enhanced." Indeed, this is an area where – in response to market participants demands – banks have provided in their 2009 reports more information on the nature of their securitisation activities, and the risks related to retained or purchased securitisation exposures.

In response to the shortcomings in the disclosure frameworks, the Basel Committee, the accounting standard setters and the securities regulators imposed additional disclosure requirements, as discussed in Section 12.2 above. One of the lessons learned from this crisis, however, is that mere compliance with the existing disclosure requirements may fail to address new risks arising from market changes. Banks will need to continuously adjust their disclosures to reflect those new risks in a proactive manner to avoid a repeat of the recent transparency and confidence crisis. In the July 2009 enhancements to the Basel II framework, the Basel Committee stressed this point by highlighting the responsibility of banks towards market participants, and requiring that "in addition to the particular information mentioned in the Pillar 3 tables, banks need to make disclosures that reflect their real risk profile as markets evolve over time".

6. Some better disclosure practices have emerged from the crisis

Some examples of best practice that allowed these institutions to differentiate themselves in the eyes of market participants have been highlighted by studies of various regulators.

In June 2008, the CEBS published a report on banks' transparency on activities and products affected by the recent market turmoil, that made a number of recommendations around disclosures. The summary of these recommended best practices is included in Appendix III.

As it relates more specifically to Pillar 3 disclosures, the June 2010 CEBS report notes a number of best practice examples beyond the observation of strict requirements, which are summarised below:

- Disclosure on own funds
    - Reconciliation of accounting equity with Tier 1 capital
    - In addition to capital resources and the capital ratio, an explicit disclosure of the additional capital requirement due to the Basel 1 floor
- Minimum capital requirements
    - Clear explanations on the interrelationship between minimum regulatory requirements and internal capital targets
    - Qualitative information on the allocation of economic capital or a measure of the group's risk taking capacity, as defined by the group's available financial resources divided by its internal capital
- Credit risk
    - Reconciliation of balance sheet and Basel II exposure amounts and reconciliation or clarification related to scope differences for impairment amounts
    - Distinction within the tables on exposures between credit risk and counterparty credit risk, or by nature of transactions (loans, derivatives, repos . . .)
    - Analytical approach through the use of percentages and narrative comments on significant changes
    - Distinction between individual and collective impairment charges and the balance on the allowance account shown within the tables
    - Separate disclosure of unrated exposure amounts and sufficient granularity of credit quality steps with no excessive concentration on one step
    - Clear delineation of the scope for the Standardised Approach
    - Analysis of expected credit model performance versus actual results over a particularly long period, or at the parameter level
    - Probabilities of default for each internal grade
    - Discussion on the approach retained for ratings with regards to the situation in the economic cycle

- ○ Quantitative information on potential future credit exposures for derivatives
- ○ Breakdown of exposure at default by exposure classes and by internal ratings
- ○ Concentration measure of counterparty risk
- ○ Breakdown of counterparty risk exposures by contract type
- ○ Table presenting the exposure amounts, the part secured by guarantees and credit derivatives, and the part secured by collateral by type of regulatory approach
- ○ Clear explanations on the Basel II treatment of the various types of CRM
- ○ Amounts of guarantees and collateral held against impaired loans
- Securitisation
  - ○ Detailed discussion on strategy
  - ○ Comments regarding the changes between periods
- Equity risk
  - ○ Quantitative breakdown of exposures by objective – strategic, capital gains, perspectives, etc.
  - ○ Information on the Basel II treatment for equity risk, and notably on the grandfathering clause, when used
  - ○ Information on the fair value hierarchy of equity instruments retained in the prudential scope of consolidation
- Market risk
  - ○ Clear and comprehensive discussion of models used
  - ○ Detailed description of valuation controls
  - ○ Graphs of VaR over the period
  - ○ Quantitative information on average, minimum and maximum VaR levels during the period as well as a comparison of the daily end-of-day VaR measures to the one-day changes of the portfolio's value
  - ○ Information provided on stressed scenarios considered as part of stress testing regime
- Operational risk
  - ○ Disclosure of the composition of operational risk sources on average over several years
  - ○ Threshold above which a loss event is recorded into the database

- Interest rate risk in the banking book
  - Presentation of interest rate gap by maturity
  - Table setting out the minimum, maximum, average and end-of-year value for the interest rate VaR
  - Principle of using several scenarios, including a steepening or a flattening of the yield curve
  - Mention of the quantitative limit used internally for the management of the interest rate risk
  - Clear discussion of the main drivers of interest rate risk

Appendix II – List of banks covered in the analysis of Pillar 3 and risk management disclosures

Danske Bank

Nordea

BNP Paribas

Credit Agricole

Societe Generale

Deutsche Bank

ING

BBVA

Barclays

HSBC

UBS

Intesa

National Australia Bank

Westpac

MUFG

SMFG

Mizuho

DBS

Bangkok Bank

Standard Bank

RBC

CIBC

Appendix III – CEBS observed good practices for disclosures on activities affected by the market turmoil (with mapping to the SSG Leading practices)

CEBS observed good practices	SSG Leading Practice Disclosures
Business model • Description of the business model (i.e. of the reasons for engaging in activities and of the contribution to value creation process) and, if applicable of any changes made (e.g. as a result of crisis). • Description of strategies and objectives. • Description of importance of activities and contribution to business (including a discussion in quantitative terms). • Description on the type of activities including a description of the instruments as well as of their functioning and qualifying criteria that products/investments have to meet. • Description of the role and the extent of involvement of the institution, i.e. commitments and obligations.	• Activities (SPE).* • Nature of exposure (sponsor, liquidity and/or credit enhancement provider) (SPE). • Qualitative discussion of policy (LF).

Risks and risk management • Description of the nature and extent of risks incurred in relation to the activities and instruments. • Description of risk management practices of relevance to the activities, of any identified weaknesses of any corrective measures that have been taken to address these. • In the current crisis, particular attention should be given to liquidity risk.	
Impact of the crisis on results • Qualitative and quantitative description of results, with a focus on losses (where applicable) and write-downs impacting the results. • Breakdown of the write-downs/ losses by types of products and instruments affected by the crisis (CMBS, RMBS, CDO, ABS and LBO further broken down by different criteria). • Description of the reasons and factors responsible for the impact incurred. • Comparison of i) impacts between (relevant) periods and of ii) income statement balances before and after the impact of the crisis. • Distinction of write-downs between realised and unrealised amounts. • Description of the influence the crisis had on the firm's share price. • Disclosure of maximum loss risk and description how the institution's situation could be affected by a further downturn or by a market recovery. • Disclosure of impact of credit spread movements for own liabilities on results and on the methods used to determine this impact.	• Change in exposure from the prior period, including sales and write-downs (CMB/LF)
Exposure levels and types • Nominal amount (or amortised cost) and fair values of outstanding exposures. • Information on credit protection	• Size of vehicle versus firm's total exposure (SPE/CDO). • Collateral: type, tranches, credit rating, industry, geographic

(e.g. through credit default swaps) and its effect on exposures.

- Information on the number of products
- Granular disclosures of exposures with breakdowns provided by;
  - level of seniority of tranches;
  - level of credit quality (e.g. ratings, investment grade, vintages);
  - geographic origin;
  - whether exposures have been originated, retained, warehoused or purchased;
  - product characteristics: e.g. ratings,share of sub-prime mortgages,discount rates, attachment points,spreads, funding;
  - characteristics of the underlying assets: e.g. vintages, loan-to-value ratios, information on liens, weighted average life of the underlying, prepayment speed assumptions, expected credit losses.
  - Movement schedules of exposures between relevant reporting periods and the underlying reasons (sales, disposals, purchases etc.).
  - Discussion of exposures that have not been consolidated (or that have been recognised in the course of the crisis) and the related reasons.
  - Exposure to monoline insurers and quality of insured assets:
  - nominal amounts (or amortized cost) of insured exposures as well as of the amount of credit protection bought;
  - fair values of the outstanding exposures as well as of the related credit protection;
  - amount of write-downs and losses, differentiated into realised and unrealised amounts;
  - breakdowns of exposures by ratings or counterparty.

distribution, average maturity, vintage (SPE/CDO/CMB/LF).

- Hedges, including exposures to monolines, other counterparties (CDO). Creditworthiness of hedge counterparties (CDO).
- Whole loans, RMBS, derivatives, other (O).
- Detail on credit quality (such as credit rating, loan-to-value ratios, performance measures) (O)
- Change in exposure from the prior period, including sales and write-downs (CMB/LF)
- Distinction between consolidated and non consolidated vehicles. Reason for consolidation (if

  applicable) (SPE).
- Funded exposure and unfunded commitments (LF)

Accounting policies and valuation issues

- Classification of the transactions and structured products for accounting purposes and the related accounting treatment.
- Consolidation of SPEs and other vehicles (such as VIEs) and a reconciliation of these to the structured products affected by the sub-prime crisis.
- Detailed disclosures on fair values of financial instruments:
  - financial instruments to which fair values are applied;
  - fair value hierarchy (a breakdown of all exposures measured at fair value by different levels of the fair value hierarchy and a breakdown between cash and derivative instruments as well as disclosures on migrations between the different levels);
  - treatment of day 1 profits (including quantitative information);
  - use of the fair value option (including its conditions for use) and related amounts (with appropriate breakdowns).
  - Disclosures on the modelling techniques used for the valuation of financial instruments, including discussions of the following:
  - description of modelling techniques and of the instruments to which they are applied;
  - description of valuation processes (including in particular discussions of assumptions and input factors the models rely on);
  - type of adjustments applied to reflect model risk and other valuation uncertainties;
  - sensitivity of fair values; and
  - stress scenarios.

- Valuation methodologies and primary drivers. (CDO).
- Credit valuation adjustments for specific counterparties (CDO).
- Sensitivity of valuation to changes in key assumptions and inputs (CDO).

Other disclosure aspects
- Description of disclosure policies and of the principles that are used for disclosures and financial reporting.

Presentation issues
- Relevant disclosures for the understanding of an institution's involvement in a certain activity should as far as possible be provided in one place.
- Where information is spread between different parts or sources clear cross-references should be provided to allow the interested reader to navigate between the parts.
- Narrative disclosures should to the largest extent possible be supplemented with illustrative tables and overviews to improve the clarity.
- Institutions should ensure that the terminology used to describe complex financial instruments and transactions is accompanied by clear and adequate explanations.

Index

Accounting standards
Basel III interaction with
balance sheet offsetting, 8.2.3
credit value adjustments, 8.2.5
deferred tax assets, 8.2.8
fair value measurement, 8.2.5
financial instruments, 8.2.1–8.2.2,
8.2.4
goodwill, 8.2.6
intangibles, 8.2.6
post-employment benefits, 8.2.7
balance sheet offsetting, 8.2.3
communication, internal and
external, 8.3.1
conclusions, 8.4
credit value adjustments
Basel III, interaction with, 8.2.5
implementation, 8.3.5
deferred tax assets, 8.2.8, 13.3.1
fair value measurement, 8.2.5
financial instruments
classification, 8.2.4
consolidation, 8.2.2
de-recognition, 8.2.2
loan loss provisions, 8.2.1
measurements, 8.2.4
goodwill, 8.2.6
implementation considerations
alignment of data, 8.3.1
communication, internal and
external, 8.3.1
credit value adjustments, 8.3.5
loan loss provisions, 8.3.2
overview, 8.3.1
pension deficits, 8.3.2
threshold deductions, 8.3.3
intangibles, 8.2.6
introduction, 8.1
leverage ratios, 7.3.4
loan loss provisions
financial instruments, 8..2.1
implementation, 8.3.2
pension deficits, 8.3.2
post-employment benefits, 8.2.7
risk-weighted assets
credit value adjustments, and, 8.2.5
goodwill and intangibles, 8.2.6
threshold deductions, 8.3.3

Tier 1 capital
classification, 8.2.4
consolidation, 8.2.2
de-recognition, 8.2.2
loan loss provisions, 8.2.1
measurements, 8.2.4
pension deficits, 8.3.2
post-employment benefits, 8.2.7
Asset value correlation
counterparty credit risk, 5.3.1.4
Back-testing
counterparty credit risk, 5.3.2.5
Balance sheet
accounting standards, 8.2.3
asset mixes, 18.2.4
liquidity, impact of, 6.3.1
Banks
code of practice
tax avoidance, 13.2.1.1
economic impact of
balance sheet asset mixes, 18.2.4
cost reductions, 18.2.3
credit pricing, 18.2.1
deposit pricing, 18.2.2
fees and charges, 18.2.7
generally, 18.2
lending, reduction in, 18.2.5
liquidity/maturity gap, 18.2.6
supply chain, 18.2.3
levies
generally, 13.2.2.1
replacement debt, and, 13.3.2
likely response of
credit pricing, 18.3.1
lending supply, 18.3.2
**Basel Committee on Banking
Supervision (BCBS)**
countries represented, 1.4
risk management, and, 17.1.2
role of, 1.4
Board, role of
risk management
commitment, 17.3.5
control functions, 17.3.2
effectiveness, 17.3.6
governance, 17.3.1
materiality, 17.3.1
qualifications, 17.3.5

risk committees, 17.3.4
risk, oversight for, 17.3.2
senior management, oversight
of, 17.3.3
Bonus bank
deferral of bonus vehicles, 14.4.3
Borrowers
stakeholders perspectives, 16.5.2
Buffers
see **Capital buffers**
Business planning
liquidity, impact of, 6.3.2.5
Business performance
risk management, 17.5.5
Business recovery officer
role of, 15.3.3
Business risk
performance measures, and, 14.3.6
Capital
Basel I and II
deductions from capital, 3.3.7
generally, 3.3
tier 1, 3.3.1–3.3.4
tier 2, 3.3.5
tier 3, 3.3.6
Basel III
deductions from capital, 3.5.7–3.5.9
generally, 3.5
tier 1, 3.5.1–3.5.4
tier 2, 3.5.5–3.5.6
capital buffers, 3.8
capital ratios, 3.6
conclusions, 3.11
contingent capital, 3.7
going concern v gone concern, 3.4
introduction, 3.1
key changes, 3.2
practical considerations
buffer-on-a-buffer approach, 3.9.2
capital planning, 3.9.1
generally, 3.9
superequivalence, 3.10
Capital adequacy
internal capital adequacy assessment
process
bank's responsibilities under, 9.2
introduction, 9.1
risk management disclosure
requirements, 12.2.2
Capital assessment
risk management, 17.5.5
Capital buffers
buffer-on-a-buffer approach, 3.9.2

capital conservation buffer
implications, 10.3.3.3
introduction, 10.3.3.1
mechanics of approach, 10.3.3.2
stress testing, 11.2.1
capital planning buffers, 10.3
countercyclical capital buffer
bank-specific requirements, 10.3.4.3
implications, 10.3.4.5
introduction, 10.3.4.1
minimum requirements, 10.3.4.4
national buffer requirements,
10.3.4.2
stress testing, 11.2.1
generally, 3.8
Pillar 2, role of
capital planning, 9.3.1
internal capital assessments,
and, 9.3.2
Tier 1 capital, and, 9.3.2
stress testing
capital conservation buffer, 11.2.1
countercyclical capital buffer, 11.2.1
Capital charges
counterparty credit risk, 5.3.1.7
Capital instruments
changes to nature of, 13.3.2
Capital market transactions
minimum holding periods, 5.3.1.5
Capital measure
leverage, 7.3.2
Capital planning
Basel II, 9.2
Basel III, 9.3.1
buffers, 10.3
forward-looking capital plan, 9.2
meaning, 3.9.1
Capital ratios
meaning, 3.6
Capital structure
risk management disclosure
requirements, 12.2.2
Cascade of economic profit
performance measures, and, 14.3.6
Cash
deferral of bonus vehicles, 14.4.3
Cash tax paid
Basel III, and, 13.3.3
Central Bank
governors and heads of security, 1.4
Chief risk officer
adequacy of resources, 17.5.3
attributes, 17.5.2

changing role of, 17.5.1
embedding risk management in
 business, 17.5.5
FSA view of role of, 17.5.1
three lines of defence, 17.5.4
Clawback
compensation, 14.4.1
Code of practice
tax avoidance, 13.2.1.1
Collateral
counterparty credit risk
 management of, 5.3.2.1
 re-use of, 5.3.2.2
liquidity, impact of, 6.3.2.6
**Committee of European Banking
 Supervisors (CEBS)**
risk disclosure requirements, 12.1
**Committee on Payment and Settlement
 Systems (CPSS)**
counterparty credit risk, and, 5.3.1.7
Communications
accounting standards, 8.3.1
risk management, 12.3.3, 17.5.5
Compensation
claw-back, 14.4.1
deferral of bonus, 14.4.1
deferral vehicles, 14.4.3
forfeiture, 14.4.1
generally, 14.4
performance adjustment, 14.4.2
Confidential information
risk management disclosure
 requirements, 12.2.1
Conservation buffer
see **Capital buffers**
Conservatism, inherent
loan loss provisions
 accounting standards, 8.3.2
Contingent capital
meaning, 3.7
stakeholders perspectives, 16.4.2
stress testing, 11.3.6
Correlation trading
market risk, and
 internal model approach, 4.6.3.6
 standardised approach, 4.6.2.1
Countercyclical capital buffer
see **Capital buffers**
Counterparty credit risk
data management, and, 5.4
FX forwards, effect on, 5.4
FX swaps, effect on, 5.4
gross market value, meaning of, 5.2

highly-leveraged counterparties
 effect on, 5.4
 qualitative requirements, 5.3.2.3
implications of new rules, 5.4
introduction, 5.1
meaning, 5.2
notional amounts, use of, 5.2
OTC derivatives, effect on, 5.4
overview, 5.2
proposals to enhance capture
 qualitative requirements, 5.3.2
 quantitative requirements, 5.3.1
qualitative requirements
 back-testing, 5.3.2.5
 collateral management
  requirements, 5.3.2.1
 generally, 5.3.2
 highly-leveraged counterparties,
  5.3.2.3
 model validation, 5.3.2.5
 re-use of collateral, 5.3.2.2
 stress testing of CCR models,
  5.3.2.4
quantitative requirements
 asset value correlation, 5.3.1.4
 capital charges for exposure to
  CCP, 5.3.1.7
 expected positive exposure based
  on stressed inputs, 5.3.1.1
 general wrong-way risk, 5.3.1.1
 generally, 5.3.1
 margin period of risk for
  collateralised trades, 5.3.1.5
 Pillar 1 charge for specific wrong-
  way risk, 5.3.1.3
 specific charge for credit value
  adjustments, 5.3.1.2
 standard haircuts for securitisation
  collateral, 5.3.1.6
risk-weighted assets, effect on, 5.4
stress testing, 11.2.2
Credit concentration
performance measures, and, 14.3.6
Credit conversion factor
leverage ratios, and, 8.2.4
Credit default swaps
exposure at default, meaning
 of, 5.3.1.3
risk adjusting TSR, 14.3.2
Credit derivatives
see **Derivatives**
Credit pricing
banks

economic impact of, 18.2.1
likely response of, 18.3.1
Credit rationing
strategic implications, 2.4.2
Credit risk
performance measures, and, 14.3.6
risk management disclosure
requirements, 12.2.2, 12.2.4,
App I
Credit value adjustments
accounting standards
Basel III, interaction with, 8.2.5
implementation, 8.3.5
counterparty credit risk, 5.3.1.2
meaning, 5.3.1.2
Data management
counterparty credit risk, 5.4
liquidity, impact of, 6.3.2.3
risk management disclosure
requirements, 12.3.2
Debt investors
stakeholders perspectives, 16.4.1
Deductions from capital
meaning, 3.5.7–3.5.9
Deferral of bonus
deferral vehicles, 14.4.3
meaning, 144.4.1
Deferred tax assets
accounting standards, 8.2.8
taxation, and, 13.3.1
Defining capital
see **Capital**
Deposit pricing
economic implications, 18.5.2
Depositors
stakeholders perspectives, 16.5.1
Derivatives
loan loss provisions
accounting standards, 8.3.2
market risk, and, 4.6.2.3
OTC derivatives
counterparty credit risk, 5.3.1.5, 5.4
resolution planning, 15.4.4
Disclosure
remuneration, 14.6
risk management
see also **Pillar 3**
communications strategy, 12.3.3
data management, 12.3.2
detailed requirements, 12.2.2
disclosure frameworks, 12.3.3
financial statement risk disclosures,
12.2.4

future of risk management
disclosures, 12.4
governance, 12.3.1
implementation, 12.3
introduction, 12.1
overarching requirements, 11.2.1
recent changes, 12.2.3
Dividends
equity investors, 16.3.2
Divisional equity
deferral of bonus vehicles, 14.4.3
Downturn adjustments
loan loss provisions
accounting standards, 8.3.2
Economic capital
meaning, 14.3.6
Pillar 2, implications of
alternative approach, 9.4.1
generally, 9.4
Economic implications
balance sheet asset mixes, 18.2.4
banks, impact of
balance sheet asset mixes, 18.2.4
cost reductions, 18.2.3
credit pricing, 18.2.1
deposit pricing, 18.2.2
fees and charges, 18.2.7
generally, 18.2
lending, reduction in, 18.2.5
liquidity/maturity gap, 18.2.6
supply chain, 18.2.3
banks, likely response of
credit pricing, 18.3.1
lending supply, 18.3.2
benefits of greater financial
stability, 18.5.2
Basel I, impact of, 18.4.1
Basel II, impact of, 18.4.1
Basel III, impact of, 18.5.5
conclusions, 18.6
cost reductions, 18.2.3
credit pricing
banks, impact of, 18.2.1
banks, likely response of, 18.3.1
crises, costs of, 18.5.1
deposit pricing, 18.2.2
fees and charges, 18.2.7
impact assessment, 18.1.1
introduction, 18.1
lending
banks, impact of, 18.2.5
banks, likely response of, 18.3.2
liquidity/maturity gap, 18.2.6

Macroeconomic Assessment
    Group, 18.1.4
macroeconomic models
    generally, 18.5.3
    results obtained from, 18.5.4
    short-term versus long-term, 18.1.3
    stability, benefits of greater, 18.5.2
    stability versus growth, 18.1.2
    supply chain, 18.2.3
Effective interest rate
loan loss provisions
    accounting standards, 8.3.2
Enforcement
risk management disclosure
    requirements, 12.2.1
Equity investors
    dividends, 16.3.2
    equity market view, 16.3.1
    generally, 16.3
Equity risk
risk management disclosure
    requirements, 12.2.2, App I.
European Commission
    rating agencies, 16.7
    recovery and resolution planning,
        15.2.2
    risk management, 17.1.2
European Systemic Risk Board
    role of, 19.8
**Expected positive exposure based on
    stressed inputs**
counterparty credit risk, 5.3.1.1
Exposure measure
    leverage, 7.3.3
Fair value
    accounting standards, 8.2.5
Financial activities tax
    see also **Taxation**
    nature of, 13.2.2, 13.2.2.2
Financial guarantors
    role of, 5.3.1.3
Financial instruments
    classification, 8.2.4
    consolidation, 8.2.2
    de-recognition, 8.2.2
    loan loss provisions, 8.2.1
    measurements, 8.2.4
Financial leverage
    see **Leverage**
Financial Reporting Standards (FRS)
    see **Accounting standards**
Financial sector contribution
    bank levies, 13.2.2.1

financial activities tax, 13.2.2, 13.2.2.2
financial stability contribution, 13.2.2
financial transactions tax, 13.2.2.3
generally, 13.2.2
Tobin tax, 13.2.2.3
Financial Stability Board
    recovery and resolution planning,
        15.2.1
    role of, 1.4
Financial stability contribution
    nature of, 13.2.2
Financial statements
    risk management disclosure
        requirements, 12.2.4
Financial transactions tax
    see also **Taxation**
    nature of, 13.2.2.3
Forfeiture
    compensation for, 14.4.1
Forward-looking provisioning
    capital plans, 9.2
    procyclicality, and, 10.2
Funding
    see **Liquidity**
Funds transfer pricing
    liquidity, and, 6.3.2.5
FX forwards
    counterparty credit risk, effect of, 5.4
FX swaps
    counterparty credit risk, effect of, 5.4
General wrong-way risk
    meaning, 5.3.1.1
**Generally Accepted Accounting
    Principles (GAAP)**
    see **Accounting standards**
Germany
    recovery and resolution planning,
        15.2.5
Goodwill
    accounting standards, 8.2.6
Governance
    liquidity, impact of, 6.3.2.1
    recovery planning, 15.3.3
    remuneration
        cascading governance, 14.5.2
        future changes, 14.5.1
        managing inputs to remuneration
            committee, 14.5.3
        remuneration oversight committee,
            14.5.2
        stakeholder roles, 14.5.1
    resolution planning, 15.4.2
    risk management

disclosure requirements, 12.3.1
risk framework, 17.5.5
role of board, 17.3.1
stress testing, 11.3.3
Government guarantees
meaning, 16.6.1
value of, 16.6.2
Governors and heads of security (GHOS)
Basel Committee on Banking Supervision, and, 1.4
Gross market value
meaning, 5.2
Highly leveraged counterparties
counterparty credit risk
effect of, 5.4
qualitative requirements, 5.3.2.3
History
introduction, 1.5
Inherent conservatism
loan loss provisions
accounting standards, 8.3.2
Institute of International Finance (IIF)
role of, 1.4
Intangibles
accounting standards, 8.2.6
International Monetary Fund (IMF)
role of, 19.8
taxation
bank levies, 13.2.2.1
banking environment, 13.2
financial activities tax, 13.2.2.2
role of, 13.1
Interest rates
loan loss provisions
accounting standards, 8.3.2
reforms in context, 2.2.4
risk management disclosure requirements, 12.2.2, App I.
Internal capital
adequacy assessment process
bank's responsibilities under, 9.2
introduction, 9.1
assessment
capital buffers, and, 9.3.2
introduction, 9.1
scope of, 9.2
Internal ratings-based framework
counterparty credit risk
asset value correlation, 5.3.1.4
International Organisation of Securities Commissions (IOSCO)

counterparty credit risk, and, 5.3.1.7
Intra-day liquidity risk
risk management, and, 6.3.2.6
Invested capital
meaning, 14.3.6
Legal entity plans
resolution planning, 15.4.3
Lending
banks
economic impact of, 18.2.5
likely response of, 18.3.2
Leverage
Basel III, and
accounting considerations, 7.3.4
capital measure, 7.3.2
exposure measure, 7.3.3
guidelines, 7.3.1
financial crisis, and, 7.2.4
financial leverage
return on equity, 7.2.2
role of, 7.2.1
future outlook, 7.4.3
introduction, 7.1
leverage-driven growth, risks of, 7.2.3
leverage ratios
accounting standards, 7.3.4
banks, impact on, 7.4.2
Basel III ratios, 7.3.1
gross ratios, 7.2.4
implementation timeline, 7.3.1
limitations on, 7.4.1
risks associated with, 7.2.3
performance measures, and, 14.3.6
risk-weighted assets, and, 7.4.2
Levies
generally, 13.2.2.1
replacement debt, and, 13.3.2
Liquidity
background, 6.1.1
balance sheet, impact on, 6.3.1
Basel III regulations
liquidity coverage ration, 6.2.1, 6.2.3
monitoring tools, 6.2.4
net stable funding ratio, 6.2.1, 6.2.3
qualitative requirements, 6.2.4
conclusions, 6.3.3
forecasting, 6.3.2.5
funds transfer pricing, 6.3.2.5
introduction, 6.1
liquidity coverage ratio
application of, 6.2.1.2
calculation of, 6.2.1.1

commercial banks, 6.2.1.2
investment banks, 6.2.1.2
liquid assets, 6.2.1.3
meaning of, 6.1.2, 6.2.1.1
net stable funding ratio, link
    with, 6.2.3
retail banks, 6.2.1.2
scenario proposed and liquidity
    driver analysis, 6.2.1.4
liquidity/maturity gap, 18.2.6
net stable funding ratio
application of, 6.2.2.2
impact of, 6.2.2.4
liquidity coverage ratio, link
    with, 6.2.3
meaning, of, 6.1.2, 6.2.2.1
scenario, 6.2.2.3
quantitative implications, of
    regulations, 6.1.2
risk management framework,
    impact on
business planning, 6.3.2.5
collateral management, 6.3.2.6
data management, 6.3.2.3
funding, 6.3.2.5
governance, 6.3.2.1
intra-day liquidity risk, 6.3.2.6
management information, 6.3.2.3
risk appetite, 6.3.2.2
senior management oversight,
    6.3.2.1
stress testing, 6.3.2.4, 11.2.4
taxation, and, 13.3.4
Liquidity coverage ratio
application of, 6.2.1.2
calculation of, 6.2.1.1
commercial banks, 6.2.1.2
investment banks, 6.2.1.2
liquid assets, 6.2.1.3
meaning of, 6.1.2, 6.2.1.1
net stable funding ratio, link
    with, 6.2.3
retail banks, 6.2.1.2
scenario proposed and liquidity
    driver analysis, 6.2.1.4
Liquidity risk
performance measures, and, 14.3.6
risk management disclosure
    requirements, 12.2.4
Loan loss provisions
accounting standards
    financial instruments, 8..2.1
    implementation, 8.3.2

Loss given default
loan loss provisions
    accounting standards, 8.3.2
Macroeconomic Assessment Group
role of, 18.1.4
Macroeconomic models
generally, 18.5.3
results obtained from, 18.5.4
stress testing, 11.3.4
Macro-prudential supervision
deployment of resources, 19.6.3
funding, 19.6.1
key principles, 19.5
organisation of resources, 19.6.2
skills, 19.6.1
supervising SIFIs, 19.6
Management information
liquidity risk, and, 6.3.2.3
Management of risk
see **Risk management**
Margin period of risk
collateralised trades, 5.3.1.5
Market risk
internal model approach
    changes to, 4.6.3
    correlation trading and
        comprehensive risk measure,
        4.6.3.6
    incremental risk charge, 4.6.3.5
    quantitative standards,
        amendments of, 4.6.3.2
    specification of risk factors,
        4.6.3.1
    stressed VaR, 4.6.3.3
    treatment of specific risk, 4.6.3.4
introduction, 4.1
performance measures, and, 14.3.6
standardised approach
    changes to, 4.6.2
    correlation trading portfolio, 4.6.2.1
    credit derivatives, 4.6.2.3
    securitisations, 4.6.2.2
stress testing, 11.2.3
trading book
    Basel II review, 4.4
    changes to definition of, 4.6.1
    financial crisis, effect of, 4.5
Materiality
risk management, 17.3.1
Mega trends
reforms in context, 2.2.3
Model validation
counterparty credit risk, 5.3.2.5

Mortgage servicing rights
loan loss provisions
accounting standards, 8.3.3
Negative carry
use of, 13.3.4
Net stable funding ratio
application of, 6.2.2.2
impact of, 6.2.2.4
liquidity coverage ratio, link with, 6.2.3
meaning, of, 6.1.2, 6.2.2.1
scenario, 6.2.2.3
Notional amounts, use of
counterparty credit risk, 5.2
**Organisation for Economic Cooperation
and Development (OECD)**
taxation, and, 13.1, 13.2
Operational risk
performance measures, and, 14.3.6
risk management disclosure
requirements, 12.2.2, App I.
OTC derivatives
see **Derivatives**
Passporting rights
bank levies, and, 13.2.2.1
Peer Review Council (PRC)
role of, 19.8
Pension deficits
accounting standards, 8.3.2
Performance measures
incorporating risk into
business risk, 14.3.6
cascade of economic profit,
14.3.6
credit concentration, 14.3.6
credit risk, 14.3.6
developing practice, 14.3.1
difficulties, 14.3.3
financial leverage, 14.3.6
liquidity risk, 14.3.6
market risk, 14.3.6
non-financial measures, 14.3.5
operational risk, 14.3.6
qualitative overview, 14.3.5
remuneration process, 14.3.1
reputation risk, 14.3.6
risk-adjusted measures, 14.3.2
suggested actions, 14.3.4
Pillar 1
charges for specific wrong-way risk,
5.3.1.3
Pillar 2
Basel II, under, 9.2
Basel III, impact of, 9.3

capital buffers
capital planning, 9.3.1
internal capital assessments, and,
9.3.2
Tier 1 capital, and, 9.3.2
capital planning
Basel II, 9.2
Basel III, 9.3.1
forward-looking capital plan, 9.2
conclusions, 9.6
economic capital, implications for
alternative approach, 9.4.1
generally, 9.4
internal capital adequacy assessment
process
bank's responsibilities under, 9.2
introduction, 9.1
internal capital assessment
capital buffers, and, 9.3.2
introduction, 9.1
scope of, 9.2
introduction, 9.1
risk management, 9.5
stress testing
Basel II, 9.2
Basel III, 9.3.1
supervisory review and evaluation
process, 9.5
Pillar 3
capital adequacy, 12.2.2
capital structure, 12.2.2
communications strategy, 12.3.3
confidential information, 12.2.1
credit risk, 12.2.2, 12.2.4, App I.
data management, 12.3.2
detailed requirements, 12.2.2
disclosure frameworks, 12.3.3
disclosure policies, 12.2.1
enforcement, 12.2.1
equity risk, 12.2.2, App I.
financial statement risk disclosures,
12.2.4
frequency of disclosures, 12.2.1
future of risk management
disclosures, 12.4
good practice, App II.
governance, 12.3.1
implementation
communications strategy, 12.3.3
data management, 12.3.2
disclosure frameworks, 12.3.3
general challenges, 12.3
governance, 12.3.1

526

suggested steps, 12.3.4
interest rate risk, 12.2.2, App I.
introduction, 12.1
liquidity risk, 12.2.4
location of disclosures, 12.2.1
market risk
   financial statement risk disclosures,
     12.2.4
   recent changes, 12.2.3
   requirements, 12.2.2
   trends, App I.
material information, 12.2.1
minimum capital requirements,
   App I.
operational risk, 12.2.2, App I.
overarching requirements, 11.2.1
proprietary information, 12.2.1
qualitative disclosures, 12.2.4
quantitative disclosures, 12.2.4
recent changes, 12.2.3
remuneration, 12.2.3
securitisations
   recent changes, 12.2.3
   requirements, 12.2.2
   trends, App I.
trends, App I.
verification process, 12.2.1
volumes of disclosures, 12.2.2
Point-in-time
loan loss provisions
   accounting standards, 8.3.2
Post-employment benefits
accounting standards, 8.2.7
Preference shareholders
position of, 16.3.2
Probability of default
cyclicality of minimum requirement,
   10.3.1
loan loss provisions
   accounting standards, 8.3.2
Procyclicality
Basel III proposals
   capital conservation buffer, 10.3.3
   countercyclical capital
     buffer, 10.3.4
   cyclicality of minimum
     requirement, 10.3.1
   forward looking provisioning, 10.3.2
   generally, 10.3
capital conservation buffer
   implications, 10.3.3.3
   introduction, 10.3.3.1
   mechanics of approach, 10.3.3.2

conclusions, 10.4
countercyclical capital buffer
   bank-specific requirements,
     10.3.4.3
   implications, 10.3.4.5
   introduction, 10.3.4.1
   minimum requirements, 10.3.4.4
   national buffer requirements,
     10.3.4.2
cyclicality of minimum requirement,
   10.1.5
forward looking provisioning,
   10.3.2
introduction, 10.1
management of
   capital planning buffers, 10.3
   generally, 10.2
   risk management, 10.2.1
risk management, 10.2.1
Rating agencies
stakeholders perspectives, 16.7
Recovery and resolution planning
conclusions, 15.6
European Commission, 15.2.2
Financial Stability Board, 15.2.1
Germany, 15.2.5
international overview
   European Commission, 15.2.2
   Financial Stability Board, 15.2.1
   Germany, 15.2.5
   Switzerland, 15.2.5
   United Kingdom, 15.2.3
   United States, 15.2.4
introduction, 15.1
lessons learned from pilots, 15.5
recovery planning
   Business Recovery Officer, 15.3.3
   contagion control, 15.3.5
   contents of plan, 15.3.4
   de-risking trading books, 15.3.5
   drafting, 15.3.2
   governance, 15.3.3
   introduction, 15.3.1
   systematic risk, 15.3.5
resolution planning
   complexity, 15.4.4
   contents of plan, 15.4.3
   derivative portfolios, 15.4.4
   governance, 15.4.2
   interdependencies, 15.4.4
   introduction, 15.4.1
   legal entity plans, 15.4.3
   retail deposits, 15.4.4

trust assets, 15.4.4
unwinding trading books, 15.4.4
Switzerland, 15.2.5
United Kingdom, 15.2.3
United States, 15.2.4
Reforms
agenda, 1.3
drivers affecting future of banking, 2.2.2
players, 1.4
Regulation
supervision contrasted, 1.4
Regulators
reforms in context, 2.2.9
Regulatory capital
meaning, 14.3.6
Remuneration
see also **Reward**
governance of
cascading governance, 14.5.2
future changes, 14.5.1
managing inputs to remuneration committee, 14.5.3
remuneration oversight committee, 14.5.2
stakeholder roles, 14.5.1
remuneration oversight committee, 14.5.2
risk management disclosure requirements, 12.2.3
Repo-style transactions
minimum holding periods, 5.3.1.5
Reputation risk
performance measures, and, 14.3.6
Resolution planning
see **Recovery and resolution planning**
Retail deposits
resolution planning, 15.4.4
Return on equity
financial leverage, and, 7.2.2
Reverse stress testing
see also **Stress testing**
introduction of, 11.1.3
methodology, 11.3.4
Reward
compensation, design of
claw-back, 14.4.1
deferral of bonus, 14.4.1
deferral vehicles, 14.4.3
forfeiture, 14.4.1
generally, 14.4
performance adjustment, 14.4.2

conclusions, 14.7
credit default swaps
risk-adjusting TSR, 14.3.2
deferral of bonus
deferral vehicles, 14.4.3
meaning, 144.4.1
disclosure of remuneration, 14.6
economic capital, meaning of, 14.3.6
forces for change, 14.2–14.2.1
governance of remuneration
cascading governance, 14.5.2
future changes, 14.5.1
managing inputs to remuneration committee, 14.5.3
remuneration oversight committee, 14.5.2
stakeholder roles, 14.5.1
introduction, 14.1
invested capital, meaning of, 14.3.6
key issues, 14.2.2
performance measures, incorporating risk into
business risk, 14.3.6
cascade of economic profit, 14.3.6
credit concentration, 14.3.6
credit risk, 14.3.6
developing practice, 14.3.1
difficulties, 14.3.3
financial leverage, 14.3.6
liquidity risk, 14.3.6
market risk, 14.3.6
non-financial measures, 14.3.5
operational risk, 14.3.6
qualitative overview, 14.3.5
remuneration process, 14.3.1
reputation risk, 14.3.6
risk-adjusted measures, 14.3.2
suggested actions, 14.3.4
regulatory capital, meaning of, 14.3.6
risk management, 17.5.5
total shareholder return
risk adjustments, and, 14.3.2
Risk appetite
liquidity risk, and, 6.3.2.2
risk management, 17.4, 17.5.5
stakeholders perspectives, 16.2
Risk assessment
scope of, 17.5.5
Risk committees
role of, 17.3.4

Risk culture
establishing, 17.2
Risk management
Basel Committee on Banking
   Supervision, 17.1.2
board, role of
   commitment, 17.3.5
   control functions, 17.3.2
   effectiveness, 17.3.6
   governance, 17.3.1
   materiality, 17.3.1
   qualifications, 17.3.5
   risk committees, 17.3.4
   risk, oversight for, 17.3.2
   senior management, oversight
      of, 17.3.3
business performance, 17.5.5
capital assessment, 17.5.5
capital management, 17.5.5
chief risk officer
   adequacy of resources, 17.5.3
   attributes, 17.5.2
   changing role of, 17.5.1
   embedding risk management in
      business, 17.5.5
   FSA view of role of, 17.5.1
   three lines of defence, 17.5.4
disclosure requirements
   see also **Pillar 3**
   communications strategy, 12.3.3
   data management, 12.3.2
   detailed requirements, 12.2.2
   disclosure frameworks, 12.3.3
   financial statement risk disclosures,
      12.2.4
   future of risk management
      disclosures, 12.4
   governance, 12.3.1
   implementation, 12.3
   introduction, 12.1
   overarching requirements, 11.2.1
   recent changes, 12.2.3
European Commission, and, 17.1.2
external communications, 17.5.5
framework, 17.5.5
governance
   disclosure requirements, 12.3.1
   risk framework, 17.5.5
   role of board, 17.3.1
implications for
   background, 17.1.2
   board, role of, 17.3
   chief risk officer, 17.5

conclusions, 17.6
overview, 17.1.1
risk appetite, 17.4
risk culture, establishing, 17.2
information required, 17.5.5
IT infrastructure, 17.5.5
leverage, and, 7.4.2
liquidity, impact of
   business planning, 6.3.2.5
   collateral management, 6.3.2.6
   data management, 6.3.2.3
   funding, 6.3.2.5
   governance, 6.3.2.1
   intra-day liquidity risk, 6.3.2.6
   management information,
      6.3.2.3
   risk appetite, 6.3.2.2
   senior management oversight,
      6.3.2.1
   stress testing, 6.3.2.4
Pillar 2, role of, 9.5
procyclicality, 10.2.1
reward, 17.5.5
risk appetite, 17.4, 17.5.5
risk assessment, 17.5.5
risk committees, 17.3.4
risk culture, establishing, 17.2
risk profile, 17.5.5
risk strategy, 17.5.5
Senior Supervisors Group, and, 17.1.2
stakeholder management, 17.5.5
Risk profile
establishing, 17.5.5
Risk strategy,
establishing 17.5.5
Risk-weighted assets
accounting standards
   credit value adjustments,
      and, 8.2.5
   goodwill and intangibles, 8.2.6
counterparty credit risk, effect
   of, 5.4
Scenarios
stress testing, 11.3.4
Secured lending
minimum holding periods, 5.3.1.5
Securities financing transactions
margin period of risk, 5.3.1.5
Securitisation
market risk, and, 4.6.2.2
risk management disclosure
   requirements
   recent changes, 12.2.3

requirements, 12.2.2
trends, App I.
stakeholders perspectives, 16.2
Senior management
liquidity risk, and, 6.3.2.1
oversight of, 17.3.3
Senior Supervisors Group
risk management, 17.1.2
Sensitivity analysis
stress testing, 11.3.4
Shadow banking
strategic implications, 2.4.4
Shares
deferral of bonus vehicles, 14.4.3
Solvency II
impact of, 16.4.1
Specific wrong-way risk
meaning, 5.3.1.3
Stakeholder perspectives
borrowers, 16.5.2
conclusions, 16.9
contingent capital, 16.4.2
debt investors, 16.4.1
depositors, 16.5.1
equity investors
dividends, 16.3.2
equity market view, 16.3.1
generally, 16.3
funding spectrum, 16.2
government guarantee
meaning, 16.6.1
value of, 16.6.2
introduction, 16.1
preference shareholders, 16.3.2
rating agencies, 16.7
risk appetite, 16.2
securitisation, 16.2
Solvency II, effect of, 16.4.1
transparency
need for, 16.8.1
wider considerations, 16.8.2
Stakeholder management
risk management, 17.5.5
Standard haircuts for securitisation collateral
counterparty credit risk, 5.3.1.6
Strategic implications
conclusions, 2.5
impact of Basel III
funding restraint, 2.3.4
higher levels of capital, 2.3.3
higher quality capital, 2.3.5
ongoing reform agenda, 2.3.6

overview, 2.3.1
strengthened liquidity
requirements, 2.3.4
summary, 2.3.2
introduction, 2.1
reforms in context
drivers affecting future of banking, 2.2.2
efficient compliance, 2.2.6
framework for response, 2.2.5
funding and capital constraints, 2.2.4
interest rates, 2.2.4
mega trends, 2.2.3
ongoing fundamental
changes, 2.2.8
regulation, 2.2.4
regulators, impact on, 2.2.9
strategic response, 2.2.7
unintended consequences, 2.2.10
western deleveraging, 2.2.4
unintended consequences
cost of credit, 2.4.3
credit rationing, 2.4.2
overview, 2.4.1
shadow banking, 2.4.4
Stress testing
actions resulting from, 11.3.6
background, 11.1.2
Basel III guidelines
capital buffers, 11.2.1
counterparty credit risk, 11.2.2
liquidity risk, 11.2.4
market risk, 11.2.3
stressed VaR, 11.2.3
capabilities of, 11.3.5
capital buffers, 11.2.1
conclusions, 11.4
contingency planning, 11.3.6
counterparty credit risk models, 5.3.2.4
crisis lessons, 11.1.3
counterparty credit risk, 11.2.2
event-driven stress testing, 11.3.4
governance, 11.3.3
implementation steps, 11.3.5
infrastructure, 11.3.5
introduction, 11.1
liquidity risk, 6.3.2.4, 11.2.4
macroeconomic stress testing, 11.3.4
market risk, 11.2.3
meaning, 11.3.1

methodologies
  reverse stress tests, 11.3.4
  scenarios, 11.3.4
  sensitivity analysis, 11.3.4
objectives, 11.3.2
outputs, 11.3.6
overview, 11.3.1
Pillar 2, role of
  Basel II, 9.2
  Basel III, 9.3.1
principal steps, 11.3.1
process, 11.3.5
quantification of impact, 11.3.4
reverse stress testing
  introduction of, 11.1.3
  methodology, 11.3.4
stressed VaR, 11.2.3
Stressed VaR
market risk, and, 4.6.3.6
stress testing, 11.2.3
trading book, 11.1.3
Subordinated debt
deferral of bonus vehicles, 14.4.3
Superequivalence
meaning, 3.10
Supervision
conclusions, 19.9
core principles, 19.2
European Systemic Risk Board, role
  of, 19.8
IMF, role of, 19.8
international oversight, 19.8
introduction, 19.1
macro-prudential supervision
  deployment of resources, 19.6.3
  funding, 19.6.1
  key principles, 19.5
  organisation of resources, 19.6.2
  skills, 19.6.1
  supervising SIFIs, 19.6
new style supervision, 19.4
Peer Review Council, role of, 19.8
regulation contrasted, 1.4
regulator, role of, 19.7
rethinking, 19.3
**Supervisory Capital Assessment
  Program (SCAP (US))**
stress testing, and, 11.1.3
**Supervisory review and evaluation
  process**
Pillar 2, role of, 9.5
Supply chain
economic implications, 18.2.3

Switzerland
recovery and resolution planning,
  15.2.5
Taxation
bank levies
  generally, 13.2.2.1
  replacement debt, and, 13.3.2
Basel III proposals, implications of
  capital instruments, changes to
    nature of, 13.3.2
  cash tax paid, 13.3.3
  deferred tax assets, 13.3.1
  definition of capital, 13.3.1
  generally, 13.3
  liquidity requirements, 13.3.4
conclusions, 13.4
environment for banks
  financial sector contribution, 13.2.2
  generally, 13.2
  tax avoidance, 13.2.1
financial activities tax, 13.2.2, 13.2.2.2
financial sector contribution
  bank levies, 13.2.2.1
  financial activities tax, 13.2.2,
    13.2.2.2
  financial stability contribution,
    13.2.2
  financial transactions tax, 13.2.2.3
  generally, 13.2.2
  Tobin tax, 13.2.2.3
financial stability contribution, 13.2.2
financial transactions tax, 13.2.2.3
IMF
  bank levies, 13.2.2.1
  banking environment, 13.2
  financial activities tax, 13.2.2.2
  role of, 13.1
introduction, 13.1
negative carry, 13.3.4
OECD, and, 13.1, 13.2
passporting rights
  bank levies, 13.2.2.1
tax avoidance
  bank losses, 13.2.1.2
  banking code of practice,
    13.2.1.1
  generally, 13.2.1
  Tobin tax, 13.2.2.3
Threshold deductions
accounting standards, 8.3.3
Through-the-cycle
loan loss provisions
  accounting standards, 8.3.2

Time horizon
loan loss provisions
accounting standards, 8.3.2
Tobin tax
introduction of, 13.2.2.3
Total shareholder return
risk adjustments, and, 14.3.2
Toxic assets
deferral of bonus vehicles, 14.4.3
Trade associations
role of in banking, 1.4
Trading book
market risk, and
Basel II review, 4.4
changes to definition of, 4.6.1
financial crisis, effect of, 4.5

recovery and resolution planning,
15.3.5, 15.4.4
stressed VaR, 11.1.3
Transparency
need for, 16.8.1
wider considerations, 16.8.2
Trust assets
resolution planning, 15.4.4
United States
rating agencies, 16.7
recovery and resolution planning,
15.2.4
Western deleveraging
reforms in context, 2.2.4